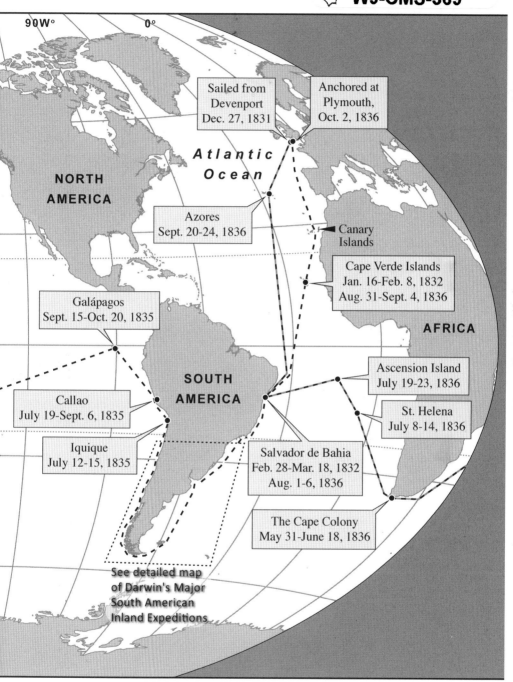

90W°   0°

Atlantic Ocean

NORTH AMERICA

Sailed from Devenport Dec. 27, 1831

Anchored at Plymouth, Oct. 2, 1836

Azores Sept. 20-24, 1836

Canary Islands

Cape Verde Islands Jan. 16-Feb. 8, 1832 Aug. 31-Sept. 4, 1836

AFRICA

Galápagos Sept. 15-Oct. 20, 1835

Ascension Island July 19-23, 1836

SOUTH AMERICA

Callao July 19-Sept. 6, 1835

St. Helena July 8-14, 1836

Iquique July 12-15, 1835

Salvador de Bahia Feb. 28-Mar. 18, 1832 Aug. 1-6, 1836

The Cape Colony May 31-June 18, 1836

See detailed map of Darwin's Major South American Inland Expeditions

ODYSSEY

ODYSSEY

YOUNG CHARLES DARWIN,
THE *BEAGLE*, AND THE VOYAGE
THAT CHANGED THE WORLD

TOM CHAFFIN

PEGASUS BOOKS
NEW YORK LONDON

ODYSSEY

Pegasus Books, Ltd.
148 West 37th Street, 13th Floor
New York, NY 10018

First Pegasus Books cloth edition February 2022

Interior design by Maria Fernandez

ISBN: 978-1-64313-908-1

10 9 8 7 6 5 4 3 2 1

Printed in the United States of America
Distributed by Simon & Schuster
www.pegasusbooks.com

To Lesly González Herrera

"grace under pressure"

CONTENTS

"I don't know anything that has gone higher than Darwin—the noble, the exalting; Darwin is to me science incarnate; its spirit is Darwin."

—Walt Whitman, August 29, 1891

Not shown: April 8-24, 1832, an approximately 200 mile roundtrip expedition from Rio de Janeiro, to visit a coffee plantation along Brazil's Macaé River.

Darwin's Major Inland Expeditions

1 Patagones to Bahía Blanca
2 Bahía Blanca to Buenos Aires
3 Buenos Aires to Santa Fé
4 Montevideo to Mercedes
5 Rio Santa Cruz
6 Valparaiso to Cerro La Campana
7 Santiago to Mendoza via the Portillo & Uspallata passes
8 Valparaiso to Coquimbo to Puerto Vierjo

PACIFIC OCEAN

Atacama Desert

30°S

Puerto Viejo
Copiapó
Huasco
Coquimbo
Herradura

Apr. 27-July 5, 1835 **8**

Rio Parand
Rio Uruguay

Coastal Range
Cerro La Campana
Valparaíso
Santiago

Uspallata Pass

Sept. 27-Oct. 2, 1833 **3**

Santa Fe

4
Nov. 14-28, 1833

Mendoza

Mar. 18-Apr. 10, 1835

7

Mercedes
Las Minas

Aug. 14-Sept. 27, 1834 **6**

Maipo River
Rancagua
Portillo Pass

Rio de la Plata
Buenos Aires
Belgrano

Maldonado
Montevideo

Concepción

PAMPAS

Sierra de La Ventana Mountains & Cerro Tres Picos

Sept. 8-20, 1833 **2**

ANDES

40°S

Valdivia

Rio Colorado
Rio Negro

Fortaleza Protectora
Bahía Blanca

Aug. 11-17, 1833 **1**

Mount Osorno

San Carlos de Chiloé

Carmen de Patagones

Chiloé Archipelago

5
Apr. 18-May 8, 1834

Rio Deseado
Port Desire

Cape Tres Montes

St. Julian

50°S

Rio Santa Cruz

Falkland Islands
Port Louis

Patagonia

Strait of Magellan

Tierra del Fuego
Isla Grande

Beagle Channel

Bay of Good Success

ATLANTIC OCEAN

Wulaia
Navarino Island
Cape Horn

70°W
60°W

Area of Detail

Rutgers Cartography 2022

HMS *BEAGLE*'S TIERRA DEL FUEGO

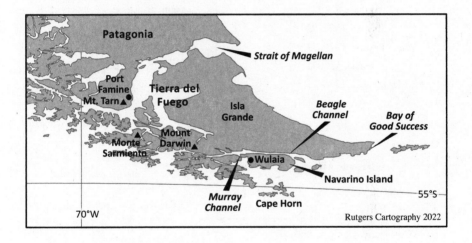

THE WEDGWOOD

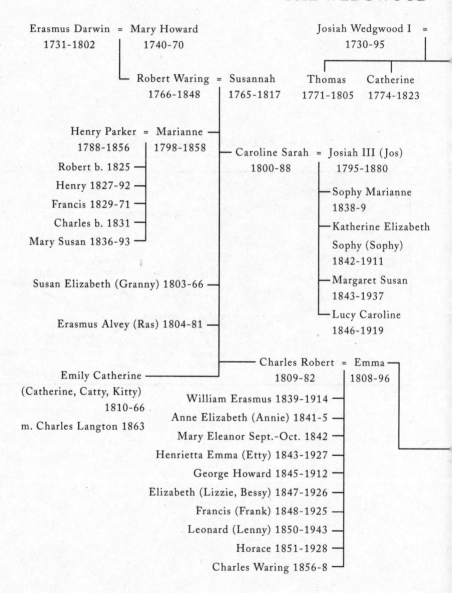

Erasmus Darwin = Mary Howard
1731-1802   1740-70

Josiah Wedgwood I =
1730-95

Robert Waring = Susannah   Thomas   Catherine
1766-1848   1765-1817   1771-1805   1774-1823

Henry Parker = Marianne
1788-1856   1798-1858

Robert b. 1825
Henry 1827-92
Francis 1829-71
Charles b. 1831
Mary Susan 1836-93

Caroline Sarah = Josiah III (Jos)
1800-88   1795-1880

Sophy Marianne
1838-9

Katherine Elizabeth
Sophy (Sophy)
1842-1911

Margaret Susan
1843-1937

Lucy Caroline
1846-1919

Susan Elizabeth (Granny) 1803-66

Erasmus Alvey (Ras) 1804-81

Charles Robert = Emma
1809-82   1808-96

Emily Catherine
(Catherine, Catty, Kitty)
1810-66
m. Charles Langton 1863

William Erasmus 1839-1914
Anne Elizabeth (Annie) 1841-5
Mary Eleanor Sept.-Oct. 1842
Henrietta Emma (Etty) 1843-1927
George Howard 1845-1912
Elizabeth (Lizzie, Bessy) 1847-1926
Francis (Frank) 1848-1925
Leonard (Lenny) 1850-1943
Horace 1851-1928
Charles Waring 1856-8

AND DARWIN FAMILIES

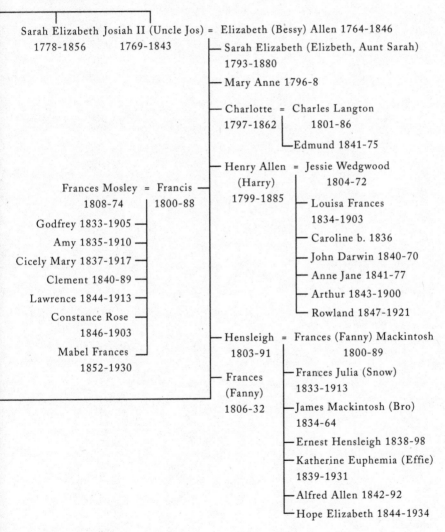

Sarah Wedgwood
1734-1815

Sarah Elizabeth Josiah II (Uncle Jos) = Elizabeth (Bessy) Allen 1764-1846
  1778-1856   1769-1843
                                   ── Sarah Elizabeth (Elizbeth, Aunt Sarah)
                                       1793-1880

                                   ── Mary Anne 1796-8

                                   ── Charlotte = Charles Langton
                                       1797-1862 │   1801-86
                                                  └─Edmund 1841-75

                                   ── Henry Allen = Jessie Wedgwood
Frances Mosley = Francis ──   (Harry)   1804-72
  1808-74   │ 1800-88   1799-1885   ── Louisa Frances
Godfrey 1833-1905 ──   1834-1903
  Amy 1835-1910 ──   ── Caroline b. 1836
Cicely Mary 1837-1917 ──   ── John Darwin 1840-70
  Clement 1840-89 ──   ── Anne Jane 1841-77
Lawrence 1844-1913 ──   ── Arthur 1843-1900
  Constance Rose ──   └─ Rowland 1847-1921
  1846-1903
Mabel Frances ──   ── Hensleigh = Frances (Fanny) Mackintosh
  1852-1930   1803-91 │   1800-89
                                                 ── Frances Julia (Snow)
                                     ── Frances   1833-1913
                                        (Fanny)   ──James Mackintosh (Bro)
                                        1806-32   1834-64
                                                 ──Ernest Hensleigh 1838-98
                                                 ──Katherine Euphemia (Effie)
                                                    1839-1931
                                                 ──Alfred Allen 1842-92
                                                 └─Hope Elizabeth 1844-1934

INTRODUCTION

HIDING IN PLAIN SIGHT

"There was nowhere to go but everywhere,
and keep on rolling under the stars . . . the western stars."
—Jack Kerouac, *On the Road* (draft)

I n Victorian-era photographs, Charles Darwin, with Isaac Newton and Albert Einstein, arguably among the world's three most famous scientists, peers at us from behind the bushy white Old Testament– prophet beard by which the world has come to know him. In the popular imagination, the older Darwin crowds out the vital younger man whose curiosities, risk-taking, and travels aboard HMS *Beagle* shaped his later theories.

We have scores of images of the older Darwin, many of them photographs. But we have only two widely-known portraits of him before age thirty, neither of them photographs: the earliest, a chalk portrait at age six, posed with his younger sister; the second, a watercolor that captured the then still cherubic-looking young man in his late twenties.

That paucity of images notwithstanding, without Darwin's travels aboard the *Beagle*, an odyssey freshly chronicled in these pages, he likely would never have formulated his paradigm-shifting theory of evolution. "The voyage of the *Beagle*," he reflected in his later years, "has been by far the most important event in my life and has determined my whole career."

By now, Darwin's journeys aboard the *Beagle* feel like familiar history. But how well do we truly *know* those travels? Readers, for instance, are familiar with how, sailing aboard a British ship called HMS *Beagle*, he visited the Pacific Ocean's remote Galápagos Islands. There, he noticed some interesting tortoises, lizards, and birds. *Voila!*—then and there, accepted lore informs us, his now famous theory burst into the great man's hirsute head.

The Voyage of the Beagle being finis, Darwin returned forthwith to England and wrote *On the Origin of Species by Means of Natural Selection*. And that book, in turn, not only transformed science, it launched a thousand recriminatory sermons, and cartoons depicting the author as a hairy, slouching ape. Gilbert and Sullivan's comic opera *Princess Ida*, captured the spirit in 1884: "Darwinian Man, though well-behaved / At best is only a monkey shaved."

But operas, cartoons, and legends make unreliable emissaries of the past. For starters, Darwin was twenty-two years old when he left England aboard the *Beagle* and twenty-six when, in 1835, he called at the Galápagos, in the fourth of five years of travels. And those islands proved, for him, initially disappointing, and provided no eureka moment. By contrast, he earlier had adjudged gloomy Tierra del Fuego the journey's most interesting stop. There, he witnessed the repatriation by his shipmates of three "Fuegians," Natives of the area kidnapped during an earlier *Beagle* voyage and brought to England to be Christianized and "civilized."

In deference to Robert FitzRoy, the *Beagle* captain with whom Darwin sailed, his published account of his five years of travels, appearing in 1839, provided only a bare-bones account of the story of the three Fuegians. "We staid there five days," he writes of the ship's visit, in 1833, to the Tierra del Fuego locale selected as the Natives' new home. "Captain FitzRoy has given an account of all the interesting events which there happened."

For the most part, Darwin deferred public reflections on the Fuegians and the issues they raised for him until 1871, when he published *The Descent of Man*. Appearing a dozen years after *Origin of Species*, that now often overlooked, two-volume work ranks among the most ambitious of his major books. Bringing, for the first time, *Homo sapiens* into his portrait of the living world, *Descent of Man* represented a bolder expression than *Origin of Species* of its author's intellectual vision.

Moreover, during Darwin's *Beagle* travels, *Origin of Species*, *Descent of Man*—and, for that matter, his patriarchal beard—remained decades away. Further undermining the legend, his call in the Galápagos and other (for him) exotic locales belonged to a five-year circumnavigation by a British survey ship, an excursion, in geography and time, of greater breadth than generally assumed.

Puncturing another common assumption, Darwin played no formal role aboard the *Beagle*. A chance invitation to serve as a meal conversation partner, on topics of natural history, for Captain FitzRoy, placed him aboard the ship. Moreover, the *Beagle* was dispatched to its far-flung destinations to conduct marine surveys (albeit mainly in South America) for commercial and military—and only incidentally *scientific*—purposes. And antecedent to those official purposes was FitzRoy's personal desire to assuage his troubled conscience over his role in the kidnapping of the Fuegians during a previous *Beagle* voyage he had led.

Moreover, Darwin, before sailing, was then a novice, an "unfinished" naturalist, and had only recently earned, from the University of Cambridge, a Bachelor of Arts degree, of the sort taken by aspirants to the Church of England's priesthood.

Even the title of the book we now know as *The Voyage of the* Beagle, first published three years after Darwin's return, distorts in fundamental ways his travels. To wit, he spent three-fifths of his five-year "voyage" on land—three years and three months on terra firma versus a total of 533 days on water. Not infrequently, arranging to meet the ship at other ports, he set out on overland excursions. During the "voyage," Darwin completed nine major overland journeys—outings, lasting weeks or months, that took him across mountains, valleys, pampas, rainforests, and deserts. In South America, he conducted those excursions during the 1830s, when few connections linked the continent's far-flung cities and towns; between them yawned thousands of unmapped miles abounding in ruthless bandits and Indigenous peoples warring with whites.

Voyage of the Beagle, originally published in 1839 under another title, belonged to a three-volume quasi-official account of the, by then, two global survey expeditions with which the *Beagle* had been associated. Captain FitzRoy, a fervent evangelical and high Tory, oversaw the publishing project. Darwin, by contrast, was a reform-minded, abolitionist Whig. And, as they had aboard the *Beagle*, the two men, during work on the volumes, shared a sometimes fraught relationship.

The book now known as *Voyage of the Beagle* drew on a lively diary kept by Darwin during his travels. Compelling writing filled many of *Voyage*'s pages. Even so, much of his diary's contents did not make it into that book. Most particularly, he excluded non-survey-related topics, personal tribulations, and materials that FitzRoy might deem irrelevant, frivolous, or offensive. Additionally, in *Voyage*, because the *Beagle* made repeated visits to several anchorages, Darwin strayed from his diary's chronological structure to organize *Voyage*'s chapters by place. In the end, those and other editorial decisions sacrificed much of his diary's drama, narrative cohesion, candor, topical breadth, and intimacy—in short what Darwin modestly called the "chit-chat details of my journal."

In creating my own narrative of Darwin's travels, I've drawn on the full breadth of his writings, published and unpublished. However, in depicting events associated with his *Beagle* travels, I've accorded primacy to writings created *during* those journeys: his diary, field notebooks, and letters. Typically, those letters, colorful and robustly detailed, were sent to family members and friends—and replete with the mangled spelling (preserved herein) that reflected his circumstances. For further illumination, I've also drawn on the correspondence, memoirs, and diaries of others he encountered or traveled with during those years.

Cumulatively, these various writings by Darwin and others constitute a pentimento* of his early years. To be sure, this lively portrait, heretofore hiding in plain sight, lurks just beneath the more public

---

* Pentimento, from the Italian *pentirsi* (to repent or change one's mind), refers to an emergence, made transparent by time, in a painting of an original element eventually painted-over by the artist.

surfaces of *Voyage of the Beagle* and *Origin of Species*. Notably, it depicts formative experiences in the naturalist's life unfound in—in some cases, deliberately excluded from—those two works.

The panorama often depicts episodes marred by false starts, impulsiveness, and the arrogance of youth. Nonetheless, it's a portrait, rendered in bold primary colors, that captures Darwin at a magical time, when his imagination, interests, and energies ranged as expansively as HMS *Beagle*'s global peregrinations.

Darwin's early career ensued before rigid specialization dominated the sciences, even before the term "science" acquired its modern usage. Moreover, it occurred before universities, foundations, governments, and corporations dominated scientific research, and before specialists walled off the sciences from the arts. Capturing that spirit, the French novelist Honoré de Balzac, in 1831, the same year that Darwin's *Beagle* set sail, praised his countryman, paleontologist George Cuvier, who had ignited public fascination with prehistoric fossils. In Balzac's estimation, Cuvier ranked as successor to Lord Byron, the late titan of that era's romantic poetry: "Is not" Balzac asked, "Cuvier the great poet of our era? Byron has given admirable expression to certain moral conflicts, but our immortal naturalist has reconstructed past worlds from a few bleached bones; has rebuilt cities . . . with monsters' teeth; has animated forests with all the secrets of zoology gleaned from a piece of coal; has discovered a giant population from the footprints of a mammoth."

Darwin eventually developed the writing skills to convey to specialized and general readers alike the often complex ideas that animated his later books. But for wit and crispness, he reflected late in life, he often preferred his earlier, more spontaneous writings to his later, more labored works: "Sentences thus scribbled down are often better ones than I could have written deliberately."

These *in situ* writings from Darwin's *Beagle* years also reveal the degree to which, beyond his expected scientific interests, a spirit of wanderlust propelled his youthful journeys. Tellingly, during those wanderings, he never set out on an overland excursion without at least one volume of poetry: "When I could take only a single small volume, I always chose Milton." At the heart of his wanderings, we thus discover a spirit, energy, and imagination not dissimilar to that which animated writers such as Lord Byron, Jules Verne, Mary Shelley—even Homer.

Beyond science and nature, myriad other topics enliven Darwin's *Beagle* writings, including politics, fashion, colonialism, race, architecture, women, South American and Australian cities, Tahitian royalty, gauchos, the British Empire, Indigenous peoples, missionaries, shopping, cuisine, and slavery. Moreover, his dispatch of those and other unexpected topics showcase his often underestimated gifts as a writer. Those talents, after all, contributed to the wide readership later won by *Origin of Species*, a work whose nominal topic, the transmutation of animal and plant species, hardly constituted standard popular fare. Moreover, the ideas expressed in *Origin*, however compelling, were already in the air. Thus, it's a fair question: Absent Darwin's writing skills, would his book have gained the prestige and influence that it achieved?

By now, it's widely acknowledged that Darwin's work influenced many authors of his own day and later—from Thomas Hardy and George Eliot (Mary Ann Evans)* to Aldous Huxley and Kurt Vonnegut. Less appreciated is the degree to which literary influencing was, in Darwin's case, a two-way street. Rarely acknowledged is the influence *on* him of authors of a literary bent; and the degree to which he consciously aspired to hone such faculties. Indeed, the *Beagle* diary and his letters of those years show him already developing the sort of literary skills more readily associated with English travelers such as Charles Dickens, Anthony Trollope, and Harriet Martineau. Likewise, in retrospect, it's easy to overlook how much, in their picaresque spirit, Darwin's *Beagle* writings share with the prose stylings of on-the-road novelists such as Miguel de Cervantes, Mark Twain, and Jack Kerouac (perhaps, in the latter case, with Argentina's potent maté standing in for Kerouac's marijuana).

Also undermining expectations, though prone to seasickness and, in later years, often beset with illnesses, Darwin, tall, lean, and fit as a young

---

* For Darwin and Eliot the admiration was mutual: Darwin was an avid reader of Eliot's works; and *Origin of Species* would influence the later novels of her career. On a personal level, the two, while not close, shared a warm relationship.

man, exemplified robust health during his *Beagle* travels. At many stops, he relished climbing the area's highest local mountain. And, thanks to years of mounted hunting excursions in England, he impressed gauchos with his marksmanship, and savored extended equestrian journeys over often difficult terrains.

In the posthumously published *Autobiography*, written in Darwin's later years, he reflected on the qualities that enabled his success as a scientist:

> I think that I am superior to the common run of men in noticing things which easily escape attention, and in observing them carefully. My industry has been nearly as great as it could have been in the observation and collection of facts. . . . From my early youth I have had the strongest desire to understand or explain whatever I observed—that is, to group all facts under some general laws. These causes combined have given me the patience to reflect or ponder for any number of years over any unexplained problem.

Even so, as Homer observed in *The Odyssey*, "The gods don't hand out all their gifts at once." Darwin, in his *Autobiography*, assessed the price paid for his mature intellectual attainments, the loss of the artistic pleasures of his youth. "My mind has changed during the last twenty or thirty years," he lamented. "Up to the age of thirty, or beyond it, poetry of many kinds, such as the works of Milton, Gray, Byron, Wordsworth, Coleridge, and Shelley, gave me great pleasure." Moreover, "music"—formerly a source of pleasure— "generally sets me thinking too energetically on what I have been at work on, instead of giving me pleasure. I retain some taste for fine scenery, but it does not cause me the exquisite delight which it formerly did." Indeed, poet William Wordsworth, born decades before Darwin, had understood that arc: "The Child," he observed, "is father of the Man."

All writing is artifice, and words can never retrieve the past. But in the pages that follow, I've tried to restore to our midst the story and spirit of the adventurous young man who evolved into the bearded patriarch whose ideas still roil and illuminate our world.

PART I

"WE PHILOSOPHERS DO NOT BARGAIN
FOR THIS KIND OF WORK," AUGUST 1833

1

LOOKING FOR THE GENERAL

"We afterwards heard, that the old major's suspicions had been very much increased by Harris's explanation of Mr. Darwin's occupation. 'Un naturalista' was a term unheard of by any person in the settlement, and being unluckily explained by Harris as meaning 'a man that knows every thing,' any further attempt to quiet anxiety was useless."

—Captain Robert FitzRoy, HMS *Beagle*,
Proceedings of the Second Expedition

From a distance, the eight horsemen, an explosive flash of color on the scruffy pampas plain, might have been religious pilgrims on some Medieval-era panel painting. It was late afternoon, August 11, 1833, and the party had left the town of Carmen de Patagones that morning. Riding north, the journey will eventually stretch, for one of the riders, over five hundred lawless miles, ending in Buenos Aires. Increasing the desolation, much of his northbound route will run two to three hundred miles inland from Argentina's Atlantic coast.

This afternoon, water from a recent storm filled the normally bone-dry wagon ruts that sufficed for roads in these parts. Although slowing the retinue's passage, the puddles provided fresh water on a journey that typically confounds travelers with a challenging aridity. That day, the men will encounter only two modest springs, both offering only brackish water.

The party consists of five gauchos, a guide, and two Englishmen: James Harris, a businessman living in Carmen de Patagones; the other Charles Robert Darwin, a twenty-four-year-old aspiring naturalist. Among the five, Darwin is the only one riding all the way to Buenos Aires.

Before arriving in South America, Darwin had assumed that his travels would occasionally take him into dangerous country. But, having yet to make his name professionally, he relished the opportunity to gather natural specimens. In England, with the popularity of natural history approaching flood stage, museums, botanic gardens, and zoos pined for exotic flora and fauna, living and stuffed, as well as fossils. And, as Darwin well knew, professional reputations in that day could be won with the right specimens—particularly fossils of prehistoric creatures.

A paradox, however, lay at the heart of how Darwin and other Europeans viewed South America. From their perspective, the continent belonged to the "New World," a reference to its "discovery," centuries earlier, by Europeans. Even so, European naturalists often viewed outings to South America as sojourns into the primeval—back into time itself. "The Tropics appear the natural birthplace of the human race," as Darwin put it in May 1832, savoring, in Brazil, his first months on the continent.

The continent's more southerly climes, particularly Patagonia, also captivated Darwin. Indeed, he believed, among all the world's places, none rivaled Patagonia as a repository of primitive life forms, or, more saliently, in its abundance of buried paleontological treasures. Though claimed by Argentina's Buenos Aires Province, in practice Patagonia was conceded by whites to be "Indian country," held by the Tehuelche, Mapuche, and other Indigenous peoples.

Since the early sixteenth century European explorers had returned with stories that, comingling ethnology and fantasy, imagined Patagonia as a land of giant Indigenous people, reputedly twice the height of Europeans. More recently, geologists had unearthed there outsized fossilized remains of extinct animals. Anticipating his own travels there, Darwin called Patagonia "an El Dorado to a Geologist."

In the distance that August, to the party's west, rose the Sierra de La Ventana range, its granitic heights an encyclopedia of blues on the otherwise drab landscape. Under other circumstances, Darwin's thoughts would have been focused on his usual priorities: the local geology and native flora and fauna—the phyla, classes, orders, families, genera, and species by which he measured typical days. And, as they rode, he did notice the occasional deer, guanaco (wild llama), and agouti (a large burrowing rodent). But he was also struck by the landscape's haunting solemnity, inhabited by few birds or other animals. Reinforcing the austral-winter pallor, the occasional trees whose silhouettes broke the monotony stood barren of leaves. "The country has one universal appearance, brown withered grass & spiny bushes," he confided to his diary. "There are some depressions & valleys."

That August marked Darwin's nineteenth month in South America. In late February 1832, at Salvador de Bahia (today's Salvador), Brazil, he had stepped off HMS *Beagle*, the Royal Navy brig that brought him to the continent. He suffered from seasickness during much of the Atlantic crossing; and, a poor student of foreign languages, his fluency in Spanish was wanting. Since arriving, however, he had leaned on compensatory advantages: he had excellent eyesight; and thanks to years of shooting excursions in England, he impressed the gauchos with his marksmanship. Moreover, today's worries notwithstanding, he generally relished sustained outings on horseback.

Among the gauchos, Darwin affected a native swagger, smoking *cigarittos* and drinking "much mate"—maté, a regional drink, potent with a caffeine-like stimulant concocted from the dried leaves of the yerba maté shrub. He likewise joined the gauchos' equestrian frolics: "I shot one day a fine buck & doe: but in this line, I never enjoyed anything so much as Ostrich hunting with the wild Soldiers, who are more than half Indians. They catch them, by throwing two balls, which are attached to the ends of a thong, so as to entangle their legs: it was a fine animated chace."

In South America, Darwin marveled at the distances he had traveled and the changes in his life since June 1831, when he had completed his studies at the University of Cambridge. When away from the *Beagle* and traveling on land, alone or with others, necessity compelled him, for the first time in his young life, to secure, on his own, his food, shelter, and personal safety. Moreover, in pursuit of those essentials and the scientific knowledge that later led to international fame, he came to rely on the kindness of a broad cast of strangers—hired guides and assistants, cattle ranchers, slave-owning planters, Native peoples, missionaries, urban merchants and entrepreneurs, government officials, and clerics.

Today, Darwin was riding toward a reunion with the *Beagle*'s captain Robert FitzRoy, expected to be with his anchored ship at southern Argentina's Bahía Blanca. But the reunion would be brief; and afterward, Darwin would continue overland to Buenos Aires. Typically, these overland treks devoted to collecting specimens were conducted after arranging to meet the *Beagle* at a later port of call. The outings took Darwin deep into jungles, mountains, forests, deserts, and pampas. Lasting weeks, even months, the journeys—there would be nine major ones in South America—crossed hinterlands mapped less well, if at all, than the ports and coasts on which the *Beagle*'s surveys focused.

And if Darwin, in August 1833 felt out of place on that day's pampas, his appearance reinforced that discordance. Six feet tall and spry, as a schoolboy he had impressed friends with his ability to jump over a bar held at a height level to his Adam's apple. Otherwise, his appearance remained that of the callow naturalist bedecked in proper English gentleman's attire—in contrast with what he described as the "very striking" appearance of his gaucho traveling companions.

> They are generally tall and handsome, but with a proud and dissolute expression of countenance. They frequently wear their moustaches, and long black hair curling down their backs. With their brightly-coloured garments, great spurs clanking about their heels, and knives stuck as daggers (and often so used) at their waists, they look a very different race of men from what might be expected from their name of Gauchos, or simple countrymen.

To be sure, today's circumstances strayed far from Darwin's usual work conditions. Writing to a friend, invoking an epithet the *Beagle*'s officers had affectionately hung on him, he lightheartedly expressed his discomfiture: "We Philosophers do not bargain for this sort of work." Worries about attacks by Native peoples and bandits particularly loomed, anxieties only partly eased by the five gauchos traveling with him.

Still later that day, August 11, 1833, the party came upon a large tree deemed sacred by local Natives—in the local Spanish argot, an *árbol del Gualicho*, a spell-possessed tree. Indigenous people, Darwin's companions explained, revered the tree, three feet in diameter, "as a God itself, or as the altar of Walleechu." Though, in his notes, the naturalist left the tree's species unidentified, he did record that it was "situated on a high part of the plain & hence is a landmark visible at a great distance. As soon as a tribe of Indians come in sight they offer their adorations by loud shouts. . . . [L]ow & much branched & thorny, [i]t stands by itself without any neighbour, & was indeed the first tree we met with." Curiously, "being winter the tree had no leaves, but in their place numberless threads, by which the various offerings, such as cigars, bread, meat, pieces of cloth, &c [were hung]."

The gauchos explained that Natives "pour spirit & mattee into a hole & likewise smoke upwards, thinking thus to afford all possible gratification to Walleechu." More ominous was another aspect, conspicuously visible that afternoon, of the Indigenous veneration of the tree: "To complete the scene the tree was surrounded by the bleached bones of horses slaughtered as sacrifices."

The tree and other signs of the Indigenous presence attested to the tenuous control government officials exercised over the area. During those years, a federation with no central leaders governed Argentina. Each of its thirteen provinces enjoyed abundant autonomy; and to travel in these environs, Darwin had been advised to seek a passport from General Juan Manuel de Rosas, until recently the dictatorial governor of Buenos Aires Province.

A classic Latin American caudillo (strong man), Rosas possessed extensive military experience, had used private militias to fuel his rise to power, and wielded personality-cult powers. The owner of vast ranches, his supporters included gauchos and Black people,* as well as other cattle ranchers who, conservative and xenophobic, tended to resent the cattle-brokers, bankers, merchants, and, more broadly, the anticlerical, centralizing liberals of the city of Buenos Aires.

Gauchos, in particular, were drawn to Rosas. Among historians, gauchos remain a fraught topic, with wide-ranging debates over their origins and defining characteristics. The gauchos drawn to Rosas, like the typical gaucho of popular imagination, tended to be of mixed race (white, Indigenous, and Black, or combinations thereof). During the colonial era, gauchos on the pampas slaughtered *cimarrones* (wild cattle) for the hide trade. But, during the nineteenth century's first decades and the coming of republican governance to South America, wealthy entrepreneurs—purchasing large tracts of recently incorporated land on the pampas—consolidated them into large estates (estancias). They also appropriated the wild cattle for themselves; and, backed by the new governments, restricted access to their newly acquired lands. Squatting was banned; and those years also saw the enactment of anti-vagrancy laws on the pampas.

The gauchos' reduced circumstances and their fears of Indigenous peoples on the pampas drove many into the employ of the ranch owners. That reduction to poorly paid hired hands notwithstanding, the gauchos stubbornly maintained their romantic self-image—maté-drinking, brawling, lassoing, guitar-playing, gambling, and independent. Even so, theirs was a reversal fated to create resentments among their numbers, irritations that Rosas—his own wealth and pampas ranches notwithstanding—skillfully exploited.

Though formally out of office in August 1833, Rosas was plotting his return to the governorship, and still wielded state-like powers in Buenos Aires Province's scarcely populated but sprawling south. That August, he was conducting a war, his infamous Desert Campaign, on Buenos Aires Province's pampas, as Darwin recalled, "for the purpose of exterminating" tribal peoples. The war was being waged on behalf of

---

* Black supporters included enslaved or formerly enslaved Argentines with various claims to manumitted status, and escaped slaves from Brazil and other countries.

Argentines of European ancestry who sought the lands, then held by Indigenous peoples, as a domain for cattle ranches.

At "wide intervals," Rosas had established twenty *postas*, each garrisoned with: five soldiers and a "small troop" of horses to bring travelers to the next station and ultimately the city of Buenos Aires. As Darwin's party journeyed over the pampas, Rosas's army was encamped on Rio Colorado's north bank, eighty miles to the north. Indeed, the gauchos traveling with Darwin had joined him because they also had business to conduct with the general.

Later that day, under the fading glow of the austral winter's light, Darwin's party stopped to camp. While gathering firewood, one of the gauchos spotted the silhouette of a solitary cow in the distance. "Off we set in chase, & in a few minutes she was dragged in by the lazo & slaughtered," recalled Darwin. For him, the killing belonged to his ongoing immersion into the rituals of gaucho life. "This was the first night which I passed under the open sky with the gear of the Recado for a bed"—a Gaucho saddle disassembled for sleeping.

> There is high enjoyment in the independence of the Gaucho life . . . to be able at any moment to pull up your horse and say here we will pass the night. The death-like stillness of the plain, the dogs keeping watch, the gipsy-group of Gauchos making their beds around the fire, has left in my mind a strongly marked picture of this first night, which will not soon be forgotten.

Indeed, for Darwin, the tableau came close to vanquishing all thoughts of marauding Natives, General Rosas's war of extermination against them, and Darwin's fears of being caught between the two warring parties.

2

"THE PERFECT GAUCHO"

wo days later, during the late afternoon of August 13, 1833, as the party continued its northern trek, the pampas's arid, sandstone landscape gave way to lusher terrain, alternately of willow groves, marshes, and swamps. By dusk, the men had reached General Rosas's camp. Set on an open riparian expanse ten miles inland from Rio Colorado's mouth, the encampment of what Darwin called "the Christian army" covered about four hundred square yards along the river's north's bank. "It consisted of a square formed by waggons, artillery, straw huts, &c."

Cavalry comprised most of Rosas's troops. "I believe such [a] villainous Banditti-like army was never before collected together: the greater number of men are of a mixed race, between Negro, Indian & Spaniard: I know not the reason, but men of such origin seldom have good expressions." Wasting no time, Darwin found Rosas's "secretary" and inquired about the passport and horses he hoped to obtain.

The secretary, in turn, began "to cross question me in a most dignified & mysterious manner." Afterward, Darwin presented him with a letter of introduction from a government official in Carmen de Patagones, as well as an assortment of passports obtained for earlier inland journeys. "This," Darwin recalled, "was taken to General Rosas, who sent me a very obliging message & the Secretary returned all smiles & graciousness."

That night, the travelers found lodging in the "Rancho or hovel of a curious old Spaniard, who had served with Napoleon in the expedition against Russia." But hopes for an audience that day with Rosas soon faded; and the following day, as a hard rain pounded the camp, Darwin again waited in vain. In the interim, he heard multiple accounts of the storied general. Admirers, praising him as "the perfect Gaucho," noted "his feats of horsemanship are very notorious"; moreover:

> He wears the Gaucho dress & is said to have called upon Lord [Arthur] Ponsonby [successively Britain's minister in Buenos Aires and Rio de Janeiro] in it; saying at the same time he thought the costume of the country, the proper & therefore most respectful dress. By these means he has obtained an unbounded popularity in the Camp, and in consequence despotic powers.

On HMS *Beagle*'s second voyage to South America, the one on which Darwin sailed, the ship had returned to complete a survey of the continent's coasts and ports, newly opened to British trade. During the nineteenth century's early decades, following the triumph of independence movements across the continent, Spain's and Portugal's former colonies stood newly opened to foreign trade. In response, the United States, France, and Britain were competing to dominate that commerce.

For that age's British navy, a circumstance of geography rendered such surveys all the more important. Prior to the 1914 opening of the Panama Canal, British mariners had two ways of reaching South America's coasts: from the Atlantic, going "Round the Horn," sailing around the continent's tip, to reach the continent's Pacific coast. Or—also sailing from the Atlantic but approaching from the opposite direction—rounding Africa's Cape of Good Hope and, with sails propelled by the "westerlies," reaching South America via Australia. Given those distances, it was no small matter that British mariners be able to navigate with reliable charts South America's coasts and ports.

On August 15, two days after Darwin's arrival at the military encampment, General Rosas summoned the twenty-four-year-old Englishman.

Forty-four years old, Rosas was a long-faced, blue-eyed man possessed of an aquiline nose and a thick mane of dark upswept hair; and during their meeting, the commander lived up to his reputation as a charismatic leader. "In conversation he is enthusiastic, sensible & very grave," Darwin reflected in his diary. "His gravity is carried to a high pitch." Even so, the naturalist's account of the meeting is exasperatingly anodyne: "My interview passed away without a smile & I obtained what I wanted, a passport and order for the government post horses, & this he gave me in the most obliging and ready manner."

Darwin's diary entry for the next day, however, if not more revealing about the general, did provide additional, even admiring, words concerning his activities: "This war of extermination, although carried with the most shocking barbarity, will certainly produce great benefits; it will at once throw open four or 500 miles in length of fine country for the produce of cattle."

In a letter two years later, Susan Darwin, by then aware of Charles's admiration of Rosas, declined to upbraid her brother for his praise of him. But she could not resist sharing the Darwin household's outrage concerning the caudillo: "We never read anything so shocking as the murderous war upon the poor Indians—one can hardly believe anything so wicked at the present day as the conduct of General Rosas," she wrote in November 1835.

Four years later, however, Charles remained unrepentant in his admiration for the general. In 1839, in the first edition of his published account of his travels, the book later known as *The Voyage of the* Beagle, he offered a coldly strategic recitation of Rosas's strategy. With assistance from Chilean allies, he noted, the general intended to drive the Natives to a common gathering point and attack them in coming summers.

> This operation is to be repeated for three successive years. I imagine the summer is chosen as the time for the main attack, because the plains are then without water, and the Indians can only travel in particular directions. The escape of the Indians to the south of the Rio Negro, where in such a vast unknown country they would be safe, is prevented by a treaty

with the Tehuelches [an Indigenous people of Patagonia] to this effect;—that Rosas pays them so much to slaughter every Indian who passes to the south of the [Rio Negro] river, but if they fail in so doing, they themselves are to be exterminated. The war is waged chiefly against the Indians near the Cordillera [the Andes]; for many of the tribes on this eastern side are fighting with Rosas. The general, however, like Lord Chesterfield, thinking that his friends may in a future day become his enemies, always places them in the front ranks, so that their numbers may be thinned.

And lest anyone miss his admiring tone, Charles explicitly praised Rosas as "a man of an extraordinary character." The general, he wrote, wielded "a most predominant influence in the country, which it seems probable he will use to its prosperity." In 1845, however, in a later edition of the same book, a contrite Darwin appended a footnote to the page on which the praise appeared: "This prophecy has turned out entirely and miserably wrong."

For Darwin, Rosas's actions presented an object lesson not immediately grasped. But it would not be the final instance during his *Beagle* years that his thoughts, straying from scientific topics, turned to matters concerning South America's politics and Indigenous peoples.

PART II

SHROPSHIRE LAD, 1809–1831

"The childhood shows the man,
As morning shows the day."

—John Milton, *Paradise Regained*

3

"GAS"

For Charles Robert Darwin, the long road that eventually led to the camp of a South American caudillo began in the market town of Shrewsbury, England, where he was born on February 12, 1809. That same day—thousands of miles to the west, in a rough-hewn log cabin in the US state of Kentucky—the infant Abraham Lincoln also first saw the light of day. Of the circumstances associated with the two men's respective births, however, those attending Darwin's could not have been more propitious than those of Lincoln's humble origins.

Charles grew up at The Mount, a handsome three-story Georgian-styled house of redbrick and white trim, whose construction his wealthy father commissioned around 1800. The future naturalist was the fifth of six children born to physician and investor Robert Waring Darwin and his wife Susannah, daughter of industrial ceramics magnate Josiah Wedgwood and his wife Sarah—also *née* Wedgwood—a third cousin.

Shrewsbury lies in Shropshire, then and today a landlocked, largely rural county, in England's West Midlands. In Shrewsbury, Shropshire's county town, Robert Darwin prospered through a medical practice that served prominent families in the area. Prudent investments augmented his wealth—stocks in railroads and canals, and ownership of local rental properties.

The Darwin-Wedgwood linkage originated in a personal friendship that grew into a business relationship between Josiah Wedgwood Sr. and Erasmus Darwin, Charles's paternal grandfather, who shared broad interests in science and invention.

In 1796, Josiah's daughter Susannah ("Sukey" or "Susan" within the family) married Erasmus's son Robert. Using the large dowry Susannah brought to the marriage, Robert purchased agricultural land in Shropshire on which he built The Mount. Like other families of Britain's ascendant professional and middle classes, the Darwins and Wedgwoods identified with that era's Religious Dissenters, a category that included most Christians outside of the state-established Church of England. Early on, accordingly, most members of both families, with the exception of freethinker Erasmus Darwin, had belonged to the Unitarian church.

By 1809, however, when Charles was born, most of the Darwins and Wedgwoods, now wealthier and gentry-like in style, had settled into more respectable religious practices. Nine months after Charles's birth, for instance, his father Robert, though privately a religious skeptic, had his son baptized at St. Chad's, the parish church of Shrewsbury's Anglican—Church of England—congregation. Nine years later, in September 1818, Charles, joining his older (by five years) brother Erasmus (named for the boys' paternal grandfather), was enrolled as a boarder at Shrewsbury School, another local Anglican establishment. Even so, during Charles's earliest years, he and his siblings accompanied their mother to services at Shrewsbury's Unitarian Chapel, on High Street.

By the late 1820s, meanwhile, as Charles was growing up, two generations of Darwin men enjoyed reputations in medicine and the natural sciences. (The future naturalist Charles Robert was named for two physicians in the family—his father and a deceased uncle.) Notably, family patriarch, physician, and author Erasmus Darwin, ranked as a prominent intellectual in eighteenth-century England, whose views on politics and religion often sparked controversy. Erasmus's book *Zoonomia* (1794–96), read by Charles during his teens, included digressions on the nature of the "evolution" of life on earth—albeit speculations vastly different in approach than Charles's later theory.[*]

A freethinker, Erasmus, in contrast with the other, typically staid Darwins, was a twice-married libertine who fathered at least fourteen children, several with unmarried women. A contemporary recalled him as "somewhat above the middle size; his form athletic, and inclined to corpulence." He also possessed a "sunny smile," stammered, wore a full wig, and his body bore the traces of a severe smallpox. And though Erasmus died seven years before Charles's birth, he loomed at The Mount as a spectral presence—and not just for Charles.

The illustrious Erasmus had also possessed a tyrannical side that shadowed the life of Charles Darwin's father Robert Waring Darwin. Robert's older brother Charles (one of the future naturalist's two namesakes) had died in 1788 while studying medicine at the University of Edinburgh. And following his death, the elder Erasmus pressured Robert into taking up what was becoming a family tradition—of preparing at Edinburgh for a career in medicine. Another son of the elder Erasmus (also named Erasmus, a solicitor) drowned himself in 1799 at age thirty-nine.

Like the Darwins, the Wedgwoods commanded wealth and social prominence. The family attained its fortune through Charles's maternal grandfather, Josiah Wedgwood, founder of the Wedgwood Company. Producing pottery and tableware for Britain's upper and middle classes, the firm pioneered modern manufacturing and marketing techniques, and helped spark Britain's Industrial Revolution. Shaping Charles's later political convictions, Josiah also became a leading philanthropist of his day, funding charities and reformist causes, particularly abolitionism.

As for Charles's father, physician Robert Waring Darwin, the naturalist recalled him as "about 6 feet 2 inches in height, with broad shoulders, and very corpulent, so that he was the largest man whom I ever saw." Robert stopped weighing himself when his weight reached 24 stone (336 pounds). But if the Doctor was plainly obese with an incongruously

---

[*] In contrast to the theory later propounded by his famous grandson, Erasmus Darwin posited that individual species evolve in a predetermined process designed by a God-like "GREAT ARCHITECT."

high-pitched voice, he also, Charles recalled, possessed, when attending patients, a kindly, reassuringly competent manner: "He was generally in high spirits, and laughed and joked with every one—often with his servants—with the utmost freedom."

But Robert Darwin also had a dark side: "He had the art of making every one obey him to the letter. Many persons were much afraid of him." Among family members, Robert was often short-tempered, given to outbursts over trivial matters. Susannah, his dutiful wife and office receptionist, often suffered the worst during his flare-ups. Moreover, after 1800, with the difficult pregnancy that had accompanied the birth of Caroline Sarah, the couple's second child, Susannah seemed to age quickly.

By 1807, two years before Charles's birth but having already given birth to four children, Susannah lamented, "Everyone seems young but me." In declining health, she gave birth a final time, in 1810, to a daughter they named Emily Catherine. By July 1817, bedridden with a painful tumor, she breathed her last on the 15th at the age of fifty-two.

Charles was eight years old when his mother died. His father would live another three decades; and Charles thus retained vivid, even affectionate, memories of the man he called "the kindest man I ever knew." Of the physician's role in shaping his son's ideas, however, Charles was less complimentary:

> My father's mind was not scientific, and he did not try to generalise his knowledge under general laws; yet he formed a theory for almost everything which occurred. I do not think that I gained much from him intellectually; but his example ought to have been of much moral service to all his children. One of his golden rules (a hard one to follow) was, "Never become the friend of any one whom you cannot respect."

By contrast, those who knew Charles's mother Susannah in her younger healthier years recalled an attractive, quick-witted woman who played the spinet and enjoyed music and following the foibles of fashionable society. Charles, however, retained only vague memories of his mother. Most singularly, and sadly, he recalled the black velvet gown in which she was dressed when he and his siblings were brought into the room to view her in bed after her husband pronounced her death. Otherwise, "I can remember hardly anything about her except her death-bed, her black velvet gown, and her curiously constructed work-table," he recalled. "I believe that my forgetfulness is partly due to my sisters, owing to their great grief, never being able to speak about her or mention her name; and partly to her previous invalid state."

After Susannah's death, Charles found himself in a household managed by his autocratic father and a matriarchy of his three older teenaged sisters—in descending order of age, Marianne, Caroline, and Susan. Two years before his mother's death, Erasmus—Charles's five years older brother—had already left home for a boarding school.

Charles, meanwhile, grew up as a compulsive collector (bird's eggs, insects, postage stamps, and rocks) with an appetite for praise for his assemblages. He also delighted in poring over books in his father's library—particularly the lavishly illustrated volumes devoted to the then fashionable topic of natural history. And beyond his father's library, he recalled, "early in my school-days," a fellow student possessed a copy of *The Hundred Wonders of the World*, an illustrated, 1821 volume by C. C. Clarke (pseudonym of Richard Phillips): "I often read and disputed with other boys about the veracity of some of the statements; and I believe this book first gave me a wish to travel in remote countries, which was ultimately fulfilled by the voyage of the *Beagle*."

Charles likewise enjoyed exploring the family's greenhouse, just off The Mount's morning room. His boyish imagination transformed the glass-enclosed garden, teeming with beautiful fancy pigeons, exotic fruit trees, and rare shrubs, into a miniature, tropical wonderland, magically transported to staid old England. And outside, at the bottom of a steep hill behind The Mount, flowed the River Severn (at 220 miles, Britain's longest) in which Charles spent hours fishing and inspecting its creatures.

Meanwhile, during his early teens, Charles grew bored with Shrewsbury School's classics curriculum. Away from school, following his older brother Erasmus, he soon took up an interest in chemistry. Eventually, the siblings even set up a makeshift laboratory inside a tool shed on The Mount's grounds.

Erasmus—"Eras" to Charles—by then had decided to follow his father into the medical profession; and, in October 1822, Erasmus left home for studies at Christ's College, at the University of Cambridge. Over the coming months, Charles spent hours in the shed alone, often late into the night. Following procedures described in Henry and Samuel Parkes's *Chemical Catechism* (1806), he mixed and heated assorted chemicals into various combinations, soon acquiring his first education in chemistry. Hearing of the experiments, Dr. Samuel Butler* Shrewsbury School's headmaster and a respected classicist, criticized him for "wasting my time over such useless subjects." But among Charles's classmates, the experiments and the fumes they often produced soon won him a nickname—"Gas."

Over those early years, Charles's interests sprouted like toadstools after an autumn shower. His formal education, by contrast, proceeded without flair. His older sister Caroline, tutoring him and his younger sister Catherine at The Mount, had been his first teacher. In spring 1817, when he was eight years old, his mother, weeks before her death, enrolled him in a local Unitarian day school operated by the Rev. George Case. But it could not compete with interests already astir:

> By the time I went to this day-school my taste for natural his-
> tory, and more especially for collecting, was well developed. I
> tried to make out the names of plants, and collected all sorts
> of things, shells, seals, franks, coins, and minerals. The passion
> for collecting, which leads a man to be a systematic naturalist, a
> virtuoso or a miser, was very strong in me, and was clearly innate,
> as none of my sisters or brother ever had this taste.

A year later, in the summer of 1818, Dr. Darwin transferred Charles to Shrewsbury School. The Anglican boarding school, with its ancient dormitories and cold baths, had been established in 1552. There, he joined his brother Erasmus. But again, the curriculum left him uninspired:

---

* Headmaster Samuel Butler was a grandfather of the novelist Samuel Butler.

"Nothing could have been worse for the development of my mind than Dr. Butler's school, as it was strictly classical, nothing else being taught except a little ancient geography and history. The school as a means of education to me was simply a blank."

> The only qualities which at this period promised well for the future, were, that I had strong and diversified tastes, much zeal for whatever interested me, and a keen pleasure in understanding any complex subject or thing. I was taught Euclid by a private tutor, and I distinctly remember the intense satisfaction which the clear geometrical proofs gave me . . . With respect to diversified tastes, independently of science, I was fond of reading various books, and I used to sit for hours reading the historical plays of Shakespeare, generally in an old window in the thick walls of the school. I read also other poetry, such as the recently published poems of Byron, Scott, and [James] Thomson's [The] Seasons.

Still other activities entailed physical exertions. "As a very young boy," Charles acquired "a strong taste for long solitary walks." At Shrewsbury School, he made a virtue of the academy's modest distance from The Mount: "I had the great advantage of living the life of a true school-boy; but as the distance was hardly more than a mile to my home, I very often ran there," soon becoming "a fleet runner."

By age fifteen, "I became passionately fond of shooting, and I do not believe that anyone could have shown more zeal for the most holy cause than I did for shooting birds. How well I remember killing my first snipe, and my excitement was so great that I had much difficulty in reloading my gun from the trembling of my hands. This taste long continued, and I became a very good shot." Several years later, "I used to practise throwing up my gun to my shoulder before a looking-glass to see that I threw it up straight. Another and better plan was to get a friend to wave about a lighted candle, and then to fire at it with a cap on the nipple, and if the aim was accurate the little puff of air would blow out the candle."

Increasingly he joined his newfound love of hunting with growing equestrian enthusiasms. He savored both at The Mount and at Maer Hall,

Charles's uncle Josiah Wedgwood II's Staffordshire estate, in the village of Maer, thirty miles, an hour's ride, from The Mount. At Maer, particularly during the autumn hunting season, Charles relished riding with assorted cousins and his generous-spirited Uncle Josiah—"Uncle Jos."

Like his father Robert, Charles grew close to Susannah Darwin's younger brother Josiah II. (A loan from Robert Darwin had enabled Jos to purchase the Maer estate in 1807.) The Wedgwood patriarch, Josiah I (Charles's maternal grandfather) had died in 1795, a year before Charles's parents married. And while growing up, Charles cherished time spent at Maer. There, presided over by their beloved Uncle Jos, the Darwin siblings found respite from the frequent severity of The Mount, where casually expressed opinions might trigger Dr. Darwin's temper. In Charles's *Autobiography*, Maer glows like lost Camelot:

> My visits to Maer during these two and the three succeeding years were quite delightful, independently of the autumnal shooting. Life there was perfectly free; the country was very pleasant for walking or riding; and in the evening there was much very agreeable conversation, not so personal as it generally is in large family parties, together with music. In the summer the whole family used often to sit on the steps of the old portico, with the flower-garden in front, and with the steep wooded bank, opposite the house, reflected in the lake, with here and there a fish rising or a water-bird paddling about. Nothing has left a more vivid picture on my mind than these evenings at Maer. I was also attached to and greatly revered my Uncle Jos.

At Maer, Charles relished galloping over green fields and hills—along the way, stopping to fire at quail and snipe. Indeed, the trails lacing Maer's ancient forests, with their Scots pines, English oaks, and sycamores, beckoned with endless horizons of pleasure.

Back at The Mount, meanwhile, Robert Darwin was growing ever more deeply distressed about what he feared was his youngest son's increasingly directionless life.

4

EDINBURGH

During the mid-1820s, as Charles's studies at Shrewsbury School foundered, Dr. Robert Darwin eventually exhausted his patience. "You care for nothing but shooting, dogs, and rat-catching, and you will be a disgrace to yourself and all your family," he exploded in a pique.

In June 1825, suspecting medicine might provide a sound career for Charles, Robert Darwin removed his sixteen-year-old son from the school and made him an apprentice doctor. "I began attending some of the poor people, chiefly children and women in Shrewsbury," Charles recalled. "I wrote down as full an account as I could of the cases with all the symptoms, and read them aloud to my father, who suggested further enquiries, and advised me what medicines to give."

With his background in chemistry, Charles often mixed those prescribed medicines himself. "At one time I had at least a dozen patients, and I felt a keen interest in the work." His hunch seemingly confirmed, the Doctor soon "declared that I should make a successful physician—meaning by this, one who got many patients. He maintained that the chief element of success was exciting confidence."

Charles was to follow his father, older brother, and grandfather (the first Erasmus Darwin) into the medical profession. But where would he train—the University of Cambridge or the University of Edinburgh? Both institutions trained doctors. Robert Darwin, as had his father, had studied at Edinburgh. But Robert's oldest son Erasmus, who had selected and was then enrolled at Cambridge, soon encouraged Charles to join him there.

Unlike Edinburgh, Cambridge, affiliated with the Church of England, required students to pledge fealty to that denomination. Consequently, generations of wealthy English dissenters had headed north to Scotland, enrolling at Edinburgh as an alternative to England's two most prominent, both Anglican, universities: Cambridge and the University of Oxford. Edinburgh-trained Robert Darwin, for instance, despite outward acceptance of Anglican conventions, remained at core a Dissenter—in his case, a Unitarian and privately a religious skeptic.

Moreover, in the training of physicians, Edinburgh enjoyed the superior reputation over Cambridge, with better staff and facilities, greater receptivity to new ideas from Europe, and a better hospital for graduates to obtain practical experience. And finally, because both Robert Darwin and his illustrious father Erasmus had been trained at Edinburgh, Charles would arrive in "the Northern Athens" assured of a place at the tables of the city's elite.

By late 1825, Charles was Edinburgh bound. Erasmus, by then had completed his course of studies at Cambridge. But, increasingly disenchanted with Cambridge and eager to allay Charles's anxiousness about moving to Edinburgh, Erasmus arranged to perform his hospital studies at the Scottish university.

Weeks shy of Erasmus's twenty-first birthday, he and Charles, then sixteen, traveled together from Shrewsbury to Edinburgh. Arriving in late October 1825, the brothers rented quarters in a privately owned building. Most Edinburgh students, Charles recalled, lived in "little holes in which there is neither air or light." In stark contrast, the brothers' rooms, on Lothian Street, were "very comfortable & near the College."

From medieval Edinburgh Castle atop high Castle Rock to the serpentine streets that sloped below and away from that fortification, Scotland's capital presented a visual banquet. "It is a beautiful city, the most beautiful I ever saw—not so much on account of the buildings as on account of its picturesque position," abolitionist Frederick Douglass would rave during an 1846 visit.

In Edinburgh, Charles and Erasmus soon called on welcoming residents who had known their father and grandfather. But Charles's studies, by contrast, proved disappointing. "The instruction at Edinburgh was altogether by Lectures, and these were intolerably dull"—particularly those by anatomist Alexander Munro. "Dr. Munro made his lectures on human anatomy as dull, as he was himself, and the subject disgusted me." Moreover, his distaste for Munro's lectures led him to forfeit an opportunity to learn proper dissection methods. That shortcoming, along with an inability to draw, became lasting regrets.

Charles likewise abhorred the university hospital's operating theater, where he watched "two very bad operations, one on a child." In those days before anesthetics, to minimize trauma on patients, surgeons worked at dizzying speeds. Operating on strapped-down, screaming patients, practitioners, with dirty hands, clutching even dirtier saws, performed their procedures, as blood poured into sawdust-packed buckets beneath operating tables.

During both surgeries observed by Charles, he "rushed" away before their completion: "Nor did I ever attend again[,] for hardly any inducement would have been strong enough to make me do so; . . . The two cases fairly haunted me for many a long year." Moreover, walks through wards of the Royal Infirmary adjacent to the college, increased worries that he would ever overcome his squeamishness.

Only through sheer will had Charles's own father overcome—in truth, learned to manage—his own squeamishness. Throughout Robert Darwin's career, his aversion to blood, recalled Charles, rendered it difficult for him to administer the still common medical procedure of "bloodletting." "The thought of an operation almost sickened him, and he could scarcely endure to see a person bled."

Thomas Charles Hope's chemistry lectures, conducted "with great éclat," constituted the sole bright spots on Charles's Edinburgh pedagogical landscape. But even those failed to win "Gas" Darwin's full approbation—"to my mind there are no advantages and many disadvantages in lectures compared with reading."

In proposing that he and his brother live together, Erasmus had envisioned a tableau in which "we can both read like horses." And by all indications, in Edinburgh, they fulfilled that expectation. During their first term, the two removed more books from the university's library than any other borrowers. Nonetheless, they also found time for their share (or, in all fairness, compared to their peers, *less* than their share) of student indulgences—from gambling to drinking, from the then popular vogue for Syrian snuff to chemistry experiments that lapsed into escapades of getting high on "laughing gas."

The brothers also relished walks along the Firth of Forth estuary, gathering sea-slugs, sea-mice, and cuttlefish. Moreover, to improve the presentation of specimens in his *Aves* collections, Charles decided to learn a new skill. "I am going to learn to stuff birds, from a blackamoor," he reported to his sister Susan. His instructor John Edmonstone, a formerly enslaved black man, had been brought from Guiana by author and traveler Charles Waterton. Edmonstone, having learned taxidermy from Waterton, lived, like the Darwin brothers, on Lothian Street, and conducted his lessons at the Edinburgh Museum. "He only charges one guinea, for an hour every day for two months." Moreover, he recalled in his autobiography, "I used often to sit with him, for he was a very pleasant and intelligent man." Evoking Charles's memories of C. C. Clarke's *The Hundred Wonders of the World*, Edmonstone shared firsthand accounts of life in tropical climes. Their exchanges were also likely Charles's first with a person held in bondage.

After his first year at Edinburgh, Charles returned to Shrewsbury. During walks there and in the nearby Welsh hills, he showed off his newly acquired techniques for gathering and preserving natural speci-mens. But, not going unreported to Robert Darwin, at Maer's annual fall shoot, Charles also demonstrated that his zeal for hunting remained incriminatingly intact—killing in the season's first week alone, three hares, a rabbit, and over forty partridges.

By November 1826, when Charles returned to Edinburgh, Erasmus had left the city to enroll in London's Great Windmill Street School of Anatomy. In early 1828, Erasmus returned to Edinburgh to sit for final examinations. By summer 1829, however, having returned from a grand tour of Europe, he elected to abandon his pursuit of a medical career. In time, Robert Darwin agreed with Erasmus that, given "his delicate frame," the physician's life would impose "severe strain upon [his] body & mind." Thus, though Erasmus was but twenty-five years old, Dr. Darwin pensioned his oldest son into a life of retirement in London. There he lived in the rooms where his brother Charles, in later years, became a regular visitor.

For Charles, meanwhile, in early 1827, now living alone in Edinburgh and bored with classes, student societies, particularly the Plinian Society, occupied much of his time. Named for Pliny the Elder, the naturalist of classical Rome, the club was founded in 1823. And through the Plinian Society, Charles met several scientists fated to have a lasting influence upon him, among them John Coldstream and Robert Edmond Grant. Coldstream, two years older than Charles, studied marine animals. And, with Coldstream, through collecting trips beside, and in trawlers on, the Firth of Forth, Charles expanded his knowledge of marine wildlife, particularly sponges.

Of the two men, however, Grant was would have the greater influence on Charles. A decade older than his English friend, Grant was an Edinburgh native. After completing his medical studies there in 1814, living off an inheritance, Grant dedicated himself to studying marine life and the zoology of invertebrates. Well-connected and traveled, he had even met Jean-Baptiste Lamarck, the French naturalist and evolution theorist whose work had inspired Charles's grandfather Erasmus. Lamarck believed that physical changes in individual species, including use of particular organs or limbs, during their lifetime could be inherited by offspring.*

Lamarck also numbered among the first intellectuals to apply the term evolution to changes over time in species. The Latin *evolutio* referred to the unrolling of an ancient scroll. Its earliest English descendent, "evolution," similarly denoted a literal unfolding or unrolling. By the eighteenth century, however, naturalists such as Charles Bonnet and Albrecht von Haller, drawing on the word's implicit reference to an

---

*   The classic example of Lamarckian evolution was his now discredited belief that the giraffe's quest over time to feed on higher tree branches resulted in the species' longer neck and front limbs.

unfolding of preexisting parts, applied it to theories by which preexisting germs, embryos, or even miniature organisms "evolve" over generations into recognized modern species.

As the Darwin-Grant friendship deepened, the two spent hours on long walks, often along the Water of Leith, the small river that runs through the city. Grant was a freethinker whose views differed from those of prominent Christian clergymen. He thus disparaged the idea that fossils attested to divine creation—and stressed that the naturalist's job was to uncover the true history of the planet told in rocks.

Grant also introduced Charles to the Wernerian Natural History Society. The club met in the university museum, in the room of another prominent Edinburgh professor, mineralogist Robert Jameson. An adherent of that age's geological school of "Neptunism," Jameson believed that rocks resulted from the crystallization of materials in the planet's early oceans. Alas, however, Darwin found Jameson's lectures "incredibly dull"; "the sole effect they produced on me was the determination [to] never as long as I lived to read a book on Geology, or in anyway to study the science."

By contrast, Charles often enjoyed the Wernerian Society meetings—particularly its visiting lecturers, including on two occasions, the American ornithologist John James Audubon. Notably, he also attended a meeting of the Royal Society of Edinburgh, Scotland's national academy, over which author Walter Scott presided as president.

After two years in Edinburgh, Charles had found a handful of kindred souls who shared his interests. But, though he attended a few geology lectures that caught his interest, his studies otherwise flagged. In his final year there, he never even joined the library.

Following the 1826–27 term, Charles spent much of the spring traveling. He toured Scotland, called on Dublin and Portrane, Ireland, and visited London for the first time. In May, he joined his uncle Josiah Wedgwood II for a trip to Paris to collect his daughters (Charles's cousins) Fanny and Emma. The visit lasted several weeks, the only trip Charles would ever make to France and, indeed, to continental Europe.

Returned to Shropshire by July, Charles resumed his nature walks, and riding and shooting. He also called on old friends, including the family of William Mostyn Owen, a retired dragoon officer and owner of Woodhouse, a forested estate fifteen miles from The Mount.*

The no-nonsense aristocrat, known locally as "Squire," and his wife had two daughters, Sarah and Frances. Charles's sisters had been close to both girls since childhood and visited Woodhouse (also called The Forest) for extended stays.

At Edinburgh, reports from his sisters reached Charles of their recent visits to Woodhouse, missives recounting balls there and how the two Owen daughters had blossomed into bright and attractive young women: "I never saw such merry, agreeable girls," gushed Catherine, Charles's only younger sister, in an 1826 letter. "Talking so easily and naturally, and so full of fun and nonsense, they are very much admired, and get plenty of partners at the Balls."**

Charles required scant persuasion to visit any estate surrounded by forests and game; and the Owens girls added still more inducement. Clinching his decision, Charles, having recently returned from Paris himself, was word that the sisters had recently lived in France, were obsessed with all things French, and talked of little else. "They are," Catherine allowed, "not at all more reconciled to England, and are longing to return to France."

After September 1, the start of the hunting season, Charles became a regular visitor at Woodhouse. There, his attentions gravitated toward Frances—Fanny to those who knew her—at twenty the oldest of the sisters. Dark-eyed, petite, raven-haired, she was quick-witted and possessed a beguiling self-confidence. Though Fanny took painting lessons to placate her father, her true joy lay in pursuits more associated with the boys, including billiards and riding. Charles was immediately attracted to Fanny. But though the attraction seemed mutual, he also knew that, until he had firmer career prospects, he dared not broach the subject of marriage with Fanny, nor ask "Squire" Owen for her hand.

---

* In 1987, true to its festive traditions, Woodhouse hosted a reception celebrating the wedding of future British prime minister Boris Johnson to his first wife Allegra Mostyn-Owen.

** Fanny refers to the estate as The Forest in later references.

In the meantime, the two commenced a lively, if sporadic, correspondence. Ebbing and flowing over the coming years, the exchange evolved, in the main, into a long-distance flirtation. Fanny's letters teemed with frisky, coded nicknames for individuals and social types (eligible young men were "shootables," female visitors to Woodhouse, "muslins"). The code names she inevitably adopted for her and Charles—"Housemaid" and "Postillion"—gave playful voice to her yearnings to more fully join in his riding and other male-associated activities. Among staff employed in a gentry household, after all, "Housemaid" and "Postillion," were polar opposites—the former, a female performing indoor, domestic work; the latter, a male, working with horses, in an outdoor, often dangerous, job.

A March 1828 letter from Fanny updated Charles on the latest gossip and asked when he planned his next trip home. It closed with an entreaty flirtatious but, chaffing in gendered claustrophobia and self-denigration, teeming with mock courtliness:

> I must conclude for I find myself getting awfully dull and prosy, but what can you expect from an unfortunate exile of the Forest pity and forgive is all I ask—& believe me my dr. Postillion ever yr faithfull Housemaid | Fanny O—
>
> For Heaven's sake burn this, or if it falls into the hands of any of the young men, what would they think, of a Housemaid writing to Mr Charles Darwin.

Before and during those months, meanwhile, Doctor Darwin again grew worried about Charles. Weary of letters from Edinburgh asking for money, he found even more disturbing reports of his son's lackluster academic performance. But for the diagnosed condition, the physician also had in mind a possible remedy: "My father," Charles recalled, "perceived or he heard from my sisters, that I did not like the thought of being a physician, so he proposed that I should become a clergyman"—more specifically, a rural parish clergyman.

Robert Darwin knew that rural parish clergymen in the wealthy Anglican church often enjoyed enviable lives with undemanding responsibilities, comfortable rectories, and abundant time to pursue other interests—including natural history. Many of that day's prominent naturalists in England held such sinecures. Moreover, the wealthy Doctor Darwin also knew that such rural parish sinecures were routinely sold to the highest bidder.

Truth be known, Robert Darwin's latest career suggestion for Charles arose less from any belief that his son was particularly suited for the ministry—more from fears of what Charles, now eighteen, might otherwise become: "He was very properly vehement against my turning an idle sporting man, which then seemed my probable destination." Furthermore, as Charles later admitted, confirming suspicions held by his father, while at Cambridge, he had grown "convinced from various small circumstances that my father would leave me property enough to subsist on with some comfort." And that "belief was sufficient to check any strenuous effort to learn medicine."

In late 1827, when Robert Darwin presented his proposal, Charles feared answering too hastily: "I asked for some time to consider, as from what little I had heard and thought on the subject I had scruples about declaring my belief in all the dogmas of the Church of England. Otherwise I liked the thought of being a country clergyman."

"Accordingly," Charles recalled, "I read with care," *Exposition of the Creed*, by John Pearson, "and a few other books on divinity." After those readings and pondering his own beliefs, Charles reached a conclusion: despite the influence upon him of Freethinkers encountered at Edinburgh, his newer perspectives on natural history could be reconciled with Anglicanism.

"I did not then in the least doubt the strict and literal truth of every word in the Bible," he recalled. "I soon persuaded myself that our Creed must be fully accepted." As he had left Shropshire School before completing his studies, so Charles would withdraw from Edinburgh University without taking his degree.

In October, 1827, Charles, on the threshold of what his father feared was his wayward son's final chance at respectability, was admitted to Cambridge University.

5

CAMBRIDGE

I n fall 1827, after agreeing to attend Cambridge University and prepare for the ministry, Charles realized he had a problem. His studies there required a familiarity with classical languages; and, upon reflection, he realized that "I had never opened a classical book since leaving [Shrewsbury] school." To refresh his knowledge, Dr. Darwin hired a tutor to work with Charles in Shrewsbury through the fall. Thus, instead of moving to Cambridge in October as he would have otherwise, his arrival there would be postponed until January of the new year.

But after the tutoring commenced, "I found to my dismay that in the two intervening years I had actually forgotten, incredible as it may appear, almost everything which I had learnt even to some few of the Greek letters." To escape the tedium of relearning materials he had detested since first encounter, Charles made two trips to Woodhouse, where he indulged in his usual riding and shooting. With the Owen girls away in Brighton, however, both outings lacked the gaiety of recent visits there.

January 1828 found Charles in Cambridge. But because he arrived midway in the academic year, lodgings were unavailable in Christ's College. So, until the following October, when quarters there would be available, he rented rooms above a tobacco shop on Sidney Street.

Academically, those first months proved promising. "I soon recovered my school standard of knowledge, and could translate easy Greek books, such as Homer and the Greek Testament with moderate facility." Alas, however, that promising trajectory soon surrendered to a familiar outcome. "During the three years which I spent at Cambridge my time was wasted, as far as the academical studies were concerned, as completely as at Edinburgh and at [Shrewsbury] school."

Charles had registered for the ordinary Bachelor of Arts degree, the conventional curriculum that preceded theological training. His initial curriculum thus included elementary mathematics, geometry, and algebra—an immersion during which he surprised himself by the "delight" he found in Euclid. He also found unexpected pleasures in various Greek and Latin texts, and a seminal book of that day, Anglican theologian William Paley's *Natural Theology, or Evidences of the Existence and Attributes of the Deity*. Paley's work emphasized the role of an "intelligent Creator" in facilitating the adaptation of organisms to environments.

"The logic of this book," Charles recalled, "gave me as much delight as did Euclid. The careful study of these works, without attempting to learn any part by rote, was the only part of the Academical Course which, as I then felt and as I still believe, was of the least use to me in the education of my mind." No doubt, more specifically, Charles's immersion in Euclid and geometry furthered his ability to think in three dimensions, always a useful gift for geologists.

On March 24, 1830, Charles passed his "Little-go," the first of two examinations required for his degree. Ten months later, between January 14 and 20, 1831, he completed his final examinations—three days of written papers, that, after being marked, landed him tenth among 178 degree candidates not seeking honors.* He later attributed the unexpected triumph to "answering well the examination questions in Paley, by doing Euclid well, and by not failing miserably in Classics."

More broadly, historian Peter J. Bowler observed, "Darwin's scientific training at Cambridge was thorough, even if it was gained outside the curriculum." To be sure, in many passages of Charles's *Autobiography*, he paints a dark view of his three years at the Anglican university. Laments

---

* Although Darwin completed his final exams in January 1831, a residency requirement for his degree kept him at the university until the following June.

the son of the abstemious Robert Darwin, "my time was sadly wasted there and worse than wasted . . . and we sometimes drank too much." Nonetheless, he allows, "There were some redeeming features in my life at Cambridge . . . Upon the whole the three years which I spent at Cambridge were the most joyful in my happy life; for I was then in excellent health, and almost always in high spirits."

A friend, John Maurice Herbert, brought Charles into a "musical set," musicians who socialized and attended concerts together. Though Charles played no instrument, through "these men and hearing them play, I acquired a strong taste for music." Another friend, Charles Thomas Whitley, who had been a classmate at Shrewsbury School, "inoculated" him "with a taste for pictures and good engravings . . . I frequently went to the Fitzwilliam Gallery [in Cambridge], and my taste must have been fairly good, for I certainly admired the best pictures, which I discussed with the old curator."

The Glutton Club, a weekly supper gathering of Charles and four other students, had a less conventional pursuit. With dishes prepared by the college's kitchen staff and washed down with generous quantities of port, the club devoted itself to the consumption of "strange flesh"—wild animals, principally birds, including bitterns and hawks. Held in its members' respective rooms, the meals came to an ignominious end the night they attempted, with unspecified disastrous consequences, to eat "an old brown owl."

But no interest Charles took up at Cambridge gave him "so much pleasure as collecting beetles." As industrialism transformed life across England, practitioners of "beetling"—weary of cities fouled by the "dark Satanic mills" cursed by poet William Blake—found sanctuary in forests and other natural settings. There, armed with nets and alcohol-filled bottles, the fad's zealots searched for their quarry beneath rocks, tree bark, and fallen leaves.

A competitive spirit drove beetling, and few pursued it as aggressively as William Darwin Fox, the naturalist who introduced Charles to the craze. A second cousin, four years younger than Charles, Fox was, like his kin, enrolled at Christ's College, preparing for the ministry. Soon spending hours in the field together, Fox imbued Charles's insect-collecting with a new sophistication. In earlier days, "It was the mere passion for collecting" beetles that propelled him—"for I did not dissect them and rarely compared their external characters with published descriptions, but got them named anyhow."

Moreover, until those Cambridge days, Charles—curiously, considering his early acquired zeal for killing birds—had retained a concern for his entomological prey's mortality. At age ten, after consulting a sister, "I concluded that it was not right to kill insects for the sake of making a collection." Under Fox's tutelage, however, Charles, abandoning such concerns, became a devotee of *An Introduction to Entomology*, a four-volume work by William Spence and William Kirby that served as the pastime's bible (a work Charles later took on his *Beagle* travels and used frequently). Moreover, during his Cambridge days, "very soon" Fox "armed me with a bottle of alcohol, in which I had to drop any beetle which struck me as not of a common kind."

On one occasion, while tearing a strip of old bark from a tree, Charles spotted "two rare beetles and seized one in each hand." Moments later, "I saw a third and new kind, which I could not bear to lose, so that I popped the one which I held in my right hand into my mouth. Alas it ejected some intensely acrid fluid, which burnt my tongue so that I was forced to spit the beetle out, which was lost, as well as the third one."

Eventually, using funds his father provided, Charles "employed a labourer to scrape during the winter, moss off old trees and place [it] in a large bag, and likewise to collect the rubbish at the bottom of the barges in which reeds are brought from the fens [marshes], and thus I got some very rare species."

Indeed, it was beetling that, in 1829, first landed the name Charles Darwin in a scientific publication. The reference appeared in *Illustrations of British Entomology*, a series authored by English naturalist James Francis Stephens. Describing several beetles recently collected by Charles, the entry was brief. But, as he later recalled, "No poet ever felt more delight at seeing his first poem published than I did at seeing in Stephen's *Illustrations* . . . the magic words, captured by C. Darwin, Esq.'"

The Rev. John Stevens Henslow, an Anglican priest and Cambridge professor, was thirty-one years old when eighteen-year-old Charles arrived at the university. And during Charles's three years at the university and later, Henslow "influenced my whole career more than any other."

Like Charles, Henslow came from a well-heeled family of professionals and, as an adolescent, acquired an interest in chemistry. But when the time arrived to select a profession, Henslow's father, as had Darwin's (eventually), dispatched him to Cambridge to train for the clergy. Other interests, however, intervened: at Cambridge, compulsive collecting interests, particularly of shells and insects, snagged Henslow's attentions.

With mathematics, chemistry, and mineralogy dominating his undergraduate studies, Henslow completed his degree in 1818. Four years later, at twenty-six, he was appointed professor of mineralogy. After marrying a year later—to supplement his meager £100 university stipend—he accepted the curacy of the nearby Little St. Mary's Church. And, in 1827, he was named Regius Professor of Botany.

Charles's brother Erasmus knew and admired Henslow. Quite possibly, during an 1828 Cambridge visit, he introduced the professor to his younger brother. But not until Charles's second and final year at Cambridge did Charles register for and attend Henslow's botany lectures—his only formal instruction in the natural sciences during his entire time at the university. More formatively, Charles recalled, "Henslow used to take his pupils, including several of the older members of the University, [on] field excursions, on foot, or in coaches to distant places, or in a barge down the river, and lectured on the rarer plants or animals which were observed. These excursions were delightful." Moreover, drawing Charles deeper into Henslow's circle, he became a regular attendee at soirees hosted by Henslow and his wife.

As a clergyman, the Rev. Henslow adhered to conventional Anglican doctrine and liturgy as expressed in the denomination's Thirty-nine Articles of Religion. But Charles, with limited passions for such matters, easily avoided exchanges concerning religion with the professor. And only after Charles, in January 1831, passed his final examination did the two establish a mentor-protégé relationship. But when they did, the bond was evident to all at the university:

> [I] took long walks with him on most days; so that I was
> called by some of the dons "the man who walks with
> Henslow"; and in the evening I was very often asked to join

his family dinner. His knowledge was great in botany, entomology, chemistry, mineralogy, and geology. His strongest
taste was to draw conclusions from long-continued minute
observations. His judgment was excellent, and his whole
mind well-balanced.

During Darwin's final Cambridge year, with Henslow's encouragement, he read *A Preliminary Discourse on the Study of Natural Philosophy*,
a recent work by English astronomer and polymath John F. W. Herschel.
The book, "stirred up in me a burning zeal to add even the most humble
contribution to the noble structure of Natural Science." During that same
period, Henslow also pressed upon his mentee another work destined to
have a lasting influence—*Personal Narrative of Travels to the Equinoctial
Regions of the New Continent during the Years 1799–1804*, by the Prussian
explorer and naturalist Alexander von Humboldt and his collaborator,
the French naturalist and explorer Aimé Bonpland.

Of the three authors, Humboldt would leave the deepest mark on
Darwin. Still alive then and in his early sixties, Humboldt had traveled
widely in tropical climes between 1799 and 1804, particularly South
America—journeys recounted in his *Personal Narrative*, a work that
merged biology, meteorology, geography, and other natural sciences.
Humboldt's writings had won admirers on both sides of the Atlantic,
including Thomas Jefferson, Napoleon Bonaparte, Simón Bolívar, Johann
Goethe, and, soon enough, Charles Darwin.

Charles grew particularly infatuated with Humboldt's account of
a 1799 visit, en route to South America, to Tenerife, the largest of the
Canary Islands, off Africa's northwestern coast. "I copied out from Humboldt long passages about Tenerife, and read them aloud" during walks
with Henslow and others. *Personal Narrative* included a vivid description of Pico de Teide, the volcano that dominated Tenerife, as well as a
colossal Dragon Tree that Humboldt had inspected. The island lay over
two thousand miles from England but still closer than most of Humboldt's exotic destinations, close enough for Charles to contemplate his
own trip to the island. "At present," he wrote in April to William Fox, "I
talk, think, & dream of a scheme I have almost hatched of going to the

Canary Islands. I have long had a wish of seeing Tropical scenery & vegetation: & according to Humboldt, Teneriffe is a very pretty specimen."

As they planned their trip, Henslow stressed to Charles the importance of his learning more geology and surveying techniques if he
intended to seriously study Pico de Teide and Tenerife's other terrestrial
wonders. Even better, as Charles soon reported to Caroline Darwin,
"Henslow promises to cram me in geology." Otherwise, Charles rhapsodized, he could barely contain himself:

> All the while I am writing now my head is running about the
> Tropics: in the morning I go and gaze at Palm trees in the hot-
> house and come home and read Humboldt: my enthusiasm is so
> great that I cannot hardly sit still on my chair. . . . I never will
> be easy till I see the peak of Teneriffe and the great Dragon
> tree; sandy, dazzling, plains, and gloomy silent forest are
> alternately uppermost in my mind. I am working regularly at
> Spanish; Erasmus advised me decidedly to give up Italian. I
> have written myself into a Tropical glow.

Henslow soon commenced the promised instruction in geology and
survey-related matters, the latter notably including tutoring in trigonometry
and the use of a clinometer, a tool for measuring the angle of slopes. Henslow
also asked his friend, geologist and theologian Adam Sedgwick, if Charles
might accompany him during part of his usual summer field work. Specifically, Henslow asked whether Charles might join Professor Sedgwick's
planned trip, expected to last a week or more, to north Wales, to conduct a
survey intended to correct suspected errors in a geological map of Britain.

Charles, by then twenty-two, and Sedgwick, forty-six, knew one another
slightly. Nevertheless, Sedgwick agreed to the request. Even by then
ranked among the founders of modern geology, Sedgwick, focused on
Britain's older rocks, would later with a colleague establish the "Cam-
brian" and "Devonian" divisions on the geological timescale.

The vicar's son from Yorkshire had risen from humble beginnings. By his early thirties, hard work and a formidable intellect elevated him to the rank of professor. Typifying that era's British geologists, throughout his life, Sedgwick remained a liberal reformer but with firm evangelical convictions.

Those latter beliefs became conspicuous in another role that he played at all-male Cambridge. In 1827, Sedgwick was named Cambridge's senior proctor, the official who represented the university in legal proceedings. In that post, with a zeal matching that of his geological investigations, he took up the cause of protecting the personal morality of Cambridge's men, young and old alike.

His attentions focused on young women who found their way to Cambridge. Usually in their teens, the girls were often in dire straits, pregnant, orphaned, hungry, or destitute. From nearby towns and villages, they flocked there in search of domestic work or simply a night on the town with well-heeled university men. Cambridge's men, in turn, often found sexual pleasure with the women. Sedgwick, for his part, soon became an expert on the young women's whereabouts. Ready to make arrests and, in court, to testify against the women, he knew where and when to find them. In January 1828, alone, his testimony sent fifteen girls to the Spinning House, the local prison and workhouse for convicted prostitutes.

By the end of July 1831, meanwhile, Charles had returned to Shrewsbury for the summer. Because the town lay on Sedgwick's route to Wales, the geologist had accepted an invitation to stay overnight at The Mount. The next morning, August 5, the two set off in a gig for northern Wales —more specifically, for "Llangollen, Conway, Bangor, and Cap[el] Curig."

Charles's exposure to Sedgwick and his methods proved formative. "This tour was of decided use in teaching me a little how to make out the geology of a country," he recalled in his *Autobiography*. "Sedgwick often sent me on a line parallel to his, telling me to bring back specimens of the rocks and to mark the stratification on a map. I have little doubt that he did this for my good, as I was too ignorant to have aided him."

But for Charles, the Welsh outing also served, in retrospect, as a cautionary tale in the follies of misreading, even ignoring, compelling evidence—in that case, dramatic signs of the role of glaciers in sculpting Wales's mountains. In those days, Sedgwick was doctrinally ill-disposed to acknowledging any major role of glaciers in sculpting the earth's surfaces. Thus, recalled Darwin, "On this tour I had a striking instance [illustrating] how easy it is to overlook phenomena, however conspicuous, before they have been observed by anyone." Indeed, even as the two explored what geologists now call the Cwm Idwal cirque and regard as a textbook case of a glacier-sculpted valley, they failed to recognize its origins:

> We spent many hours in Cwm Idwal, examining all the rocks with extreme care, as Sedgwick was anxious to find fossils in them; but neither of us saw a trace of the wonderful glacial phenomena all around us; we did not notice the plainly scored rocks, the perched boulders, the lateral and terminal moraines. Yet these phenomena are so conspicuous that, as I declared in a paper published many years afterward in the *Philosophical Magazine*, a house burnt down by fire did not tell its story more plainly than did this valley. If it had still been filled by a glacier, the phenomena would have been less distinct than they now are.

Parting with Sedgwick on around August 12, Charles traveled alone to northwest Wales's coastal town of Barmouth to join friends from Cambridge. There, by then even more obsessed with Tenerife, he playfully badgered his friend John Maurice Herbert with jests about how many days he could wear a shirt there without washing it.

During those same days, word reached Charles of the passing of his Cambridge friend Marmaduke Ramsay. His friend, who weeks earlier, had died of a blood infection, had planned to accompany Charles to Tenerife. Over the past months, Henslow and another Cambridge friend Richard Dawes had also agreed to join the trip to Tenerife—only to, in succession, withdraw from the contemplated journey—and now, Ramsay, Charles's most recent prospect for the trip, was dead.

The would-be voyager faced a quandary: should he postpone the trip until he could find a companion? Or plow ahead with plans for a solo outing? Or perhaps just accept this latest setback as an omen and abandon the entire idea?

Such decisions, he eventually decided, could await another day. For now, soon leaving Barmouth, Charles looked forward to returning to Shrewsbury and to Maer. At the latter, he eagerly anticipated catching up with some sorely missed shooting with his Uncle Jos—"for at that time I should have thought myself mad to give up the first days of partridge-shooting for geology or any other science."

Upon arriving, on August 29, at The Mount, however, a pair of startling letters awaited Charles—both in the same large envelope, postmarked London: one, written on the 24th was from Henslow, the other penned two days later, came from George Peacock, a Cambridge friend of Henslow's. Both letters concerned what Henslow described as an "offer which is likely to be made you of a trip to Terra del Fuego & home by the East Indies."

At that instant, for twenty-two-year-old Charles Darwin, the snow-crowned heights of Tenerife's Pico de Teide suddenly shrinking in his mind's eye, became far less beguiling.

6

"YOU ARE THE VERY MAN
THEY ARE IN SEARCH FOR"

On August 29, 1831, Charles Darwin, twenty-two years old, read the two momentous letters that, exceeding his wildest fantasies, offered him passage on a two-year global voyage. The missive from the Rev. John Stevens Henslow, written five days earlier, commenced with a cursory lament for the recent "loss of our inestimable friend poor Ramsay"—Marmaduke Ramsay who was to have accompanied Charles to Tenerife.

Dispensed of that "painful subject," Henslow turned toward "the offer" that he "fully expect[ed]" Charles to "eagerly catch"—to accompany an expedition that would take his former student to Tierra del Fuego and other exotic climes.

Relayed by Henslow, the invitation originated in London, in the Office of the Admiralty and Marine Affairs that oversaw the Royal Navy. It reached Henslow via a letter from George Peacock, a mutual Cambridge friend of Henslow and Charles. Henslow's letter to Charles, worth quoting at length, summarized the offer:

> I have been asked by Peacock who will read & forward
> this to you from London to recommend him a naturalist as

companion to Capt [Robert] Fitzroy employed by Government to survey the S. extremity of America. I have stated that
I consider you to be the best qualified person I know of who
is likely to undertake such a situation. I state this not on the
supposition of your being a *finished* Naturalist, but as amply
qualified for collecting, observing, & noting any thing worthy
to be noted in Natural History. Peacock has the appointment
at his disposal & if he can not find a man willing to take the
office, the opportunity will probably be lost. Capt. F. wants a
man (I understand) more as a companion than a mere collector
& would not take any one however good a Naturalist who was
not recommended to him likewise as a *gentleman*. Particulars
of salary &c I know nothing. The Voyage is to last 2 y^{rs}. & if
you take plenty of Books with you, any thing you please may
be done. You will have ample opportunities at command. In
short I suppose there never was a finer chance for a man of
zeal & spirit. Capt F. is a young man.

Henslow urged Charles to come "instantly" to Cambridge and
meet with Peacock to "learn further particulars." During that meeting,
Henslow advised, "Don't put on any modest doubts or fears about your
disqualifications for I assure you I think you are the very man they are
in search of." The letter filled the entire page; and on its other side,
Henslow scrawled a postscript: "The expedn. is to sail on 25 Sept: (at
earliest) so there is no time to be lost."

Peacock's letter, written a few days after Henslow's, added further
inducements for Charles to join the venture: "The expedition is entirely
for scientific purposes & the ship will generally wait your leisure for
researches in natural history &c. Peacock described Captain FitzRoy
as a "public spirited & zealous officer, of delightful manners. . . . greatly
beloved by all his brother officers."

To illustrate FitzRoy's good-heartedness, Peacock noted that in
association with an earlier expedition, he had "spent 1500£ in bringing
over & educating at his own charge 3 natives" of Tierra del Fuego.
Moreover, for the upcoming expedition, FitzRoy had already engaged

"at his own expense an artist at 200[£] a year to go with him: you may be sure therefore of having a very pleasant companion, who will enter heartily into all your views."

Henslow in *his* letter had urged Charles to come to Cambridge to meet with Peacock. But Peacock, assuming Charles's acceptance of the proposal, suggested instead that he hasten to London and meet with the Admiralty's Captain Francis Beaufort, render his answer official, and "complete your arrangements."

The hunt for "a naturalist as companion" to the expedition's commander had actually originated with Captain FitzRoy, who would be conducting the voyage aboard a small, two-masted warship HMS *Beagle* then being refitted for the outing.* In search of the companion, FitzRoy had spoken to Francis Beaufort, chief hydrographer in the Admiralty Office, who, in turn, had written to mathematician George Peacock, a Cambridge lecturer and tutor, who, in turn, had relayed the solicitation to Henslow.

Due to a misunderstanding, however, Henslow originally thought the Admiralty was seeking a seasoned naturalist, a qualification that would have excluded Charles. Acting on that misconception, and unmentioned in his letter to Charles, Henslow had briefly considered offering himself for the voyage, a temptation soon abandoned due to familial obligations. Also unbeknownst to Charles, Henslow, before writing to Charles, had tried to recruit his own brother-in-law, naturalist and clergyman Leonard Jenyns, for the voyage. But Jenyns—a decade older than Charles and saddled with responsibilities in the rural parish where he served as vicar—likewise, to his lasting regret, declined.

Upon reading the two letters on August 29, Charles recalled, "I was instantly eager to accept the offer." The following morning, however, "My father strongly objected." To Dr. Darwin, the entreaty sounded quixotic—its timing conveniently serving as his son's latest dodge in a long history of avoiding the responsibilities of career and family.

---

* The *Beagle*'s name reflected a predilection of that day's British navy to name ships after animals. Darwin's later friend Thomas Huxley would travel the world as assistant surgeon and de facto naturalist aboard HMS *Rattlesnake*.

Additionally, Dr. Darwin and Charles's sisters argued that he underestimated the miseries and perils of life at sea, including disease, drowning,
filthy conditions, and shipwreck. The following morning Charles wrote
to Henslow:

> Mr. Peacocks letter arrived on Saturday, & I received it late
> yesterday evening. As far as my own mind is concerned, I
> should I think, *certainly* most gladly have accepted the oppor-
> tunity, which you so kindly have offered me. But my Father,
> although he does not decidedly refuse me, gives such strong
> advice against going that I should not be comfortable, if I did
> not follow it. My Fathers objections are these; the unfitting me
> to settle down as a clergyman. My little habit [inexperience]
> of seafaring, the *shortness of the time* & the chance of my not
> suiting Captain Fitzroy. It is certainly a very serious objection,
> the very short time for all my preparations, as not only body
> but mind wants making up for such an undertaking. But if
> it had not been for my Father, I would have taken all risks.

Done with his letter to Henslow, Charles set off that same morning
for Maer, for some badly needed riding and shooting with Uncle Jos.
Before Charles departed, however, his father, having further reflected
on the offer, hinted of a possible compromise. "If you can find any man
of common sense, who advises you to go," he told his son, "I will give
my consent."

Both understood a "man of common sense" as a clear reference to
Uncle Jos. Indeed, a note that the doctor sent to Maer with his son to his
brother-in-law underscored that assumption: "Charles will tell you of
the offer he has had made to him of going for a voyage of discovery
for 2 years," Robert Darwin wrote. "I strongly object to it (on var)ious
grounds." Even so, he avowed, "I will not detail my reasons that he may
have your unbiassed opinion on the subject, & if you think differently
from me I shall wish him to follow your advice."

At Maer, Charles described the offer and his father's reaction to it.
But Uncle Jos had an entirely different, uniformly positive, reaction to

the opportunity being dangled before his nephew. By late afternoon, their conversation turned toward how to dissuade Dr. Darwin from his opposition. Toward that end, Uncle Jos eventually suggested that Charles write out a list of his father's objections. Afterward, Jos would write a letter to his brother-in-law, responding to each objection.

Jos also suggested that Charles write his own letter to Robert Darwin—conciliatory in tone, treading carefully, and avowing respect and gratitude. Taking up the suggestion, Charles commenced the letter. "I am afraid I am going to make you again very uncomfortable," he wrote to his father. "But upon consideration, I think you will excuse me once again stating my opinions on the offer of the Voyage." After delicately alluding to "the different way all the Wedgwoods view the subject from what you & my sisters do," Charles came to the heart of his letter:

> I have given Uncle Jos, what I fervently trust is an accurate & full list of your objections, & he is kind enough to give his opinion on all. The list & his answers will be enclosed. But may I beg of you one favor. it will be doing me the greatest kindness, if you will send me a decided answer, yes or no. If the latter, I should be most ungrateful if I did not implicitly yield to your better judgement & to the kindest indulgence which you have shown me all through my life.—& you may rely upon it I will never mention the subject again.

A separate page—soon sent to The Mount in the same envelope as Charles's letter to his father—detailed Charles's encapsulation of Doctor Darwin's objections to the expedition:

(1)   Disreputable to my character as a Clergyman hereafter
(2)   A wild scheme
(3)   That they must have offered to many others before me, the place of Naturalist
(4)   And from its not being accepted there must be some serious objection to the vessel or expedition
(5)   That I should never settle down to a steady life hereafter

(6)   That my accomodations would be most uncomfortable
(7)   That you should consider it as again changing my
         profession
(8)   That it would be a useless undertaking

Still later that day, with Charles's list before him, Uncle Jos commenced his own letter to the doctor, one-by-one answering each of
Robert Darwin's eight objections. Knowing his no-nonsense brother-in-
law well, Jos took care to steel the letter with a hard-nosed, business-like
practicality:

> My dear Doctor
> I feel the responsibility of your application to me on the
> offer that has been made to Charles as being weighty, but as
> you have desired Charles to consult me I cannot refuse to give
> the result of such consideration as I have been able to give it.
> Charles has put down what he conceives to be your principal
> objections & I think the best course I can take will be to state
> what occurs to me upon each of them.
>
> 1—I should not think that it would be in any degree disrepu-
> table to his character as a clergyman. I should on the contrary
> think the offer honorable to him, and the pursuit of Natural
> History, though certainly not professional, is very suitable to
> a Clergyman
>
> 2—I hardly know how to meet this objection, but he would
> have definite objects upon which to employ himself and might
> acquire and strengthen, habits of application, and I should
> think would be as likely to do so in any way in which he is
> likely to pass the next two years at home.
>
> 3—The notion did not occur to me in reading the letters &
> on reading them again with that object in my mind I see no
> ground for it.

4—I cannot conceive that the Admiralty would send out a bad vessel on such a service. As to objections to the expedition, they will differ in each mans case & nothing would, I think, be inferred in Charles's case if it were known that others had objected.

5—You are a much better judge of Charles's character than I can be. If, on comparing this mode of spending the next two years, with the way in which he will probably spend them if he does not accept this offer, you think him more likely to be rendered unsteady & unable to settle, it is undoubtedly a weighty objection—Is it not the case that sailors are prone to settle in domestic and quiet habits.

6—I can form no opinion on this further than that, if appointed by the Admiralty, he will have a claim to be as well accommodated as the vessel will allow.

7—If I saw Charles now absorbed in professional studies I should probably think it would not be advisable to interrupt them, but this is not, and I think will not be, the case with him. His present pursuit of knowledge is in the same track as he would have to follow in the expedition.

8—The undertaking would be useless as regards his profession, but looking upon him as a man of enlarged curiosity, it affords him such an opportunity of seeing men and things as happens to few.

You will bear in mind that I have had very little time for consideration & that you & Charles are the persons who must decide.

Both letters went out the next day with the September 1 mail. Charles and Uncle Jos, meanwhile, intended to devote that morning to riding and hunting. By ten o'clock, however, recognizing that both were too distracted for such sport, they slipped into Jos's carriage. Shrewsbury-bound, they would press their case in person.

But their worries were unjustified. Having read Jos's letter, Robert Darwin's opposition to the venture had already crumbled. "When we arrived," Charles recalled, "all things were settled, and my Father most kindly gave his consent." The doctor had even written a letter to his brother-in-law, thanking him for "taking so much trouble and interest" in Charles's plans. Moreover, he pledged, as those plans progressed, to "give him all the assistance in my power."

7

CAPTAIN FITZROY

During the late summer of 1831, as Charles Darwin navigated the shoals of his father's opposition to his joining the *Beagle* expedition, he feared jeopardizing the prize that fate was dangling before him. More particularly, he worried that his delay in answering Captain Beaufort's letter might send the invitation to another young man. Beyond the delay caused by his father's misgivings, after all, Beaufort's letter had been written, mailed, and reached The Mount days before Charles returned home and read it. He likewise worried that, via George Peacock, word might have reached Beaufort of Doctor Darwin's opposition to his joining the voyage.

Thus, on September 1, immediately after Uncle Jos left The Mount, Charles wrote to Beaufort. Accepting the offer, he apologized for his delayed response, attributing it the Welsh trip and his father's now assuaged concerns. Charles assured Beaufort he would go to Cambridge the following morning, meet with Henslow, and "thence will proceed immediately to London" to call at the Admiralty. Before leaving, Charles asked family members not to share word of the venture in town; "The reason I dont want people told in Shrops: in case I should not go, it will make it more flat."

Hours later, at 3:30 A.M., Charles left Shrewsbury in a stagecoach. In Cambridge, Henslow provided more details about the offer—revealing that he and Leonard Jenyns had both considered taking the spot now being offered to Charles. Adding to the woes of his "tremendous hard week," while Charles was in Cambridge, a "discouraging letter" from FitzRoy arrived. Sent to Charles Wood, a friend of both Charles and Henslow, it notified Charles that, due to a misunderstanding between himself and Peacock, FitzRoy had offered the spot on the voyage to a friend. But if the friend declined, FitzRoy promised, the position was Charles's to claim. For Charles, FitzRoy's note felt like a final blow. Even so, he pressed on to London—albeit having, as he put it, *"entirely* given it up" and now feeling the pain of a jilted suitor.

When Charles arrived in London on Monday, September 5, the city buzzed with excitement over Whig-sponsored reform legislation snaking through Parliament. The Whigs had triumphed in the general election the previous year and their legislation, if passed, promised to expand voting rights and otherwise liberally refurbish political life throughout the United Kingdom. And although the Whigs had largely gained control over the broader Reform movement across the country, widespread rioting by farmworkers persisted. Simultaneously, however politically incongruous, London was otherwise in a celebratory spirit, anticipating that Thursday, the coronation of sixty-six-year-old King William IV who had ascended the throne a year earlier.

Because his brother Erasmus was out of town, Charles found lodgings on Spring Gardens, a dead-end street near the Admiralty building. From there, he immediately walked around the corner to London's busy Whitehall thoroughfare. There, he entered the three-storied Admiralty building, a handsome Queen Anne–styled edifice of redbrick with white limestone trim.

Inside, he found both Beaufort and FitzRoy, the latter, "a slight figure . . . dark but handsome." At twenty-six, the captain was four years older than Charles. Moreover, with his aquiline nose, slight mustache, and high forehead, FitzRoy's presence, in contrast to the callow Charles, projected world-weariness and aristocratic hauteur. He was, after all, directly descended from, among other eminences, King Charles II.

Upon greeting Charles, FitzRoy shared important news: five minutes earlier, he explained, he had received a letter from the friend to whom he had offered the extra spot on the expedition.

The friend had declined the invitation. Given that, the captain asked, was Charles still interested?

Later that day, writing to Henslow, Charles playfully suggested a hymn that summarized the day's meeting: "Gloria in excelsis [Deo] is the most moderate beginning I can think of," he mused. "Cap. FitzRoy is every thing that is delightful, if I was to praise half so much as I feel inclined, you would say it was absurd, only once seeing him. I think he really wishes to have me."

Even better, Charles added, FitzRoy had made clear that, during the voyage, he desired to share with him his dining table, and when assigning cabins, "he will take care I have such room as is possible."

Unbeknownst to Charles, the captain's first impressions of that morning's caller had been ambivalent. His reservations concerned Darwin's nose. FitzRoy was a devotee of Johann Kaspar Lavater, the eighteenth-century proponent of physiognomy, the belief that physical traits, particularly facial features, reveal traits of character. And during that first meeting, Charles later learned, "I had run a very narrow risk of being rejected, on account of the shape of my nose! . . . He doubted whether anyone with my nose could possess sufficient energy and determination for the voyage. But I think he was afterward well-satisfied that my nose had spoken falsely."

Charles, then and later, apparently thought little of physiognomy. Four decades later, after world fame had blessed his name, he received a book in the mail sent by its author Joseph Simms, an American exponent of physiognomy. The work, *Nature's Revelations of Character*, included a flattering reference to Darwin, asserting that he possessed the quality of "Observativeness Large," an attribute it defined as the "quality or disposition to look closely and with rigid care at every object." Enclosed with the book was a note requesting a favor: if, to Darwin, the volume "prove[ed] sufficiently interesting," Simms asked that he "say a word in . . . [the book's] favour for print."

Simms also asked if Darwin might take pencil and paper in hand, kneel, trace an outline of his right foot, and send it to Simms. No response to the request has been located; and no reference to Simms's book appears in any of Darwin's publications. The introduction to his 1872 book *Expression of the Emotions in Man and Animals*, however, opens with a dismissive view of physiognomy: works on the topic, he wrote, "which I have consulted, have been of little or no service to me."

FitzRoy's concerns about Charles's nose, meanwhile, caused no lasting damage to their relationship. Throughout that week of their first meeting, the two could be seen dining together and riding around London in FitzRoy's gig—"going about the town & ordering things," as Charles recalled to Henslow.

Charles's personal inventory of equipment acquired for the voyage eventually included a microscope and a pocket compass. In Charles's mind, his purchases, the spending of his father's money on the venture, confirmed the reality, now as tangible as a sales receipt, of an imminent adventure that a week earlier felt like a lost dream: "By this," he crowed to Henslow, "you will perceive it is all settled; that is to say I cannot possibly conceive any cause happening of sufficient weight to alter my determination."

Not that the captain expected Charles to supply all of the items that he would need for the voyage. Or that FitzRoy and the Admiralty did not already possess their own substantial inventory of relevant items: "Fitzroy has an immense stock of instruments & books."

There was, however, one category in which Charles spent profligately. "I have ordered pistols & a rifle, both of which by Fitzroys account I shall have plenty of use for. These really are nearly the only expensive things I shall want." To another friend, Charles gushed that he actually *enjoyed* purchasing items for the expedition—particularly guns: "It is such capital fun ordering things, to day I ordered a Rifle & 2 pair of pistols; for we shall have plenty of fighting with those d——Cannibals: It would be something to shoot the King of the Cannibals Islands."

Outward bonhomie aside, FitzRoy harbored a dark history, as did HMS *Beagle*. The expedition that Charles had been invited to join would, in fact, not be the *Beagle*'s first survey voyage to South America. Five years earlier, in May 1826, accompanied by the larger HMS *Adventure*, the *Beagle*, leaving from Plymouth, England, had sailed to the continent on its first survey. The outing was conducted under the overall command of Phillip Parker King, captain of the *Adventure*, with Pringle Stokes commanding the *Beagle*.

Two years later, however, in August 1828, while the ships were anchored at Tierra del Fuego, the region's desolation and puzzling waters overwhelmed the *Beagle*'s Captain Stokes. His dejection was memorialized in his shipboard journal: "The place being destitute of inhabitants, is without that source of recreation, which intercourse with any people, however uncivilized, would afford a ship's company after a laborious and disagreeable cruise in these dreary solitudes." Days later, on August 12, locking himself in his cabin, Stokes put a bullet in his head. As gangrene set in, the thirty-five-year-old captain lingered for eleven days before breathing his last.

Over the coming months, the *Beagle* and *Adventure* remained in South America, continuing their survey work. In December 1828, however, while the *Beagle* lay anchored at Rio de Janeiro, Robert Otway, commander of the British navy's South America Station* ordered the *Beagle*'s acting captain replaced by an officer from HMS *Ganges*, another British ship anchored at Rio.

Robert FitzRoy became the *Beagle*'s new captain. A stellar graduate of the Portsmouth naval college, FitzRoy rose to his new post, his first command, from the rank of flag lieutenant (an assistant) to the admiral supervising the South America Station. FitzRoy was twenty-three years old when Otway promoted him to command the *Beagle*. Hard work, and, to be sure, skilled seamanship had driven his rise, from midshipman to captain in nine years. But influential political connections also aided that ascent. And, as the *Beagle*'s new commander, FitzRoy quickly established a reputation as a stern taskmaster, fair but willing to order floggings to recalcitrant seamen to enforce shipboard discipline.

---

* A formation, based in Rio, existing from 1808 to 1834, of British naval ships.

The captain also possessed a volatile temper. Years later, Darwin recalled that officers starting shifts aboard the *Beagle* routinely asked about FitzRoy's mood that day, inquiring of their peers, "'whether much hot coffee had been served out this morning,'—which meant how was the Captain's temper?"

From late 1828, when FitzRoy assumed command of the *Beagle*'s first expedition and over the next two years, all of his hallmark personality traits came into play as he worked to complete the vessel's survey orders. Acting on those instructions, he eventually returned the ship to Tierra del Fuego. And, while anchored there in May 1830, an incident occurred of far-reaching consequences. While conducting survey work, one of the ship's whaleboats—the small two-masted open boats carried aboard the *Beagle* and used in waters for which that larger vessel was ill-suited—was stolen by a group of Indigenous people.

A chase ensued. But the *Beagle* failed to overtake the culprits and recover the boat. Following a scuffle, however, its crew did capture and eventually bring aboard the *Beagle* five relatives of the thieves, hostages that the ship's crew intended to hold as ransom for the return of the stolen boat.

One of the captives later escaped. The other four, however, after none arrived to bargain for their release, remained aboard the *Beagle* as it sailed to other spots along Tierra del Fuego's coast. But at each successive location, FitzRoy failed to find what he considered a suitable landing spot to place the Natives ashore.

Eventually, he decided to bring them to England. There, he decided, their lives would be improved through exposure to Christianity and English society. Afterward, they could be returned to their home in the expedition that FitzRoy assumed would be dispatched to complete the current voyage's work.

In the end, their survey work left unfinished, the *Adventure* and *Beagle* returned to Plymouth, England, in October 1830, months earlier than planned. Upon returning, FitzRoy placed all four Fuegians in the local naval hospital—one because he was displaying symptoms of smallpox, the other three for vaccination against the disease and thereafter for the mandatory quarantine.

Weeks later, the young man whom the crew had named Boat Memory died of the pox. The other three, their hospital stays successfully concluded, remained FitzRoy's responsibility.

At his own expense, FitzRoy soon enrolled all three—a young girl about nine years old, a boy about fifteen, and a young man in his midtwenties—in a church-sponsored school in the town of Walthamstow, outside of London. There, they acquired English fluency and the trappings of "civilized" Christian culture. The evangelical Anglican FitzRoy believed that those who remained unconverted to that faith faced an eternity in Hell.

The captain, meanwhile, was resolute that the three not be exploited as exotics from a distant land. Even so, he did arrange for the heads of all three to be inspected by a phrenologist, a practitioner of a body of lore similar to physiognomy. And as word of their presence circulated, eventually reaching St. James's Palace, the three, in late 1831, were presented to King William IV and Queen Adelaide.

By mid-1831, meanwhile, with no immediate plans afoot for a second South American expedition, FitzRoy grew preoccupied with the political reforms the Whigs hoped to enact in Parliament—"innovations which," in his view, "now threaten . . . and tend to destroy that Communion, which has raised us to the first rank among nations." Resolving to bring his Church-and-King conservatism to the civilian sphere, he stood for a seat in the House of Commons from a borough in Suffolk's market town of Ipswich. But that May, when the votes were counted, FitzRoy placed third. Observed Darwin biographers Adrian Desmond and James Moore, "Just 145 Ipswich votes stopped Robert FitzRoy" from winning a seat in the Commons, thus enabling "Charles Darwin to take his place in history."

Beaufort, meanwhile, though declining to commission a second South American survey expedition, did eventually offer to provide the Fuegians, under FitzRoy's care, passage on the next navy vessel bound for their native land. FitzRoy, however, refused to entrust their well-being to others. In late spring—taking a twelve-month leave of absence from his naval responsibilities—he booked passage on a private ship to Tierra del Fuego for himself and the three Fuegians.

Before that ship sailed, however, an intervention with the Admiralty by George FitzRoy, the Duke of Grafton, a politically connected uncle of Robert's, brought a welcome change in plans. Beaufort authorized a second South American survey, to be led by FitzRoy aboard HMS *Chanticleer*. But when *Chanticleer* was deemed unsuitable for the voyage, the commission was assigned to another, for FitzRoy, more familiar, vessel: HMS *Beagle*.

Beaufort's act spared FitzRoy the burden of personally bankrolling a voyage. Gladdening him still more, plans soon materialized for the Church Missionary Society, an Anglican-affiliated organization that usually sent missionaries to Africa and Asia, to dispatch one aboard the *Beagle* to Tierra del Fuego.

Because, however, the society could not afford the funding with which it usually supported missions, it had trouble recruiting a candidate for the distant posting. In the end, the job went to Richard Matthews, a volunteer still in his late teens and inexperienced as a missionary. Even so, FitzRoy, after meeting Matthews, was impressed. In the captain's eyes, the young man, however objectively unqualified, deserved credit for volunteering for a task so "difficult and trying."

Over the summer of 1831 arrangements for the new expedition moved forward propitiously. But FitzRoy had another request for Beaufort. He had not been aboard the *Beagle* when Stokes took his life. He did, however, know firsthand, from his subsequent return with the ship to Tierra del Fuego, the forlornness that led to his predecessor's suicide. Furthermore, he knew firsthand the loneliness that stalks *any* commander, particularly those tasked with global expeditions.

Equally foreboding, FitzRoy himself was prone to depression. It ran in his family. An uncle, Robert Stewart, Viscount Castlereagh, a prominent diplomat and statesman, had, in 1822, slit his own throat. Moreover, FitzRoy recalling his own morose feelings while at Tierra del Fuego, viewed Stokes's fate as a cautionary tale. Reinforcing such fears, FitzRoy, by disposition, was something of a loner. While often sociable, his personality also had a severe, private, even brooding side. And his ready willingness to flog seamen never won him any shipboard friends. By Royal Navy tradition, lest he undermine his authority, a ship's captain was well advised to limit fraternization with subordinates. To relieve the isolation that otherwise would accompany his command, FitzRoy struck upon an idea: why not invite a civilian to join the voyage—someone outside the ship's chain of command with whom he might share his dining table? Even better, find one who shared his interests in natural history. Such regular company, FitzRoy reasoned, might reduce his own odds of following Stokes's downward spiral.

Years later, in *Narrative of the Surveying Voyages of His Majesty's Ships Adventure and Beagle between the Years 1826 and 1836*, FitzRoy's contribution to the three-volume *Journal of Researches*, the semi-official, published account of the survey expeditions, the captain, would omit reference to Darwin's companion role on the second voyage. Instead, he summarized the origins of the budding naturalist's participation and its expected benefits—for Darwin and for the expedition:

> Anxious that no opportunity of collecting useful information, during the voyage, should be lost; I proposed to the Hydrographer that some well-educated and scientific person should be sought for who would willingly share such accommodations as I had to offer, in order to profit by the opportunity of visiting distant countries yet little known. Captain Beaufort approved of the suggestion, and wrote to Professor Peacock, of Cambridge, who consulted with a friend, Professor Henslow, and he named Mr. Charles Darwin, grandson of Dr. Darwin the poet, as a young man of promising ability.

Meanwhile, even as Charles, in early September 1831, reveled in his purchases of guns for the expedition, he had yet to commit to the venture. Over those days, however, with FitzRoy and Beaufort, he did negotiate his terms. "The conditions," FitzRoy recalled, "asked by Mr. Darwin were, that he should be at liberty to leave the *Beagle* and retire from the *Expedition* when he thought proper, and that he should pay a fair share of the expenses of my table."

Charles's attempts, however, to alter the ship's planned route back to England, found Beaufort inflexible. The fifty-seven-year-old Ireland-born Huguenot-descended naval commander and scientist was not about to take directions from a twenty-two-year-old landlubber. Reaching back to his youth, maps and marine surveys were, for Beaufort, serious business: His father had produced an admired map of Ireland; and Francis, as a fifteen-year-old sailor, had been shipwrecked due to an inaccurate chart.

After enlisting as a sailor for the East India Company, Francis Beaufort had eventually commanded ships for that global enterprise and, still later, for the British navy—including, for the latter, warships during the Napoleonic wars, where he was seriously wounded. Later, returning to naval service, he spent most of the subsequent decades involved in marine surveys—directing ships in far-flung locales around the world, and eventually, from a desk in London. There, in 1829, by then an admiral, the self-educated scientist became the Royal Navy's chief hydrographer. In that post, Beaufort won praise for wide-ranging innovations in disciplines ranging from astronomy to meteorology. In 1833, the formula he developed for estimating and classifying wind-forces, the Beaufort wind scale, became mandatory on British navy vessels.

Charles, while meeting with FitzRoy and Beaufort, tried persuading Beaufort to permit the *Beagle* to make a broader-ranging circumnavigation of the globe. As Charles made his case, however, FitzRoy, in a sotto voce aside, advised silence on the matter with Beaufort. As FitzRoy later explained to Darwin, politically, "he [FitzRoy himself] has interest enough" among influential Tories. And assuming Prime Minister Earl Grey's Whig government, then in its second year, "is not everlasting," the Tory FitzRoy believed, he would be able, at a later date, to "get the ship ordered home by whatever track he likes." ("I shall soon turn Tory!" Charles, recounting the aside, later joked to Susan Darwin.)

Over those days, meanwhile, as the two grew closer, FitzRoy increasingly confided in the younger man, even admitting, as Charles recounted to Susan Darwin, that his earlier note about having mistakenly promised Charles's spot to a friend had been a ruse.

> Cap. Fitz first wished to have [a] naturalist & then he seems to
> have taken a sudden horror of the chances of having somebody
> he should not like on board the Vessel: he confesses, his letter
> to Cambridge, was to throw cold water on the scheme.

By September 9, Charles, having formally agreed to join the voyage, was describing FitzRoy as "my beau ideal of a Captain." Indeed, upon learning that FitzRoy had become aware of his newest recruit's Whig loyalties, Charles even believed that the two might, if not transcend, then at least avoid, partisan differences: "I dont think we shall quarrell about politics."

During those weeks, FitzRoy also finalized arrangements with Richard Matthews, the twenty-one-year-old missionary with the Church Missionary Society, who had agreed to remain in Tierra del Fuego with the three Fuegians—known to the crew as Fuegia Basket, Jemmy Button, and York Minster.

Plans called for Matthews to assist the Fuegians' resettlement. He was to help them build and furnish houses, establish a vegetable garden, and raise pigs, chickens, and goats; as well as continue their education, religious and otherwise. The instructions, consigning Matthews to a life of desolation, further called for him to establish a mission in Tierra del Fuego, an outpost dedicated to providing hospitality to passing British seamen, and more generally, to spreading the gospel of Jesus Christ and the Bible among the region's Indigenous peoples.

Matthews, along with Charles Darwin, numbered among at least eight supernumeraries—civilians recruited by FitzRoy who were outside of the *Beagle*'s military chain of command. Particularly for Charles, the coming years would provide abundant lessons in the vagaries of life outside of that formal hierarchy.

8

HMS *BEAGLE*

On September 11, 1831, Captain FitzRoy decided the time had arrived for Charles Darwin to see HMS *Beagle*. Leaving London that morning, the two, over the next three days, sailed aboard a steam packet ship—east down the Thames, then west in the English Channel along England's South Coast to Devonport, in Plymouth Sound.

Besides giving FitzRoy a look at the sea legs of his newest recruit, the trip allowed time for him to unspool for Darwin the entire doleful tale of the *Beagle*'s earlier voyage and his quest to repatriate the three Fuegians. Likewise, the days provided opportunity for FitzRoy to detail the political and economic forces driving the *Beagle*'s work: British merchants and other investors were eager to compete against the United States, France, and Spain for access to South America's markets. They thus required up-to-date charts of the continent's coasts and ports. And those charts would provide better information for getting to those entrepôts, as well as practical sailing routes through Tierra del Fuego.

In late 1831, HMS *Beagle*, eleven years old and in rickety, weathered condition, was undergoing a conversion from a ten-ton brig into a three-masted bark. Thus, at Devonport, when Darwin first saw and boarded the vessel, he and FitzRoy necessarily raised their voices to hear one another above the din of hammers, mallets, and saws wielded by the carpenters, painters, caulkers, joiners, and riggers refitting the ship.

The renovation, funded largely by the navy but with contributions from FitzRoy, would eventually equip the *Beagle* with new upper-deck skylights, a reinforced copper bottom, and a patent galley stove (whose fire did not have to be extinguished during turbulent weather). Its features also included a windlass (a device for lowering and lifting anchors), chains rather than ropes (as needed), a more modern rudder, state-of-the-art lightning conductors, and, to lessen interference with the ship's compasses, cannons of brass rather than iron. The refitting also raised by about a foot the ship's upper deck. To assist its tasks, the *Beagle* would carry seven small, open boats—a two-masted twenty-six-foot yawl, a single-masted twenty-three-foot cutter, four oar-propelled whaleboats (each about twenty-five feet long), and a twenty-five-foot oar-propelled dingy (or jolly boat).

Moreover, as a Royal Navy vessel, FitzRoy's ship sailed well armed: "The *Beagle* was designed to carry eight 18 lb. carronades and two 6-pound long guns," wrote paleontologist and naval historian Keith Stewart Thomson. "Her bulwarks were pierced with six gunports on each side and two at the stern. In normal times, the carronades were mounted down the sides, and the long guns were used as stern or bow 'chasers.'" Provoking protests from the Admiralty, the *Beagle* eventually sailed from England with seven guns on its main deck—two shy of FitzRoy's original request. At Rio de Janeiro, he would purchase, at his own expense, two more nine-pounders.

For all that, however, Darwin's first glimpse of his own quarters aboard the *Beagle* left him crestfallen. "My own private corner looks so small that I cannot help fearing that many of my things must be left behind." he lamented. Days later, however, recently installed cabin-nameplates provided a welcoming reintroduction: "My cabin"—the ship's poop cabin—"is the drawing one, & in the middle is a large table, over which we 2 sleep in hammocks, but for the first 2 months there will be no drawing to be done, so that it will be quite a luxurious room & good deal larger than the Captains cabin."

The ship's chart table devoured most of the ten-by-eleven-foot area of the poop cabin (from *le poupe*, French for "the stern"). Chests and seats for officers working on surveys lined its port wall; and filling its entire forward wall were a washstand, a cabinet for storing instruments, and a chest of drawers for storing charts.

Against the cabin's aft and starboard walls were the bookshelves of the ship's library, with its hundreds of volumes. Most of the books belonged to FitzRoy and had been on the *Beagle*'s first voyage. As the captain had crowed to a sister, "I flatter myself I have a complete library in miniature, upward of 400." On the *Beagle*'s second expedition, FitzRoy accorded all officers, as well as Darwin, library privileges. Travel and natural history books dominated the collection.* And FitzRoy's rules governing the library indicate the seriousness that he brought to the assemblage:

> The books in the Poop Cabin are at the Service of all the Officers of the Beagle who will comply with the following regulations:
>
> Books are to be taken from, and returned to their places by the Person appointed for that purpose.
>
> Every Book, whether *Old* or *New*, *bound* or *Unbound*, is to be covered, temporarily, by the person who has it in use.
>
> Books are not to [be] transfered from one Officer to another without the knowledge of the person who has it in charge.
>
> Two Catalogues will be kept, one for general use, the other for the Cabin.
>
> The names of those who take Books are to be written in a list kept for that Purpose.
>
> Any Officers who have books which they think will be generally useful and of which there are not already Duplicates in the Catalogue will confer a general benefit by lending them in a similar manner, inserting their names in the Catalogue, and if more convenient keeping them in the Poop Cabin.
>
> Books are to be taken, or returned in morning before ½ past 8.

---

* Two "catalogs"—lists—that once existed of the library's books have since gone missing. But scholars in recent decades have reconstructed a list of most of its volumes.

Books are never on any account to be taken out of the
Vessel.

In front of the chart table in Charles's quarters, rising through the
cabin, was the *Beagle*'s mizzenmast (the aft-most of the ship's three
masts). A newly installed skylight brought into the space natural light, a
precious amenity aboard ships of that day. Directly above the cabin was
the *Beagle*'s poop deck, a high platform, ideal for taking observations.
Uniquely among his shipmates, Darwin also enjoyed the use of a sofa in
the captain's cabin; and, when FitzRoy was out, he often retreated to it
to recline when seasick or to read.

Inevitably, of course, once the cruise was underway, Darwin would
find his own cabin less capacious than recently imagined. His personal
collections took up space; and the only other storage area assigned to
him was a locker, where he stored specimens, in the *Beagle*'s fo'c's'le
(or forecastle), an enclosure in the most forward section of the ship's
main deck. That extra space, however, as Charles's daughter Henrietta
later recalled, apparently failed to assuage the irritations of the *Beagle*'s
punctilious second-in-command: "My Father used to describe how John
Clements Wickham the first Lieutenant—a very tidy man who used to
keep the decks so that you c[oul]d eat your dinner off them—used to say
'If I had my way, all your d.d. mess would be chucked overboard & you
after it, old Flycatcher.'"

During his first visits aboard the *Beagle*, Darwin was delighted to
learn that his cabinmate was to be nineteen-year-old John Lort Stokes,
the ship's assistant surveyor. Stokes—of no relation to the late Captain
Stokes—had sailed on the *Beagle*'s first voyage. Before reaching Devonport, Darwin had met and liked his future cabinmate; and considered
him his favorite among the *Beagle*'s officers.

As the two men became familiar with their cabin, however, they discovered that, once in their hammocks, only about two feet lay between
their faces and the deck above. Moreover, because Darwin was over six
feet tall, getting the extra length to accommodate his height required his
hanging one end of the hammock on a hook inside his cabin's forward-
wall cabinet. Thus, each time prior to slipping into the hammock, he faced

the tedium of removing the cabinet's top drawer. Moreover, because the poop cabin projected over the *Beagle*'s stern, the two men could feel—and hear—the ship's sounds and movements on a magnified level. Little did he then know, but that proximity would bode ill for the seasick-prone recent Cambridge graduate.

9

DEVONPORT

F rom Plymouth in mid-September 1831, Darwin rushed overland via
a night coach back to London, arriving on the 17th. From there, he
left for Cambridge, where he spent two days updating Henslow on
recent developments. Afterward, he hastened to Shrewsbury, arriving
there on the twenty-second. Over the coming days, Darwin paid a quick
visit to Maer and otherwise completed his packing and saying goodbye
to Shropshire residents. Plans fixed, he now spoke openly of the voyage.

Moreover, providing an inspirational passport of sorts for the voyage,
Henslow had recently given Darwin a volume of Humboldt's writings.
Darwin had first encountered the explorer in a volume borrowed from
Henslow. And now, also thanks to Henslow, he had his own copy to
bring aboard the *Beagle*—of the 1822 English translation of volumes
one and two of the *Personal Narrative*. The book, which gathered both
volumes into a single volume, was inscribed: "J. S. Henslow to his friend
C. Darwin on his departure from England upon a voyage around the
World. 21 Sept. 1831."

From The Mount, on October 2, Darwin left for London. There,
he met with landscape painter Augustus Earle, another supernumerary
recruited by FitzRoy. The Royal Academy–trained artist hand been
enlisted to create paintings of the *Beagle*'s various stops. At thirty-eight,
Earle already ranked as a seasoned world traveler, with extended sojourns

in South America; and like Darwin, he had permission to spend extended time away from the ship.

In London, Darwin also met with specialists holding expertises relevant to his journey, from taxidermy to natural history collecting. Arrangements for the natural history specimens that Darwin expected to send back to England from his travels, after all, weighed much on his mind. For that age's naturalists, such collections constituted an established route to professional prestige. He also knew that a collection's prestige derived, in part, from the prominence of the institution which displayed it. Writing to Henslow, Darwin was already strategizing: "I do not think the Admiralty would approve of my sending them to a Country collection, let it be ever so good,—& really I doubt myself, whether it is not more for the advancement of Nat. Hist. that new things should be presented to the largest & most central collection."

From London, Darwin hastened to Plymouth and Devonport.* He reached Plymouth on the evening of October 24, and the following morning boarded the *Beagle*. Though still not prepared to sail, the ship, since he last saw it, had been hauled out of the dockyard and slipped into the harbor. In his mind, however, the ship, including his cabin, once again appeared too small. "The absolute want of room is an evil, that nothing can surmount," he complained to Henslow.

Even so, it dawned on Charles hours later, those weeks of labors *had* transformed the once rotting hulk. The following morning, the 25th, he captured the transformation in the diary that he'd begun keeping the night before: "The men were chiefly employed in painting the fore part & fitting up the Cabins. The last time I saw her on the 12th of Septr she was in the Dock yard & without her masts or bulkheads & looked more like a wreck than a vessel commissioned to go round the world."

By mid-November, he was raving to Henslow, "She looks most beautiful, even a landsman must admire her. *We* all think her the most perfect vessel ever turned out of the Dock yard. One thing is certain no vessel

---

* Though often used interchangeably in contemporary documents, the neighboring ports of Devonport and Plymouth were separate towns in Darwin's day. In 1914, the two, along with the town of East Stonehouse, were combined to form what eventually became the City of Plymouth.

has been fitted out so expensively & with so much care. Everything that can be made so is of Mahogany, & nothing can exceed the neatness & beauty of all the accomodations."

Darwin had arrived at Devonport expecting to sail on November 4. But over the coming weeks, as the ship's refitting dragged on, projected sailing dates came and went. He used the enforced limbo to catch up on correspondence—including, on November 17, summarizing for his cousin William Fox "an outline of the Instructions, which came down yesterday." The directions, Darwin approvingly noted, "leave a great deal to the Captains judgement, & I am sure they could not leave it to a better one." While crossing the Atlantic, there would be stops in the Canary Islands, (including, he hoped, Tenerife!), the Cape Verde Islands, and the Fernando de Noronha archipelago. In Brazil they would call at Salvador de Bahia and Rio de Janeiro. At the latter port, Darwin was already anticipating a climb up Corcovado Mountain, site of today's *Christ the Redeemer* statue, "for I hear there is no view in the world at all equal to it."

From Rio, plans called for the *Beagle* to plunge south to Montevideo, Uruguay, for an extended stay. While each of the earlier stops was expected to last about a week, the Montevideo anchorage would be of longer duration. During the ship's toils along South America's Atlantic coast, work expected to "consume about [a] year & half," FitzRoy expected Uruguay's capital to serve as the ship's "headquarters," the port to which it would "often return for fresh provisions &c."

South of Montevideo, the *Beagle* would commence its "regular work." At the heart of this voyage, after all, lay the unfinished labors of the *Beagle*'s first expedition, surveys required to update charts of Argentina's and Uruguay's Rio de la Plata estuary, the Patagonian coast, eastern Tierra del Fuego, and the Falkland Islands. And, after rounding Cape Horn, at the tip of South America, the *Beagle*, finding its way into the Pacific, had still more assigned survey work, along Chile's Chiloé Archipelago and that country's mainland ports. Afterward, wrote Darwin with Byronic aplomb, "we are to proceed as far Northward as Captain likes (I daresay to California)."

But however northerly the *Beagle* sailed, eventually it would bend to a westerly course, through the Pacific and Indian oceans. En route, there were to be stops at Tahiti and other South Pacific islands, New South Wales (in Australia), Tasmania, and other locales. Eventually, rounding Africa's Cape of Good Hope and bending northward, returning to the Atlantic, the *Beagle* would find its way back to England. "Time, which no one can alter, is the only serious inconvenience," Darwin reflected to William Fox. "Why, I shall be an old man, by the time I return, far too old to look out for a little wife." To Henslow, however, over those same days, he offered a less lighthearted expression of such concerns: "I grieve to say time is unlimited, but yet I hope we shall not exceed the 4 years." A measure of the expedition's elasticity, an outing originally presented to Darwin as "to last 2 years," in mere weeks, had doubled in its projected duration.

In early December, as its refitting continued to stall the *Beagle*'s departure, Darwin managed a brave face, writing to Henslow, on the third, "My time passes away very pleasantly." Even so, the delays left him with little to do. "My chief employment is to go on board the Beagle & try to look as much like a sailor as ever I can. I have no evidence of having taken in man, woman or child." But though frustrated, he remained smitten with the travels ahead. "When I think of all that I am going to see & undergo, it really requires an effort of reasoning to persuade myself, that all is true," he confided to Fox. "That I shall see the same land, that Captain Cook did."

During those same days, Darwin asked Henslow to resolve a matter that seemed, for the departing prodigal son, to ratify his father's worst characterization of his spendthrift habits. Embarrassed, Charles delicately inquired, "I am going to ask you to do one more commission & I trust it will be the last." The matter concerned what was effectively a double billing that his father had paid. "When I was in Cambridge," he explained, "I wrote to Mr. Ash, asking to send my college account to my Father after having subtracted about 30£ for my furniture. This he has forgotten to do, & my Father has paid the bill, & I want to have the Furniture money transmitted to my Father. Perhaps you would be kind enough to speak to Mr. Ash. I have cost my Father so much money. I am quite ashamed of myself."

During the delay, Darwin not only wrote letters. He also received them—including one from Fanny Owen. Over the past years, their relationship—ambiguous and proceeding erratically, usually at distances—had ebbed and flowed. Moreover, it had hardly helped that while Charles was at Cambridge, Fanny accepted a marriage offer from the Rev. John Hill, a local clergyman. The marriage, for reasons now unclear, was soon called off. But it underscored the sad fact that if the bond shared by Charles and Fanny had ever blossomed into true romance, it had remained star-crossed. And, to be sure, the letter from Fanny that reached Charles in early December, though hinting of a future together, underscored the sadness of their four past years of missed opportunities:

> I hope *not* that this may reach you in time, for I want to have one bit more chat with you. . . . Pray my dear Charles do write me one last adieu if you have a spare half hour before you sail. I should like very much to send you some account of us now & then during yr. absence if I knew where to direct to you? You cannot imagine how I have *missed* you already at the Forest [Woodhouse], & how I do long to see you again. May every happiness & pleasure attend you dear Charles, and return to us as soon as *you can* I *selvishly* say!

By December 2, the *Beagle*'s refitting was complete. FitzRoy had designated the fifth as their latest sailing date, and Charles was expecting his brother Erasmus's arrival in Devonport for a farewell visit. Their expected imminent departure, necessitating final packing, further brightened his spirits, a change in mood reflected in his diary entries for those days:

> *2nd* Worked all day long in arranging & packing my goods in the drawers. Erasmus arrived in the afternoon & I spent with him a very pleasant evening.
> *3rd* Incessantly busy in ordering, paying for, packing all my numberless things; how I long for Monday even sea-sickness must be better than this state of wearisome anxiety. Erasmus being here is a great pleasure, but I do not see much of him.

4th I am writing this for the first time on board, it is now about one oclock & I intend sleeping in my hammock. I did so last night & experienced a most ludicrous difficulty in getting into it; my great fault of jockeyship was in trying to put my legs in first. The hammock being suspended, I thus only succeded in pushing [it] away without making any progress in inserting my own body. The correct method is to sit accurately in centre of bed, then give yourself a dexterous twist & your head & feet come into their respective places. After a little time I daresay I shall, like others, find it very comfortable. I have spent the day partly on board & partly with my brother: in the evening, Cap King & son, [John Lort] Stokes, my brother & myself dined with Cap FitzRoy.

Alas, however, the next morning, December 5, brought "a heavy gale from the south." Once again, their departure was canceled and rescheduled for the next day. That evening, after dining ashore with Erasmus, Charles returned to the dockside lodging where he had slept for the past weeks. "I returned home very disconsolate, but mean to treat myself with sleeping, for the last time, on a firm flat steady bed."

But, over the coming weeks, the gale's persistence and other weather-related delays kept the *Beagle* bottled up at Devonport. Christmas Day, with Darwin, FitzRoy and likely Matthews and the Fuegians away from the ship, was set aside for shipboard celebrations. Moreover, the day after Christmas, though "beautiful . . . & an excellent one for sailing," was "lost owing to the drunkedness & absence of nearly the whole crew."

The ship has been all day in state of anarchy. One days holiday has caused all this mischief; such a scene proves how absolutely necessary strict discipline is amongst such thoughtless beings as Sailors. Several have paid the penalty for insolence, by sitting for eight or nine hours in heavy chains. Whilst in this state, their conduct was like children, abusing every body & thing but themselves, & the next moment nearly crying. It is an unfortunate beginning, being obliged so early to punish

so many of our best men there was however no choice left as
to the necessity of doing it.

The December 27 sunrise brought "a beautiful day" and a welcome
east wind. The *Beagle* stood luminous in the harbor, freshly painted in
that day's standard Royal Navy fashion, black sides with a broad white
stripe stretching along its upper parts. And upon the relay of FitzRoy's
orders to prepare to sail, the whistle of a fife, the sounds of men working
hawsers (thick nautical ropes), the unfurling of canvas, and the crisp
ripple of sails billowing in the wind suddenly filled the morning.

At eleven o'clock, after HMS *Beagle*'s anchors rose from the harbor,
the ship began tacking toward Devonport's breakwaters. Darwin and his
friend Lieutenant Bartholomew James Sulivan, meanwhile, ashore, completed "a farewell luncheon" of "mutton chops & champage," pleasures
Darwin "hope[d] excuse[d]" a "total absence of sentiment . . . experienced
on leaving England."

Afterward, borrowing a ride on a local dignitary's yacht, "We joined
the Beagle about 2 o'clock outside the Breakwater, & immediately with
every sail filled by a light breeze we scudded away at the rate of 7 or
8 knots an hour. I was not sick that evening but went to bed early."
Plowing south-southeast into the blue Atlantic, the expedition, at long
last, was South America–bound.

PART III

ODYSSEUS UNBOUND, 1832

10

MARINE LIFE

"If a person suffers much from sea sickness, let
him weigh it heavily in the balance: I speak from
experience, it is no trifling evil cured in a week."
                    —Charles Darwin, *Beagle* diary,
                                September 25, 1836

The following day, December 28, 1831, found Darwin again bat-
tling seasickness. Compounding the neophyte sailor's miseries,
FitzRoy chose that day to address some unfinished business from
Devonport. "My thoughts most unpleasantly occupied with the flogging
of several men for offences brought on by the indulgence granted them
on Christmas day." Indeed, it had been Darwin's discomfiture at pain
inflicted upon others that had led him to abandon his medical studies.
Worse, "I am doubtful whether this makes their crime [of] drunkedness
& consequent insolence more or less excusable."

By noon the following day the *Beagle*, plowing southward through
the Bay of Biscay, lay 380 miles from Plymouth. Fair weather persisted
but so too, intermittently, did Darwin's seasickness. "I found . . . the
only thing my stomach would bear was biscuit & raisins: but of this as I
became more exhausted I soon grew tired & then the sovereign remedy is

Sago"—a remedy concocted from the trunk of a sago cycad palm—"with wine & spice & made very hot."

Before boarding the *Beagle*, Darwin's only oceanic travel had been a handful of brief sea passages—his 1828 trips to Ireland and France, and the previous September's three-day packet trip with FitzRoy from London to Plymouth. And at Devonport, Darwin knew to employ the universal method of lessening the agonies of seasickness—to lie on his back and remain in a horizontal position. But once the *Beagle* was underway, he came to appreciate that his hammock's location, directly underneath the ship's newly installed skylight, allowed him, while cocooned in his canvas cradle, to hasten time's passage during the sickness's miseries: "There is one great difference between my former sea sickness & the present," he wrote. "Indeed it is rather amusing whilst lying in my hammock to watch the moon or stars performing their small revolutions in their new apparent orbits."

Over the coming days, when not seasick or otherwise occupied on deck, Darwin settled into a routine: breakfast at eight; afterward reading, writing, and working with his collections; lunch at one; then return to work; and tea at five. Otherwise, he reveled in observing natural marvels previously unfamiliar to him—habits evidenced in his December 31 diary entry, his coda for 1831:

> In the morning very uncomfortable; got up about noon & enjoyed some few moments of comparative ease. A shoal of porpoises dashing round the vessel & a stormy petrel skimming over the waves were the first objects of interest I have seen. I spent a very pleasant afternoon lying on the sofa [in FitzRoy's cabin], either talking to the Captain or reading Humboldts glowing accounts of tropical scenery. Nothing could be better adapted for cheering the heart of a sea-sick man.

Darwin rued how life at sea rendered simple tasks complicated. "Nothing can be done without so much extra trouble," he griped. "Even a book cannot be taken from the shelves or a piece of soap from the washing stand, without making it doubtful whether in the one case it is worth while to wash ones hands, or in the other to read any passage."

For the most part, however, his diary includes few details concerning those quotidian details of shipboard life—bodily functions, daily ablutions, the washing of clothes, and the like. Typifying that "extra trouble" of which Darwin complained, crewmen on that age's ships answered nature's call at the "head"—a raised platform that extended from the base of the vessel's bowsprit. In Darwin's case, however, he also had use of a private water closet just off his poop-cabin quarters. Fresh water for drinking and washing was rationed daily to each passenger. But, to conserve fresh water, the washing of clothes was generally done with soap and salt water. That regimen, however, with each successive wash, left a growing accumulation of salt in each garment, thickening the fabric, rendering it increasingly stiff and uncomfortable, causing irritation to the skin. Alternatively, individuals set out their own casks on the ship's deck to collect rainwater for washing purposes; or simply waited for the next anchorage and its presumably, more plentiful supply of fresh water.

By FitzRoy's count, the *Beagle* sailed from Devonport with seventy-four people. (Darwin counted seventy-six.) More specifically, while such tabulations differ slightly, the ship departed with about thirty-four seamen, fourteen commissioned officers, two petty (noncommissioned) officers, one marine sergeant and eight marine privates, ten "idlers" (crew members such as cooks and sailmakers who, due to their duties, were not required to keep watches), and at least eight supernumeraries—including Darwin, painter Augustus Earle, FitzRoy's steward Henry Fuller, missionary Richard Matthews, the three Fuegians, and instrument maker George Stebbings, hired to attend to FitzRoy's chronometers. The *Beagle* carried twenty-four chronometers—highly reliable timepieces which, used with solar observations taken with a sextant, allowed mariners to accurately determine longitude.

By tradition, aboard the *Beagle* and that era's other sailing ships, the limited shipboard space was divided and allocated by rank. Seamen and other low-ranking crewmen lived, ate and worked "before the mast," on the main and lower decks of the ship's fore or front section. Access to the ship's hold, in which water, sails, and other goods (including many of Darwin's specimens) were stored, was gained via hatches in the ship's main and fore sections. Passages called companionways and scuttles linked the ship's rooms, cabins, and other spaces.

Although prior agreement exempted Darwin from the stricture, the captain, by tradition, in his lower deck quarters at the ship's stern, dined alone or with any invited guest or guests. Other officers, along with the ship's surgeon, purser, and chaplain, took meals in the gun room, the traditional name for the midship space designated as the dining room or quarters for midshipmen and other junior officers. Seamen took meals in the ship's more forward, mess room.

Officers worked throughout the ship but ate and slept on the lower and main decks of the vessel's "aft" (rear) section. Only officers were permitted on the quarterdeck, the raised deck near the ship's stern. Even the highborn Darwin honored the latter rule, if on occasion more in the breach than in the observance. In February 1832, he asked his father to tell his brother Erasmus "that in the night I have actually sat down in the sacred precincts of the Quarter Deck."

During the voyage, Darwin occasionally took meals in the ship's gun room with the *Beagle*'s officers, the cohort who accorded him the affectionate nickname "The Philosopher." And, in one instance, his diary breaks its usual silence shrouding such interactions—an exception made all the more interesting given Darwin's ambiguous status within the ship's society. He, after all, sailed as a civilian—a supernumerary outside the ship's chain of command. All aboard, however, knew that Darwin came from a prominent family, was close to the captain, and, by prior arrangement, dined with him and enjoyed the run of his cabin.

Of the *Beagle*'s officers, Darwin noted, they "are all good friends yet there is a want of intimacy, owing I suppose to gradation of rank, which much destroys all pleasure in their society." In his diary, pondering the beehive of the *Beagle*'s shipboard society, he was already deploying the powers of observation and dispassionate analysis on which his later fame would rest:

> The probability of quarrelling & the misery on ship board consequent on it produces an effect contrary to what one

would suppose. Instead of each one endeavouring to encourage habits of friendship, it seems a generally received maxim that the best friends soon turn out the greatest enemies. It is a wonder to me that this independence one from another, which is so essential a part of a sailors character, does not produce extreme selfishness. I do not think it has this effect, & very likely answers their end in lessening the number of quarrels which always must necessarily arise in men so closely united.

Nonetheless, he still wondered: why did such men, who have experienced and seen so much, remain, by his lights, such lackluster interlocutors? "Let the cause be what it may, it is quite surprising that the conversation of active intelligent men who have seen so much & whose characters are so early & decidedly brought out should be so entirely devoid of interest."

The most singularly unique souls sailing aboard the *Beagle* were, of course, the three Fuegians. Moreover, their plight, or FitzRoy's desire to atone for his role in their kidnapping, had prompted the current expedition. In arranging for their education, the captain had contemplated their welfare and life upon their return to Tierra del Fuego. But, as the *Beagle*'s sailing date approached, he also pondered the Fuegians' usefulness to the planned mission in Terra del Fuego, including assistance they might render passing British seamen.

At the Walthamstow school, FitzRoy had asked its schoolmaster, a "Mr. Jenkins," to develop a curriculum for the three focused on instruction in English and conservative Anglican Christianity. They also received instruction in the use of simple tools and the essentials of mechanics, gardening, and animal husbandry.

The Alakaluf people, to whom Fuegia Basket and York Minster belonged, and Jemmy Button's Yaghans, were both hunter-gatherer cultures. Both peoples traveled by birchbark canoes and clothed themselves—albeit, to European eyes, scandalously close to naked—in animal hides. Moreover, both subsisted on a diet of shellfish, seals, and the occasional whale and vegetables, along with terrestrial game such as guanaco and foxes.

For shelter, both peoples constructed circular dwellings, roughly ten feet in diameter and six feet high. Called "wigwams" by Europeans, the structures were fashioned from sticks, grass, and sealskin, with a hole at their tops for venting smoke. Despite their similar material cultures, however, the Alakaluf and the Yaghan had separate languages. FitzRoy, for his part, though having all three of his Fuegian charges instructed in English, also learned a smattering of their respective tongues. He even compiled a small vocabulary that included about 200 English words, mostly nouns, translated into both the Yaghan and Alakaluf tongues.

Several men aboard the *Beagle* in 1831 had sailed on the ship's first expedition and thus knew the three Fuegians from that outing's return voyage to England. Those first expedition veterans included Lieutenants Wickham and Sulivan, carpenter Jonathan May, assistant surgeon Benjamin Bynoe, assistant surveyor John Lort Stokes, and midshipmen Arthur Mellersh and Philip Gidley King (son of the first expedition's Captain Philip Parker King).

Darwin, for his part, after November 13, when the Fuegians boarded the ship, wasted little time in introducing himself to the three. The Fuegians and their world captivated him, attentions they gladly reciprocated. But how often Darwin conversed with the three, or the level of their respective fluencies in English, remains unclear. "Although all three could both speak and understand a good deal of English," he recalled, "it was singularly difficult to obtain much information from them, concerning the habits of their countrymen."

York Minster was known as Elleparu by the Alakaluf people of western Tierra del Fuego whence he came. In his late twenties when the *Beagle* sailed from Devonport, he was the oldest of the three Fuegians aboard the ship. Darwin recalled him as "a full-grown, short, thick, powerful man. His disposition was reserved, taciturn, morose, and when excited violently passionate; his affections were very strong toward a few friends on board; his intellect good."

Jemmy Button was about fifteen years old when the *Beagle*'s second expedition sailed from Devonport. His fellow Yaghan people of southern

Tierra del Fuego, called him Orundellico. Though, by Darwin's account, the young man was, "short, thick, and fat," he was also "vain of his personal appearance." Even so, Darwin added, Button ranked among the ship's crew and officers as "a universal favourite." Echoing that assessment, "Jemmy was the favourite," remembered Lieutenant Bartholomew James Sulivan,

> and his progress in civilization was most evident in his excessive dandyism. In his own country two years previously, he was a naked savage, but, even then, even in weather that made the officers thankful for their rough coats and greased boots, he would make his appearance on deck with polished boots and well brushed broad cloth.

During Button's stay in England, he had, noted Darwin, acquired a taste for fine clothes; and aboard the *Beagle* he would usually "wear gloves, his hair was neatly cut, and he was distressed if his well-polished shoes were dirtied. He was fond of admiring himself in a looking-glass." Moreover, Button was also "passionate": "The expression of his face at once showed his nice disposition." With evident affection, the naturalist recalled a young man who was typically "merry," "often laughed," and "remarkably sympathetic with any one in pain." Remembering his own frequent bouts with seasickness, Darwin recalled how Button, during those ordeals, "used to come to me and say in a plaintive voice, 'Poor, poor fellow!'"

With similar affections, Darwin also remembered, "He [Button] was of a patriotic disposition; and he liked to praise his own tribe and country, in which he truly said there were 'plenty of trees,' and he abused all the other tribes: he stoutly declared that there was no Devil in his land."

> It seems yet wonderful to me, when I think over all his many good qualities, that he should have been of the same race, and doubtless partaken of the same character, with the miserable, degraded savages whom we first met here.

Fuegia Basket, about eleven years old when the *Beagle*'s second expedition sailed, belonged, like York Minster, to the Alakaluf people of Tierra del Fuego's west, where she was known as Yokcushlu. She was, Darwin noted, "a nice, modest, reserved young girl, with a rather pleasing but sometimes sullen expression." Moreover, she was "quick in learning anything, especially languages. This she showed in picking up some Portuguese and Spanish, when left on shore for only a short time at Rio de Janeiro and Monte Video, and in her knowledge of English."

More provocatively, Darwin also recalled, "York Minster was very jealous of any attention paid to her; for it was clear he determined to marry her as soon as they were settled on shore." But complicating Minster's affections for the girl two decades his junior, according to one shipboard source, of the other two Fuegians, "Jemmy was evidently her favorite."

According to Jemmy Button biographer Nick Hazlewood, York Minster's infatuation with Fuegia Basket—reaching back to shared days at the Walthamstow school, where the two alarmed their teachers—may even have included sexual intimacies. Moreover, aboard the *Beagle*, Minster's perception of Button as a rival for Basket's attentions, rendered him, according to Lieutenant Sulivan, "so jealous at times, as to require the interference of the captain."

What Darwin deemed the "remarkably acute" eyesight of the three Fuegians likewise intrigued him: "It is well known that sailors, from long practice, can make out a distant object much better than a landsman; but both York and Jemmy were much superior to any sailor on board."

> Several times they have declared what some distant object has been, and though doubted by every one, they have proved right, when it has been examined through a telescope. They were quite conscious of this power; and Jemmy, when he had any little quarrel with the officer on watch, would say, 'Me see ship, me no tell.'

11

IN HUMBOLDTIAN CLIMES

"The only sounds are the waves rippling on the stern & the
sails idly flapping round the masts. Already can I understand
Humboldts enthusiasm about the tropical nights, the sky is
so clear & lofty, & stars innumerable shine so bright that
like little moons they cast their glitter on the waves."
                                          —Charles Darwin, *Beagle* diary,
                                                          June 20, 1832

A week after leaving Devonport, as the *Beagle* sailed southwesterly, the island of Porto Santo rose before the ship's bow at daybreak on January 4, 1832. Still later that morning, the island of Madeira appeared. FitzRoy had long considered stopping at that largest of the two Portuguese islands. Weeks earlier at Devonport, Darwin and several officers, competing in a shooting match onshore, had even wagered on planned purchases, during the stop, of the island's famous wines.

Even so, that morning, deeming the island's anchorage "bad & the landing difficult," FitzRoy elected to forgo the visit. "I was so sick that I could not get up even to see Madeira when within 12 miles," Darwin lamented. "In the evening [I was] a little better but much exhausted."

Over the coming days, Darwin consoled himself with thoughts of their next possible port, Tenerife; and to his delight, at daybreak, on January 6, the *Beagle* sailed within sight of that largest of the Canary Islands. "Every thing has a beautiful appearance: the colours are so rich & soft," he observed before, moments later spotting Pico de Teide, the volcano celebrated by Humboldt. "It towers in the sky twice as high as I should have dreamed of looking for it. A dense bank of clouds entirely separates the snowy top from its rugged base."

By eleven o'clock that morning, the *Beagle*, with its officers planning to anchor there, stood about a half mile from the island's capital of Santa Cruz. It was around that moment—"Oh misery, misery," Darwin recalled—"when a boat came alongside bringing with it our death-warrant." A government official aboard the boat informed the Englishmen that, before being cleared to go ashore, they must conduct a shipboard quarantine for twelve days.

FitzRoy instead ordered First Lieutenant Wickham to set a course south toward the Cape Verde archipelago. For two years, Darwin had fantasized about Tenerife, but in an instant his Humboldtian dream lay shattered: "Those who have never experienced it can scarcely conceive what a gloom it cast on every one," he sighed. "We have left perhaps one of the most interesting places in the world, just at the moment when we were near enough for every object to create, without satisfying, our utmost curiosity."

Even so, that evening, as night's starry dome shrouded the south-bound *Beagle*—on January 10 it would cross the Tropic of Cancer—Darwin found solace in the heavens above: "Already can I understand Humboldts enthusiasm about the tropical nights, the sky is so clear & lofty, & stars innumerable shine so bright that like little moons they cast their glitter on the waves."

Moreover, on January 15, even before the *Beagle*'s first landfall, Darwin, noting the flora and fauna they were passing, was already speculating on topics more often associated with his later visit to the Galápagos Islands, what a later era would call biogeography: "Some few birds have been hovering about the vessel & a large gay coloured cricket found an insecure resting place within the reach of my fly-nippers. He must at the least have flown 370 miles from the coast of Africa."

Darwin's first impressions of the place that he called "Jago"—Santiago Island, in the Cape Verde archipelago—were far from positive. On the morning of January 16, shortly after eleven o'clock, the *Beagle* approached the port of Praia, capital of the island group. From a distance, to Darwin, the ten-square-mile island, four hundred miles off Africa's coast, appeared "desolate."

As the *Beagle* approached the island, crew members crowding the deck spotted on the island a series of volcano-formed plateaus from which rose "truncate[d] conical hills." Completing the scene, "the horizon is bounded by an irregular chain of more lofty & bolder hills." But if Darwin had often romanticized tropical landscapes, for Jago he willingly violated that inclination: "The Volcanic fire of past ages & the scorching heat of a tropical sun have in most places rendered the soil sterile & unfit for vegetation."

By three o'clock, when the *Beagle* anchored at Praia, his opinion of Cape Verde's capital was equally dismissive. "I went with a party to announce our arrival to the 'Governador,'" he recalled. "After locating the governor's official residence—a "house . . . not suited to the grandeur of his title"—the English visitors, "were ushered into a room where the great man most courteously received us." By Darwin's account, the meeting quickly foundered into Babel-like confusion:

> After having made out our story in a very ludicrous mixture of Portuguese, English & French, we retreated under a shower of bows. We then called on the American Consul who likewise acts for the English. The Portugeese might with great advantage have instilled a little of his well-bred politesse into this quarter.

Afterward, a stroll through Praia's other corridors confirmed first impressions: "The town is a miserable place, consisting of a square & some broard streets, if indeed they deserve so respectable a name."

> In the middle of these "Ruas" are lying together goats, pigs & black & brown children: some of whom boast of a shirt, but quite as many not: these latter look less like human being than I could have fancied any degradation could have produced.

There are a good many black soldiers, it would be difficult I should think to pick out a less efficient body of men. Many of them only possess for arms a wooden staff.

Even local fruit disappointed Darwin. While the oranges he sampled were tasty, the bananas, to his palate, were "maukish & sweet with little flavor."

Unmentioned by Darwin, however, was Praia's status as a notorious slave-trading center. Cape Verde's Portuguese colonial overseers—deeply enmeshed in the transport to Brazil of enslaved people captured on the African coast—played a vital role in that era's transatlantic slave trade.

That same day, the 16th, before returning to the *Beagle*, Darwin and his companions, leaving Praia, found their way into a deep valley. "Here I first saw the glory of tropical vegetation," he wrote. "Tamarinds, Bananas & Palms were flourishing at my feet . . . I expected a good deal, for I had read Humboldts descriptions & I was afraid of disappointments: how utterly vain such fear is, none can tell but those who have experienced what I to day have."

Jago's spell reached beyond tropical plants. In time, the island's entire volcanic geography bore, for him, a sublime majesty. Later, while returning to the *Beagle*, he found himself "treading on Volcanic rocks, hearing the notes of unknown birds, & seeing new insects fluttering about still newer flowers." Indeed, "It has been for me a glorious day, like giving to a blind man eyes. He is overwhelmed with what he sees & cannot justly comprehend it."

The following morning Darwin accompanied FitzRoy to what they called Quail Island (today's Santa Maria Island), "a miserable desolate spot, less than a mile in circumference" and close to Jago. FitzRoy had selected the island as the site for an observatory, at which, over the coming weeks, tents would be erected as he and others conducted surveys and astronomical observations. As FitzRoy went about his work, Darwin examined at close range the volcanic surfaces that now commanded his attention. "Uninviting as its first appearance was, I do not think the impression this day has made will ever leave me. The first examining of Volcanic rocks must to a Geologist be a memorable epoch."

Possibly undergirding Darwin's newfound interest in volcanic rocks was a book, *The Principles of Geology*, which FitzRoy had given him in December. Its author, Charles Lyell, was a thirty-five-year-old geologist whose work was challenging long-held precepts in the natural sciences.

Born to a prosperous Scottish family, Lyell was educated at Oxford University, where he had studied classics and law. During the 1820s, however, he grew infatuated with newly emerging trends in geology. Two years later, he presented his first scientific paper; and, a year later, he was elected joint secretary of London's prestigious Geological Society. By 1827, having abandoned the legal profession, Lyell was devoting himself full-time to geology. And, by 1830 when the first volume of *Principles of Geology* appeared, his name was widely known among geologists. Indeed, as Darwin was devouring Lyell's *Principles*, its author was already preparing the second of that work's eventual three volumes.

During the eighteenth century and into the early 1800s, Biblical-minded geologists such as Englishmen Granville Penn and George Bugg exerted great influence among that day's scientists. Taking the Bible's stories literally, they and other "Biblical" or "scriptural" geologists calculated the earth's age to be only a few millennia, six thousand years by one widely accepted calculation. As geologists, they thus saw their challenge as explaining how the earth and its features were created within that limited timeline. Their theories, moreover, purported to explain the earth's history by resort to Biblical events—particularly Noah's flood. Put another way, in their gathering of rocks and in their studies of geological formations, Biblical geologists sought evidence to support Biblical explanations of the earth's history.

By the 1820s, George Cuvier and other geologists had developed another approach to their field called "catastrophism." Unwed to Biblical timetables and eschewing supernatural events to support their theories, catastrophism's adherents brought a more empirical approach to geology. Nonetheless, like Biblical geologists, Cuvier and his ilk argued that a series of "catastrophes" (mainly floods), albeit of natural not supernatural origin, had befallen the earth and largely explained its history. And those processes, Curvier further believed, also explained the successive animal and plant extinctions that he deduced from fossil specimens.

By contrast, Lyell, as had his fellow Scottish geologist James Hutton a generation earlier, rejected both Biblical geology and catastrophism. (Owing in part, however, to Hutton's often obscure writing style, his works had limited impact among other geologists.) Along the way, both Hutton and Lyell sought to recast geology as a rigorous science wedded to disciplined attention to "natural causes," without resort to the supernatural to explain the earth's history. Indeed, Lyell's *Principles of Geology* called for geologists to abandon what he called "the Mosaic account" of the planet's history and fully embrace the empirical sciences:

> Geology is intimately related to almost all the physical sciences, as is history to the moral. An historian should, if possible, be at once profoundly acquainted with ethics, politics, jurisprudence, the military art, theology; in a word, with all branches of knowledge, whereby any insight into human affairs, or into the moral and intellectual nature of man, can be obtained. It would be no less desirable that a geologist should be well versed in chemistry, natural philosophy, mineralogy, zoology, comparative anatomy, botany.

Likewise rejecting catastrophism, Lyell, like Hutton, argued that still active and readily observable natural processes, rather than rare catastrophes, best explain the earth's history. Soon a rival to catastrophism, the school associated with Hutton and Lyell became known as "uniformitarianism."

Ranging across the planet and its history, from ancient to modern times, Lyell's *Principles of Geology* examined how earthquakes, wind, rain, snow, rivers, oceans, subterranean pressures, and volcanoes, not distant Biblical events, shaped and continue to shape the earth. The work's subtitle underscored its departure from that era's geological establishment: *Being an Attempt to Explain the Former Changes of the Earth's Surface, by Reference to Causes Now in Operation.*

Significantly, however, while Lyell assumed the earth older than did most geologists of his era, he accorded no such vintage to *Homo sapiens*.

"We need not dwell on the proofs of the low antiquity of our species, for it is not controverted by any geologist," he wrote in *Principles*. "Indeed, the real difficulty which we experience consists in tracing back the signs of man's existence on the earth to that comparatively modern period when species, now his contemporaries, began to predominate."

Likewise, Lyell, a devout Anglican and, in the 1830s, a firm believer in what Darwin later called the fixity of species, rejected all claims that the earth's living organisms had changed over time. Lyell believed rather that the planet's biological history included countless, often localized, extinctions and creations of new species. "It is," he wrote, "clear, that there is no foundation in geological facts, for the popular theory of the successive development of the animal and vegetable world, from the simplest to the most perfect forms." Put simply, while Lyell rejected the Bible's Noah, he accepted its Adam; to him, fossils presented evidence of extinctions, not evolutions.

Even so, for Darwin, Lyell's recognition that rocks and landforms gradually change over time proved instructive and contributed to his later controversial speculations concerning biological life. Darwin's mentor, the Rev. John Henslow (a Lyell friend) was aware of the potentially heretical influence of the geologist on the young man. Henslow, after all, admired Lyell's intellectual rigor as a field geologist and encouraged Darwin to read him. But his endorsement had come with a caveat: read Lyell, Henslow advised, "but on no account . . . accept the views therein advocated."

A dozen years later, acknowledging Lyell's influence, Darwin reflected:

> I always feel as if my books came half out of Lyell's brains & that I never acknowledge this sufficiently, nor do I know how I can, without saying so in so many words—for I have always thought that the great merit of the Principles, was that it altered the whole tone of one's mind & therefore that when seeing a thing never seen by Lyell, one yet saw it partially through his eyes.

In 1845, when Darwin's published *Beagle* travels appeared for the second time, this time as a separate volume—the book originally published as *Journal and Remarks** but known today as *The Voyage of the Beagle*, it commenced with a dedication to a Fellow of the Royal Society, Britain's prestigious learned society of scientists and mathematicians:

TO

CHARLES LYELL, ESQ., F.R.S.,

THIS SECOND EDITION IS DEDICATED WITH GRATEFUL

PLEASURE, AS AN ACKNOWLEDGMENT THAT THE CHIEF

PART OF WHATEVER SCIENTIFIC MERIT THIS JOURNAL AND

THE OTHER WORKS OF THE AUTHOR MAY POSSESS, HAS

BEEN DERIVED FROM STUDYING THE WELL-KNOWN AND

ADMIRABLE PRINCIPLES OF GEOLOGY.

Darwin, in his *Autobiography*, would later claim that, "the very first place which I examined, namely St. Jago in the Cape Verde islands, showed me clearly the wonderful superiority of Lyell's manner of treating geology, compared with that of any other author, whose works I had with me or ever afterwards read."

Scholars accept Lyell's role as a major influence on Darwin. However, the assertion in his *Autobiography*, a work written decades after his visit to Jago, that the island was the first place where he discerned "the wonderful superiority of Lyell's manner of treating geology" has been called into question. According to recent scholarship, neither contemporary correspondence nor the field notebook Darwin kept while on Jago indicate that he had read very far, if at all, in the copy of Lyell's *Principles* given him by FitzRoy.

Even so, regardless of Darwin's familiarity with *Principles* while at Jago—and whether it came through recent readings or earlier conversations with Henslow—one point appears indisputable: In retrospect, the well-exposed, relatively straightforward geology of the first volcanic island that

---

*   To avoid confusion, all references to and quotations from Darwin's published account of his *Beagle* travels, unless otherwise stipulated, derive from that work's first edition, published in 1839, and which is referred to herein by the title under which that edition appeared—*Journal and Remarks*.

Darwin visited prepared him for the infinitely more complex geologies of Tierra del Fuego, the Andes, and other future *Beagle* anchorages.

Moreover, beyond Darwin's newfound infatuation with volcanic rocks, Jago marked another milestone: "It then first dawned on me that I might perhaps write a book on the geology of the various countries visited, and this made me thrill with delight." The inspiration struck as he rested amid a chaos of volcanic rocks: "How distinctly I can call to mind the low cliff of lava beneath which I rested, with the sun glaring hot, a few strange desert plants growing near, and with living corals in the tidal pools at my feet."

Darwin spent the rest of January 17 examining and collecting rocks in Jago's interior. Along the island's shoreline and from its tidal pools and coastal waters, he also gathered "numerous animals," including corals. By sunset, enthralled with his new way of understanding landscapes, he joyfully beheld what, days earlier, he had dismissed as an expanse "sterile & unfit for vegetation." As if daring posterity, he exclaimed to his diary: "Let those who have seen the Andes be discontented with the scenery of St Jago. I think its unusually sterile character gives it a grandeur which more vegetation might have spoiled." The musing echoed another from weeks earlier, penned aboard the *Beagle*, as he pondered the haul from a small "plankton net" he had fashioned:

> The number of animals that the net collects is very great & fully explains the manner so many animals of a large size live so far from land [presumably whales and other marine animals that feed on plankton]. Many of these creatures so low in the scale of nature are most exquisite in their forms & rich colours. It creates a feeling of wonder that so much beauty should be apparently created for such little purpose.

Pondering species distribution and adaptation, concerns that loom large in his later work, as geographer Patrick Armstrong observed, "Darwin was already beginning to think ecologically."

On January 19, walking along Jago's western coast, Darwin, like a man possessed, returned to his meditation: "My imagination never pictured so utterly barren a place as this is," he wrote. "It is not the absence of vegetation solely that produces this effect: every thing adds to the idea of solitude: nothing meets the eye but plains strewed over with black & burnt rocks rising one above the other: And yet there was a grandeur in such scenery & to me the unspeakable pleasure of walking under a tropical sun on a wild & desert island." Nonetheless, "It is quite glorious the way my collections are increasing. I am even already troubled with the vain fear that there will be nobody in England who will have the courage to examine some of the less known branches."

On January 20, hiking with ship surgeon Robert McCormick, Darwin encountered a large baobab tree (*Adansonia digitata*), a celebrated deciduous species native to Africa. "I had forgotten its existence, but the sight immediately recalled a description of it which I had formerly read." Thrilled, he recounted in his diary that the tree's namesake, eighteenth century French naturalist Michel Adanson, had noted that baobabs can live up to six thousand years. Two days later, FitzRoy and Darwin returned to the site. There, the captain, carrying a sextant, climbed the tree to measure its height (45 feet) and circumference (13 feet).

At Jago, though Darwin had permission to remain ashore, he returned to the *Beagle* at each day's end. On Sunday, January 29, he witnessed, on the ship's main deck, his first shipboard church service. "It is a striking scene & the extreme attention of the men renders it much more imposing than I had expected," he recalled. "Every thing on board on Sunday is most delightfully clean. The lower decks would put to shame many gentlemens houses." Over the coming years, when living aboard the *Beagle*, the Sunday "divine service" became a regular feature of Darwin's Sunday mornings. Led by FitzRoy, the services, depending upon weather conditions, were conducted on the ship's main or lower deck.

By early February, after further hiking and collecting, and repeated visits to Praia and Ribeira Grande, Darwin was eager to move on. Indeed, on the seventh, their departure's eve, he confessed to his diary, "I am becoming rather impatient to see tropical Vegetation in greater luxuriance than it can be seen here." He likewise recalled a pertinent insight from an esteemed writer: "During the first week every object was new & full of uncommon interest & as Humboldt remarks the vividness of an impression gives it the effect of duration. In consequence of this, those few days appeared to me a much longer interval than the whole three weeks does now."

And when the *Beagle* sailed the next day, February 8, four days before his twenty-third birthday, Darwin praised the island and its capital, both of which, three weeks earlier, he had disdained: "Again I admired the varied outline of the hills round Praya; the memory of which will never be effaced from my mind."

Over the next three weeks, hastening on a southeasterly course toward South America, HMS *Beagle* covered over two thousand miles. Approaching Brazil's coast, the ship made brief stops in the St. Paul's Rock and Fernando de Noronha archipelagos. During those weeks, the ship also crossed the Equator. To mark the passage, uninitiated sailors, those new to the crossing, traditionally submit to an unpleasant ritual: costumed "Neptunes," using a gruesome concoction—the *Beagle*'s recipe was tar and paint—shave and wash out the mouths of the hapless novitiates.

Accordingly, on February 17, at nine o'clock in the morning, four Neptunes appeared; and, one by one, led scores of blindfolded "griffins" from the lower to the main deck. Darwin, with dread, had anticipated the ritual for the past four months:

> I was . . . placed on a plank, which could be easily tilted up
> into a large bath of water. They then lathered my face &
> mouth with pitch and paint, & scraped some of it off with
> a piece of roughened iron hoop. A signal being given I was
> tilted head over heels into the water, where two men received
> me & ducked me.

Moments into the hazing, however, he wrested away from and, unlike others among the uninitiated, escaped his tormentors. "Most of the others were treated much worse, dirty mixtures being put in their mouths & rubbed on their faces. The whole ship was a shower bath: & water was flying about in every direction: of course not one person, even the Captain, got clear of being wet through."

12

TROPIC OF SLAVERY

On the morning of February 28, 1832, Charles Darwin got his first glimpse of South America's mainland. "About 9 o'clock," he recorded, "we were near to the coast of Brazil; we saw a considerable extent of it, the whole line is rather low & irregular, & from the profusion of wood & verdure of a bright green colour."

By eleven o'clock, the *Beagle* had entered the bay on whose eastern shore sprawled the town of Salvador de Bahia, a realm that actually comprised two towns—one dominated by the port, the other, the *Cidade Alta* (Upper Town), above the port and well-described by Darwin: "It would be difficult [to] imagine, before seeing the view, anything so magnificent," he marveled. "The town is fairly embosomed in a luxuriant wood & situated on a steep bank overlooks the calm waters of the great bay of All Saints."

The architecture of the town he called "Bahia" likewise enchanted him: "The houses are white & lofty & from the windows being narrow & long have a very light & elegant appearance," he observed. "Convents, Porticos & public buildings vary the uniformity of the houses: the bay is scattered over with large ships; in short the view is one of the finest in the Brazils." Later that same day, finding his way inland, he found still greater enchantments. Bahia's "beauties are as nothing compared to the Vegetation," he noted. Alas, even "Humboldt's glorious descriptions" left him "unprepared" for the "tropical scenery."

The delight one experiences in such times bewilders the mind. If the eye attempts to follow the flight of a gaudy butter-fly, it is arrested by some strange tree or fruit; if watching an insect one forgets it in the stranger flower it is crawling over. If turning to admire the splendour of the scenery, the individual character of the foreground fixes the attention. The mind is a chaos of delight, out of which a world of future & more quiet pleasure will arise. I am at present fit only to read Humboldt; he like another Sun illumines everything I behold.

Longer outings the following day and the next brought deeper pleasures. "The day has passed delightfully," he confided to his diary on the first of the two excursions. "Delight is however a weak term for such transports of pleasure: I have been wandering by myself in a Brazilian forest: amongst the multitude it is hard to say what set of objects is most striking."

The general luxuriance of the vegetation bears the victory, the elegance of the grasses, the novelty of the parasitical plants, the beauty of the flowers. The glossy green of the foliage, all tend to this end. A most paradoxical mixture of sound & silence pervades the shady parts of the wood. The noise from the insects is so loud that in the evening it can be heard even in a vessel anchored several hundred yards from the shore. Yet within the recesses of the forest when in the midst of it a universal stillness appears to reign. To a person fond of Natural history such a day as this brings with it pleasure more acute than he ever may again experience.

Later that afternoon, while returning to the *Beagle*, he experienced his first tropical storm on land. "I tried to find shelter under a tree so thick that it would never have been penetrated by common English rain, yet here in a couple of minutes, a little torrent flowed down the trunk." But even as he exulted in the storm's grandeur, more analytically, he contemplated its role in the forest's life. "It is to this violence we must attribute the verdure in the bottom of the wood. If the showers were like those of a colder clime, the moisture would be absorbed or evaporated before reaching the ground." Summarizing his paean, the next day, he added, "Brazilian scenery is nothing more nor less than a view in the Arabian Nights, with the advantage of reality."

But idylls inevitably end; and for Darwin, Brazil's tropical bliss evaporated with a speed that matched its commencement. The serpent in his Brazilian garden was slavery. Brazil, the first South American country he visited—like others there through which he later passed, with the exception of Chile—had yet to outlaw slavery. Moreover, in the next two countries that he would visit, Uruguay and Argentina, slavery was already a moribund institution, ill-fitted to a ranching economy; and few expected it to survive. In Brazil, by contrast, the institution thrived. Europeans, after all, had decided that sugar, the country's main export, was a necessity not a luxury. Still later in the century, its trading partners would render the same judgment about another main export, coffee—thus incentivizing slavery's survival in Brazil until 1888.

Given those circumstances, Darwin eventually realized that, beyond the quaint stucco residences and Renaissance-style public buildings of what he initially praised as "the glorious city of Bahia," the town played a dark role in South America's past and present. From 1549 to 1763, as Brazil's first capital, Bahia numbered among the New World's most active slave markets; and during Darwin's visit, it remained a robust entrepôt for such commerce. Curiously, however, that enterprise—along with the many enslaved persons of African descent that he no doubt saw in Bahia's port district—had gone unmentioned in his diary's praise of the city upon landing there.

The coup de grâce for Darwin's Brazil infatuation came during a dinner aboard the *Beagle* for the captain of a Royal Navy ship anchored in Bahia for a sustained stay. Over those days, Charles Henry Paget, the twenty-six-year-old commander of the twenty-eight-gun frigate HMS *Samarang*, was a frequent guest aboard the *Beagle*.

Darwin found the young captain "amusing" and a welcome dinner companion. Moreover, Paget shared Darwin's opposition to slavery and the naturalist listened attentively as the officer shared his firsthand observations concerning human bondage. The "facts about slavery [were] so revolting," he recalled, "that if I had read them in England, I should have placed them to the credulous zeal of well-meaning people." More pointedly, he confided to his diary, "The extent to which the trade is carried on; the ferocity with which it is defended; the respectable (!) people who are concerned in it are far from being exaggerated at home."

In 1807, Britain had banned the slave trade throughout its empire; and in 1833, two years after Darwin set sail, Parliament would outlaw the institution itself in most of the British empire. Throughout those years, British abolitionists and a growing roster of allies in and outside of government exerted pressure on both the British and foreign governments to end the slave trade and the institution itself. And, among the world's polities, Brazil—as a Portuguese colony and, after 1825, as an independent state—proved most resistant to such reforms. An 1819 census found that slaves of African descent constituted about one-third of the country's total 3.6 million population. Moreover, when Darwin landed in Salvador de Bahia, Brazil, with its booming sugar and coffee plantations, was still importing thousands of slaves annually.

Generally, when Captain Paget visited the *Beagle*, Captain FitzRoy listened without comment to his harrowing tales of slavery's cruelties. Absent other evidence, it seems doubtful that FitzRoy, though a Tory, was an actual defender of slavery, as Darwin later claimed; more likely, he merely questioned Paget's depictions of it. Whatever the case, FitzRoy's political views *were* starkly more conservative than those of the Whigs Paget and Darwin. And on one particular evening, FitzRoy clearly disputed Paget's accounts of the institution's brutality. Purportedly drawing on his own visit to a local plantation, FitzRoy, according to Darwin, avowed that, "he had just visited a great slave-owner, who had called up many of his slaves and asked them whether they were happy, and whether they wished to be free, and all answered 'No.'"

That evening's exchange, described in Darwin's diary, would go unmentioned in the two men's respective published accounts of the *Beagle*'s travels. But, decades later, Darwin, in his *Autobiography*, provided a lively account of the rest of his exchange with the commander whose temper had earned him the epithet "hot coffee" among his crew: "I then asked him," remembered Darwin, "perhaps with a sneer, whether he thought that the answers of slaves in the presence of their master was worth anything."

This made him excessively angry, and he said that as I doubted his word, we could not live any longer together. I thought that I should have been compelled to leave the ship; but as soon as the news spread, which it did quickly, as the captain sent for the first lieutenant [John Clements Wickham] to assuage his anger by abusing me, I was deeply gratified by receiving an invitation from all the gun-room officers to mess with them. But after a few hours Fitz-Roy showed his usual magnanimity by sending an officer to me with an apology and a request that I would continue to live with him.

By outward appearances, the rift between the two quickly healed. The two, after all, faced a long voyage together, and it was in neither's interest to prolong discords. But neither forgot the exchange. Darwin, for his part, regretted the flare-up but took satisfaction in having stood up for his convictions: "The Captain does every thing in his power to assist me, & we get on very well," he wrote weeks later to Henslow. "But I thank my better fortune he has not made me a renegade to Whig principles: I would not be a Tory, if it was merely on account of their cold hearts about that scandal to Christian Nations, Slavery."

Moreover, for the 1845 edition of Darwin's published account of the voyage, he elaborated on the horrors he witnessed in Brazil:

To this day, if I hear a distant scream, it recalls with painful vividness my feelings, when passing a house near Pernambuco [a northern Brazilian port the *Beagle* visited Aug. 12–17, 1836], I heard the most pitiable moans, and could not but suspect that some poor slave was being tortured, yet knew that I was as powerless as a child even to remonstrate. I suspected that these moans were from a tortured slave, for I was told that this was the case in another instance. Near Rio de Janeiro I lived opposite to an old lady, who kept screws to crush the fingers of her female slaves. I have staid in a house where a young household mulatto, daily and hourly, was reviled, beaten, and persecuted enough to break the spirit of the lowest animal. I have seen a little boy, six or seven years old, struck thrice with a horse-whip (before I could interfere) on his naked head, for having handed me a glass of water not quite clean; I saw his father tremble at a mere glance from his master's eye.

Beyond slavery, however, another matter weighed on Darwin during his weeks at Bahia—misgivings, shared with his father, in early 1832, over joining the expedition:

Hitherto the voyage has answered admirably to me, & yet I am now more fully aware of your wisdom in throwing cold water on the whole scheme: the chances are so numerous of it turning out quite the reverse. To such an extent do I feel this that if my advice was asked by any person on a similar occasion I should be very cautious in encouraging him.

On March 17, a "bright & exceedingly clear evening," Darwin with midshipman Philip Gidley King took a farewell stroll through the center of Brazil's former capital. By that hour, the city lay quiet with no Atlantic breezes rustling the leaves of the palms that lined its streets. "Nothing," Darwin recalled, "could be better adapted for fixing in the mind the last & glorious remembrances of Bahia." Two weeks earlier, Bahia's natural wonders had delighted him. But now, on the eve of his leave-taking, his thoughts turned toward what seemed, morally, a squandered opportunity:

If to what Nature has granted the Brazils, man added his just & proper efforts, of what a country might the inhabitants boast. But where the greater parts are in a state of slavery, & where this system is maintained by an entire stop to education, the mainspring of human actions, what can be expected; but that the whole would be polluted by its part[s].

13

RIO

"The Tropics appear the natural birthplace of the human
race; but the mind, like many of its fruits seems in a
foreign clime to reach its greatest perfection."
                    —Charles Darwin, *Beagle* diary, May 27, 1832

Weighing anchor from Bahia, the *Beagle*, on March 18, 1832,
sailed south for Rio de Janeiro. During that transit, at each
day's end, as the tropical sun surrendered to the star-powdered
night, Darwin savored what was, after four months in the Southern
Hemisphere, becoming a familiar pleasure.

At night in these fine regions of the Tropics there is one certain & never failing source of enjoyment, it is admiring the
constellations in the heaven. Many of those who have seen
both hemispheres give the victory to the stars of the North.
It is however to me an inexpressible pleasure to behold those
constellations, the first sight of which Humboldt describes
with such enthusiasm. I experience a kindred feeling when I
look at the Cross of the South, the phosphorescent clouds of
Magellan & the great Southern Crown.

During the days, meanwhile, a week after leaving Bahia, Darwin recorded, "The labours of the expedition have commenced." The ship's hydrographers had begun the work for which the *Beagle* had returned to these waters—the completion of the survey begun by the ship's first expedition and to otherwise correct errors and fill gaps left by earlier surveyors.

Because high rates of scurvy had afflicted the *Beagle*'s first expedition, FitzRoy resolved that that the second voyage's crew would be free of that traditional mariner's disease. Although now understood to result from deficiencies of vitamin C specifically, the disease in that day was already known to be caused by a lack of selected produce. Thus, as FitzRoy recalled, the ship's provisions included "various antiscorbutics—such as pickles, dried apples, and lemon juice—of the best quality, and in as great abundance as we could stow away."

Early on, FitzRoy was also proud of the ship's supply, between five and six thousand cans, of preserved (salted) meat that he had obtained. "We had," he recalled, "on board a very large quantity of Kilner and Moorsom's preserved meat." And rounding out the ship's provisions were copious supplies of dried peas, beans and soup, suet (animal fat), oatmeal, vinegar, raisins, bread, rice, cocoa, tea, rum, and tobacco.

Unfortunately, most of the preserved-meat canisters, after contact with salt water, exploded before they could be consumed. On a brighter note, FitzRoy's efforts to combat scurvy proved successful. More generally, during most of the expedition, timely stops at well-stocked ports allowed the ship to maintain a supply of reasonably palatable foodstuffs. At successive ports, FitzRoy purchased bread, fresh meat, and produce, as well as live animals—goats, pigs, sheep, and chickens who lived on the ship's main deck until being slaughtered and eaten.

Moreover, whether under sail or swinging at anchor, the *Beagle*'s men, using poles and nets, also caught fresh fish. And, while at remote landfalls, officers and crew often conducted overland hunts that returned with a wide array of local, often (to the *Beagle*'s men) exotic, game—including ducks, rheas, geese, turtles, armadillos, and seals. For Darwin, the hunts for victuals, sometimes operating at cross-purposes with his scientific collecting objectives, on occasion left him lunging, to comic effect, to rescue a rare species' carcass from the cooking pot or even a shipmate's mouth.

The maintenance of an adequate supply of fresh water, however, constituted a unique challenge. To expand the ship's range, FitzRoy had ordered it equipped with iron tanks capable of holding up to nineteen tons of water. Maps of that age often marked sources of potable (as opposed to sulfurous or brackish) water. And upon anchoring near such sources, typically above a beach or the distant end of an estuary, FitzRoy would dispatch small parties in whaleboats bearing empty casks. Upon reaching their destinations, the men conducted the exhausting work of digging for and ladling the water into the barrels.

On March 27, Darwin watched as Brazil's Abrolhos Archipelago hove into view on the *Beagle*'s starboard bow. Aside from visiting fishermen, the five islands were uninhabited and, except for occasional palms, barren of trees. From a distance, fringed by dark-sanded beaches set against the turquoise Atlantic, the islands resembled oil paints on an artist's palette—visually pleasing daubs of grays, browns, and greens.

On the morning of the twenty-ninth, Darwin numbered among two groups of *Beagle* crew members joyously landed to hunt for food upon the islands—though, in his case, he tended to other priorities:

> I commenced an attack on the rocky [island's] . . . insects & plants. The rest began a more bloody one on the birds. Of these an enormous number were slaughtered by sticks, stones & guns; indeed there were more killed than the boats could hold. We all returned for dinner & after that a boat was given to the midshipmen in order that they might see the islands. I took the opportunity & had another ramble on this solitary spot. Whilst pulling back to the ship we saw a turtle; it immediately went down, nothing certainly could be imagined worse for surprising an animal than a boat full of midshipmen.

Darwin's diary offers vivid views of his *Beagle* travels. Beyond that, in ways that he could not then have anticipated, the chronicle would play a major role in establishing his later career. For that reason alone, the circumstances of its creation warrants explanation. The naturalist wrote out his diary, which he actually called his "Journal," in ink with a favorite Brahma pen, on gatherings of faintly lined paper folded into 8 x 10-inch pages.*

During those five years, he began each diary entry with a date and placename. Those headings, however, were often more conceits than accurate records of the date and place of the respective entries' actual writing. To wit, Darwin seldom risked carrying the diary on excursions away from the *Beagle*; or, when living ashore, away from his residence. To further safeguard the diary, he periodically gathered its pages and mailed them to his sisters.

To compose the entries, Darwin drew on memory and the often cryptic notes that he jotted with a pencil in the successive pocket notebooks that he carried ashore and on overland ventures. As a consequence, though he aspired to give the diary's entries a sense of *en plein air* composition, they were often composed hours, even days or weeks, after their depicted incidents.

Darwin had also agreed to write regular letters to his three unmarried sisters (Caroline, Susan, and Catherine) still living at The Mount.** They, in turn, agreed to swap turns writing monthly, family letters to their absent brother. For Charles, the sisters' letters, affectionate and brimming with gossip and local news, served as an emotional lifeline. (His father, Robert, and brother, Erasmus, by contrast, seldom wrote.) Surprisingly, however, during periods when Charles was away from the *Beagle*, Captain FitzRoy also became a frequent correspondent. Likewise, Charles also corresponded regularly with English relatives and friends, particularly John Henslow.

For Charles, therefore, his diary, besides adding to the burdens of his voluminous correspondence, constituted a new writing challenge. And,

---

* Brahma pens, which first appeared in 1809, were the first pens with separate quill nibs slipped into a holder to gain wide usage

** Charles's oldest sister Marianne Darwin Parker, who married physician Henry Parker in 1824, had already left home.

as he soon confessed to Caroline Darwin, an anxiety, akin to a man befuddled in a house of mirrors, initially attended its creation.

> I am looking forward with great interest for letters, but with very little pleasure to answering them. It is very odd, what a difficult job I find this same writing letters to be. I suppose it is partly owing to my writing everything in my journal: but chiefly to the number of subjects; which is so bewildering that I am generally at a loss either how to begin or end a sentence.

Three weeks later, again writing to Caroline, Charles was still castigating himself about the diary. But he was also growing more comfortable with the challenges of creating a narrative of his travels:

> I send in a packet, my commonplace Journal. I have taken a fit of disgust with it & want to get it out of my sight, any of you that like may read it. A great deal is absolutely childish: Remember however this, that it is written solely to make me remember this voyage, & that it is not a record of facts but of my thoughts.—& in excuse recollect how tired I generally am when writing it. . . . Be sure you mention the receiving of my journal, as anyhow to me it will [be] of considerable future interest as it [is] an exact record of all my first impressions, & such a set of vivid ones they have been, must make this period of my life always one of interest to myself. If you speak quite sincerely, I should be glad to have your criticisms.

Susan Darwin often chastised her brother for careless spelling. Otherwise, the sisters were generally flattering of Charles's diary. In response, however, to his April 1832 solicitation for criticism, Caroline Darwin did eventually offer some gentle advice:

> I am very doubtful whether it is not pert in me to criticize, using merely my own judgement, for no one else of the family have yet read this last part—but I will say just what I think—I

mean as to your style. I thought in the first part (of this last journal) that you had, probably from reading so much of Humboldt, got his phraseology & occasionly made use of the kind of flowery french expressions which he uses, instead of your own simple straight forward & far more agreeable style. I have no doubt you have without perceiving it got to embody your ideas in his poetical language & from his being a foreigner it does not sound unnatural in him. Remember, this criticism only applies to parts of your journal, the greatest part I liked exceedingly & could find no fault, & all of it I had the greatest pleasure in reading.

Their March 27 outing on Brazil's Abrolhos Archipelago provided a welcome respite for the *Beagle*'s crew. In a broader, historical sense, however, for British navigators, the archipelago and similar others constituted a presence anything but benign: geologically, the islands were a collection of submerged and barely above water coral reefs. During the 1820s, the French admiral and explorer Albin Roussin had surveyed the Abrolhos Archipelago. But those measurements, part of a larger reconnoitering of Brazil's coast, had been left unfinished. Thus, the Admiralty, in commissioning FitzRoy's return to South America, included instructions for the *Beagle* to obtain precise measurements of the islands' longitudinal and latitudinal positions, as well as soundings of their coral-ringed waters.

April 28 thus found the *Beagle*, while keeping a safe distance, cautiously edging alongside the archipelago. Over the coming days, as Darwin watched attentively, his crewmates repeatedly, from successive positions around the islands, uncoiled iron chains into the surrounding waters. "We have laid down the soundings on parts of the Abrolhos, which were left undone by Baron Roussin," he noted. "The depth varied to an unusual extent: at one cast of the lead there would be 20 fathoms & in a few minutes only 5. The scene being quite new to me was very interesting."

Whence the British navy's interest in coral reefs? Stretching back to the eighteenth century, reports by explorers such as Louis Antoine de

Bougainville and James Cook of coral reefs, particularly circular-shaped reefs (now called atolls) in the Pacific and Indian oceans, had inspired both fascination and terror. And by the 1830s, the Admiralty had grown concerned about hazards they posed for ships.

Moreover, the growth of the reefs, not understood then, even raised questions about the lasting value of marine surveys. Due to the increasingly recognized speed of the reefs' growth, some wondered whether maritime surveys were a pointless expenditure of time and money. More bluntly, might the Admiralty's efforts, through surveys and the commissioning of updated charts, intended to render the seas safer for mariners, be all for naught?

Darwin was frequently away from the *Beagle* and, even when aboard, was often aloof from shipboard activities. Not infrequently, however, he made an exception for his shipmates' survey-related labors. He observed and eventually adopted for his own purposes hydrographic expertise, which he had learned from them. In fact, prior to the voyage, more enamored with the writings of Charles Lyell and geology than biology, he expected to eventually make his professional name as a geologist rather than a specialist in flora and fauna. Thus Darwin's attentions to coral, simultaneously both rock and animal, synthesized for him geology and biology—furnishing his expanding interests a natural bridge between those two disciplines. In a similar intellectual linkage, as his biographers Adrian Desmond and James Moore observed, by the final years of Darwin's *Beagle* travels, he would "come round to the position of his Lamarckian teacher Robert Grant" at Edinburgh a decade earlier that, "the plant and animal kingdom had a common starting point."

On April 3, the *Beagle*'s crew began preparing for their arrival at Rio de Janeiro, capital of the Empire of Brazil. "All day we ran along the coast & in the evening drew near to the harbour of Rio," wrote Darwin. "The whole line is irregularly mountainous, & interspersed with hills of singular forms. The opening of the port is recognised by one of these, the well known Sugar-loaf [Pão de Açúcar]." In preparation for Rio, teams of sailors soon scrubbed and mopped the *Beagle*'s decks and polished its brass fixtures; still others climbed the ship's riggings to trim its sails. In the end, however, Darwin recalled, because the *Beagle*'s navigators determined they could not reach the port before sundown, FitzRoy postponed their landfall:

> As it would be impossible to get a good anchorage or enjoy the view so late in the evening, the Captain has put the ships head to the wind & we shall, to my great joy, cruize about for the night. We have seen great quantities of shipping; & what is quite as interesting, Porpoises, Sharks & Turtles; altogether, it has been the most idle day I have spent since I left England. Everybody is full of anxiety about letters & news papers, tomorrow morning our fates will be decided.

The postponement, however, only enhanced the magnificence of the *Beagle*'s arrival at Rio the following day—an entry rendered even more dramatic by the presence in the port of the flagship HMS *Warspite* and two other British warships, the *Tyne* and the *Lightning*, as well as the British packet—a mail and passenger ship—*Calypso*. "In most glorious style did the little Beagle enter the port & lower her sails alongside the Flag ship," wrote Darwin. "We were hailed that from some trifling disturbances we must anchor in a particular spot."

FitzRoy, meanwhile, by then, had grown eager to defuse growing shipboard tensions issuing from the rivalry between Jemmy Button and York Minster for the affections of Fuegia Basket. Accordingly, shortly after the *Beagle* anchored at Rio, he placed her in the care of a local family of English expatriates for whom she soon served as a nanny to the couple's children and tutored them in English. It was during that stint that Basket impressively learned enough Portuguese to communicate in it.

Eighteen years earlier, Scottish merchant J. P. Robertson passing through Rio, had found himself both dazzled and repulsed by the contradictory energies still pulsing when Darwin, in 1832, first glimpsed the city.

> The merchandise of Tyre could not have been more cumbrous and varied than that of Rio de Janeiro. The hubbub and the fatigue of everything connected with the custom-house, made me hasten away from a place so unbearable, at once from its confusion, effluvia, heat, and deafening din. I wondered how any organization of human senses and susceptibilities could be found equal to the work going on within this monstrous Babel. I now threaded my way through streets so narrow that it was with the greatest difficulty one carriage could pass another in them. The houses were from two to four stories high. Not a pane of glass was to be seen in any one of them. Instead of this, the openings in the house for light and air, were shrouded by balustrades of latticed woodwork. From under these the inhabitants, chiefly females, raising the jalousies, or lowering them down at pleasure, peeped out upon passengers, without in return being seen by them. The whole town looked like a large darkened convent.

On the morning of April 4, the day after the *Beagle* reached Rio, Darwin and painter Augustus Earle, leaving the ship, "landed . . . at the Palace steps," those of the *Paço Imperial*, the royal palace, close to the waterfront. Erected in 1774, the three-story palace, with its white, grey-trimmed exterior and terra-cotta roof, had been, during the colonial era, the home of Brazil's viceroy. But now it housed the independent country's Emperor Pedro II, then six years old and his powers vested in a board of regents. Like his predecessors, Pedro was descended from members of Portugal's royal family who, in the wake of Napoleon Bonaparte's Iberian Peninsula invasion of 1807, exiled themselves to Brazil.

From the palace, Darwin and Earle wandered through the streets, admiring their gay and crowded appearance. The plan of the town is very regular, the lines, like those in Edinburgh, running parallel, and others crossing them at right angles. The principal streets leading from the squares are straight and broard; from the gay colors of the houses, ornamented by balconies, from the numerous churches and convents and from the numbers hurrying along the streets, the city has an appearance that bespeaks the commercial capital of Southern America.

For four years in the 1820s, Earle had lived in Rio and thus had much to share with the until recently little-traveled Darwin. "Earl[e] makes an excellent guide," he noted. Among other matters, the painter warned of the pernicious effects of drink (and presumably, sexually transmitted diseases) in such climes.

> Earls enquiries about the number of young men whom he left in health & prosperity, the most frequent answer is he is dead & gone. The deaths are generally to be attributed to drinking: few seem able to resist the temptation, when exhausted by business in this hot climate, of strongly exciting themselves by drinking spirits.

Possibly through Earle, Darwin also learned of Botafogo, a tiny hamlet a few miles south of Rio (today *within* that sprawling metropolis). And as the two young men explored Rio that day, April 5, they finalized a plan. As neither's presence were required on the *Beagle* for the next two weeks, they, with FitzRoy's blessings, would find and rent a house together at Botafogo. There, Earle would paint local scenes; and Darwin would collect natural specimens and plan trips into Brazil's interior.

By the day's end, the two, venturing to Botafogo, had found and rented a cottage. To his diary, Darwin exulted: "What can be imagined more delightful than to watch Nature in its grandest form in the regions of the Tropics? We returned to Rio in great spirits."

14

A NIGHT AT THE VENDA DA MATTO

D arwin's "great spirits" of April 5, 1832, proved short-lived. The following morning, a letter from his sister Caroline, written months earlier, reached him in Rio with hurtful news concerning Fanny Owen. The young woman whom Charles cautiously assumed, even after her canceled betrothal to John Hill, he would marry upon his return to England, was now engaged to Robert Myddelton Biddulph, a young aristocrat and member of Parliament. Adding to the sting, the couple's betrothal had occurred within twelve days of Charles's departure from England. Months later, Caroline, writing again, would suggest that Charles consider marrying his cousin Fanny Wedgwood, "an excellent Clerg[y]man's Wife . . . she would be."

Upon learning of Fanny Owen's marriage, Charles, writing to Caroline, tried to sound stoic: "I feel much inclined to philosophize but I am at a loss what to think or say; whilst really melting with tenderness." Compounding his woes, however, on April 6, the day after learning of Fanny's wedding, Charles experienced, for the first but not the last time, the frustrations that would attend most of his interactions with South American governments.

The day has been frittered away in obtaining the passports for my expedition into the interior. It is never very pleasant to submit to the insolence of men in office; but to the Brazilians who are as contemptible in their minds as their persons are miserable it is nearly intolerable. But the prospect of wild forests tenanted by beautiful birds, Monkeys & Sloths, & Lakes by Cavies [a guinea-pig-like rodent] & Alligators, will make any naturalist lick the dust even from the foot of a Brazilian.

The passports, eventually obtained, were for a visit to a coffee plantation along Rio Macaé, one hundred miles north of Rio. His host there, Patrick Lennon, the estate's owner, was an outgoing Irish-born merchant whom Darwin had met during his first days in Rio. As recounted by Darwin, Lennon,

when the Brazils were first opened to the English made a large fortune by selling spectacles, Thermometers &c. About eight years since he purchased a tract of forest country on the Macae & put an English agent over it. Communication is so difficult that from that time to the present he has been unable to obtain any remittances. After many delays Mr Patrick resolved in person to visit his estate. It was easily arranged that I should be a companion & certainly in many respects it has been an excellent opportunity for seeing the country & its inhabitant.

For Charles, the journey would realize a cherished dream: "I shall thus see," he wrote to Caroline, "what has been so long my ambition, virgin forest uncut by man & tenanted by wild beasts. You will all be terrified at the thought of my combating with Alligators & Jaguars in the wilds of the Brazils."

By April 8, when the party, all on horseback, departed Rio, its numbers included a half-dozen or so Europeans, all relatives or acquaintances of Lennon, with a "black boy" as their guide. Their wilderness passage, Charles confided to his diary, immediately revived his enthusiasm for Brazilian scenery.

The colours were intense & the prevailing tint a dark blue, the sky & calm waters of the bay vied with each other in splendor. After passing through some cultivated country we entered a Forest, which in the grandeur of all its parts could not be exceeded. As the gleams of sunshine penetrate the entangled mass, I was forcibly reminded of the two French engravings after the drawings of [Johann Moritz] Rugendas & Le Compte de [Clarac].

As was the custom for whites of social standing when traveling through such country, at each day's end, they ate and lodged at estancias (ranches) along their route. Darwin, for his part, found the overnight hospitality wanting and the travel conditions even worse. April 11 marked a particularly difficult day in the saddle:

Passed through several leagues of a thick wood. I felt unwell, with a little shivering & sickness: crossed the Barra de St Jaôa in a canoe, swimming alongside our horses: could eat nothing at one oclock, which was the first time I was able to procure anything. Travelled on till it was dark, felt miserably faint & exhausted; I often thought I should have fallen off my horse.

And nightfall brought still deeper despair; "Slept at the Venda da Matto," he wrote in his diary. "All night felt very unwell; it did not require much imagination to paint the horrors of illness in a foreign country, without being able to speak one word [of Portuguese] or obtain any medical aid." Weeks later to Caroline Darwin, he added, "My horror of being left utterly destitute in a Venda will be better than any schoolmaster to make me learn Spanish, as soon as we get into those countries."

One aspect of the journey, however, did please Darwin. Even more than earlier tropical outings, its natural bounties inspired "sublime devotion [as] the prevalent feeling." Indeed, praise of those bounties often overwhelmed his ability to capture his thoughts in the small notebook he carried—producing a rush of words resembling a later age's surrealistic poetry: "twiners entwining twiners. tresses like hair beautiful lepidoptera.

silence hosannah. (Frog habits like toad. slow jumps. Iris copper coloured colours become fainter Snake. Cobris de Corrall Fresh water fish."

As in Bahia, however, Darwin's disgust over Brazil's slavery soon eclipsed his admiration of its nature. On April 12, the party lodged at Socego, a fazenda*—a large coffee plantation owned by Manuel Figuireda, "a relation of one of our party." Recording in his diary, the conditions under which Socego's enslaved laborers toiled, Darwin noted, "The slaves here appeared miserably over-worked & badly clothed. Long after it was dark they were employed." However, seven years later, in 1839, Darwin's published account of his *Beagle* travels, labor conditions at Socego had inexplicably improved: "On such fazendas as these, I have no doubt the slaves pass happy and contented lives."

Whence Darwin's retreat from his former outrage? Perhaps an olive branch to FitzRoy to ease wounded feelings over their dustup at Salvador de Bahia? Or perhaps the about-face issued from a fundamental ambivalence beating in the heart of the privileged young Englishman, an ambivalence revealed three sentences earlier in that 1839 recounting of his Socego visit: "As long as the idea of slavery could be banished, there was something exceedingly fascinating in this simple and patriarchal style of living; it was such a perfect retirement and independence of the rest of the world."

But slavery's visceral cruelty was less easily banished from Darwin's mind. From April 14 to the 15th, the party stayed at Patrick Lennon's fazenda, a coffee plantation (not far from Socego) two a half miles long, worked by a now unknown number of slaves, under the management of a "Mr. Cowper." Memorably during their stay, their host transmogrified from charming raconteur—a chap "above the common run of men," as Darwin had described him—into a vile tyrant. Displaying a heretofore unseen temper, Lennon repeatedly harangued Cowper and the plantation's enslaved laborers. He even vowed to separate the latter's menfolk from their wives and children—including a mulatto child fathered by the estate's agent—and sell them "separately at the market at Rio." For

---

* The Portuguese term *fazenda* indicates a large plantation devoted to coffee or sugar, but is sometimes applied to a cattle ranch.

Darwin, Lennon's cruelty illustrated slavery's powers to diminish the humanity of entrepreneurs who profit from its moral outrages: "How strange & inexplicable is the effect of habit & interest! Against such facts how weak are the arguments of those who maintain that slavery is a tolerable evil!"

In 1839, in his published account of his visit to Lennon's estate, Darwin's outrage over the slaves' treatment remained undiminished. But the name of the estate's owner, his fellow British subject Lennon, was nowhere to be found.

By April 24, Darwin was back in Rio. While back aboard the *Beagle* to collect possessions for his move to Botafogo, he learned of recent shipboard discords: "Mr Maccormick"—the *Beagle*'s surgeon—"has been invalided, & goes to England by the [HMS] *Tyne*." Thirty-one-year-old Robert McCormick had grown jealous of Darwin's closeness to FitzRoy. He was also resentful, not without cause, of Darwin's de facto role as the ship's naturalist, a title traditionally accorded a ship's surgeon. He also learned that Darwin, contrary to the stated terms of his joining the expedition, was receiving free meals.

McCormick had earned his place in the Royal Navy through hard work and adherence to rules; and, as a naturalist, he cultivated ambitions similar to Darwin's; furthermore, also like Darwin, McCormick knew that reputations for naturalists were often made through collections. But the surgeon also knew that Darwin's family and prominent associations afforded powerful advantages that he lacked; and beyond that—the final straw—he had learned that Darwin was to be permitted to send his specimens gratis to England.

Darwin, however, for his part, felt no sentimentality nor remorse over McCormick's departure: "He is no loss," he wrote to Caroline.

15

BOTAFOGO IDYLL

"In vain may we look amidst the glories of this
almost new world for quiet contemplation."
—Charles Darwin, *Beagle* diary,
Botafogo Bay, Brazil, May 9, 1832

U pon returning from Brazil's interior to Rio, an exhausted Charles
Darwin, now twenty-three years old, made a confession to his
decade-older sibling Caroline: "Although I like this knocking
about, I find I steadily have a distant prospect of a very quiet parsonage,
& I can see it even through a grove of Palms."

Weary from sixteen days of inland travel, he spent his first night back
in Rio, the evening of April 24, 1832, aboard the *Beagle*. The following
morning, his possessions piled into a rowboat, he set out on the short
trip to his rented cottage at Botafogo. Before reaching his destination,
however, the same powers of nature he routinely praised rudely ambushed
him: "Two or three heavy seas swamped the boat," he recalled, "& before
my affrighted eyes were floating books, instruments & gun cases &
everything which was most useful to me. Nothing was lost & nothing
completely spoiled, but most of them injured."

Mishap overcome, Darwin at Botafogo over the coming days arranged the animal, rock, and plant specimens he had gathered in the interior. And, poring over his field notebook notes from the trip, drawing on them for details and to jog memories, he composed his diary's longer, more fluid, account of the excursion.

Otherwise, Darwin and painter Augustus Earle settled into their respective Botafogo routines. "Earl[e] & myself are now living in this most retired & beautiful spot," he rhapsodized to Caroline Darwin. "I trust to spend a most delightful fortnight." Even better, when FitzRoy on April 26, knocked on their door, their planned fortnight at the cottage lengthened to a stay of undetermined duration: "The Captain has just paid us a visit" and "communicated to me an important piece of news." FitzRoy explained that the *Beagle*, on May 7, would be leaving Rio to return to Bahia, Brazil, on a cruise of undetermined length.

> The reason is a most unexpected difference is found in the Longitudes it is a thing of great importance, & the Captain has written to the Admiralty accordingly. . . . Most likely, I shall live quietly here, it will cost a little, but I am quite delighted at the thought of enjoying a little more of the Tropics.

During those same days, Darwin likewise learned of the death of three crew members who, while hunting snipe ashore, had contracted "Fevers."

At Botafogo, meanwhile, the austral winter's days "quietly glided away"; "A great deal of rain falls, but chiefly by night," Darwin noted. "In other respects the weather is most delightful & cool. The temperature in a room generally varies from 70°–75° [21°–24°C]."

During his Botafogo residency, Darwin generally enjoyed robust health. Even so, the benign weather couldn't insulate him from mishaps or their medical consequences. Early May thus found him suffering from an incident that occurred during a recent collecting outing: "These four days I have been almost laid up by an inflammation in my arm. Any small prick is very apt to become in this country a painful boil." By then, the number of souls from HMS *Beagle* living in the Botafogo cottage had expanded to four: joining Darwin and Augustus Earle (by then ailing from rheumatism) were a Sergeant Beazeley who commanded the seven Royal Marines aboard the ship; and, as Darwin recalled, "Miss Fuegia Basket, who daily increases in every direction except height."

Darwin relished Botafogo's proximity to forests, bodies of water, and mountains. He also cherished having time to study and classify the specimens he gathered each day. The focus of his ever-widening collecting varied from week to week, even day to day. May 1, for instance, found him focused on "a host of fresh water animals with which every ditch abounds." A week later, he was "chiefly collecting spiders." Still later, he "took a long ride, in order to geologize some of the surrounding hills."

The free time at Botafogo proved well needed: "The naturalist in England enjoys in his walks a great advantage over others in frequently meeting with something worthy of attention; here he suffers a pleasant nuisance in not being able to walk a hundred yards without being fairly tied to the spot by some new & wondrous creature." Moreover, "I find one hour's collecting keeps me in full employment for the rest of the day."

On May 25, Darwin, Earle, and Alexander Derbyshire, the *Beagle*'s first mate, guided by a local host, a "Mr Bolga," climbed Corcovado.* For Darwin, the mountain, the site of today's *Christ the Redeemer* statue, was a long-coveted destination. The ninety-eight-foot art deco statue, today a celebrated Rio icon, would not be erected until 1931. But even in 1832 when Darwin ascended the 2,330-foot mountain just two miles from Botafogo, it ranked among the continent's most storied landmarks:

> At every corner alternate & most beautiful views were presented to us. At length we commenced ascending the steep sides, which are universally to the very summit clothed by a thick forest. . . . We soon gained the peak & beheld that view, which perhaps excepting those in Europe, is the most celebrated in the world. If we rank scenery according to the

---

* The mountain's name derives from a Portuguese word for "hunchback."

astonishment it produces, this most assuredly occupies the highest place.

Savoring the view, Darwin imagined how sublime the mountain would appear if viewed from that age's most advanced aeronautical conveyance: "The view from a Balloon would be exceedingly striking." Later, recounting the outing in his diary, he concluded with a macabre coda: "Some years ago a poor insane young woman threw herself from this summit; in few places could a more horrible lovers leap be found. Our present host, Mr Bolga, was one of the first who found the corps[e] dashed into pieces amongst the trees & rocks."

Weeks later, recounting another visit to the mountain, Darwin added another grisly anecdote: "The Caucovado is notorious for Maroon or run-away slaves [*quilombo*, in Portuguese] last time we ascended, we met three most villanous looking ruffians, armed up to the teeth." The latter men—"Maticans" or slave-hunters—"receive so much for every man dead or alive whom they may take. In the former case they only bring down the ears."

Not infrequently, as Darwin inspected local scenes, his mind turned toward the morose and melancholic. On May 9, visiting one of the area's many saltwater inlets and ponds—slipping into what a later generation of readers would call a Proustian revelry—it struck him that, the scene's beauty notwithstanding, something, for him, remained amiss.

Many of the views were exceedingly beautiful; yet in tropical scenery, the entire newness, & therefore absence of all associations, which in my own case . . . are unconsciously much more frequent than I ever thought, requires the mind to be wrought to a high pitch, & then assuredly no delight can be greater; otherwise your reason tells you it is beautiful but the feelings do not correspond. I often ask myself why can I not calmly enjoy this; I might answer myself by also asking, what is there that can bring the delightful ideas of rural quiet & retirement, what that can call back the recollection of childhood & times past, where all that was unpleasant is forgotten;

untill ideas, in their effects similar to them, are raised, in vain
may we look amidst the glories of this almost new world for
quiet contemplation.

Typically, at Botafogo, Darwin spent evenings reading and catching
up on his diary and correspondence. "The number of friends to whom
I am in debt keeps me in full employment." Books by explorers such
as Britain's George Anson were favorites: "I have just finished Ansons
voyage. My pleasure in reading such works is at least trebled by expecting
to see some of the described places & in knowing a little about the sea."

Not that all of the naturalist's Botafogo pleasures, as a May 2
entry attests, pertained to nature: "Walked to Rio: the whole day has
been disagreeably frittered away in shopping." There were also social
outings—including calls on British expatriates, government officials,
and an array of compatriots conducting, or trying to conduct, business in
those climes. "Called on a Mr. Roberts, one of the endless nondescript
characters of which the Brazils are fullbroken down agents to speculation companies; officers who have served under more flags than one: &c
to all of whom I am charitable enough to attribute some little peccadillo
or another." On May 3, calling on more respectable company, Darwin
ventured into Rio and boarded HMS *Warspite* to witness its inspection
by Rear Admiral Thomas Baker, commander of the Royal Navy's South
America Station. "It was one of the grandest sights I ever witnessed."

> When the Admiral arrived the yards were manned by about
> 400 seamen; from the regularity of their movements & from
> their white dresses, the men really looked more like a flock
> of wild-fowl than anything else. . . . In the evening dined
> with the Admiral & afterwards enjoyed the calmer pleasure
> of reading letters from Shropshire.

The next day, with the previous day's visit to the *Warspite* still in mind,
Darwin "worked away at my usual employments, & filled up the cracks
in the time by building castles in the air about the 'pomp & circumstance
of war.'"

At Botafogo Darwin cherished walks at sundown alongside a nearby lagoon. Thus, that walk on the evening of June 25, after he received word of the *Beagle*'s long-postponed but now imminent departure, marked a bittersweet milestone: "In the evening took a farewell stroll to the Lagoa, & saw for the last time its waters stained purple by the last rays of twilight."

16

"LAUGHABLE REVOLUTIONS"

On July 5, 1832, HMS *Beagle*, finally slipping away from Rio, sailed south, bound for Montevideo, capital of the República Oriental del Uruguay. There, Darwin would finally have the chance to try out the Spanish that he had begun studying fourteen months earlier, when he believed himself Tenerife-bound.

By July 22, after three weeks of smooth sailing, the *Beagle* was nearing Rio de la Plata. "We have had this morning a true specimen of the Plata weather," wrote Darwin, inevitably, once again, ravaged by seasickness. Though nominally a river, Rio was actually an estuary formed by the Paraná and Uruguay rivers, a realm mariners traditionally associated with devilish weather. "The lightning was most vivid, accompanied by heavy rain & gusts of wind. The day has been exceedingly cold & raw."

Simultaneously, a sight universally welcomed as a good omen by mariners greeted the crew. "A wonderful shoal of Porpoises at least many hundreds in number, crossed the bows of our vessel. The whole sea in places was furrowed by them; they proceeded by jumps, in which the whole body was exposed; & as hundreds thus cut the water it presented a most extraordinary spectacle."

As they drew still closer to the Rio de la Plata estuary, the world's largest, penguins and seals now abounded, the latter barking so loudly that one seaman mistakenly assumed the ship was passing a cattle pasture. Additionally, Darwin recalled, "We passed through large flocks of different sea-birds & some insects & a bird very like a yellow hammer flew on board." More dramatically, nightfall brought his first glimpse of the natural phenomenon christened St. Elmo's Fire:

> The night presents a most extraordinary spectacle. The darkness of the sky is *interrupted* by the most vivid lightning. The tops of our masts & higher yards ends shone with the Electric fluid playing about them. The form of the vane might almost be traced as if it had been rubbed with phosphorus. To complete these natural fireworks, the sea was so highly luminous that the Penguins might be tracked by the stream of light in their wake.

Bending by late July to a westerly course into Rio de la Plata ("river of silver"), the *Beagle* for four days battled stiff breezes, often direct headwinds, and the estuary's powerful currents. On July 26, at about nine o'clock in the morning, the *Beagle* approached Montevideo's harbor. Minutes later, however, "As we were coming to an anchor, signals were made from the Druid," a British warship lying in the harbor. "To our utter astonishment & amusement," HMS *Druid* "ordered us to 'Clear for action'"—to prepare for an attack "& shortly afterward [to] Prepare to cover our boats." The precaution, however, soon proved unnecessary. "We set sail again & the latter part of [the] order was shortly explained by the arriving of 6 boats heavily armed with Carronades [short, smooth-bore, iron cannon] & containing about 40 marines, all ready for fighting, & more than 100 blue-jackets."

In the quickening action, the *Druid*'s commander, Captain G. W. Hamilton, boarded Darwin's ship with bad news: "The present government," he said, "is a military usurpation" and one of its leaders "had seized upon 400 horses, the property of a British subject." The standoff ended hours later, after a promise by the responsible party to return the seized horses.

But Darwin, for his part, had his doubts: "I do not think [it] is very clear [that the promise] will be kept." He further resented the confrontation's likely effect on the *Beagle*'s stay at Montevideo and his own expectations of inspecting the local nature: "I am afraid, it is not impossible that the consequences will be very unpleasant to us: The Druids officers have not for some weeks been allowed to go on shore, & perhaps we shall be obliged to act in the same manner. How annoying will be the sight of green turf plains, whilst we are performing a sort of quarantine on board."

Rio de la Plata's politics during the 1830s were often as muddy and dark—and bedeviled with confusing currents—as the estuary itself. Underscoring those circumstances, Uruguay's nominal, and fragile, independence was only four years old when the *Beagle* reached Montevideo, and had issued from a peace treaty between Brazil and Argentina. The two countries had warred from 1825 to 1828 for control of Uruguay, then known as Banda Oriental (Eastern Bank), a realm east of the Uruguay River and north of Rio de la Plata.

Mediated by Britain, the Argentina-Brazil armistice created a buffer state (Uruguay) to prevent a recurrence of war. But though Uruguay was formally independent when the *Beagle*, in 1832, sailed into the estuary, Montevideo remained riven by poisonous military and political factionalism. Likewise, west of Uruguay, turmoil roiled Argentina's domestic politics. In 1820, the central government had collapsed. Afterward, its thirteen provinces became independent from one another—linked only by treaties, until 1824, when they reunited in Congress. That body, in 1826, produced a constitution, but it ultimately failed to win ratification by the provinces. And with the Congress's collapse in 1827, the provinces, soon again linked only by treaties, reverted to independent status.

Darwin, for his part, in late July 1832, was marking his fifth month on the South American continent. Already, however, as his diary attests, he held a cynical view of the continent's politics:

The revolutions in these countries are quite laughable; some
few years ago in Buenos Ayres, they had 14 revolutions in 12
months. Things go as quietly as possible [in Montevideo]; both
parties dislike the sight of blood; & so that the one which
appears the strongest gains the day. The disturbances do not
much affect the inhabitants of the town, for both parties find
it best to protect private property. The present governor has
about 260 Gaucho cavalry & about same number of Negro
infantry. The opposite party is now collecting a force & the
moment he enters the town the others will scamper out.
Mr Parry (a leading merchant here) says he is quite certain
a 150 men from the Frigate could any night take M: Video.

Darwin's views of South America's politics typified those of the
era's upper-class Englishmen. Often unaware of underlying causes ani-
mating conflicts, many dismissed the continent's politics as the stuff of
opera buffa. Darwin's comments on political instability in the Plata, for
instance, overlooked London's ongoing aspirations to create informal
empires in the region. Likewise, his views minimized the role of British
diplomatic interference in Buenos Aires and Montevideo—mischief
punctuated by military actions in 1806 and 1807.

By the early 1820s, following the wars of independence that created South America's republics, British interests, often sparking local
irritation, sought to fill voids created by the withdrawal of Spanish and
Portuguese overseers. Indeed, it has even been argued that, during those
years, British interests simply took over where the Spanish and Portuguese left off.

While Montevideo and Buenos Aires, for instance, welcomed
British merchants, by the 1830s the continuing presence of British
warships—and, to a lesser degree, those of France, Spain, and Italy—in
both ports fueled growing resentments. To wit, during that era, international laws concerning national sovereignty remained vague. And,
exploiting that circumstance, foreign merchants, when enmeshed in dis-
putes with local officials, routinely called upon their respective consuls for
satisfaction. And those diplomats, in turn, particularly those of Britain,

often successfully called upon the captains of their nation's warships to militarily intervene in disagreements.

Not until July 27, the day after the *Beagle* reached Montevideo, did Darwin go ashore. Accompanying FitzRoy, he visited Isla de Rata (Rat Island), where the captain took sextant sightings from a small rise that dominated the tiny island. Rising to 450 feet, the modest elevation was the source of the name Montevideo ("mountain view"). On Rat Island, as FitzRoy took his solar sightings, Darwin inspected phenomena closer to the ground—soon finding a species of legless lizard called a skink. "At first sight," he recorded, "every one would pronounce it to be a snake: but two small hind legs or rather fins marks the passage by which Nature joins the Lizards to the Snakes."

The skink fascinated Darwin, but the harbor vantage from Rat Island left him underwhelmed: "The view from the summit is one of the most uninteresting I ever beheld. Not a tree or a house or trace of cultivation give cheerfulness to the scene. An undulating green plain & large herds of cattle has not even the charm of novelty." A later stroll with FitzRoy through Montevideo's center left him even more unimpressed: "The appearance of the place does not speak much in its favor; it is of no great size; possesses no architectural beauties, & the streets are irregular & filthily dirty."

On July 29, two days after visiting Rat Island, FitzRoy, still in Montevideo, learned about documents in the state archives at Buenos Aires that allegedly contained hydrographic data compiled by the Spanish government. Assuming them worth inspecting, he decided that a quick run up the Plata to the Argentine capital was in order. Thus, as Darwin recorded, on July 31, "at one oclock we stood out of the Bay with a light fair wind."

Two days later, Buenos Aires appeared before the *Beagle*'s bow. "On entering the outer roadstead, we passed a Buenos Ayres guard-ship." But, as in Montevideo, a surprise loomed for the *Beagle*'s crew. As they passed the guard-ship, "she fired an empty gun."

The salvo, Darwin recalled, left the *Beagle*'s complement momentarily nonplussed. But, "We not understanding this sailed on." Minutes later, however, "another discharge was accompanied by the whistling of a shot over our rigging. . . . We certainly are a most unquiet ship; peace flies before our steps." Fortunately, however, before the Argentine ship "could get another gun ready we had passed her range." Moreover, "when we arrived at our anchorage, which is more than three miles distant from the landing place; two boats were lowered, & a large party started in order to stay some days in the city."

Hoping to locate Henry Stephen Fox, Britain's minister in Buenos Aires, and file a formal complaint about the incident, Lieutenant John Wickham and Darwin found spots in one of two boats lowered from the *Beagle*. But before their boat reached the docks, an Argentine "Quarantine boat" pulled alongside with strict instructions: "We must all return on board, to have our bill of health inspected, from fears of the Cholera."

Irate, dismissing the cholera concerns as a subterfuge masking belligerent motives, FitzRoy ordered the *Beagle*'s return to Montevideo. For good measure, Darwin recorded, "We then loaded & pointed all the guns on one broadside, & ran down close along the guard-ship. Hailed her, & said that when we again entered the port, we would be prepared as at present & if she dared to fire a shot we would send our whole broadside into her rotten hulk."

Two days later, however, when their ship reached Montevideo—"an eventful day in the history of the *Beagle*," in Darwin's words—political upheaval once again stirred that port.

> At 10 oclock in the morning the Minister for the present military government came on board & begged for assistance against a serious insurrection of some black troops. Cap FitzRoy immediately went ashore to ascertain whether it was a party affair, or that the inhabitants were really in danger of having their houses ransacked. The head of the Police (Damas) has

continued in power through both governments, & is considered
as entirely neutral; being applied to, he gave it as his opinion
that it would be doing a service to the state to land our force.

In the end, acceding to the request, FitzRoy dispatched fifty-two
armed men to capture and hold the fort until the arrival of expected
government reinforcements. Even Darwin—armed with pistols and
a cutlass, in his life's only known military deployment—joined their
numbers. The *Beagle*'s men easily took the fort. Over the next few hours,
however, Darwin, suffering a headache, returned to the ship. There, he
helped prepare for a feared attack. The following day, as reinforcements
arrived at the fort but auguries of violence multiplied near their ship,
FitzRoy ordered all hands back to the *Beagle*.

Over the coming days, as gunfire filled Montevideo's center, the
Beagle's men watched the exchanges from their anchorage. "In the paltry
state of Monte Video, there are actually about 5 contending parties for
supremacy," noted Darwin. "It makes one ask oneself whether Despotism
is not better than such uncontrolled anarchy."

After the fighting subsided, the *Beagle*'s men spent the coming days
conducting soundings near Montevideo. Darwin, meanwhile, courtesy of
the Royal Navy, finally dispatched his first box of specimens to Henslow,
a motley assemblage whose contents ranged from rocks to birds, lichens
to crabs. And, on August 19, after four weeks in the Plata, the *Beagle*
weighed anchor and sailed south.

PART IV

AUSTRAL CLIMES, 1832–1833

17

"NO PAINTER EVER IMAGINED
SO WILD A SET OF EXPRESSIONS"

"The result, therefore, of this physical inquiry is, that we
find no vestige of a beginning—no prospect of an end."
—James Hutton,
Theory of the Earth, 1795

By early September 1832, the *Beagle* was nearing Bahía Blanca
("White Bay"), which traditionally marked Buenos Aires Province's
southern edge, below which semiarid Patagonia began. Taking its
name from the salt-laden soil fringing its shores, the bay was actually an
estuary. In Bahía Blanca, the waters of Arroyo Napostá (Naposta stream),
rising from the Sierra de La Ventana range and flowing seventy-five
northeasterly miles, met those of the Atlantic.

But the bay and the coastal approaches to it, as the *Beagle*'s men soon
learned, could be perilously shallow. On September 3, roughly forty miles
north of Bahía Blanca, they almost ran aground: "Our bottom was then
only two feet from the ground," Darwin recorded. "If we had struck, it
is possible we should have gone to the bottom; & the long swell of the
open ocean would soon dash the strongest timber into pieces."

Altering course and by evening finding temporary anchorage in deeper waters, the *Beagle* resumed its southward journey the next morning. By the fifth, the ship lay anchored just outside the mouth of Bahía Blanca. The following morning, "we stood into the bay; but soon got entangled in the midst of shoals & banks." Once again, however, after managing to free the ship, they found nearby, deeper waters and safe anchorage.

On the morning of September 7, FitzRoy, leading several of the *Beagle*'s open boats, set out to find a safe passage to Port Belgrano inside the larger bay. But once again, "Our boats were soon stopped by shoal water, and I found, to my vexation, that the Beagle was anchored at the head of an inlet, between the shore and a large bank extending far towards the south-east."

Returning to the *Beagle*, FitzRoy issued orders to reverse the ship's course, leave the bay, and reenter it through another, deeper, passage. "This," he recalled, "was an unexpected dilemma; but our prospect was improved by the appearance of a small schooner running towards us, from Port Belgrano, with a Buenos Ayrean (or Argentine) flag flying."

The *Beagle* approached the schooner, whose passengers included an Englishman, James Harris, with whom FitzRoy talked and eventually struck a deal. A part owner of the schooner, Harris was a "sealer," a businessman invested in seal-hunting. He lived in Carmen de Patagones, on Rio Negro, 170 miles to the south, to which his schooner that day was sailing.*

Harris told FitzRoy about another schooner, berthed deep in Bahía Blanca's backwaters, a few miles from an inland Argentine fort. The schooner would be leaving in two days for the same Rio Negro destination. But the boat's current anchorage, Harris explained, was too shallow for the *Beagle* to reach. So, if FitzRoy agreed to later take Harris in one of the *Beagle*'s open boats to the schooner's anchorage near the fort, Harris would pilot the *Beagle* to a safe harbor inside the bay.

By the day's end, thanks to Harris's piloting, the *Beagle* lay safely anchored at Port Belgrano. The following morning, true to his word,

---

* Patagonia's Rio Negro (Black River) should not be confused with at least nine other South American rivers of the same name, including one other in Argentina and six in Brazil.

FitzRoy set out in an open boat for the Argentine fort. The party included FitzRoy, Darwin, Harris, and *Beagle* purser George Rowlett. Their destination lay about twenty miles from Port Belgrano. After reaching a distant edge of the estuary, Darwin recalled, "We took by chance the first creek we could find: but following this for some miles, it gradually became so narrow that the oars touched on each side & we were obliged to stop."

Over the coming hours, the party confronted a maze of narrow, often muddy, creeks and channels. That evening, recalled Darwin, "we arrived at the creek which is about four miles distant from the Settlement [the fort]. Here was a small schooner lying & a mud-hut on the bank." Ominously, at the same spot, "several of the wild Gaucho cavalry [were] waiting to see us land."

> They formed by far the most savage picturesque group I ever beheld. I should have fancied myself in the middle of Turkey by their dresses. Round their waists they had bright coloured shawls forming a petticoat, beneath which were fringed drawers. . . . They all wore the Poncho, which is [a] large shawl with a hole in the middle for the head. Thus equipped with sabres & short muskets they were mounted on powerful horses. The men themselves were far more remarkable than their dresses; the greater number were half Spaniard & Indian. Some of each pure blood & some black. The Indians, whilst gnawing bones of beef, looked, as they are, half recalled wild beasts. No painter ever imagined so wild a set of expressions.

Added FitzRoy, "the assemblage of grotesque figures . . . I shall not easily forget."

But the suspicions were mutual. Among those meeting the *Beagle* party was the Argentine fort's commander; and, as FitzRoy recalled, the officer initially believed, "we were bringing supplies from Buenos Ayres for the needy colony." But "finding that we were neither Buenos Ayreans, nor traders from any other place, it was supposed that we must be spies sent to reconnoitre the place previous to a hostile attack."

Harris joined the exchange but to no avail. "Neither the explanations nor assertions of Mr. Harris had any weight," recalled FitzRoy, "for as he was our countryman, they naturally concluded he was in league with us." Even so, "the commandant had some idea that we might, by possibility, be what we maintained . . . and offered to carry us to the settlement for a night's lodging."

Exhausted, the Englishmen accepted the invitation. Recalled Darwin, "We all mounted behind the Gauchos & started at a ha[rd] gallop for the Fort."

Set on a flat plain, pentagon-shaped Fortaleza Protectora Argentina, 282 yards in diameter, had adobe walls and bastions at its corners. "In some places," wrote FitzRoy, "the walls are almost twenty feet high but in others . . . there is a mere ditch, over which a man could jump. It is, however, said by the gauchos, that a ditch six feet wide will stop a mounted Indian, and that their houses require no further defence from attacks of the aborigines."

Inside and beyond the citadel's walls, FitzRoy recalled, "were huts (ranchos) and a few small houses: more were not required for the inhabitants, who, including the garrison, only amounted to four hundred souls. Some half-dozen brass guns were in a serviceable condition; and two or three other pieces occupied old carriages, but did not seem to be trustworthy."

Once inside the fort, Darwin wrote, "Our reception here was not very cordial. The Commandant was inclined to be civil; but the Major, although second in rank, appears to be the most efficient. He is an *old* Spaniard, with the old feelings of jealousy. He could not contain his surprise & anxiety at a Man of War having arrived for the first time in the harbor."

The major, FitzRoy added, "thought we were very suspicious characters, especially Mr. Darwin, whose objects seemed most mysterious." More vexing, "We afterwards heard, that the old major's suspicions had been very much increased by Harris's explanation of Mr. Darwin's occupation. 'Un naturalista' was a term unheard of by any person in the settlement, and being unluckily explained by Harris as meaning 'a man that knows every thing,' any further attempt to quiet anxiety was useless."

The *Beagle* party soon learned that Fortaleza Protectora Argentina (from which today's city of Bahía Blanca grew) was constructed four years earlier to provide "an advanced post, at which to watch and check the Indians, rather than as a colony likely to increase rapidly." The outpost's officers attributed its strategic importance to its proximity to Port Belgrano—"the only port, between 25° S. and Cape Horn, capable of receiving in security any number of the largest ships."

Fortaleza Protectora Argentina lay at the strategic heart of a vast expanse in which the troops commanded by caudillo Juan Manuel de Rosas were conducting his Desert Campaign. With the tacit blessings of his successor Juan Ramón Balcarce, Buenos Aires Province's current governor, Rosas was at war with the region's Indigenous peoples—determined to usurp their lands and open them to white settlers and cattle ranching. His battle-theater was a broad six-hundred-mile north-to-south swath of pampas, at its north roughly parallel with Buenos Aires and dropping south to Carmen de Patagones, on Rio Negro. Over that broad swath, in successive actions that year, columns of Rosas's troops fanned out east-to-west over the plains toward and into the Andes foothills.

In the breadth of his destruction, the general aspired to nothing less in scale than the persecution inflicted centuries earlier by his Iberian forebears on Spain's Jewish and Muslim populations.

———※———

That evening, mutual suspicions between the fort's commander and the *Beagle* party deteriorated into veiled threats, and, in FitzRoy's case, a brazen, outlandish bluff. The fort's commander, Darwin recalled, "asked endless questions about our force &c., & when the Captain, praising the bay, assured him he could bring up even a line of battle ship[s], the old gentleman was appalled & in his minds eye saw the British Marines taking his fort."

The following morning, September 8, Harris stayed behind at the fort to await the departure of the Rio Negro–bound schooner.

The *Beagle*'s men, meanwhile, leaving at daybreak, returned to their ship. At Port Belgrano that evening and over the coming days, FitzRoy found the *Beagle* shadowed by gauchos lurking on nearby mudflats. Through it all, however, his men conducted their Bahía Blanca survey work undaunted.

Unbeknownst to others aboard the *Beagle*, however, during FitzRoy's outing to the fort, he and Harris had discussed FitzRoy's growing doubts about the ship's ability to complete, within its allotted time, the southerly sections of its Argentine coast survey—from Bahía Blanca south to the mouth of Rio Negro. Moreover, FitzRoy recalled, "after a few days' examination of Port Belgrano, and making inquiries of Harris, as well as those persons at Argentina who knew something of the neighbouring waters and shores, I was convinced that the Beagle alone could not explore them."

> What then was to be done? Open boats could not explore the seaward limits of those numerous shoals which lie between Blanco Bay [Bahía Blanca] and the river Negro, because there are dangerous 'races', and often heavy seas. The Beagle herself, no doubt, could do so, and her boats might explore the inlets; but, the time that such a proceeding would occupy was alarming to contemplate.

Eventually, from Harris, Fitzroy arranged to hire two schooners, *La Paz* and *La Liebre*, to assist the *Beagle*. "Mr. Harris was to be in the larger [schooner, *La Liebre*], as pilot to Lieutenant Wickham—and his friend Mr. Roberts, also settled at Carmen de Patagones, on the river Negro, was to be Mr. Stokes's pilot in the smaller vessel." For FitzRoy, the arrangement left but one nagging concern, his lack of authorization from the Admiralty to hire extra vessels. Hoping for later reimbursement, he thus would use his own funds to hire the extra boats. Otherwise, by FitzRoy's lights, the arrangement seemed ideal, freeing the *Beagle* to tend to other assigned survey areas, including Tierra del Fuego, where the Fuegians would be repatriated: "These small craft [belonging to Harris], of fifteen and nine tons respectively, guided by their owners, who had for years frequented this complication of banks, harbours, and tides, seemed to me capable of fulfilling the desired object."

Darwin likewise praised the new strategy: "By this means the time spent on the Eastern coast will be much shorter & this is hailed with joy by everybody. Mr Harris will immediately go to Rio Negro to bring the vessels & soon after that we shall return to the Rio Plata."

Darwin's presence, as usual, would not be required during the *Beagle*'s upcoming survey work. Indeed, since returning on September 9 to Port Belgrano, he had spent much of his time away from the ship—shooting, among other game, deer, ostriches, and agouti (the large rodent). Carcasses not hauled back to the *Beagle* for consumption by its crew, he bartered or sold to nearby Argentine soldiers. As he recalled on the fourteenth:

> I am spending September . . . much in the same manner as I should in England, viz in shooting; in this case however there is the extra satisfaction of knowing that one gives fresh provisions to the ships company. To day I shot another deer & an Agouti or Cavy. The latter weighs more than 20 pounds; & affords the very best meat I ever tasted.

FitzRoy admired—in truth, *envied*—the joy Darwin took in his outings ashore. Writing to his sister Frances ("Fanny"), he praised the naturalist as, "a good pedestrian, as well as a good horseman; he is a sensible, shrewd, and sterling good fellow. While I am about pottering in the water, measuring depths and fixing positions, he wanders over the land, and frequently makes long excursions where I cannot go, because my duty is Hydro- not 'Geo-graphy.'"

As for Darwin, as much as he savored his "Geo-graphy"-driven excursions away from the *Beagle*, by late 1832, having during the voyage collected few significant specimens, he was growing anxious. Compounding worries, reports were reaching him that French naturalist Alcide d'Orbigny was also in Argentina searching for specimens. To Henslow, Darwin fretted, "I am very selfishly concerned that he will get the cream of all the good things."

On Sunday, September 22, FitzRoy, Darwin, Bartholomew Sulivan, and Syms Covington were enjoying what Darwin called "a pleasant cruize" in one of the *Beagle*'s open boats. During the outing, FitzRoy, with mock understatement, recalled: Darwin's "attention was soon attracted to some low cliffs near Point Alta [Punta Alta, near Port Belgrano], where he found some of those huge fossil bones . . . and notwithstanding our smiles at the cargoes of apparent rubbish which he frequently brought on board, he and his servant [apparently Syms Covington] used their pick-axes in earnest, and brought away what have since proved to be most interesting and valuable remains of extinct animals."

His luck abruptly redeemed, Darwin spent several days at Punta Alta. That first day, the twenty-second, he recorded in his diary, produced results sufficiently encouraging ("numerous shells & the bones of large animals") to bring him back the next day: "I walked on to Punta alta to look after fossils," he noted on the twenty-third, "& to my great joy I found the head of some large animal, imbedded in a soft rock. It took me nearly 3 hours to get it out: As far as I am able to judge, it is allied to the Rhinoceros. I did not get it on board till some hours after it was dark."

Over the coming years, Charles Darwin's theories tended to arrive slowly, in increments, rather than as blinding Saul of Tarsus epiphanies. Even so, as physiologist Richard Darwin Keynes, a great-grandson of the naturalist observed, Sunday, September 23, 1832, marked a milestone—for Charles and for the history of science: "This was," wrote Keynes, "truly a red-letter day for biology, marking the initial discovery of the first of the lines of evidence that eventually led CD to question and ultimately to reject the doctrine of the fixity of species."

At Punta Alta, Darwin, in September 1832, had discovered a fossil of a giant animal that resembled in all but size a living species with which he was familiar. However, not until after the *Beagle*'s return and the specimen's examination by zoologist Richard Owen did Darwin learn that his fossil was a *Megatherium*, a now extinct giant ground sloth. (In 1842, by then an old hand in prehistoric matters, Owen repeatedly coined the term "dinosaur," from the Greek *deinos* for terrible, *sauros* for lizard.)

Indeed, Richard Darwin Keynes added, "In July" 1837, after learning of Owen's identification of the fossil's species, Charles Darwin "opened

[his] first note book on 'Transmutation of Species.'" Although Darwin would require Owen to correctly identify his fossil's species, he knew immediately, in September 1832, that he had unearthed something important: as he wrote to Henslow, "I have just got scent of some fossil bones of a Mammoth!, what they may be, I do not know, but if gold or galloping will get them, they shall be mine."

By early fall, James Harris had returned to Rio Negro. There, joined by Lieutenant Wickham, he was working to refit the two schooners promised to FitzRoy. By mid-October, both vessels and the *Beagle* lay at Bahía Blanca. And there, on October 18, the *Beagle* and the schooners *La Liebre* and *La Paz* parted ways—the *Beagle* for Rio Plata for survey work and to take on fresh provisions; and Harris's two schooners, for the south to complete the more southerly surveys.

Darwin, sailing aboard the *Beagle*, welcomed the return to Rio de la Plata as an opportunity, earlier denied, to spend time in cosmopolitan Montevideo and Buenos Aires. In the latter that November, fresh from his *Megatherium* discovery, he even managed to find and purchase a copy of volume II of Charles Lyell's *Principles of Geology*. He also visited Buenos Aires's natural history museum (today's Bernardino Rivadavia Museum of Natural Science), saw a dentist, had his watch repaired, dined with the British chargé d'affaires, purchased a new belt and thermometer, and refreshed his supply of notebooks and Brahma pens. He also bought "some enormous bones" which he was assured, "belonged to the former *giants!*" In Buenos Aires, Darwin presumably also conducted a usual ritual performed upon his arrival at any major port—of finding his way to a bank or local English agent and, through the international banking system, withdrawing cash from his father's account.

While Darwin enjoyed both Buenos Aires and Montevideo, the former left the better impression.

> [Nov.] *6th* . . . Buenos Ayres is an excellent place for making purchases; there are many shops kept by Englishmen full of English goods. Indeed the whole town has more of an Europæan look than any I have seen in S. America. One is called back to the true locality, both by the Gauchos riding

through the streets with their gay coloured Ponchos & by the dress of the Spanish ladies. This latter, although not differing much from an English one, is most elegant & simple. In the hair (which is beautifully arranged) they wear an *enormous* comb; from this a large silk shawl folds round the upper part of the body. Their walk is most graceful, & although often disappointed, one never saw one of their charming backs without crying out, "how beautiful she must be."

In Buenos Aires, Charles's frequent shore companion was Robert Nicholas Hamond, a midshipman in his early twenties who, that November, had been loaned to the *Beagle* from HMS *Druid*. "Our chief amusement was riding about & admiring the Spanish Ladies," Charles wrote to Caroline Darwin. "After watching one of these angels gliding down the streets; involuntarily we groaned out, 'how foolish English women are, they can neither walk nor dress'. And then how ugly Miss sounds after Signorita; I am sorry for you all; it would do the whole tribe of you a great deal of good to come to Buenos Ayres."

As a naturalist, however, Charles found both Buenos Aires and Montevideo—and indeed much of what he had seen of Argentina's coast—wanting. "In sad reality," he lamented to Henslow, "we coasted along 240 miles of sand hillocks; I never knew before, what a horrid ugly object a sand hillock is." Moreover, "The famed country of the Rio Plata in my opinion is not much better; an enormous brackish river bounded by an interminable green plain, is enough to make any naturalist groan."

He thus looked forward to the *Beagle*'s more southerly wanderings. "So hurrah for Cape Horn & the land of storms," he exclaimed, noting that he expected "to find the wild mountainous country of Terra del. [Fuego] very interesting." And, on December 2, 1832, the *Beagle*, to Charles's delight, departing Montevideo, set sail for the bottom of the world.

18

TIERRA DEL FUEGO

"O, wonder!
How many goodly creatures are there here!
How beauteous mankind is! O brave new world,
That has such people in't!"

—William Shakespeare, *The Tempest*

B y 1832's final weeks, Captain FitzRoy's thoughts had turned toward
the Tierra del Fuego survey and repatriating the three Fuegians
there. The afternoon of December 10, early summer in those austral climes, thus found his ship scudding along with a "strong breeze,"
approaching Port Desire on southern Patagonia's Atlantic coast.

Two days later, however, what Darwin called "the heaviest squall I
have ever seen" battered the ship. And though it was early summer in
that latitude, "the air has the bracing fear of an English winter day."
Further confounding expectations, three days later, the fifteenth, found
the *Beagle*, sailing under "very foggy" conditions. "Every thing," Darwin
complained, "conspires to make our passage long."

But the *Beagle* persevered; and, on Sunday, December 16, south of
Cape St. Sebastian but still in Atlantic waters, "We made the coast
of Tierra del Fuego." A few men aboard that day had been on the ship's
earlier visits to Tierra del Fuego. But, noted Darwin, "The *Beagle* had

never visited this part before; so that it was new to every body." No one aboard thus knew whether the area was inhabited.

But the mystery soon lifted. "Our ignorance whether any natives lived here, was soon cleared up by the usual signal of a smoke," Darwin wrote. Furthermore, FitzRoy recalled, Natives soon appeared on the shore, calling across the bay's waters, "waving skins, and beckoning to us with extreme eagerness."

Explorer Ferdinand Magellan, in 1520, reputedly named the archipelago Tierra del Fuego ("land of fire") after the torches that Indigenes brought to the islands' shores as his ships passed. Now, three centuries later, the *Beagle*'s officers, squinting into spyglasses, could clearly "see a group & some scattered Indians evidently watching the ship with interest." Speculated Darwin, in his diary, "They must have lighted the fires immediately upon observing the vessel, but whether for the purpose of communicating the news or attracting our attention, we do not know." Later, recalling that first sighting to Caroline Darwin, Charles elaborated,

> An untamed savage is I really [I] think one of the most extraordinary spectacles in the world. The difference between a domesticated & wild animal is far more strikingly marked in man. In the naked barbarian, with his body coated with paint, whose very gestures, whether they may be peacible or hostile are unintelligible, with difficulty we see a fellow-creature. No drawing or description will at all explain the extreme interest which is created by the first sight of savages.

More admiringly, FitzRoy reflected, "I have often been astonished at the rapidity with which the Fuegians produce this effect (meant by them as a signal) in their wet climate, where I have been, at times, more than two hours attempting to kindle a fire."

Terra del Fuego, at the "Bottom of the World," occupied an austere, even terrifying, zone in the European imagination. For centuries of Old

World–born travelers, the archipelago constituted a realm beset with real and imagined perils—ship-pulverizing storms, disorienting labyrinths of channels and islands, starvation and cannibalism, nightmarish cold and darkness, and suicide-inducing isolation. Bearing witness to those dangers, European travelers left place-names there that doubled as cautionary tales: Desolation Bay, Fury Bay, Devil Island, Useless Bay, Port Famine.

Situated between Latitudes 52° and 56° South, the archipelago sprawled over 28,000 square miles, an area roughly the size of Ireland. The Strait of Magellan separates Terra del Fuego from the South American mainland. Isla Grande, the archipelago's (and South America's) largest island, dominates its east and north, where the terrain tends to be relatively low-lying. In the west, geologically an extension of the Andes, several mountains exceed 7,000 feet.

As the *Beagle* sailed south on December 17, a "strong wind" and obliging tides blessed its passage. "But even thus favoured," Darwin noted, "it was easy to perceive how great a sea would rise were the two powers opposed to each other. The motion from such a sea is very disagreeable; it is called 'pot-boiling', & as water boiling breaks irregularly over the ships sides."

Hugging the coast, the *Beagle* passed "high hills clothed in brownish woods [which] take the place of the [earlier passed, steep] horizontal formations." Still further south, now along Isla Grande's east coast, the ship, that afternoon, entered a bay whose history and name evoked safe anchorage—the Bay of Good Success.

On December 17, 1832, when the *Beagle* reached the bay, the days were growing longer, though not always brighter. Indeed, a "gloomy" sky hung over the cape's waters at the next daybreak, at just after 3:00 A.M. The scene captivated Darwin: "The country is not high, but formed of horizontal strata of some modern rock, which in most places forms abrupt cliffs facing the sea. It is also intersected by many sloping vallies. These are covered with turf & scattered over with thickets & trees, so as to present a cheerful appearance." In the distance, to the south, rose "a chain of lofty mountains, the summits of which glittered with snow."

"Here," noted Darwin, "we intend staying some days." FitzRoy's decision to linger in the bay notwithstanding, the *Beagle*'s crew was already aware they were not alone. Earlier that day, while entering the bay, they had noticed, "a party of Fuegians . . . watching us." The observers were "perched on a wild peak overhanging the sea & surrounded by wood."

> As we passed by they all sprang up & waving their cloaks of skins sent forth a loud sonorous shout. This they continued for a long time. These people followed the ship up the harbor & just before dark we again heard their cry & soon saw their fire at the entrance of the Wigwam which they built for the night. After dinner the Captain went on shore to look for a watering place; the little I then saw showed how different this country is from the corresponding zone in the Northern Hemisphere.

When Darwin later that day, still December 17, joined the captain to go ashore to search for freshwater sources, the young naturalist was weeks away from his twenty-fourth birthday. Over those hours and the coming days, that looming milestone prompted reflections on the physical distances he'd traveled over the past twelve months.

Far from Shrewsbury, he was now journeying in the paths of explorers whose adventures he'd marveled over as a boy in books, such as C. C. Clarke's *Hundred Wonders of the World*. Indeed, the Bay of Good Success in which the *Beagle* lay anchored, named by explorer García de Nodal, had been later visited by, among other celebrated travelers, English explorer James Cook. "To me it is delightful being at anchor in so wild a country as Tierra del F.," Darwin reflected. "The very name of the harbor we are now in, recalls the idea of a voyage of discovery; more especially as it is memorable from being the first place Capt. Cook anchored in on this coast."

More prosaically, Darwin described the bay as "a fine piece of water & surrounded on all sides by low mountains of slate." Some of the landscape's features even brought to mind the Welsh mountains in which sixteen months earlier he assisted Professor Sedgwick's fieldwork. "These are of the usual rounded or saddle-backed shape, such as occur in the less wild parts of N: Wales. They differ remarkably from the latter in being clothed by a very thick wood of evergreens almost to the summit."

That night, a gale rose from the shoreward mountains—pounding with wind and rain the *Beagle*, swinging at anchor in the bay. Inside, meanwhile, just above the ship's stern, Darwin, snug in his cherished poop cabin, found ironic comfort in the vessel's rocking, and the creaking of its wooden planks, in the storm-roiled waters. Drifting in and out of sleep in his hammock, he found added solace in the bay's name and history.

> Those who know the comfortable feeling of hearing the rain & wind beating against the windows whilst seated round a fire, will understand our feelings: it would have been a very bad night out at sea, & we as well as others may call this Good Success Bay.

The next day, December 18, FitzRoy, seeking to establish direct contact with the Fuegians, dispatched a boat to the shore, its passengers including Darwin, Jemmy Button, and several officers. The encounter began amicably. "As soon as the boat came within hail," Darwin recalled, "one of the four men who advanced to receive us began to shout most vehemently, & at the same time pointed out a good landing place."

By the time the Englishmen dragged their boat ashore, however, the women and children had scurried away. The remaining men on the beach "looked rather alarmed, but continued talking & making gestures with great rapidity. It was without exception the most curious & interesting spectacle I ever beheld." Then, returning to a familiar theme, Darwin added, "I would not have believed how entire the difference between savage & civilized man is. It is greater than between a wild & domesticated animal, in as much as in man there is greater power of improvement."

Apparently, the group the *Beagle* party saw was a family—its patriarch, an old man who remained on the shore. Beside him stood three "young powerful men," each "about 6 feet high." "From their dress &c &c,"

Darwin was taken aback—to him, the four resembling, "Devils on the Stage," from Carl Maria von Weber's 1821 opera *Der Freischütz*, which he'd seen in Cambridge.

> The old man had a white feather cap; from under which, black long hair hung round his face. The skin is dirty copper colour. Reaching from ear to ear & including the upper lip, there was a broard red coloured band of paint. & parallel & above this, there was a white one; so that the eyebrows & eyelids were even thus coloured; the only garment was a large guanaco skin, with the hair outside. This was merely thrown over their shoulders, one arm & leg being bare; for any exercise they must be absolutely naked.

For their part, the Fuegians seemed equally startled by the Europeans' appearance. To assuage their fears, the *Beagle*'s men offered pieces of red cloth which, Darwin noted, "they immediately placed round their necks." Right away, "We became good friends," he recalled. "This was shown by the old man patting our breasts & making something like the same noise which people do when feeding chickens."

> I walked with the old man & this demonstration was repeated between us several times: at last he gave me three hard slaps on the breast & back at the same time, & making most curious noises. He then bared his bosom for me to return the compliment, which being done, he seemed highly pleased.

The parties tried to converse but to no avail. ("Their language," Darwin noted dismissively, "does not deserve to be called articulate: Capt. Cook says it is like a man clearing his throat.") As both groups soon resorted to pantomime, the Englishmen inferred that the Fuegians wanted knives. "This they showed by pretending to have blubber in their mouths, & cutting instead of tearing it from the body."

But no knives were proffered that day. Still later, the *Beagle*'s men were reassured that the Fuegians apparently recognized the power of the firearms they carried. "They knew what guns were & much dreaded them," Darwin noted. And "nothing would tempt them to take one in their hands."

Haunting the *Beagle*'s men during those interactions were fears of cannibalism, a perennial concern of that age's British seamen in encounters with those they deemed "savages." (Such fears stretched back to Christopher Columbus's reports of allegedly cannibalistic Carib Indians.) Indeed, Darwin, FitzRoy and others aboard the *Beagle* claimed to have heard—on multiple occasions, from all three Fuegians aboard the ship—graphic descriptions of cannibalism practiced by Tierra del Fuego's Indigenous peoples. As FitzRoy later wrote:

> It is proved that they eat human flesh upon particular occasions, namely, when excited by revenge or extremely pressed by hunger. Almost always at war with adjoining tribes, they seldom meet but a hostile encounter is the result; and then those who are vanquished and taken, if not already dead, are killed and eaten by the conquerors. The arms and breast are eaten by the women; the men eat the legs; and the trunk is thrown into the sea.

FitzRoy, moreover, claimed to have heard from Jemmy Button, by then about seventeen years old, a particularly hair-raising winter's tale—that when snows interfered with the Fuegians' hunting, they would sometimes "lay violent hands on the oldest woman of their party . . . choke her" and "devour every particle of her flesh." According to FitzRoy, "Jemmy Button, in telling this horrible story as a great secret, seemed to be much ashamed of his countrymen, and said, he never would do so—he would rather eat his own hands. When asked why the dogs were not eaten, he said, 'Dog catch iappo' (*iappo* means otter)." Furthermore, added FitzRoy, "York [Minster] told me that they always eat enemies whom they killed in battle; and I have no doubt that he told me the truth."

The truth or falsity of the alleged incidents of Fuegian cannibalism are impossible to assess. Moreover, we have no direct reports from the three

Fuegians themselves. Even so, in his 1947 memoir *Uttermost Part of the Earth*, author Lucas Bridges—who spoke English and Yaghan, and grew up in Tierra del Fuego as the son of an Anglican missionary—rejected assertions that cannibalism was ever been practiced there. Indeed, Bridges dismissed all such reports as "lurid stories . . . told by self-styled explorers who had been more influenced by a desire to feature as heroes of sensational adventures than by any love of veracity."

FitzRoy biographer Peter Nichols added that "Cannibalism was known to have been practiced in Africa, Polynesia, and Australasia; any dark-skinned face was presumed to be capable of it." And whether or not cannibalism was ever practiced in Tierra del Fuego, for FitzRoy and his ilk the belief that it was, "underscored the moral imperative that God-fearing Englishmen felt to improve the condition of Native cultures everywhere." Even as a fiction, the cannibalism narrative thus had a purpose.

During their December 18 encounter with the Fuegians at Good Success Bay, meanwhile, the *Beagle*'s Englishmen took particular notice of exchanges between Button and the Natives. Button, after all, was dressed in English clothes and spoke with the *Beagle*'s Englishmen in their native tongue. But, noted Darwin, observing Button's interactions with the Indigenes on the beach, "It was interesting to watch their conduct to him." And without knowing the language of the Fuegians standing before him, Darwin nonetheless deduced their apparent entreaty to Button:

> They immediately perceived the difference & held much conversation between themselves on the subject. The old man then began a long harangue to Jemmy; who said it was inviting him to stay with them: but the language is rather different & Jemmy could not talk to them.

The *Beagle* party's first encounter with the Fuegians eventually concluded. But later that same day, after dinner, Darwin returned to the same spot on the shore—with a party that now included Captain FitzRoy, midshipman Robert Hamond, missionary Richard Matthews, and the Fuegian York Minster—older than Button and by then in or approaching his life's third decade. This time, Darwin recalled, "They received us with less distrust & brought with them their timid children." Taking note of Minster, "[t]hey examined the color of his skin; & having done so, they looked at ours. An arm being bared, they expressed the liveliest surprise & admiration. Their whole conduct was such an odd mixture of astonishment & imitation, that nothing could be more laughable & interesting."

FitzRoy, describing the Fuegians assembled on the shore, recalled, "five or six stout men, half-clothed in guanaco-skins," nearly six feet in height "and confident in demeanour." "Except in colour and class of features," he recalled, they bore no resemblance to the three Fuegians aboard the *Beagle*. Recalled FitzRoy, "I can never forget Mr. Hamond's earnest expression, 'What a pity such fine fellows should be left in such a barbarous state!'"

Hammond's comment, FitzRoy recalled, "told me that a desire to benefit these ignorant, though by no means contemptible human beings, was a natural emotion, and not the effect of individual caprice or erroneous enthusiasm." More personally, the captain reflected, Hammond's "feelings were exactly in unison with those I had experienced on former occasions." And those sentiments led to the remorse that, in turn, "had led to my undertaking the heavy charge of those Fuegians whom I brought to England."

Whimsically turning the tables, FitzRoy later compared the impression the Fuegians left that day on the *Beagle*'s men to that left at Dover, England, in 55 B.C.E., by native Britons, on Julius Caesar and his cohort, the first official representatives of the Roman Empire to arrive on British shores.

"Disagreeable," FitzRoy wrote, "indeed painful, as is even the mental contemplation of a savage, and unwilling as we may be to consider ourselves even remotely descended from human beings in such a state, the reflection that Cæsar found the Britons painted and clothed in skins, like these Fuegians, cannot fail to augment an interest excited by their childish ignorance of matters familiar to civilized man, and by their healthy, independent state of existence."

At the Bay of Good Success, meanwhile, the *Beagle* party's second attempt of the day—December 18—to communicate with Fuegians gathered ashore, at first, proved futile. Without a shared language, the exchange initially collapsed into charade, replete with pantomimes, mock displays of aggression, nervous laughter, and tentative snatches of dancing and singing. Amidst the displays, "Two or three of the officers, who are both fairer & shorter than the others (although possessed of large beards) were, we think, taken for Ladies," Darwin surmised. "I wish they would follow our supposed example & produce their 'squaws.'" By the evening, however, "we parted very good friends; which I think was fortunate, for the dancing & 'sky-larking' had occasionally bordered on a trial of strength."

The next day, December 19, intrigued by the dense beech forest rising behind the Bay of Good Success's rock-strewn beach, Darwin and a *Beagle* seaman, unnamed in the diary, set off "to penetrate some way into the country." But the landscape proved inhospitable. Lamented the naturalist, "There is no level ground & all the hills are so thickly clothed with wood as to be quite impassable." Furthermore, "The trees are so close together & send off their branches so low down, that I found extreme difficulty in pushing my way even for gun-shot distance."

The two eventually found a narrow stream that they hoped might provide a passable course through the vegetation. But their "mountain torrent" soon grew hopelessly wide, eventually overflowing its banks. Abandoning the channel, they ascended into higher country. But that gambit too, leading to more difficult terrain, soon ended in frustration, denying the climbers the elevation's peak. Even so, Darwin consoled himself with the belief, however naive, "that this part of the forest had never before been traversed by man."

Returning to the *Beagle* that day, Darwin described his outing to FitzRoy. After consulting books and maps, the captain concluded that the mountain Darwin attempted to ascend was the same (Banks Hill) climbed, in January 1769, by botanist Joseph Banks of James Cook's expedition.

Among the *Beagle*'s officers and other officers on similar expeditions, the names of often obscure places and the dates of visits to them by earlier explorers constituted a shared and revered body of knowledge. Indeed, in that milieu, familiarity with such lore brought a pride similar to that of Christian clergymen secure in their command of Biblical scripture.

The following day, December 20, inspired by FitzRoy's hunch, Darwin completed the climb. To his delight, the summit rewarded him with a view of the eastern half of Isla Grande and the oceans to its east and south. "The view was superb, & well was I repaid for the fatigue." Moreover, unmentioned in his diary but a noteworthy milestone, Darwin had begun to expand his naturalist repertoire to include up-close, firsthand observations of Tierra del Fuego's flora, fauna, and geology—the hallmarks of which ranged from trees stunted and deformed by punishing westerly winds to the thunderous boom of calving glaciers crashing from craggy mountains into cobalt-blue seas.

Among the archipelago's wonders, however, none fascinated the naturalist more than the Fuegians themselves. During that season's anchorages in Tierra del Fuego, Darwin—drawing on firsthand observations, past readings, and conversations aboard the ship, many with the three Fuegians—contemplated the archipelago's Natives and their world. Testament to that obsession, his diary entries on the topic combined crisp ethnographic observations, pithy practical insights—and unvarnished English imperial arrogance:

> If their dress appearance is miserable, their manner of living is still more so. Their food chiefly consists in limpets & muscles, together with seals & a few birds; they must also catch occasionally a Guanaco. They seem to have no property excepting bows & arrows & spears: their present residence is under a few bushes by a ledge of rock: it is no ways sufficient to keep out rain or wind & now in the middle of summer it daily rains & as yet each day there has been some sleet. The almost impenetrable wood reaches down to high water mark.

So that the habitable land is literally reduced to the large stones on the beach.& here at low water, whether it may be night or day, these wretched looking beings pick up a livelihood. I believe if the world was searched, no lower grade of man could be found. The South sea Islanders are civilized compared to them, & the Esquimaux, in subterranean huts may enjoy some of the comforts of life.

During those same weeks, meanwhile, FitzRoy grew increasingly obsessed with the return of the three Fuegians to their respective native regions of Tierra del Fuego. For him personally, after all, that objective remained the (however unofficial) raison d'être of the entire expedition. Jemmy Button came from the archipelago's east, relatively speaking, close to the *Beagle*'s then current position. But repatriating York Minster and Fuegia Basket, both of the Alakaluf people, required sailing to Tierra del Fuego's west.*

On December 21, the day after Darwin's successful climb, the *Beagle*—bound for western Tierra del Fuego—departed the Bay of Good Success. Weighing anchor at 4:00 A.M., the first day of sailing went well; indeed, by 3:00 P.M. the next day, the ship had even doubled "old-weather-beaten Cape Horn."

For the *Beagle*'s passengers, the passage brought a heart-swelling moment. Cape Horn, the headland on the southern side of the southernmost island in the Tierra del Fuego archipelago, traditionally marked the demarcation between the Atlantic and Pacific oceans. Thus, after reaching the other side of Cape Horn—upon, that is, reaching Pacific waters—all breathed a sigh of relief: "The evening was calm & bright & we enjoyed a fine view of the surrounding isles." Darwin wrote. "The height of the hills varies from 7 or 800 to 1700, & together they form a grand irregular chain."

---

* Visually dominating the southwestern Tierra del Fuego island from which Minster hailed was the mountain that inspired the name given him by the *Beagle*'s earlier crew. That mountain, in turn, had been accorded *its* name by explorer James Cook, after a celebrated cathedral in York, England—York Minster.

In his diary, Darwin noted the solemnity of the *Beagle*'s passage by the storied promontory. Hours later, however, "Cape Horn . . . demanded his tribute & by night sent us a gale right in our teeth." Over the next three weeks, hard rain and winds pummeled the ship. Blowing north and south, east and west, the turbulences ricocheted the *Beagle* through Tierra del Fuego's maze of waters and shorelines.

Discouraged, FitzRoy soon abandoned hopes of reaching York Minster's and Fuegia Basket's western environs. Sailing eastward, he found, on January 15, 1833, secure anchorage in a place called Goree Sound. An inlet along Navarino Island's eastern shore, it was located on the opposite side of the island from which Button had been abducted. Moreover, by coincidence, the inlet was also just south of the eastern end of a 150-mile east-west strait linking Tierra del Fuego's Atlantic and Pacific edges—a passage named Beagle Channel by their own ship's first expedition.

Further gladdening spirits, upon reaching Goree Sound, welcome news greeted the crew. "The object of our disastrous attempt to get to the Westward was to go to the Fuegian York Minster[']s, country," Darwin recalled. "Luckily," he added, "York Minster from his free choice intends to live here with Matthews & Jemmy." Neither FitzRoy's nor Darwin's various accounts of the expedition mention Fuegia Basket's thoughts concerning the decision to settle all three Fuegians in the east. Like York Minster, after all, Basket hailed from the archipelago's west. But if she opposed the decision to again dislocate her from her native soil, her preferences, if solicited, went unheeded.

FitzRoy had first visited Navarino in 1829 on the *Beagle* voyage that named the island (after the decisive naval battle in the then recent Greek War of Independence). Given his earlier visit, FitzRoy thus assumed a familiarity with the island. And, wasting no time, he resolved to find a site there for Matthews and the three Fuegians to establish their mission. Poring over maps, the captain located what appeared to be a suitable spot. Beyond lying close to their current anchorage, recalled Darwin, FitzRoy speculated that the site possessed another commending significance. "It is," he noted, "the only piece of flat land the Captain has ever met with in Tierra del F & he consequently hoped it would be better fitted for agriculture."

19

NAVARINO ISLAND

O n January 16, 1833, FitzRoy, leading a two-boat party, set out from the *Beagle*'s Goree Sound anchorage for the "piece of flat land" he had selected on a map as the site for Richard Matthews's mission. But those hopes proved short lived. Darwin numbered among the party's participants; and upon reaching the site, he recalled, "it turned out to be a dreary morass only tenanted by wild geese & a few Guanaco."

> The section on the coast showed the turf or peat to be about 6 feet thick & therefore quite unfit for our purposes. We then searched in different places both in & out of the woods, but nowhere were able to penetrate to the soil; the whole country is a swamp. The Captain has in consequence determined to take the Fuegians further up the country.

Upon returning to the *Beagle* that day, FitzRoy concluded that, to find a suitable site for the mission, the next party should sail to the opposite side, the west coast, of Navarino Island (since 1881 recognized by a bilateral Argentine-Chilean treaty as a Chilean possession).

To get there, starting from the *Beagle*'s Goree Sound anchorage on Navarino's eastern shore, they would sail north, then bend to a westerly course in the Beagle Channel, sailing along the island's northern coast. Upon reaching Navarino's west coast, leaving the Beagle Channel, they would dip south, into the Murray Channel, and sail halfway down that coast. There, they would find the cove and settlement called Wulaia from whence Jemmy Button came—the place that Darwin spelled as Woollÿa or otherwise called "J. Buttons country."

Because FitzRoy's latest plan covered more distance than his first and thus required several days of travel, the new expedition eventually involved twenty-eight souls and four of the *Beagle*'s seven open boats—the yawl and three whaleboats. Moreover, FitzRoy decided, the outing, beyond locating a mission site, would also transport to it Matthews, the three Fuegians, and the future mission's "outfit"—the supplies provided by the Church Missionary Society for the Tierra del Fuego outpost.

Decision made, FitzRoy ordered the mission's items loaded on to the twenty-six-foot long, two-masted yawl. Those labors, however, stalled as the goods weighed down and consumed all available space on the yawl. To accommodate the cargo, FitzRoy ordered the installation of a "temporary deck" on the yawl; afterward, passengers and cargo that still lacked space were assigned to the three whaleboats. Each of the whaleboats, all without masts and propelled by oars, were about twenty-five feet in length.

Recalled Darwin of the new expedition's January 19 launch, "The yawl, being heavily laden, stayed towed by the other three boats, and, while her sails were set, went almost as fast as they did." From Goree Sound, the expedition sailed north, then bent to its westward Beagle Channel course along Navarino's northern shore. There headwinds forced crew members to deploy ropes and "drag her" (the yawl), as FitzRoy later recounted, "along by strength of arm against wind and current."

Darwin, meanwhile, stayed fixated on the landscapes he was observing on both shores of the Beagle Channel. "Slate hills," he noted, "thickly clothed by the beech woods run nearly parallel to the water." Even so, he complained, "the low point of view from a boat," blinkered his view of the "beautiful succession of ridges" and was "nearly destructive to picturesque effect."

During the next day's "pull," on the twentieth, the party confronted a problem more worrisome than challenging wind and currents, the first in a series of encounters with Natives that Button commented were "not his friends, and often made war upon his people." Recalling that day, Darwin described fires, "lighted on every point to attract our attention & spread the news" and men running along for miles along the shore in pursuit of the tiny convoy. "I shall never forget how savage & wild one group was."

> Four or five men suddenly appeared on a cliff near to us. They were absolutely naked & with long streaming hair; springing from the ground & waving their arms around their heads, they sent forth most hideous yells. Their appearance was so strange, that it was scarcely like that of earthly inhabitants.

By early evening, after FitzRoy ordered the boats ashore for dinner, the party's pursuers suddenly appeared in their midst. Recalled Darwin, they "were not at first inclined to be friendly," keeping "their slings in readiness." But, tensions reduced, "We soon delighted them by trifling presents such as tying red tape round the forehead." Even so, he noted, "It is very easy to please but as difficult to make them content; the last & first word is sure to be 'Yammerschooner' which means 'give me.'"

Confirming Darwin's premonition, the following morning of the twenty-first brought more challenges. "A fresh party [of Fuegians] having arrived, they became troublesome," he recalled. As their women and children vanished from sight, the remaining Fuegian men began gathering stones. A show of firearms by the Europeans soon averted any confrontation that morning. But for Darwin the close call served as a cautionary tale:

> I was very much afraid we should have had a skirmish; it would have been shocking to have fired on such naked miserable creatures. Yet their stones & slings are so destructive that it would have been absolutely necessary. In treating with savages, Europæans labor under a great disadvantage, until the cruel lesson is taught how deadly firearms are. Several times when the men have been tired & it was growing dark, all the things have been packed up to remove our quarters; &

this solely from our entire inability to frighten the natives. One night the Captain fired double barrelled pistols close to their faces, but they only rubbed their heads & when he flourished his cutlass they were amused & laughed. They are such thieves & so bold Cannabals that one naturally prefers separate quarters.

Later reflecting on those days, FitzRoy particularly recalled York Minster's reaction to the pursuing Fuegians: "York laughed heartily at the first we saw, calling them large monkeys; and Jemmy assured us they were not at all like his people, who were very good and very clean. Fuegia was shocked and ashamed; she hid herself, and would not look at them a second time."

More broadly, it seemed clear that the years since FitzRoy visited those climes had done nothing to diminish his English gentleman's arrogance:

It was interesting to observe the change which three years only had made in their ideas, and to notice how completely they had forgotten the appearance and habits of their former associates; for it turned out that Jemmy's own tribe was as inferior in every way as the worst of those whom he and York called 'monkeys—dirty—fools—not men.'

By January 22, after a full day and night of un-menaced movements, Darwin assumed that the *Beagle* party had reached "neutral ground, between the people we saw yesterday & Jemmys." Moreover, "we enjoyed a delightful pull through . . . calm[er] water."

The Northern mountains have become more lofty & jagged. Their summits are partially covered with snow & their sides with dark woods: it was very curious to see as far as the eye ranged, how *exact* & truly horizontal the line was at which the trees ceased to grow. It precisely resembled on a beach the high-water mark of drift sea-weed.

That night, Darwin recalled, "we took up our quarters with a family belonging to Jemmys . . . people"—by FitzRoy's count, three men and two women. Still later that night, the *Beagle* party joined Jemmy Button's friends around a communal fire. "Although naked," Darwin noted, "they streamed with perspiration at sitting so near to a fire which we found only comfortable."

The following morning, January 23, their hosts dispatched a canoe toward Wulaia to alert its inhabitants to Jemmy's return and to guide the *Beagle* party to his home. Within a few hours, responding to the alert, a dozen canoes, each bearing four or five passengers, paddled into the cove.

That same day, the *Beagle* party resumed the final miles of its own journey to Wulaia. But the multi-canoe escort, soon overtaken by the *Beagle*'s swifter boats, proved, Darwin recalled, entirely unnecessary. "Jemmy Button now perfectly knew the way & he guided us to a quiet cove where his family used formerly to reside." A day earlier, Jemmy had been saddened to learn that, during the year he had lived in England, his father had died. Equally disheartening, according to Darwin, during Jemmy's absence, he had "forgotten his language."

> It was pitiable, but laughable, to hear him talk to his brother in English & ask him in Spanish whether he understood it. I do not suppose, any person exists with such a small stock of language as poor Jemmy, his own language forgotten, & his English ornamented with a few Spanish words, almost unintelligible.

More painful, according to FitzRoy, when the party, on January 22, had arrived at the cove to meet the family that later dispatched the canoe to Wulaia, Jemmy's linguistic deficit grew painfully evident: "Jemmy and York then tried to speak to them," the captain recalled. "But to our surprise, and much to my sorrow, we found that Jemmy had almost forgotten his native language, and that, of the two, York, although belonging to another tribe, was rather the best interpreter."

On a brighter note, Jemmy Button's native country seemed to satisfy everyone's fondest hopes. "When we arrived at Woolliah (Jemmys cove) we found it far better suited for our purposes, than any place we had hitherto seen," Darwin recalled. "There was a considerable space of cleared & rich ground, & doubtless Europæan vegetables would flourish well."

As before, the *Beagle* party befriended a family living beside the cove, who, in turn, summoned Jemmy's relatives. Soon enough, "the Fuegians began to pour in," a cohort that included Jemmy's mother, a brother and an uncle. And thus, Darwin recalled, over the coming days, "the labors of our little colony commenced."

All the while, Darwin had suppressed voicing his thoughts concerning an irritation that had rankled him since at least January 19, when the party left Goree Sound. The Fuegian mission was, for FitzRoy, a cherished cause. And, in the months after their argument in Rio over slavery, Darwin had avoided troublesome topics with the captain.

In this case, Darwin's reticence concerned the Fuegian mission, specifically the "kit" the Church Missionary Society had provided to furnish the outpost. To be sure, it was the same weighty cargo that, filling the yawl to its gunwales, had slowed the boat's passage to Wulaia. To Darwin's unspoken disgust, the kit, upon the opening of the boxes containing it, was revelaed to include wine glasses, butter dishes, soup tureens, tea trays, a mahogany cabinet, and an "endless variety of similar things." To him, all bore witness to "how little was thought about the country where they were going to." Indeed, as if invoking the frugality of Dr. Robert Darwin, his son confided to his diary, "The means absolutely wasted on such things would have purchased an immense stock of really useful articles."

But, in the end, that day, Darwin kept his misgivings to himself, eventually even conceding that, at Wulaia, "Everything went on very peacibly for some days."

Many of the party's labors went into constructing what FitzRoy called wigwams, traditional Fuegian lodgings:

> Their height is not above four or five feet above the ground; but an excavation is usually made within, which gives another foot, making about five feet and a-half of height, inside, and they are

two, three, or four yards in diameter. Branches of trees stuck in the ground, bent together towards the top, form the structure, upon which skins, pieces of bark, and bunches of coarse grass are roughly fastened.

Over those days, Darwin recorded, "3 houses"—wigwams—"were built, & two gardens dug & planted & what was of most consequence the Fuegians were very quiet & peacible; at one time there were about 120 of them."

> The men sat all day long watching our proceedings & the poor women working like slaves for their subsistence. The men did not manifest much surprise at anything & never even appeared to look at the boats. Stripping for washing & our white skins seemed most to excite their attention. They asked for every thing they saw & stole what they could. Dancing & singing absolutely delighted them. Things thus remained so quiet, that others & myself took long walks in the surrounding hills & woods.

On January 27, however, nearly all the Fuegian men, women, and children suddenly left the settlement. And those few souls remaining behind soon became aware of being watched by Fuegians perched on a nearby hill. "We were," Darwin remembered, "all very uneasy at this, as neither Jemmy or York understood what it meant; & it did not promise peace for the establishment." Added FitzRoy, "Even Jemmy's own family, his mother and brothers, left us."

Immediately, some in FitzRoy's cohort speculated that a recent show of force by the Englishmen had prompted the exodus. "Our party," he recalled, "were employed for a short time in firing at a mark, with the three-fold object of keeping our arms in order—exercising the men—and aweing, without frightening, the Natives." During the display, "the Fuegians sat about on their hams, watching our proceedings, and often eagerly talking to each other, as successful shots were made at the target, which was intentionally placed so that they could see the effect of the balls." Or perhaps, others speculated, the exits resulted from a recent argument between a *Beagle* sailor standing sentry and an old Fuegian—the incident that, in fact, had prompted the target practice.

Whatever the cause, Darwin recalled, "the Captain thought it advisable not to sleep another night there." Matthews and FitzRoy, meanwhile agreed that the time had arrived for Matthews and the three Fuegians to spend their first night ashore, at their new mission.

That evening, FitzRoy recalled, Matthews and his party, Button, Minster, and Basket, went to their respective abodes amid the three new wigwams. In Jemmy's shelter, in an overhead space concealed by boards taken from the *Beagle*, the ship's men hid most of the mission's stores. "But," recalled FitzRoy, "the most valuable articles were deposited in a box, which was hid in the ground underneath the wigwam, where fire could not reach."

Before departing that evening, Darwin silently took his measure of the visibly nervous young missionary preparing to spend his first night away from the *Beagle*'s crew on terra firma at the bottom of the world. "Matthews," he wrote, "behaved with his usual quiet resolution: he is of an eccentric character & does not appear (which is strange) to possess much energy & I think it very doubtful how far he is qualified for so arduous an undertaking."

The following morning, January 28, when FitzRoy and his cohort returned to Wulaia, a welcome sight greeted them. "We found everything quiet," recalled Darwin. "The canoes were employed in spearing fish & most of the people had returned. We were very glad of this & now hoped everything would go on smoothly." FitzRoy dispatched the yawl and one of the whaleboats back to the *Beagle*, still anchored in Goree Sound. As for those men, including the captain and Darwin, remaining aboard the other two whaleboats, they sailed north, then west. Recalled Darwin, "We reentered the Beagle channel in order to examine the islands around its Western entrance."

Over the coming days, FitzRoy, still sailing west, savored his return to the sea. On January 30, in a magnanimous mood, he even found time to honor a cherished shipmate. On that day, the captain recalled, "we passed into a large expanse of water, which I named Darwin Sound—after my messmate, who so willingly encountered the discomfort and risk of a long cruise in a small loaded boat."

No doubt, FitzRoy's warm feelings were also inspired by the role, a day earlier, of Darwin and a handful of other shipmates, during a visit ashore, in saving several of the *Beagle*'s open boats from being destroyed by colossal waves heaved by a calving glacier. Recalled FitzRoy, "By the exertions of those who grappled them or seized their ropes, they were hauled up again out of [the waves'] reach."

But the captain's solace proved short-lived. Amid the wanderings of FitzRoy's boats, on February 5, on a shore opposite a place that he called Shingle Point, a group of Fuegians caught his attention: "All of them appeared in full dress, being bedaubed with red and white paint, and ornamented, after their fashion, with feathers and the down of geese."

Among the group was a woman wearing "a loose linen garment, evidently one that had belonged to Fuegia Basket," FitzRoy recalled. "The sight of this piece of linen, several bits of ribbon, and some scraps of red cloth, apparently quite recently obtained, made me feel very anxious about Matthews and his party."

> There was also an air of almost defiance among these people, which looked as if they knew that harm had been done, and that they were ready to stand on the defensive if any such attack as they expected were put into execution. Passing therefore hastily on, we went as far as the light admitted, and at daybreak next morning (6th) were again hastening towards Woollӯa.

En route, heightening FitzRoy's worries, his cohort spotted other Native parties with individuals "ornamented with strips of tartan cloth or white linen, which we well knew were obtained from our poor friends." Later that day, the party's return to Wulaia confirmed FitzRoy's fears. Finding Matthews ashore, FitzRoy invited him into his boat. Afterward, "We pushed out a short distance to be free from interruption, and remained till I had heard the principal parts of his story." Darwin later summarized Matthews's harrowing story:

From the moment of our leaving, a regular system of plunder commenced, in which not only Matthews, but York & Jemmy suffered. Matthews had nearly lost all his things; & the constant watching was most harassing & entirely prevented him from doing anything to obtain food &c. Night & day large parties of the natives surrounded his house. One day, having requested an old man to leave the place, he returned with a large stone in his hand: Another day, a whole party advanced with stones & stakes, & some of the younger men & Jemmys brother were crying.

By FitzRoy's account of Jemmy's story, "York and Fuegia fared very well; they lost nothing; but Jemmy was sadly plundered, even by his own family." Moreover,

Our garden, upon which much labour had been bestowed, had been trampled over repeatedly, although Jemmy had done his best to explain its object and prevent people from walking there. When questioned about it, he looked very sorrowful, and, with a slow shake of the head, said, 'My people very bad; great fool; know nothing at all; very great fool.'

Assessing the outrages, FitzRoy decided to accede to Matthews's request to be removed from Wulaia:

I considered that he had already undergone a severe trial, and ought not to be again exposed to such savages, however willing he might be to try them farther if I thought it right. The next difficulty was how to get Matthews's chest and the remainder of his property safely into our boats, in the face of a hundred Fuegians, who would of course understand our object, and be much more than a match for us on land; but the less hesitation shown, the less time they would have to think of what we were about; so, dividing our party, and spreading about a little to create confidence—at a favourable moment the wigwam was quickly cleared, the cave emptied, and the contents safely placed in our boats. As I stood watching the proceedings, a few anxious moments passed, for any kind of skirmish would have been so detrimental to the three who were still to remain. When the last man was embarked, I distributed several useful articles, such as axes, saws, gimblets, knives and nails, among the natives, then bade Jemmy and York farewell, promising to see them again in a few days, and departed from the wondering throng assembled on the beach.

By the day's end, with Matthews now aboard one of FitzRoy's boats, the captain pined to resume the *Beagle*'s survey and mapping work. Toward that end, recalled Darwin, the captain, "to save time determined to go to the South & outside of Navarino Island, instead of our returning by the Beagle channel."

Accordingly, later that same day, February 6, 1833, as the two boats sailed from the cove and Wulaia faded behind their sterns, FitzRoy imagined the thoughts crowding the missionary mind: "Matthews," he speculated, "must have felt almost like a man reprieved, excepting that he enjoyed the feelings always sure to reward those who try to do their duty, in addition to those excited by a sudden certainty of his life being out of jeopardy."

Darwin, meanwhile, witnessing the same moment, offered his own departing lament:

> It was quite melancholy leaving our Fuegians amongst their barbarous countrymen: there was one comfort; they appeared to have no personal fears. But, in contradiction of what has often been stated, 3 years has been sufficient to change savages, into, as far as habits go, complete & voluntary Europæans. York, who was a full grown man & with a strong violent mind, will I am certain in every respect live as far as his means go, like an Englishman. Poor Jemmy, looked rather disconsolate, & certainly would have liked to have returned with us; . . . I am afraid whatever other ends their excursion to England produces, it will not be conducive to their happiness. They have far too much sense not to see the vast superiority of civilized over uncivilized habits; & yet I am afraid to the latter they must return.'

20

EL DORADO LOST

"According to a strangely transformed variety of Darwinism
sanctioned by Darwin himself, the modern Orientals
were degraded remnants of a former greatness."
                                        —Edward Said, *Orientalism*, 1978

By February 8, 1833, four days before Charles Darwin's twenty-fourth birthday, the *Beagle* had returned to Goree Sound. Two days later, after the ship anchored along Navarino Island's south coast, Captain FitzRoy set out with a small party in an open boat—to conduct surveys in the area but also to check on the Fuegians. On February 14, "with considerable anxiety," he arrived at Wulaia. As his party entered the settlement, FitzRoy recalled, the few Fuegians present took little notice of the Englishmen. "Several canoes were out fishing, women only being in them, who did not cease their occupation as we passed: this augured well."

A few minutes later, "we saw Jemmy, York, and Fuegia, in their usual dress." After greetings were exchanged, "Jemmy complained that the people had stolen many of his things." York and Fuegia, however, "had contrived to take better care of theirs." Visiting the wigwams constructed three weeks earlier, the captain found "very little change." Moreover, "Fuegia looked clean and tidily dressed, and by her wigwam was a canoe, which York was building out of planks left for him by our party. The garden was uninjured, and some of the vegetables already sprouting."

> Jemmy told us that strangers had been there, with whom he and his people had 'very much jaw,' that they fought, threw 'great many stone,' and stole two women (in exchange for whom Jemmy's party stole one), but were obliged to retreat. Jemmy's mother came down to the boat to see us; she was decently clothed, by her son's care. He said that his brothers were all friendly, and that he should get on very well now that the 'strange men' were driven away. I advised Jemmy to take his mother and younger brother to his own wigwam, which he promised to do, and then, finding that they were all quite contented and apparently very happy, I left the place, with rather sanguine hopes of their effecting among their countrymen some change for the better.

That day, as FitzRoy's party returned to his boat, his conscience remained troubled by his role in the abduction of the Fuegians. However wistful, he still entertained hopes that the three would eventually understand his motives in the drama that had upended their lives. "I hoped that through their means our motives in taking them to England would become understood and appreciated among their associates." Indeed, already contemplating another call at Wulaia before leaving South America, FitzRoy even allowed himself to hope that such a "future visit might find them so favourably disposed towards us, that Matthews might then undertake, with a far better prospect of success, that enterprise which circumstances had obliged him to defer, though not to abandon altogether."

By February 15, FitzRoy's party had returned to the *Beagle* and again reported on the Fuegians' condition. As the news won a welcoming shipboard reception, even Darwin took a sanguine view of the returned exiles' future. "If the garden succeeds," he wrote, "this little settlement may be yet the means of producing great good & altering the habits of the truly savage inhabitants."

Following survey work in east Tierra del Fuego, the *Beagle*, from February 21–25, again lay anchored in the Bay of Good Success. A gale kept the men confined to the ship for most of that anchorage. But on their final full day at Good Success, during a break in the weather, Darwin seized the opportunity to go ashore and climb and measure the height of Banks Hill (by Darwin's reckoning 1,472 feet), the mountain he ascended during their earlier anchorage in the bay. "I was surprised that nine weeks had not effaced our footsteps so that we could recognize to whom they belonged."

⸺

Weighing anchor from the Bay of Good Success on February 25, HMS *Beagle* sailed for the Falkland Islands. Four-hundred-and-twenty northeasterly miles from Cape Horn and three hundred miles east of the Patagonian coast, the Falklands occupied a murky position in international diplomacy.* The archipelago received its first recorded visits by Europeans during the late seventeenth century. Since those years, it had become the object of rival claims by England, France, Spain, and, more recently, Argentina. Indeed, Argentina had been the claimant to the islands group in November 1831, when Francis Beaufort instructed FitzRoy, before "finally quit[ing] the eastern coast of South America," to conduct a "rigorous survey" of the archipelago. Though small, Beaufort noted, the islands "are the frequent resort of whalers" and are of "immense consequence to a vessel that has lost her masts, anchors, or a large part of her crew."

Marking FitzRoy's first visit to the archipelago, as the island of East Falkland, on March 1, rose before the *Beagle*'s prow, the sight confounded expectations. "The aspect of the Falklands rather surprised me," he recalled. "Instead of a low, level, barren country, like Patagonia, or a high woody region, like Tierra del Fuego, we saw ridges of rocky hills, about a thousand feet in height." Beneath the treeless hills, a "black, low, and

---

* Still contested, the Falklands remain, as of this writing, a British colony—but called by their rival Argentine claimants *las islas Malvinas*.

rocky coast, on which the surf raged violently" ominously fringed the island. Darkening the doomful aura, "the strong wind against which we were contending, did not tend to improve our first impressions of those unfortunate islands—scene of feud and assassination, and the cause of angry discussion among nations."

"We arrived early in the morning at Port Louis, the most Eastern point of the Falkland Islands," recalled Darwin. "The first news we received was to our astonishment, that England had taken possession of the Falklands Islands & that the Flag was now flying."

The most recent confrontation had arisen from an Argentine initiative in 1829 to colonize the then largely uninhabited islands. For three years afterward, Buenos Aires ignored protests by London; and so, in December 1832, weeks before the *Beagle*'s arrival, two British warships arrived in the archipelago. But the confrontation proved short-lived. Ashore, the Union Jack replaced the Argentine flag, and life there continued much as before. Wrote Darwin, "The present inhabitants consist of one Englishman, who has resided here for some years, & has now the charge of the British Flag, 20 Spaniards & three women, two of whom are negresses."

Over the coming weeks, as FitzRoy led the *Beagle*'s survey of the area, Darwin, as he recalled, slipped into his usual routines, "wandering about the country, breaking rocks, shooting snipes, & picking up the few living productions which this Island has to boast of." Over those days, the island confirmed his first impressions. "The whole landscape from the uniformity of the brown color, has an air of extreme desolation."

On March 4, *Beagle* crew member Edward H. Hellyer died from drowning, apparently while trying to retrieve from the surf a bird he had shot. The ship's clerk numbered among crewmen who, inspired by their shipmate, had begun collecting natural specimens. The following day, Darwin recalled, "Mr Hellyer was buried on a lonely & dreary headland. The procession was a melancholy one: in front a Union jack half mast high was carried, & over the coffin the British ensign was thrown; the funeral, from its simplicity was the more solemn, & suited all the circumstances."

FitzRoy, meanwhile, still questioning the expedition's ability to complete its assigned tasks, was arranging to add yet another vessel, again at his own expense, to their flotilla. From a visiting sealer discouraged after an unproductive hunting season, he purchased a schooner called the *Unicorn*:

> I had often anxiously longed for a consort, adapted for carrying cargoes, rigged so as to be easily worked with few hands, and able to keep company with the Beagle; but when I saw the Unicorn, and heard how well she had behaved as a sea-boat, my wish to purchase her was unconquerable. A fitter vessel I could hardly have met with, one hundred-and seventy-tons burthen, oak built, and copper fastened throughout, very roomy, a good sailer, extremely handy, and a first-rate sea-boat.

Moreover, with salvaged ropes, canvas, and cables purchased from two damaged ships that had limped into Port Louis, FitzRoy soon refitted the *Unicorn*.

In early April, the two ships set sail for the mouth of Rio Negro, 775 miles to the north, on Patagonia's coast. There, plans called for the *Beagle* and *Unicorn* to join *La Paz* and *La Liebre* and perform survey work along the Patagonia coast. During the *Beagle*'s earlier, southward passage down that coast, Darwin had gazed longingly at the cliffs cradling Rio Negro. And, on April 16, 1833, as they again approached the area, the landward view from the *Beagle*'s deck toward what he presumed were fossil-rich cliffs, still captivated him: "What we saw of the coast consisted entirely in horizontal cliffs; in these, the divisions of the strata run for miles together exactly parallel to the surface of the sea. It looks an El Dorado to a Geologist; such modern formations must contain so many organic remains."

Alas, however, turbulence at sea—"baffling winds and a heavy swell," in FitzRoy's words—scuttled the four ships' planned rendezvous at Rio Negro. And, on April 15, after standing for two days off the river's mouth, FitzRoy followed the *Unicorn* north, toward Montevideo. Instead of his geological El Dorado, the *Beagle*, to Darwin's consternation, was returning to the Rio de la Plata country which, as he had grumbled to Henslow, "was fit to make any naturalist groan."

The day after arriving in Montevideo, the *Beagle*, on April 27, weighed anchor for another Uruguayan port—Maldonado, seventy miles to the east, where Rio de la Plata met the Atlantic. Reaching Maldonado before noon that day, they found, Darwin recalled, the *Unicorn* "safe and snug" in the harbor. Because the ship needed a new copper bottom, FitzRoy had ordered its captain to sail to Maldonado for the refitting.

Aware that the *Beagle*'s survey work in the area and the *Unicorn*'s refitting would take weeks, Darwin, eager for a break from his cramped cabin and the endless rocking of life at sea, began searching for lodgings ashore, a quest that soon brought frustrations. "The day has been miserably spent in attempts to transact business by the aid of vilely bad Spanish." Beyond that, he knew the odds were slim of replicating in Maldonado the domestic pleasures of his shore-life idyll with Earle at their Botafogo cottage.

Concluding a "day . . . spent in vain efforts to make any sort of comfortable arrangements," Darwin eventually settled on austere lodgings owned by an elderly town lady. "The rooms are very high & large," he wrote. "They have but very small windows & are almost destitute of furniture. They are all on the ground floor & open into each other. The very existence of what an Englishman calls comfort never passed through the builders mind."

The next day, however, further exploration of the area lifted his spirits. "The country is exceedingly similar to that of M: Video," he noted, "but rather more hilly. We here have the same fine grass plain, with its beautiful flowers & birds, the same hedges of Cactus & the same entire absence of all trees." To his surprise, he enjoyed, for the most part, the next two months. Exploring the countryside on trips brief and extended, Darwin conducted his usual observational and collecting rituals. Birds particularly engaged his attentions, especially bountiful flocks of the flightless ostrich-like rhea.

On May 9, accompanied by two hired guides ("Don Francisco Gonzales & Morante, a sort of servant of his"), Darwin embarked on a twelve-day mounted trip into the Uruguayan countryside, eventually covering two-hundred miles. On all but one night, the three, beneficiaries of rural hospitality, lodged in private homes. A year earlier, at Bahía Blanca's Fortaleza Protectora Argentina, Darwin had briefly encountered South America's gaucho culture. But it was during those spring 1833 evenings in the Uruguayan hinterlands that he had his first sustained exposure to that unique world:

> During the evening a great number of young Gauchos came in to drink spirits & smoke cigars. They are a singularly striking looking set of men—generally tall, very handsome, but with a most proud, dissolute expression. They wear their moustachios & long black hair curling down their necks. With their bright coloured robes; great spurs clanking on their heels & a knife, stuck (& often used) as a dagger at their waist, they look a very different race of men from our working countrymen. Their politeness is excessive, they never drink their spirits, without expecting you to taste it; but as they make their exceedingly good bow, they seem quite ready, if occasion offered, to cut your throat at the same time.

Darwin returned to Maldonado on May 20. From his most recent and earlier outings, he now possessed scores of birds he had shot, in total about eighty species: and, afterward, another twelve additional species each week. In his rented Maldonado rooms, he busied himself labeling the specimens and meticulously recording in a notebook the song, habits, and habitats of each. He also skinned each bird and carefully slit its stomach to examine its barely digested contents.

The work was made manageable by the assistance of Syms Covington to whom, over the past few months, Darwin had taught to shoot and to skin birds. Indeed, during those weeks at Maldonado, the naturalist, with

FitzRoy's permission, formally hired Covington as his personal assistant. (For £30 a year, the captain agreed to allow Darwin Covington's services.) Though Darwin's employment of Covington would last until 1839, three years beyond the *Beagle*'s five-year voyage, the relationship, on Darwin's part, proceeded without personal affections. "I do not very much like him; but he is, perhaps from his very oddity, very well adapted to all my purposes," he wrote to Catherine Darwin soon after hiring Covington.

Moreover, beyond Covington's skills, another factor, described to Catherine, commended him to Charles: "There is a standing order, in the Ship, that no one, excepting in civilized ports, leaves the vessel by himself. By thus having a constant companion, I am rendered much more independent, in that most dependent of all lives, a life on board."

On June 29, trading his Maldonado rooms for the now welcome familiarities of his old poop-cabin, Darwin reboarded the *Beagle*. And, after a week swinging at anchor, the ship returned to Montevideo. There, the *Beagle*'s men welcomed the arrival of a packet ship bearing mail from England. As always, Darwin savored letters from relatives and friends—depending on them for the latest (albeit, at least three months old) news and gossip from London, Shropshire, and other precincts.

From Susan, Charles learned that his Uncle Jos, in December 1832, had been elected, as a Whig, to the House of Commons. More generally, Susan joked, the winds of political reform across the United Kingdom were blowing so hard as to discomfit their own father. "The Radicals are getting so fierce & licentious in the Debates, that Papa gets more & more of a Tory every day." Turning to Charles's *Megatherium* fossil, she wrote, "I congratulate you on your luck in finding those curious remains of the Monster M—. I think Geology far the most interesting subject one can imagine & now I have found a very easy way of learning a little smattering of it. The penny Magazines give a few pages (which the most foolish person can understand) in every Number on the subject."

Otherwise, Susan, along with Charles's other correspondents, updated him on births, marriages, tribulations, and general gossip. Several, including Caroline Darwin, informed him of the death by "a sort of billious fever" of their beloved cousin Fanny Wedgwood. A year earlier, after Fanny Owen's unexpected marriage, Caroline, writing to Charles, had suggested that Fanny Wedgwood would make for him an "excellent" spouse. But now too, that potential spousal candidate—in her case, by death—had been eliminated.

Charles, in turn, from Montevideo, dispatched letters to England, to assorted relatives and Henslow. To his mentor, Charles recounted his recent activities but also aired hopes for the coming months:

> After the Beagle returns from this short cruize, we take in 12 months provisions & in beginning of October proceed to Tierra del F.; then pass the Strait of Magellan & enter the glorious Pacific: The Beagle after proceeding to Conception or Valparaiso, will once more go Southward, (I however will not leave the warm weather) & upon her return we proceed up the coast, ultimately to cross the Pacific. I am in great doubt whether to remain at Valparaiso or Conception: at the latter beds of Coal & shells, but at the former I could cross & recross the grand chain of the Andes.

To Henslow, from Montevideo, Charles also dispatched the latest bounties from his collecting—four barrels containing skins, rocks, pickled fish, and other specimens.

On the evening of July 13, Darwin, again ensconced aboard the *Beagle*, albeit freshly enlightened on the latest (however dated) news from home, departed Montevideo and returned to Maldonado. There he and the *Beagle*'s other men found the *Unicorn*, freshly girded with its new copper bottom and its crew preparing to sail. For good measure, FitzRoy soon renamed the schooner—rechristening it the *Adventure*. The new name, Darwin noted, commemorated the ship, "employed in the former voyage with the *Beagle*, & likewise as being the name of one of Captain Cooks ships & therefore classical to all Surveying vessels."

And, on the evening of July 24, 1833, defying an electrical storm, the two ships weighed anchors and departed Maldonado. Plowing southward, they sailed toward Rio Negro, Darwin's elusive geological El Dorado. "The whole sky," he wrote, "was brilliant with lightning; it was a wild looking night to go to sea, but time is too precious to lose even a bad portion of it."

21

IN PATAGONIA

"The surging of my mind is ebbing fast,
Borne on fresh tides to ocean's furthest reaches
Here at my feet the shining waters stretch away,
And to a new shore beckons now a bright new day!"
—Heinrich Faust, in *Faust, A Tragedy*,
by Johann von Wolfgang Goethe

On August 3, 1833, having sailed south from Maldonado ten days earlier, the *Beagle* and the *Adventure* reached the mouth of northern Patagonia's Rio Negro. Shots from a signal gun aboard the *Beagle* soon summoned the schooner *Le Lievre* toward the larger ships. And, as the *Beagle* and its auxiliary ship prepared to head back to sea to survey the Argentine coast from Rio Negro north to Bahía Blanca, Darwin boarded *Le Lievre*.

Darwin had finally arrived at Rio Negro and the Patagonian coast he longed to geologize. But the twenty-four-year-old naturalist was also well aware of Rio Negro's remove from the other, more settled, places of that day's Argentine state (or more accurately, Buenos Aires Province). Indeed, south of Rio Negro, that polity faded into a cartographic conceit, a dominion claimed but hardly controlled. As

Darwin put it, "To the northward of the Rio Negro, between it and the inhabited country near Buenos Ayres, the Spaniards have only one small settlement, recently established at Bahía Blanca"—with the straight-line distance from Bahía Blanca to Buenos Aires stretching to 350 miles.

Le Lievre, along with *La Paz*, James Harris's other schooner hired by FitzRoy, had spent the past weeks surveying the Argentine coast; and Darwin, after boarding *Le Lievre*, listened attentively as its crew recounted their recent work. The schooner, that day, eventually anchored at Rio Negro's mouth, and Darwin spent that night in the pilot's house on the river's south bank.

The following morning, after crossing the river, he hiked north along the Atlantic coast, inspecting the perpendicular cliffs that rose above the white sandy beaches. The headlands rose to about 120 feet, almost per-pendicularly from the beach. After a few miles, Darwin found a break in the cliffs, climbed to their top and viewed the scrubby—and, to his taste, uninviting—landscape that overlooked the beach.

> This plain has a very sterile appearance it is covered with thorny bushes & a dry looking grass, & will for ever remain nearly useless to mankind. It is in this geological formation that the Salinas or natural salt-pans occur; excepting imme-diately after heavy rain no fresh water can be found. The sandstone so abounds with salt, that all springs are inevitably very brackish. The vegetation from the same cause assumes a peculiar appearance; there are many sorts of bushes but all have formidable thorns which would seem to tell the stranger not to enter these inhospitable plains.

The next day, August 5, Darwin and assistant surveyor John Lort Stokes, fresh from commanding *La Paz*, set out from the mouth of Rio Negro toward the town of Carmen de Patagones, eighteen miles upstream. En route, they passed scenes said to be associated with violent confrontations between Indigenous peoples and recent arrivals of Euro-pean ancestry, variously called by Darwin "Spaniards" and "Christians."

The often macabre stories heard that day and over the coming days involved surprise appearances by Native people. Typically, as in one story heard that day, the assailants were said to have arrived in overwhelming numbers, in various states of undress: "The Indians were Araucanians from the South of Chili; several hundred in number & highly disciplined. They first appeared in two bodies on a neighbouring hill; having there dismounted & taken off their fur mantles, they advanced naked to the charge."

The military theater into which Darwin had stumbled pitted white soldiers and settlers against an informal alliance of tribal peoples from southern Argentina and Chile. Basing themselves in the Andes foothills to the west, the Natives, it was said, were using guerrilla war tactics against whites, including prospective settlers, on the pampas of Buenos Aires Province. Stories recounted by whites often involved alleged thefts by Indigenes of horse and cattle from white settlers, and these incidents frequently culminated in grisly acts of violence by the Natives.

An episode recounted in Darwin's diary typified those he and Stokes heard during their ride to Carmen de Patagones:

> The only weapon of an Indian is a very long bamboo or Chusa [*Chusquea culeou*] ornamented with Ostrich feathers and pointed by a sharp spear head. My informer seemed to remember with the greatest horror, the quivering of these Chusas as they approached near.

"When close," Darwin was told, the attackers' leader, "hailed the besieged to give up their arms or he would cut all their throats."

Accurate or not, such stories—predictably one-sided and presumably originating from either Spanish- or English-speaking informants—left a deep impression on Darwin. Consequently, his concerns over the coming days shifted from fossils to protecting himself during a long-planned south-to-north overland journey, from Rio Negro to Buenos Aires.

Indeed, before leaving the *Beagle* at Carmen de Patagones, Darwin, as he recorded in his diary, had told FitzRoy of his plans to proceed overland and meet the *Beagle* in Buenos Aires (or perhaps elsewhere) at some now unclear date:

[August] *9th* Some months ago the government of B: Ayres
sent out an army, under the command of General Rosas to
exterminate the Indians. They are now encamped on the Rio
Colorado, in consequence the country is now very tolerably
safe from Indians. The only danger is meeting with a few
stragglers; but a week since a man lost his whole troop of mares
but it was on the Southern shore of the river. As the *Beagle*
intended to touch at Bahía Blanca, I determined to pass over
land to that place.

I made arrangements with a guide for a troop of horses, &
Mr Harris (of the little Schooner) who was going to take a passage to Buenos Ayres in the *Beagle*, agreed to accompany me.

10th The weather was bad, so would not start: our party was
increased by five more Gauchos who were going on business
to the Encampment. Every body seemed glad of companions in
this desolate passage.

Almost exactly three years earlier, in September 1831, amid his
London gun-buying spree, a bravado-besotted Darwin had fantasized
"fighting with those d—Cannibals." He boasted of how it would be
"something to shoot the King of the Cannibals Islands." And now, for the
first time during his *Beagle* travels, he had real cause to fear for his life.

Moreover, he was now soliciting armed protection from, among
others, the notorious caudillo Juan Manuel de Rosas, until the previous
December, governor of Buenos Aires Province. Though out of office,
Rosas remained, that summer of 1833, a politically formidable leader
with aspirations to return to formal rule. In the meantime, comporting
himself as an ad hoc head of state, he issued passports over lands held
by his army in Buenos Aires Province's pampas plains and northern
Patagonia. Organized by Rosas and executed by himself and a handful
of field generals, his Desert Campaign sought to violently push Native
populations away from farms and haciendas on the frontier and thereby
to gain control over more land for cattle raising by white settlers.

Darwin had arrived at Carmen de Patagones on August 5. Situated on Rio Negro's north bank, the town was established in 1779. A Spanish fort was constructed soon thereafter; and by the 1820s, its strategic importance to Argentine officials had led to the creation of a naval base along its waterfront.

Darwin found the town agreeable but with a curious appearance. "It is built on the face of a cliff which fronts the river, and many of the houses are excavated even in the sandstone. The river is about two or three hundred yards wide, and is deep and rapid." Similarly, FitzRoy found Carmen de Patagones "irregularly built": "The houses are small, one only having two stories; and glass windows are seldom seen," he wrote. "A square enclosure of some extent, formed by walls of unbaked bricks (adobes), is called the fort, and within it are the church, the governor's house, lodgings for the officers, and public stores."

Over those early August days of 1833, as Darwin lingered around Rio Negro, the *Beagle* sailed for other waters. Even so, after the *Beagle*'s departure surely other ships were arriving at Rio Negro, vessels bound for Buenos Aires, Montevideo, and other ports safer than the lawless country through which Darwin planned to pass. So why, after learning of the dangers along his planned overland route, did he not remain at Rio Negro and wait for such a ship?

Alas, none of his extant writings answer that question. Available evidence, however, suggests that Darwin over those days grimly pondered his options, weighing reasonable fears of being killed by Natives against the pleasures of exploring his geological "El Dorado," a country that in his mind shone with a magical luster. In the end, choosing magic over fear, he steeled himself for the journey ahead.

Darwin's eventual eight-man party, himself, James Harris, five gauchos, and a hired guide (unnamed in his writings), departed Carmen de Patagones on August 11. They reached General Rosas's Rio Colorado encampment two days later. As planned, after the gauchos met with Rosas, they left Darwin's party. And on August 14, during Darwin's own eventual meeting with the general, Rosas agreed to provide him a passport and other travel protections. The following morning, Darwin and the guide, leaving an ailing Harris in the camp, set off for Bahía Blanca. There, though "not knowing when the ship would be there," he nonetheless entertained hopes of seeing the *Beagle* and its crew before he continued overland to Buenos Aires.

Beyond facilitating external travels, that era's passports often, like letters of introduction, eased the passage of foreign visitors through host countries. And Darwin's procurement that August at Rio Colorado of a passport from Rosas would not be the last time the general's beneficence safeguarded his travels. Indeed, Darwin wrote, in 1839, in *Journal and Remarks*, "I am bound to express, in the strongest terms, my obligation to the Government of Buenos Ayres for the obliging manner in which passports to all parts of the country were given me, as naturalist of the *Beagle*."

Rosas also granted Darwin use of the chain of twenty armed postas (post-houses) his army had erected: At each posta, Darwin could lodge and obtain fresh horses for the next day's ride. "The horses &c were all gratis," he elaborated to Caroline Darwin, "My only expense (about £20) was hiring a trusty companion, but in that depends your safety, for a more throat-cutting gentry do not exist than these Gauchos on the face of the world."

Such perils notwithstanding, Charles's daily passages were smoothed by a title that Rosas, combining a Spanish male honorific and that language's cognate for Charles, bestowed upon the English visitor. Charles later described calling at a posta soon after obtaining the passport:

> In the evening it rained heavily: on arriving at a post-house, we were told by the owner that if we had not a regular passport we must pass on, for there were so many robbers he would trust no one. When he read, however, my passport, which began with "El Naturalista Don Carlos, &c." his respect and civility were as unbounded, as his suspicions had been before. What a naturalist may be, neither he nor his countrymen, I suspect, had any idea; but probably my title lost nothing of its value from that cause.

Leaving General Rosas's encampment on the morning of August 16, Darwin and his guide that afternoon arrived at the first of the twenty postas on their route, its location, like Rosas's base, along the Rio Colorado corridor. Having over the past days heard more stories of alleged atrocities by Natives, Darwin, gazing upon the green riparian landscape on which the posta sat, contemplated Rosas's vision of the area's future: "The diluvial plains on the side appeared fertile & it is said are well adapted for the growth of corn: the advantage of having willow trees will be very great for the Estancias which General Rosas intends making here."

By August 17, having passed through four postas, Darwin and his guide were approaching Bahía Blanca. Failing to find the *Beagle* in the bay, the two stayed that night in familiar digs, inside Fortaleza Protectora Argentina's pentagonal adobe walls. There, after saying goodbye to the guide, Darwin quickly grew bored: "The *Beagle* had not arrived. I had nothing to do, no clean clothes, no books, nobody to talk with. I envied the very kittens playing on the floor."

Two days later, with a soldier-guide and horses obtained from the fort's comandante, he set out for the bay to see if the *Beagle* had arrived, ostensibly a one-day outing. Mishaps, however, turned the excursion into a two-day fiasco: A late start on their return trip prevented them from getting back to the fort before sundown. They thus spent the night without food, sleeping on ground "thickly encrusted with saltpetre & of course no water." The following morning, an armadillo they caught made a "poor breakfast & dinner for [the] two men."

Moreover, when the two decamped for their return to the fort, their "horses could hardly walk." Equally disconcerting,

> The road was full of little puddles from some recent rain, yet every drop quite undrinkable. At last I could walk no more, & was obliged to mount my horse, which was dreadful inhumanity as his back was quite raw. I had scarcely been 20 hours without water & only part of the time with a hot sun; yet my

thirst rendered me very weak. . . . I do not know whether the
poor horse or myself were most glad to arrive at the Fort.

After a night's rest, the following morning, on August 21, Darwin
purchased, for "4£ . . . 10S," a "fine powerful young horse" and spent the
day riding the plains surrounding the fort. The following day—"tired of
doing nothing" and hiring the same guide from his earlier star-crossed
outing to the bay—he headed back to Punta Alta, site of his *Megatherium*
discovery. Their destination, Darwin noted, was "not so distant" and
"commands a good view of the harbor." And when the two returned to
the fort the next day, he was gladdened to find there his friend James
Harris, whom he had last seen at General Rosas's camp.

Among other topics, the two commiserated over recent news that
"the Indians had murdered every soul in one of the Postas," news that,
for them, confirmed the reports heard weeks earlier around Carmen de
Patagones.

On August 24, news reached the fort that the *Beagle* was in the harbor.
But the following day, when Darwin rode down to the water's edge and
waved to his shipmates, high winds prevented them from sending a
boat ashore. The next day, however, brought better luck, "A boat with
Mr [Edward Main] Chaffers [the *Beagle's* master] arrived from the ship."

Over the coming hours, Darwin waited as the boatmen searched
ashore "for a cow to be killed, to take fresh meat aboard." Consequently,
"We did not start till late." Finally—"at ½ after one oclock"—he boarded
the *Beagle*. Hours later, after the sun rose, the "whole day" was "consumed
in telling my travellers tales." The day after that—the twenty-eighth—
was spent "actively employed in arranging things, in order to start to
Buenos Ayres by land. The feeling of excitement quite delightful after
the indolence of the week spent at the fort of Bahía Blanca."

On August 29, joining several shipmates in the ship's yawl, Darwin
returned to Punta Alta. The following day, preoccupied with finding a
guide to escort him from Bahía Blanca to Buenos Aires, he returned to
the fort. But, taking maximum advantage of his dwindling days of access
to Punta Alta, he left Syms Covington at the site to continue hunting
for fossils.

Darwin's late August Punta Alta days proved productive. As recalled to Caroline Darwin, he excavated "some more bones more perfect than those" of the *Megatherium*—"indeed one is nearly an entire skeleton."

Punta Alta's latest gift to Darwin appeared to be a giant horselike quadruped. Later, the fossil—from the Late Pleistocene, the most recent ice age—was identified as a giant ground sloth. Eventually, zoologist Richard Owen named it *Scelidotherium*. More generally, the identification by Owen and others of fossils Darwin unearthed on the pampas, and their resemblance to still living inhabitants there eventually led Darwin to what by 1839 he called his "law of the succession of types." The axiom posited biological linkages between fossils recovered in a given area and the same area's present inhabitants—in retrospect, an intellectual way station on Darwin's journey toward his eventual theory of evolution.

As his days at Bahía Blanca drew to a close, Punta Alta became for Darwin sacred ground, a geological Temple of Delphi: "It is a quiet retired spot & the weather beautiful; the very quietness is almost sublime, even in the midst of mud banks & gulls, sand hillocks & solitary Vultures." Still later, in *Journal and Remarks*—coining an epithet worthy of his overland travel companion and favorite poet John Milton—Darwin described Punta Alta as "a perfect catacomb for monsters of extinct races." Alas, however, Darwin's "perfect catacomb" no longer exists: an early twentieth-century expansion of the Argentine Navy's Puerto Belgrano base destroyed the Punta Alta fossil bed.

By early September 1833, as Darwin prepared to resume his journey to Buenos Aires, his fears of attacks by Natives were newly inflamed by reports of their ever closer presence north and west of the fort. With the reports, the still unfulfilled task of securing a guide for his upcoming trip now weighed even heavier on Darwin. Compounding anxieties, between September 4 and 7, a misunderstanding related to that search confined him to Fortaleza Protectora Argentina. "These four days were lost in miserable ennui," he complained. "A man, whom I had engaged to be my Vacciano.* disappointed me & ultimately at some risk & much trouble I hired another."

Typifying his upper-class hauteur, in Darwin's overland travel chronicles, his various hired assistants, guards, and guides often remain nameless, almost invisible, entities, their presence given away, in many cases, only by the pronoun "we" in his sentences. In other instances, a single mention of the individual's name reveals his presence, or the name appears on a payment voucher located by a later historian. In all of Darwin's travel writings, however, a constant obtains: those assisting him rarely, if ever, get speaking parts. Indeed, in 1837, FitzRoy, during the final labors on their published account of the *Beagle* expedition, would take Darwin to account for failing, in a preface to that work, to acknowledge contributions by the ship's officers to his achievements during the voyage, an omission Darwin soon corrected.

Biding his time in August 1833, at Fortaleza Protectora Argentina, Darwin, meanwhile, missed the *Beagle*'s library, whose books often brought him through perilous or boring times. At the fort, by contrast, "My only amusement was reading a Spanish edition published at Barcelona of the trial of Queen Caroline!"—consort of George IV, tried and ultimately acquitted of charges of infidelity. Unfortunately, the lull also provided time to contemplate disturbing reports drifting through the fort from General Rosas's war. "I heard many curious anecdotes respecting the Indians. The whole place was under great excitement."

---

* Darwin here and elsewhere in his diary misspells the noun *Baquiano* (sometimes rendered as *Baqueano*), a term used in Rio de la Plata Spanish that refers to someone who is an expert guide, or who otherwise knows his way around in the countryside.

22

CERRO TRES PICOS

///

On September 8, 1833, Charles Darwin and the gaucho guide he eventually hired, nameless to posterity, set out on their 350-mile journey to Buenos Aires. Ascending from the coastal plain, they soon reached the Sierra de La Ventana mountains. "I do not think Nature ever made a more solitary desolate looking mountain [range]," he wrote.

> It is very steep, rough & broken . . . so completely destitute of
> all trees, that we were unable to find even a stick to stretch out
> the meat for roasting, our fire being made of dry thistle stalks.
> The strangeness of its appearance chiefly is caused by its abrupt
> rise from the sea-like plain, which not only comes up to the foot
> of the mountain, but separates the parallel ridges or chains.

Whether in Wales, Brazil, Tierra del Fuego, Uruguay, Chile, Australia, Tasmania, or Mauritius, Darwin relished opportunities to climb any area's highest or otherwise most notable mountain, ostensibly for scientific purposes. But the sheer joy of the ascents also compelled him. Thus, on September 9, his second day in the Sierra de La Ventana, with his guide's encouragement, he set out to conquer Cerro Tres Picos—at 4,065 feet, the range's and Buenos Aires Province's highest mountain. "The guide, told me to ascend the ridge & that I could walk along its edge to the very summit." Providing still more inducement was an unverifiable assumption: "I am not aware that any foreigner, previous to my visit, had ascended this mountain."

But, as its name ("Three Peaks Hill") indicates, Cerro Tres Picos actually comprises three peaks. And when, after several hours of climbing, Darwin reached a summit, he saw that it overlooked "a precipitous valley, as deep as the plain," a chasm separating him from Cerro Tres Picos's other, truth be known, higher peaks. Returning to the mountain's base, "I proceeded cautiously on my second ascent. It was late in the day, & this part of the mountain, like the other was steep & very [jagged]."

By two o'clock, he had reached the second peak, "but got there with extreme difficulty. Every twenty yards I had the cramp in the upper parts of both thighs." Worried that the condition might augur trouble for a third climb that day, he decided, once off the mountain, to forgo the final peak: its "altitude was but little greater & every purpose of geology was answered; it was not therefore worth the hazard of any further exertion."

Equally dispiriting, before climbing Cerro Tres Picos, Darwin had heard the mountain touted as a realm of "caves, of forests, of beds of coal, of silver & gold &c." Instead, he found "a desert mountain of pure quartz rock." Worse, "I had hoped the view would at least have been imposing; it was nothing; the plain was like the ocean without its beautiful colour or defined horizon." Even so, the day's exertions brought their consolations.

A little danger, like salt to meat, gave . . . [the day] a relish. That the danger was very little was clear, by my two companions* making a good fire, a thing never done when it is suspected Indians are near."

After sundown, "drinking much mattee & smoking several little cigaritos," he "made up . . . [his] bed for the night." The wind "blew furiously, but I never passed a more comfortable night."

---

* Darwin's diary and his 1839 *Journal and Remarks* are both inconsistent concerning the number of guides accompanying him during the Cerro Tres Picos episode. By the end of his diary's September 8 entry, the "Gaucho [hired to] accompany me" has inexplicably become "the Gauchos."

23

"I THANK PROVIDENCE I AM HERE
WITH AN ENTIRE THROAT"

O ver those nervous days, General Rosas's succession of postas eased Darwin's passage through the Sierra de La Ventana. Moreover, stopping at a posta on September 12, 1833, he was joined the following day by "a troop of soldiers, which, General Rosas had the kindness to send to inform me, would shortly travel to Buenos Ayres. . . . He advised me to take the opportunity of such an escort." Indeed, by September 20, Rosas's soldiers had brought him and his two guides all the way to Buenos Aires. Although the *Beagle* was not in port there, he learned from a FitzRoy letter awaiting him that he would find the ship in Montevideo. His poop cabin thus unavailable, the naturalist arranged lodging in Buenos Aires in the home of English merchant Edward Lumb and his family.

The Lumbs' home in the city's fashionable Calle Florida district afforded the road-weary sojourner a welcome taste of familiar comforts. "I am now living in the house of a most hospitable English merchant," Charles wrote to Caroline Darwin. "It appears quite strange writing in an English furnished room, & still more strange to see a lady making tea."

The association with the Yorkshire-born merchant soon proved otherwise fortuitous. Lumb's mercantile associations allowed him to arrange to receive from a Darwin friend in Argentina and forward to Henslow a shipment of *Megatherium* bones. Moreover, Lumb's family ties across South America provided Darwin a helpful social entree.

———

Syms Covington soon joined Darwin in Buenos Aires. And, as the two contemplated their circumstance, Charles concluded that, before rejoining the *Beagle* in Montevideo, there remained time for more travel. To Caroline Darwin, he announced his plan to tour "the Northern parts of this [Buenos Aires] Province." Accordingly, on September 27, he departed Lumb's Calle Florida residence.

The two guides and Rosas's soldiers who escorted Darwin to Buenos Aires had, by then, departed. Thus, for his travels' next leg, he had hired a new guide, a "peon," as he wrote to Caroline, engaged through Francis Bond Head, an English-born Argentine mining entrepreneur.

By October 2, Darwin, Covington, and the newly hired guide had reached the town of Santa Fe, three hundred miles northwest of Buenos Aires. But that distance, he soon discovered, failed to convey the natural contrasts between the two places. Though "the difference in latitude between" the two locales was, "about 3 degrees; the change in climate is much greater": "Everything shows it. The dress & complexion of the inhabitants, the increased size of the Ombus [Umbú, *Phytolacca dioica*, a large evergreen tree common to South America], many new cacti, the greater beauty of the birds & flowers; all proves the greater influence of the sun."

That same day, according to his diary, Darwin came down with a fever, an affliction that inexplicably becomes a "headach[e]" in *Journal and Remarks*. Whatever the malady, Darwin, in both accounts, remained bedridden for two days. Once recovered, he resolved to visit Buenos Aires Province's neighboring province of Entre Rios, just east, across the Paraná River from Santa Fe. During several days in Entre Rios, however, as Charles lamented to Caroline Darwin, "so much time lost" weighed on him. Worried about missing the *Beagle*'s departure from Montevideo, he resolved to return to the city of Buenos Aires forthwith and, there, find a packet boat to the Uruguayan capital.

Darwin, Covington, and their guide thus booked passage on the *Bal-andra*, a small, one-masted sloop bound via the Paraná River for the Argentine capital. For five days, however, delays dogged the *Balandra*'s departure. But when the boat did sail, the passage, after five days, proved unbearable for Darwin: Gales, mosquitoes, and a cabin too small for the six-foot tall naturalist—too puny to even sit up in—eventually led the men to abandon the boat and complete their journey to Buenos Aires by canoe.

On the morning of October 21, however, their second day in the canoe, as the three neared Buenos Aires, they learned that a blockade impeded their entry into the city. Moreover, turmoil arising from conflicts between Juan Ramón Balcarce, Buenos Aires Province's current governor, and his predecessor (and Darwin's protector) General Rosas engulfed the capital. To Caroline Darwin, Charles described the next few days:

> By riding about (at a ruinous expence) amongst the different generals, I at last obtained leave to go on foot without passport into the city: I was thus obliged to leave my Peon & luggage behind; but I may thank kind providence I am here with an entire throat. Such a set of misfortunes I have had this month, never before happened to poor mortal. My servant (Covington by name & most invaluable I find him) was sent to the Estancia of the Merchants [Edward Lumb and family] whose house I am staying in. He [Covington] the other day nearly lost his life in a quicksand & my gun completely.

Eventually, Charles found his way into an encampment of soldiers aligned with General Rosas. Finding the general's brother, "I soon began to talk about the Generals civility to me at the R. Colorado."

> Magic could not have altered circumstances quicker than this conversation did. At last they offered me the choice to enter the city on foot without my Peon[,] horses &c &c & without a passport: I was too glad to accept it, & an officer was sent to give directions not to stop [me at] the bridge. The road, about a league in length, was quite deserted; I met one party of soldiers;

but I satisfied them with an old passport. I was exceedingly glad when I found myself safe on the stones of B. Ayres.

Eventually, in March 1835, reelected as governor, an emboldened Juan Manuel de Rosas did nothing over the coming years to diminish his reputation for ruthlessness. Dispatching spies and death squads against his opponents or otherwise forcing them into exile, he remained in power for another seventeen years.

Following his return to office, Rosas awarded allies with grants of land seized from Natives during his Desert Campaign. But, his populist image notwithstanding, as a wealthy representative of the landed class, he failed to improve conditions for the gauchos and blacks whose numbers had swelled his army and political rallies. His political career ended ingloriously in February 1852 when, the province facing economic crisis and his powers collapsing, he exiled himself to England.

There, the once feared caudillo lived as a farmer near Southampton until his death in 1873. Though Rosas's farm lay one hundred miles from the village of Down, where Darwin spent his later years, only one report exists of the two men's paths crossing during those years—apparently in Southampton, in 1862. Rosas would have been about seventy years old, Darwin about fifty-three, Alas, however, little is known about the alleged meeting, neither its duration or what they discussed.*

In October 1989, over a century after Rosas's death, in an intended act (however misguided) of national reconciliation ordered by Peronist

---

* Conjecture concerning the alleged Darwin-Rosas encounter in Southampton, in 1862, rests on a June 27 letter, possibly from 1863, to Charles from his oldest son William Erasmus Darwin. William worked in Southampton, from 1862 to 1877 in the banking industry; and presumably the meeting occurred while Charles was visiting William. "I tried to explain that you had met him last year and spoke to him, and I think he understood," wrote William. "He took your paper and read it carefully through making me read each word, and then he said he would write the answer and give it to his servant for me." Later, presumably that same day, the servant informed William that Rosas "was very busy & should not be able to write for some few days." Alas no letter from Rosas has ever surfaced.

president Carlos Menem, the caudillo's body was repatriated from Southampton to Buenos Aires.

Charles Darwin, meanwhile, in fall 1833, in Buenos Aires, after arranging passage on a packet boat bound for Montevideo, reached the Uruguayan capital on November 3. The next day, "I went on board the *Beagle*." There, he "was astonished to hear we were not to sail till the beginning of December: the cause of this great delay was the necessity of finishing all charts, the materials for which had been collected by the Schooners." Indeed, "The poop-cabin being full of workers, I took up my residence on shore, so as to make the most of this additional month."

24

TIERRA DEL FUEGO REDUX

"Whence have these people come? Have they remained in
the same state since the creation of the world? What could
have tempted a tribe of men leaving the fine regions of
the North to travel down the Cordilleras the backbone of
America, to invent & build canoes, & then to enter upon
one of the most inhospitable countries in the world?"

—Charles Darwin, *Beagle* diary,
Tierra del Fuego, February 25, 1834

From Buenos Aires, Charles Darwin had hastened to Montevideo
to reach the *Beagle* before it sailed, arriving on November 4, 1833,
only to learn that its departure was postponed for a month. The
Beagle's tender ship, the *Adventure*, also in port, was still being refitted
for the two ships' upcoming passage around Cape Horn. But the main
reason for the delay was the success of the *Beagle*'s recent surveys, activities so productive that the ship's hydrographers were left busy for weeks,
for hours on end, reducing survey measurements to mathematical tables.
And because the hydrographers were working round-the-clock in the
Beagle's chart room, otherwise Darwin's poop cabin, he found himself
exiled to lodgings ashore.

The naturalist, for his part, hardly lacked for ways to fill his own time over those weeks. As always, there were letters to write. There was also the task of packing and sending to England specimens gathered over the past months. That sprawling collection now included the *Megatherium* bones that Covington, at Darwin's request, had loaded onto the *Beagle* and were thus in the ship's hold awaiting Darwin's attention.

To reduce shipping costs, he sent the *Megatherium* bones—for inventory purposes, with each bone carefully numbered in ink—in a separate box to Robert Armstrong, a physician at the Royal Hospital in Plymouth. (In fall 1830, Armstrong, at FitzRoy's request, had tended to the Fuegians.) Otherwise, the rest of the latest cache—two boxes and a cask, a shipment teeming with birds, rocks, mice, fish, bones, and seeds—was dispatched to the Rev. Henslow.

But even as Darwin dispatched his skins and fossils across the Atlantic, he longed to gather more specimens. "There is nothing like geology," he wrote to his sister Catherine. "The pleasure of the first days partridge shooting or first days hunting cannot be compared to finding a fine group of fossil bones, which tell their story of former times with almost a living tongue." Accordingly, with unexpected time on his hands, Darwin began searching Montevideo and environs for fossils. Indeed, on November 14, he embarked on a four-hundred-mile excursion to western Uruguay's town of Mercedes.

There, he lodged for three nights at an estancia owned by Englishman George Keen, to whom Darwin's Buenos Aires host Edward Lumb had provided a letter of introduction. Otherwise, during the trip, the naturalist unearthed fossils and pondered sights, expected and unexpected—some among the latter inspiring equally unexpected insights: "A naked man on a naked horse is a very fine spectacle; I had no idea how well the two animals suited each other: as the Peons were galloping about they reminded me of the Elgin marbles." But Darwin's favorite incident occurred during his return to Montevideo, his purchase, on November 26, at an estancia—for 18 pence, roughly $30 in early twenty-first-century US dollars—of "a part, very perfect, of the head of a *Megatherium*."

During the *Beagle*'s August 1833 Montevideo anchorage, painter Augustus Earle, beset with declining health, had resigned from the ship. By happenstance, Conrad Martens, an English-born painter in his early thirties, while passing through Rio, soon learned of Earle's resignation.

An artist aboard HMS *Hyacinth*, then anchored in Rio, Martens later found his way to Montevideo and came to terms with FitzRoy for Earle's old position. Only months later, however, did Earle join the ship—on November 25, 1833, while Darwin was away on his trip to Mercedes.

Writing to Darwin after hiring Martens, FitzRoy suggested the two men were kindred spirits. Moreover, the captain, knowing Darwin's weakness for exuberant souls, praised Martens as a "a stone pounding artist who exclaims in his sleep 'think of me standing upon a pinnacle of the Andes, or sketching a Fuegian Glacier!!!'" And, indeed, over the coming months Martens, confirming FitzRoy's prescience, demonstrated formidable artistic talents, and also became fast friends with the ship's naturalist.

On November 28, Darwin returned to Montevideo and, at 4:00 A.M. on December 5, the *Beagle* and the *Adventure*, bound for Tierra del Fuego, both weighed anchor from Montevideo. And, on December 23, after two weeks of sailing, the two ships, to celebrate the coming holidays, anchored at Port Desire (today's Puerto Deseado). Six hundred miles north of Cape Horn, the "harbor," Darwin wrote, consisted of "a creek which runs up the country in the form of a river: the entrance is very narrow; but with a fine breeze, the Beagle entered in good style."

But their "good style" arrival notwithstanding, Darwin found Port Desire wanting. "The Beagle is anchored opposite to a fort erected by the old Spaniards. It was formerly attempted to make a settlement here; but it quite failed from the want of water in the summer, & the Indians in the winter," he recalled. "The fate of all the Spanish establishments on the coast of Patagonia, with the exception of the R. Negro, has been miserable."

The bleakness, to his mind, extended to the landscape:

I thought I had seen some desart looking country near
B. Blanca; but the land in this neighbourhead so far exceeds
it in sterility, that this alone deserves the name of a desart.
The plain is composed of gravel with very little vegetation &
not a drop of water. In the vallies there is some little, but it
is very brackish.

At Port Desire, Captain FitzRoy dispatched a party in the *Beagle*'s yawl
to find fresh water and game. Over the next five days, Darwin, with
others and on solo hunts, likewise helped replenish the ship's provisions,
killing, among other game, a large rhea that became the main course
for a Christmas feast in the ship's gun room: "Wretched looking as the
country is, it supports very many Guanacoes," he noted. "By great good
luck I shot one; it weighed without its entrails &c 170 pounds."

Conrad Martens, meanwhile, had also killed a rhea while at Port
Desire. And his quarry, soon cooked, was also served in the gunroom. But
as Darwin was eating his serving of the avian, he realized, to his horror,
that it was not the species of rhea he usually encountered. Recalling a
conversation with gauchos at Rio Negro concerning a rarer bird, a smaller
species of rhea (the "petise"), he realized that the latter was the very species
he and the other men were eating, for his purposes a new (uncollected)
species. "Fortunately," he recalled, part of the rhea remained uneaten; and
"the Head neck legs, one wing & many of the larger feathers" were salvaged
and soon preserved and packed away—becoming a specimen of the species
eventually known as *Rhea darwinii*, "Darwin's Rhea."

Meanwhile, beyond the expected festivities, Christmas Day at Port
Desire harbored still other pleasures for the *Beagle*'s naturalist and his
shipmates:

After dining in the Gun-room, the officers & almost every
man in the ship went on shore. The Captain distributed prizes
to the best runners, leapers, wrestlers. These Olympic games
were very amusing; it was quite delightful to see with what

school-boy eagerness the seamen enjoyed them: old men with long beards & young men without any were playing like so many children—certainly a much better way of passing Christmas day than the usual one, of every seaman getting as drunk as he possibly can.

Upon the arrival of the *Beagle* and the *Adventure* at Port Desire, FitzRoy, noticing damages to the latter's sails, ordered their repair before the ship left the port. Over those days, as the *Adventure* underwent its ordered repairs, FitzRoy perceived an opportunity in the ongoing delay: Aboard the *Beagle*, he would "run down" to Port Julian, 110 miles to the south, and conduct surveys there and along the nearby coast.

Leaving Port Desire on January 4, Darwin recalled, the *Beagle* over the next five days "surveyed the coast & at night either anchored or stood out to sea." Reaching their destination on the ninth, the nascent geologist found Port St. Julian yet another uninviting landscape. Even so, its coastal cliffs soon yielded treasures before his rock-hammer: "I found some very perfect bones of some large animal, I fancy a Mastodon," he later gloated to Henslow. "The bones of one hind extremity are very perfect and solid. This is interesting, as the latitude is between 49° and 50°, and the site far removed from the great Pampas, where bones of the narrow toothed Mastodon are so frequently found. By the way this Mastodon and the Megatherium, I have no doubt, were fellow brethren in the ancient plains." Slowly but inexorably, Darwin continued to stumble toward what he would later call his law of the succession of types.

January 22 found both expedition ships sailing from Port Desire—the *Beagle* toward Tierra del Fuego, the *Adventure* toward the West Falklands to conduct surveys there. Four days later, the *Beagle* reached the Strait of Magellan; and, on January 29, anchored in St. Gregory Bay. From the ship, Darwin recalled, the *Beagle's* men spotted "a large tribe of Patagonian Indians." Venturing ashore, FitzRoy and Darwin received "a very kind reception."

These Indians have such constant communication with the Sealers, that they are half civilized. They talk a good deal of Spanish & some English. Their appearance is however rather wild. They are all clothed in large mantles of the Guanaco, & their long hair streams about their faces. They resemble in their countenance the Indians with Rosas, but are much more painted; many with their whole faces red, & brought to a point on the chin, others black. One man was ringed & dotted with white like a Fuegian.

Equally noteworthy to Darwin and FitzRoy, and seeming to confirm legends of Patagonian "giants," "The[ir] average height appeared to be more than six feet," recalled Darwin. Equally disconcerting, "The horses who carried these large men were small & ill fitted for their work."

Shortly thereafter, the two confronted a discomfiting predicament. "When we returned to the [open] boat, a great number of Indians got in; it was a very tedious & difficult operation to clear the boat." After FitzRoy agreed to take three Indigenes into the boat, "every one seemed determined to be one of them. At last we reached the ship with our three guests." To Catherine Darwin, Charles described the Natives' shipboard visit. "One of them, who dined with us eat [sic] with his knife & fork as well as any gentleman," he wrote. "Many of them could talk a little Spanish."

The following day, a larger party ventured ashore to trade with the Natives. "The whole population of the Toldos* were arranged on a bank, having brought with them Guanaco skins, ostrich feathers &c &c," recalled Darwin. Initially, the Natives demanded firearms in exchange for their items, "& of course not giving them these, tobacco was the next." And when the *Beagle*'s men obliged, offering generous amounts of tobacco, their negotiating partners responded enthusiastically. "Indeed knives, axes &c were of no esteem in comparison to tobacco."

It was an amusing scene & it was impossible not to like these mis-named giants, they were so throughily good-humoured &

---

*   *Toldos*, a Spanish noun applied to Native shelters in Latin America, was, along with "wigwams," used by English visitors to refer to the Fuegians' distinctive huts.

unsuspecting. An old woman, well known by the name of Santa Maria, recognized Mr Rowlett as belonging formerly to the Adventure & as having seen him a year & a half ago at the R. Negro, to which place a part of this tribe had then gone to barter their goods. Our semi-civilized friends expressed great anxiety for the ship to return & one old man wanted to accompany us.

On February 2, the *Beagle* entered Port Famine (today's Puerto del Hambre, Chile), a star-crossed locale in the ship's history. The name of the anchorage, on the Magellan Strait's northern shore, came from English privateer and explorer Thomas Cavendish who, stopping there in 1587, found only the ruins of an earlier settlement.

Of greater moment for the spot's current visitors, it was at Port Famine, that, in 1828, a despondent Captain Pringle Stokes, the *Beagle*'s first commander, locked himself in his cabin and put a bullet in his head. And indeed, when the *Beagle* returned to Port Famine six years later, the pounding rainfall churning its waters over the following three days provided scant reason for the ship's men to believe the intervening years had vanquished whatever curse haunted the inlet.

FitzRoy had not been at Port Famine when Stokes killed himself. Nonetheless—based on the sphinxlike concision the normally prolix captain later adopted in describing his visit there—Stokes's death apparently haunted him when he stepped ashore: "On the 2d of February we anchored in Port Famine, and on the 10th, having obtained chronometric observations for which I went there, we sailed for the neighbourhood of the First Narrow and Lomas Bay."

On February 6, after the rains ceased at Port Famine, Darwin got ashore early, at 4:00 A.M. With compass in hand and joined by an unspecified companion (probably Covington), he was determined to climb nearby Mt. Tarn. At 2,707 feet, Tarn was hardly a towering peak. Even so, Darwin had heard it described as the area's highest, and weary of shipboard life, he longed for a bracing climb.

Seeming to confirm suspicions of a Port Famine jinx, the outing proved initially disorienting. "For the two first hours I never expected to reach the summit." He consulted his compass, but steep, angular terrain—dense with trees and thicker tangles of roots, vines, and brush—blinded his navigation. "It is barely possible to see the sky & every other landmark which might serve as a guide is totally shut out."

Hours later, "I at last found myself amongst the stunted trees & soon reached the bare ridge which conducted me to the summit," he recalled. "Here was a true Tierra del Fuego view; irregular chains of hills, mottled with patches of snow; deep yellowish-green valleys; & arms of the sea running in all directions." Equally gratifying, he seemed to find confirming evidence of Charles Lyell's theory of oceanic floors rising to create continents: "I had the good luck to find some shells in the rocks near the summit."

Alas, however, curses are curses; and, in the end, the view from Mt. Tarn's peak proved disappointing. The day's other pleasures notwithstanding, "the atmosphere was not . . . clear, & indeed the strong wind was so piercingly cold, that it would prevent much enjoyment under any circumstances."

Leaving Port Famine on February 10, the *Beagle* spent the next three weeks surveying Tierra del Fuego's eastern waters. By March 2, recalled Darwin, Captain FitzRoy, contemplating non-survey-related matters, decided to make "the bold attempt of beating against the Westerly winds & proceeding up the Beagle channel . . . to Jemmy Buttons country."

Two days later, with the *Beagle* anchored en route to that destination, FitzRoy surprised Darwin with a tribute, perhaps a belated gift honoring his twenty-fifth birthday two weeks earlier. Recalled the honoree in his March 2 diary entry: "The mountains, which we passed today, on the Northern shore of the Channel are about 3000 feet high. They terminate in very broken & sharp peaks; & many of them rise in one abrupt rise from the waters edge to the above elevation." One peak, however, one with "a very grand, appearance," had caught FitzRoy's attention; and "the Captain has done me the honour to call [it] by my name." Even more flattering, FitzRoy, using "angular measurement," had determined Mt. Darwin to be "the highest in Tierra del Fuego."

In his November 1831 instructions to FitzRoy, Captain Francis Beaufort, concerning the naming (in truth, often renaming) of geographic features and places, had counseled respect for established appellations. "Trifling as it may appear, the love of giving a multiplicity of new and unmeaning names tends to confuse our geographical knowledge," Beaufort wrote. "The name stamped upon a place by the first discoverer should be held sacred by the common consent of all nations." Moreover, it was, he advised, often better, "to adopt the native appellation, than to exhaust the catalogue of public characters or private friends at home."

But Beaufort also appreciated the power of such license to boost shipboard morale: "Officers and crews, indeed, have some claim on such distinction, which, slight as it is, helps to excite an interest in the voyage."*

Alas, however, a century later, that "highest" accolade FitzRoy assigned to Mt. Darwin (7,999 feet) passed, after a recalculation, to nearby Mt. Shipton (8,460 feet). In, however, a consolation of sorts for the naturalist's memory, both mountains lie in the same range along the Beagle Channel's north shore that FitzRoy, in yet another act of homage, named the Cordillera Darwin.

By March 2, the *Beagle* was nearing Jemmy Button country. Plowing westward in the Beagle Channel, it then dropped south in the Murray Channel. And, as the ship approached Wulaia, Fuegians crowded the surrounding waters: "We had at one time 10 or 12 canoes alongside; a rapid barter was established Fish & Crabs being exchanged for bits of cloth & rags."

On March 5, with the *Beagle* securely anchored, Darwin joined a party in one of the ship's open boats and headed for the shore. "This

---

* The deference FitzRoy and other Europeans showed to "first discoverers" in the naming of places and geographical features obviously did not extend to Indigenous peoples whose own names for such locales antedated the arrival of their "discoverers."

being a populous part of the country, we were followed by seven
canoes."

> When we arrived at the old spot; we could see no signs of our
> friends, & we were the more alarmed, as the Fuegians made
> signs of fighting with their bows and arrows. Shortly after-
> wards a canoe was seen coming with a flag hanging up: untill
> she was close alongside, we could not recognise poor Jemmy.

"It was quite painful to behold him," Darwin recalled. When the
naturalist last saw Jemmy, he had been dressed in the attire of a proper
English gentleman. "When he left us he was very fat, & so particular
about his clothese, that he was always afraid of even dirtying his shoes;
scarcely ever without gloves & his hair neatly cut."

Now standing before the *Beagle*'s men, Button was "thin, pale,
& without a remnant of clothes, excepting a bit of blanket round his
waist," with "hair, hanging over his shoulders."

"I thought he was ill," recounted FitzRoy.

More telling, by Darwin's lights, Button had seemed "so ashamed
of himself . . . [that] he turned his back" to the *Beagle*'s men earlier that
day as they approached.

Upon the captain's instructions, Button was brought aboard the *Beagle*.
"We hurried him below," recalled FitzRoy, and "clothed him immediately."

Minutes later, Button reappeared on the main deck." I never saw so
complete & grievous a change," recalled Darwin. "When . . . he was clothed
& the first flurry over, things wore a very good appearance. He had plenty
(or as he expressed himself too much) to eat. [He] was not cold; his friends
were very good people; could talk a little of his own language!"

Hours later, Button left the *Beagle* but soon returned; and that night,
the ship's men learned that, since their visit a year earlier, he "had got a
young & very nice looking squaw." Moreover, he had undergone a change
of heart concerning a vital matter. During the *Beagle*'s February 1833
visit to Wulaia, as Darwin had then put it, "Poor Jemmy, looked rather
disconsolate, & certainly would have liked to have returned with us."
But now, in 1834, "We were rather surprised to find he had not the least
wish to return to England." To Catherine Darwin, Charles soon wrote,

"The Captain offered to take him to England, but this, to our surprise, he at once refused."

Equally surprising, and disturbing, to Darwin was a deterioration that, to his ears, each passing word from their former shipmate bore witness. "The strangest thing is Jemmys difficulty in regaining his own language. He seems to have taught all his friends some English. When his wife came, an old man announced her, 'as Jemmy Buttons wife'!"

But what of Fuegia Basket and York Minster? The *Beagle*'s men apparently learned little about those two that day, and the little they did learn suggested perfidy and ill-fortune: "York Minster," Darwin wrote, "returned to his own country several month ago, & took farewell by an act of consummate villainy: He persuaded Jemmy & his mother to come to his country, when he robbed them of every thing & left them. He appears to have treated Fuegia very ill."

Although much about the reunion disquieted Darwin, the meeting did have its tender moments. "Poor Jemmy with his usual good feeling brought two beautiful otter skins for two of his old friends & some spear heads & arrows of his own making for the Captain." For the *Beagle*'s men, the encounter even presented reasons for optimism. "He had also built a canoe. & is clearly now well established. The various things now given to him he will doubtless be able to keep."

Button slept ashore that night. The following morning, March 6, he came aboard the *Beagle* for breakfast. "The Captain," recalled Darwin, "had some long conversations with him & extracted much curious information." That exchange, Darwin later learned, cleared up some of the mysteries concerning the fate of the Fuegians since the *Beagle*'s men last saw them. "They had left the old wigwams & crossed the water in order to be out of the reach of the Ohens men who came over the mountains to steal." Recalling the Natives the *Beagle*'s men encountered at St. Gregory Bay, Darwin surmised, "They clearly are the tall . . . Patagonians of the East coast."*

That morning, Button lingered aboard as the crew readied the ship to sail, staying so long that his "frightened" wife "did not cease crying

---

* The Indigenous people that Darwin called the "Ohens"—the Ona or Oensmen—are also called the Selk'nam.

till he was safe out of the ship with all his valuable presents." And eventually, the moment came for their honored guest to return to the shore. "Every soul on board was as sorry to shake hands with poor Jemmy for the last time, as we were glad to have seen him," wrote Darwin. "I hope & have little doubt he will be as happy as if he had never left his country; which is much more than I formerly thought."

Later, as the *Beagle* sailed from Wulaia, its men spotted a faint light ashore. Button, Darwin recalled, had "lighted a farewell signal fire as the ship stood out of [Wulaia] . . . on her course to East Falkland Island."

Neither Darwin or FitzRoy ever saw Jemmy Button again. In 1855, representatives of the recently founded Patagonian Missionary Society, based in the Falklands, visited Wulaia. Sailing aboard the society's ship the *Allen Gardiner*, they were heartened upon arriving to find Button and that he retained a serviceable grasp of English.

Four years later, in November 1859, however, another Patagonian Missionary Society delegation to Wulaia, also sailing aboard the *Allen Gardiner*, failed to return. Months later, the society dispatched another ship, the *Nancy*, to the settlement to search for its missing ship. There, in March 1860, the delegation aboard the *Nancy* learned that all but one of the men aboard the *Allen Gardiner* had been massacred by Fuegians.

The lone survivor was a young man named Alfred Coles who greeted the *Nancy* at Wulaia and shared a harrowing tale: Coles, the cook aboard the *Allen Gardiner*, had escaped the massacre by fleeing into the forest. Weeks later, after initially suffering their abuse, he befriended several Fuegians. Coles also shared a stunning accusation: Jemmy Button, he said, had directed the massacre.

Button, meanwhile, had arrived in Wulaia, after the *Nancy*'s arrival and soon boarded the ship. But after hearing Coles's report, and by then feeling threatened by Fuegians gathering in canoes around his ship's bow, the *Nancy*'s captain, with Button still aboard, ordered the vessel's immediate return to the Falklands.

At an 1861 public inquiry at Port Stanley overseen by the Falkland's governor, Button denied any role in the killings. Other Fuegians, he testified, members of the Selk'nam (the Ona) tribe who lived "over the mountains," carried out the massacre.

Coles stuck by his allegation. Under questioning, however, he conceded he had not personally witnessed the massacre and that his accusation against Button rested on second-hand accounts heard from the Fuegians he befriended. Moreover, Coles acknowledged, he did not speak the Yaghan language. He had heard the accusation against Button in broken English, and thus could not vouch to understanding it accurately. In the end, the governor adjudged the evidence against Button insufficient, and he returned to Wulaia.

Three years later, in 1864, Button's son Wammestriggens ("Threeboys"), visiting Wulaia, learned that his father and the area's other Yaghans had died during an epidemic.

During the 1870s, picking up where General Rosas had left off, the Conquest of the Desert,* led in large part by General Julio Argentino Roca, consolidated and extended Rosas's depredations, projecting Argentina's dominion into deepest southern Patagonia. Among other consequences of Roca's campaign, it opened coastal Patagonia's river valleys to white settlers, irrigation, and the cultivation of wheat and other cereals.

Moreover, by the nineteenth century's final decades, white settlers, drawn to Tierra del Fuego by the lure of gold and land for cattle- and sheep-raising, were paying bounties to Chilean and Argentine mercenaries to hunt and kill the Selk'nam there. Among Tierra del Fuego's last surviving Native peoples, the Selk'nam poignantly, along with the Tehuelches, numbered among several tribes reputed to have been

---

* A similar campaign in Chile, the Pacification of Araucanía (1861–83), likewise, clearing the way for white settlement and agriculture at the expense of Native peoples, extended the Chilean republic's dominion into much of today's central Chile.

Magellan's "giants." Indeed, the noun *patagón** the explorer applied to the Natives that he saw (whomever they were) was, in time, adopted by Europeans as their name for the country that Magellan's giants ostensibly dominated—Patagonia.

Causing more deaths, priests attempting to protect Indigenous peoples sheltered them in confined spaces—inadvertently exposing them to the rapid spread of smallpox and other deadly contagious diseases. By the early twentieth century, all but a scarce few of Tierra del Fuego's Indigenous peoples, those Darwin called the "Fuegians," dispossessed of their lands, had been killed by whites or European diseases.

Consummating Juan Manuel de Rosas's brutal prophecy, his genocidal long arm reaching beyond the grave, "the fine territories which extend from the Andes to the coast and down to the Magellan Strait" were, at last, laid "wide open" for his "children."

---

*   *Patagón* was the name of a monster creature in the knight-errantry tale *Primalean*, published in 1512 by Spanish writer Francisco Vázquez.

25

RIO SANTA CRUZ ASCENT

W hen the *Beagle*, on March 10, 1834, returned to East Falkland's Port Louis, its crew members again found a town recovering from turmoil—in this case a rebellion orchestrated the previous summer by gauchos and Indigenes against a handful of British overseers. In the uprising's aftermath, in January 1834, the warship HMS *Challenger*, arrived, chased down, and jailed the insurrection's instigators. The uprising's leader, Antonio Rivero, however, remained at large, hiding on a nearby islet. And soon after the *Beagle*'s arrival, the Navy lieutenant acting as the archipelago's governor asked FitzRoy to sail to that speck in Berkeley Sound and capture the culprit. Complying, FitzRoy soon captured Rivero, and placed him in the ship's brig.

Darwin, meanwhile, was appalled by what he considered the consequences of lax governance that had left the port woefully ungarrisoned. "How different from old Spain," with its dispatch of conquistadors to, and construction of strong citadels in, the New World," he inveighed to Catherine Darwin. By contrast, he noted, London had left the distant colony protected by, "a Lieutenant, with four sailors, without authority or instructions."

Otherwise, Port Louis—in truth the letters awaiting him there boosted Charles's spirits—Caroline Darwin expressed relief that his travels were going well but feared memories of them would complicate his adjustment, following his return, to life as a rural parish priest, if indeed he still planned to enter the clergy. "I cannot help being rather grieved when you speak so rapturously of the Tropics and . . . have great fears how far you will stand the quiet clerical life you used to say you would return to."

Caroline otherwise updated her brother on the comings and goings of relatives and friends, including Frances "Fanny" Biddulph (*née* Owen). His former paramour, though of late "very unwell," nonetheless seemed in good spirits when Caroline recently saw her. "She talked a good deal about you very affectionately & warmly, & said how much she wished to see you again, & how very much she wished for your happiness."

A letter from Henslow, meanwhile, acknowledged receipt of a shipment of specimens. "I have popped the various animals that were in the Keg into fresh spirits in jars & placed them in my cellar," he wrote. "The more delicate things as insects, skins &c. I keep at my own house, with the precaution of putting camphor into the boxes. The plants delight me exceedingly, tho' I have not yet made them out." But, Henslow added, with help from Charles's friend, botanist Joseph Dalton Hooker, "I hope to do so before long."

Beyond that, "The fossil portions of the *Megatherium* turned out to be extremely interesting as serving to illustrate certain parts of the animal which the specimens formerly received in this country & in France had failed to do." For good measure, Henslow entreated, "Send home every scrap of *Megatherium* skull you can set your eyes upon—& *all* fossils."

Henslow added that William Buckland, president of the British Association for the Advancement of Science, had exhibited some bones Darwin had sent at a recent meeting of the organization's Geological Section. Another letter, from Frederick Hope, a former beetling companion of Charles's, describing the meeting, predicted "your name is likely to be immortalized . . . [it] was in every mouth & Buckland applauded you as you deserved."

Darwin, however, was distressed to learn that the Megatherium bones had been sent to a curator at the Hunterian Museum, a repository associated with London's Royal College of Surgeons. The curator intended to "pick them out carefully repair them, get them figured, & return them" with a learned description of the species.

Soon responding to Henslow, Darwin declared himself, "alarmed by the expression cleaning all the bones, as I am afraid the printed numbers will be lost."

> The reason I am so anxious they should not be [cleaned], is that a part were found in a gravel with recent shells, but others in a very different bed. Now with these latter there were bones of an Agouti, a genus of animals I believe now peculiar to America & it would be curious to prove some one of the same genus coexisted with the Megatherium; such & *many other* points entirely depend on the numbers being carefully preserved.

Overall, however, reports that his collections were winning positive receptions in England thrilled Darwin. Indeed, he seemed on the cusp of becoming, as Frederick Hope had predicted, "immortalized" among his country's geologists. If nothing else, he could now resume his travels, confident that he enjoyed in Britain a rapt audience for his future collecting and observations.

The weather, meanwhile, during the *Beagle*'s April–May (austral fall) anchorage at Port Louis proved as dismal as the ship's March 1833 stay there. Once again, the *Beagle*'s men even faced the grim task of again burying a drowned British seaman, albeit this time from another ship.

A few days after the *Beagle* reached Port Louis, Darwin reported, "The Adventure arrived, after an exceedingly prosperous voyage." By March 20, however, FitzRoy's "consort" had departed to resume survey work. And, on April 7, the *Beagle*—its departure delayed by the wait for a cutter that never arrived to transport their prisoner Antonio Rivero to Rio—finally weighed anchor for Patagonia. For now, Rivero and a second captured insurrectionist would remain aboard the ship.

A week later, on April 13, the *Beagle* anchored at its next destination, the mouth of southern Patagonia's Rio Santa Cruz. The following day, Captain FitzRoy began executing a plan that, weeks earlier at Port Louis, Charles had described in a letter to Catherine Darwin: The captain feared that at Port Desire the *Beagle*, upon striking a rock, had torn its hull's copper sheathing. At Rio Santa Cruz, he thus intended to anchor the ship at high tide at the river's mouth; and after the tides rolled out, a team would repair the exposed copper bottom.

On April 16, three days after the *Beagle* reached Rio Santa Cruz, Darwin took pleasure in the plan's successful execution: "One tide was sufficient to repair her & after noon she floated off & was again moored in safety. Nothing could be more favourable than both the weather & place for this rather ticklish operation." In a stroke of good fortune for posterity, shipboard artist Conrad Martens memorialized the repair in a drawing later rendered as a detailed engraving. The image, a rich source for historians, depicts the *Beagle* on the estuary's beach—prow-forward, tilted at a 45° angle and supported by braces.

In his letter to Catherine, Charles, beyond detailing the plan to repair the *Beagle*, described a second plan that FitzRoy had in mind: "the Captain has a glorious scheme . . . to go to the very head, that is probably to the Andes, of this river. It is quite unknown. . . . I cannot imagine anything more interesting."

The idea of ascending the Santa Cruz to its Andes headwaters captured Darwin's imagination. But if FitzRoy's plan seemed "a glorious scheme," it was not an original idea. The same ascent, led by Captain Pringle Stokes, had been attempted, without success, in 1829, during the *Beagle*'s first expedition.

But how to explain FitzRoy's apparent sudden interest in an inland excursion, about which Darwin first learned mere days earlier at Port Louis? The Admiralty had mandated no such outings. And Darwin's writings shed no light on the matter. Moreover, FitzRoy himself, when later addressing the matter, retreating in his *Narrative* into the passive voice, does little to resolve the mystery: "An examination, or rather a partial exploring, of the River Santa Cruz had long been meditated." Lacking further clues, speculations are tempting: was FitzRoy lured by the prospect of succeeding where his predecessor Stokes had failed? Or was he simply jealous of Darwin's frequent outings on terra firma? While both motivations are plausible, conjecture tilts toward the latter.

On April 18, leaving the rest of the crew aboard the *Beagle*, FitzRoy and twenty-four men set off in three of the ship's whaleboats. (FitzRoy recalled that he was joined by "Mr. Darwin, Mr. Chaffers, Mr. Stokes, Mr. Bynoe, Mr. Mellersh, Mr. Martens, and eighteen seamen and marines.") Additionally, "Three chronometers were carried in the boats, with other necessary instruments: among them two mountain barometers, with which Mr. Darwin and myself wished to measure the height of the river above the level of the sea, and the heights of the neighbouring ranges of hills above the level of the river."

Setting out on April 18, incoming tides assisted the first leg of their upriver passage. But as they moved upriver, increasingly distant from the estuary, the river's channel grew narrower, more serpentine, and its currents stronger. By their second day out, defeating their sails and oars, the currents forced the men to leave their boats, haul them ashore, and tie them together. Over the coming days, two party members would man each of the three boats. Otherwise, standing on a riverbank, the rest of the men, FitzRoy and Darwin included, working in teams in ninety-minute shifts, pulled the boats upstream.

On April 20, they passed the point on the Santa Cruz where Stokes's party had turned back, a calculation confirmed by their discovery of an abandoned boat hook bearing markings from the earlier expedition. Over the next two weeks, the ascent proceeded ploddingly; and the party survived on guanaco and other scarce game. All the while, keeping a wary eye out for occasionally glimpsed Natives, the men, Darwin recalled, settled into a routine. Each night, they pitched tents and cooked on the river shore. "The officers of each boat lived with, eat the same food, & slept in the same tent with their crew; so that each boat was quite independent of the others."

By early May, however, the men were increasingly confronting rocky obstructions in the river. Moreover, the stream's grade was growing steeper, its currents fiercer. On May 4, conceding the inevitable, FitzRoy ordered the ascent abandoned.

By Darwin's estimate, the party, when FitzRoy issued his order, was about 140 miles from the Atlantic, and roughly sixty miles from the closest stream that empties into the Pacific. After ordering the boats placed ashore, the naturalist recalled, "The Captain & a large party set off to walk a few miles to the Westward. We crossed a desert plain which forms the head of the valley of S. Cruz, but could not see the base of the mountains. . . . We had however the satisfaction of seeing in full view the long North & South range of the Cordilleras."

Inspired by what he saw over those days and diving into Lyellian speculation concerning the origins of landmasses, Darwin soon wrote to Henslow. The Andes, he theorized, were, geologically, recently formed mountains; and before their creation, the Santa Cruz had been an Atlantic-to-Pacific channel: "The valley of S. Cruz appears to me a very curious one, at first it quite baffled me. I believe I can show good reasons for supposing it to have been once a Northern Stts. like that of [the Strait of] *Magellan*."

On May 5, the day after FitzRoy ordered the ascent abandoned, "before sun-rise, we began our descent," Darwin recalled. "We shot down the stream with great rapidity; generally at the rate of 10 miles an hour; what a contrast to the laborious tracking. We effected in this day what had cost us five days & a half." On May 8, three days after turning back, the men had returned to the river's mouth: "From passing over so much country," Darwin reflected, "we, as it were, condensed all the birds & animals together & they appeared much more numerous."

Four days later, on May 12, the *Beagle*'s full complement, its inland adventurers returned from their Quixotic outing, returned to Atlantic waters. Sailing south, they were bound for the Strait of Magellan—and, beyond those waters' storied perils, the Pacific Ocean and Chile.

PART V

ROUND THE HORN, 1834–1836

"Little by little, and also in great leaps,
Life happened to me."
　　　　—Pablo Neruda, "October Fullness"

26

THE HEIGHTS OF CERRO LA CAMPANA

///

"As soon as Don Quixote entered those mountains
his heart filled with joy, for it was a landscape that
seemed suited to the adventures he was seeking."
—Miguel de Cervantes, *Don Quixote*

Sailing south on May 22, 1834, ten days after leaving Rio Santa Cruz, the *Beagle* encountered a British warship. In a gam, a meeting in open waters of parties in open boats sent from the two ships, the *Beagle* transferred its two prisoners to the man-of-war. The latter vessel, in turn, passed along a bundle of mail, collected in the Falklands, for the *Beagle*'s men.

By June 1, keeping its southward course, the *Beagle* lay anchored at Port Famine (Puerto del Hambre), on the Strait of Magellan's north shore. And from Darwin's perspective, the place where Captain Pringle Stokes shot himself in 1828 remained as dismal as it seemed during their previous visit there, five months earlier.* "I never saw a more cheer-less prospect," he wrote. "The dusky woods, pie-bald with snow, were only indistinctly to be seen through an atmosphere composed of two thirds rain & one of fog."

A week earlier, on May 23, the *Beagle*, encountering the *Adventure*, had arranged to meet the auxiliary ship at Port Famine. Thus, while awaiting the *Adventure*'s arrival at that forlorn spot, FitzRoy, making the best of the

---

* Stokes's grave remains there today.

delay, ordered the crew to gather wood in local forests to replenish their supply of fuel for the ship's galley stove. Not incidentally, during the coming days, the Englishmen abandoned any pretense of concord with the local Natives. On that single day, Darwin wrote, "The Fuegians twice came & plagued us. . . . As there were many instruments, clothes &c & men on shore, the Captain thought it necessary to frighten them away."

Occasional English musket fire, albeit out of range of the Natives, was promptly answered. "As the shot splashed up the water, they picked up stones in return & threw them towards the ship which was then about a mile & a half off," Darwin recalled. "Every time a musket was pointed towards them, they in return pointed an arrow. I feel sure they would not have moved till more than one had been wounded. This being the case we retreated."

On June 8, the *Beagle* weighed anchor from Port Famine. Its course now set for Pacific waters, the survey ship soon reunited with the *Adventure*—the latter, recalled Darwin, "after having examined the East side of this part of the [Magellan] Strait."

FitzRoy planned to bypass the Magellan Strait's western section by leaving that passage and slipping south through the Magdalena Channel into open sea. The following day, having left the Magellan Strait and entered the Magdalena Channel, the *Beagle*'s shipmates, downcast after days of dreary weather, found their spirits lifted by a welcome sight. "We were delighted in the morning by seeing the veil of mist gradually rise from & display Sarmiento."

Rising from the Magdalena Channel's eastern shore, Monte Sarmiento (7,369 feet) had been named, for sixteenth-century Spanish explorer Pedro Sarmiento de Gamboa, by Captain Phillip Parker King. And though clouds often obscured its pyramidal summit, the *Beagle*'s men had glimpsed the celebrated mountain on earlier occasions. But on this passage, Darwin recalled, a particularly splendid view greeted the two ships' men. "I cannot describe the pleasure of viewing these enormous, still, & hence sublime masses of snow which never melt & seem doomed to last as long as this world holds together."

With the next day's sunrise, June 10, both ships reached open waters, both still west-bound but bending to a northwesterly course up Chile's southern coast. But though finally in Pacific waters, Darwin was far from joyous. "The Western coast generally consists of low, rounded, quite barren hills of Granite," he noted. "Outside the main islands, there are numberless rocks & breakers on which the long swell of the open Pacific incessantly rages. . . . The sight of such a coast is enough to make a landsman dream for a week about death, peril, & shipwreck."

Two weeks later, on June 27, deepening Darwin's melancholy, George Rowlett, the *Beagle*'s purser, breathed his last. Thirty-eight years old, Rowlett had served aboard the *Adventure* during the *Beagle*'s first expedition; and on the current expedition, he had been the *Beagle*'s oldest officer. Moreover, Darwin noted, Rowlett had been "an old friend to many in this ship; by whom & everyone else he was warmly respected." Poignantly, "He had been for some time gradually sinking under a complication of diseases; the fatal termination of which were only a little hastened by the bad weather of the Southern countries."

On June 28, the day after Rowlett's death, FitzRoy read a funeral service on the *Beagle*'s quarterdeck, after which the decedent's body was lowered into the Pacific. "It is, noted Darwin, "an awful & solemn sound, that splash of the waters over the body of an old ship-mate."

Hours later, on the evening of the twenty-eighth, the *Beagle* anchored in the port of San Carlos de Chiloé, Chile. The port (today's Ancud) on the island of Chiloé was then the capital of the Chilean archipelago of the same name. The following morning, as most of the *Beagle*'s men, weary of shipboard confinement, joyfully spilled ashore, townspeople in boats rowed alongside the anchored ship for a closer look.

Darwin, for his part, going ashore that day and leaving San Carlos, soon found himself following a winding creek into Chiloe's forested interior. A day earlier, as he gazed from the *Beagle*'s deck, the island, except for occasionally spotted human dwellings, had seemed grimly familiar. "Seen from a considerable distance the country bears a very close resemblance to T. del Fuego. The country is hilly & entirely clothed in thick wood, excepting a few scattered green patches which have been cleared near to the Cottages."

But now, following the creek into the island's lushly forested interior, a more inviting tableau beckoned. "The high thatched roofs of the cottages with the little railed paddocks of grass surrounded by lofty evergreens, reminded me of some drawings of the houses in the S. Sea Islands." Moreover, "The woods are incomparably more beautiful than those of T. del Fuego. Instead of the dusky uniformity of that country we have the variety of Tropical scenery; excepting in Brazil I have never seen such an abundance of elegant forms." To his chagrin, however, as Darwin observed days later, the island warranted another superlative: "I do not suppose any part of the world is so rainy as the Island of Chiloe."

Two days after the *Beagle*'s arrival at San Carlos, the *Adventure*, on June 29, still commanded by John Wickham, had joined the *Beagle* at San Carlos de Chiloé. "Her main-boom," FitzRoy observed, had "broken in a heavy squall on the 27th, in consequence of which she got to leeward." After a month at San Carlos reprovisioning the two ships, Captain FitzRoy, on July 13, ordered both to sail north, for Chile's larger, mainland port of Valparaiso.

Ten days and six-hundred northerly miles later, on the evening of July 23, the *Beagle* and the *Adventure* arrived at Valparaiso. And, by Darwin's account, the next daybreak revealed a city, the first he had visited in six months, worthy of its name ("valley of paradise"): "After Chiloe & T. del Fuego we felt the climate quite delicious; the sky so clear & blue, the air so dry & the sun so bright, that all nature seemed sparkling with life."

There were also flowers abloom in brilliant hues, scented bushes, the Pacific Ocean—and, to the east, verdant foothills and, beyond them, the glorious Andes. And, at each day's end, sunsets bathed both the foothills and the Andes in shimmering, golden light.

Valparaiso was South America's largest Pacific port. The city itself consisted of a single winding street facing the bay, recalled Darwin,

"on the very foot of [a] range of hills, which are 1600 feet high, &
tolerably steep."

> The surface is worn into numberless little ravines, which
> exposes a singularly bright red soil between patches of light
> green grass & low shrubs. It is perhaps for this reason &
> the low white-washed houses with tile roofs, that the view
> reminded me of Teneriffe & others of Madeira.

Days later, as Darwin settled into the city of 25,000 souls, it brought
to mind, in ways welcome and unwelcome, two other places he had
known. "Valparaiso is [more] a sort of London or Paris, [compared] to
any place we have been to," he wrote to Catherine Darwin. "It is most
disagreeable to be obliged to shave & dress decently."

For the coming months, as seasonal storms roiled the Pacific, FitzRoy,
using Valparaiso as his sanctuary, intended to have the *Beagle* and the
Adventure refitted—both having been mangled by Tierra del Fuego's
punishments. In the meantime, Darwin, recalling his Botafogo cottage's
pleasures, found lodgings ashore with merchant Richard Henry Corfield,
a friend from Shrewsbury School. Corfield, to whose home Darwin
moved on August 2, numbered among four hundred British subjects
who, during the early 1820s, lived in Valparaiso.

Corfield, Darwin wrote, went to "the most obliging pains to render
me all assistance in my pursuits." His house sat in the Almendral, a
suburb set on what Darwin, invoking Lyellian perspective, described as
a "small sand-plain" that until "very recently has been a sea-beach." The
house, "very pleasant" by Darwin's lights, was,

> one story high, with all the rooms opening into a quadrangle,
> there is a small garden attached to it, which receives a small
> stream of water 6 hours in the week. Another gentleman lives
> with Mr Corfield; the expences of the house, table, wine,
> 2 men servants, 3 or 4 horses, is about 400 pounds sterling per-
> annum. I should think this same establishment in England
> would at least cost double this sum.

By August 5, his third day at *casa* Cornfield, Darwin was enjoying long walks in the area. Soon venturing into the surrounding countryside, he delighted in its abundance of species of colorful flowers and aromatic bushes, all the while noting its relative paucity of insects, birds, and quadrupeds. As he ascended to higher elevations, so too did his Lyellian speculations: "I have already found beds of recent shells, yet retaining their colors at an elevation of 1300 feet; & beneath this level the country is strewed with them. It seems not a very improbable conjecture that the want of animals may be owing to none having been created since this country was raised from the sea."

On August 14, accompanied by Syms Covington, both on horseback, Darwin set off on his first outing through Chile's Central Valley to the country's inland capital of Santiago. Stopping at a hacienda, they acquired fresh horses and a guide (a gaucho or, to use the Chilean term, a *huaso**) named Mariano Gonzalez, destined to play a sustained role in Darwin's Chilean travels.

The next day, savoring the lush valley, Darwin found the country "exceedingly pleasant, just what I fancy Poets mean by Pastoral." He particularly adored its "little square gardens . . . crowded with orange & olive trees & every sort of vegetable." Moreover, "on each side huge bare mountains arise & this contrast renders the patch-work valley the more pleasing."

The following day, the sixteenth, succumbing to the lure that celebrated mountains held for Darwin, the three began climbing Cerro la Campana. Rising from the Coast Range (*Cordillera de la Costa*) that parallels central Chile's shoreline, the mountain soared to 6,170 feet and took two days to ascend. "The paths were very bad, but both the geology & scenery amply r[e]paid the trouble." The mountain's peak particularly rewarded their exertions:

---

* "The [H]uassos of Chili, which correspond to the Gauchos of the Pampas, are however a very different set of beings. Chili is the more civilized of the two countries; & the inhabitants in consequence have lost much individual character. Gradations in rank are much more strongly marked; the Huasso does not by any means consider every man his equal."—Charles Darwin, *Beagle* diary, Aug. 17, 1834.

We spent the whole day on the summit, & I never enjoyed one more throughily. Chili & its boundaries the Andes & the Pacifick were seen as in a Map. The pleasure from the scenery, in itself beautiful was heightened by the many reflections which arose from the mere view of the grand range, its lesser parallel ones and of the broard valley . . . which directly cuts these in two.

The coming days found Darwin besotted with Lyellian conjectures. Two years earlier, he had imagined soaring in a balloon over Brazil's Corcovado Mountain. In a similarly expansive spirit, he now launched himself in lofty theories concerning the origins of the Andes, the world's longest mountain range: "Who can avoid admiring the wonderful force which has upheaved these mountains, & even more so the countless ages which it must have required to have broken through, removed & levelled whole masses of them?"

"I skirt sierras, my palms cover continents / I am afoot with my vision," poet Walt Whitman, decades later, soared in visionary reverie. In a similarly dizzying leap, Darwin envisioning the Andes' origins, skirted the plains to that range's east and indeed the *entire* South American continent. All three, he theorized, in stages, had been pushed upward, out of the sea, by forces deep in the earth. To Henslow, he soon admitted his speculations transcended established geological knowledge. Except for the few volumes devoted to geology aboard the *Beagle*, he noted, he had no access to books that might otherwise constrain his speculative leaps. "In consequence I draw my own conclusions, & most gloriously ridiculous ones they are, I sometimes fancy I shall persuade myself there are no such things as mountains."

For the budding geologist, Chile's mountains and valleys, particularly the former, offered a sumptuous feast. "I throughily enjoyed rambling about, hammer in hand, the bases of these great giants, as independently as I would the mountains in Wales," he wrote to Caroline Darwin. Over the coming days, Darwin, Covington, and Gonzalez, after riding through the Quillota Pass, visited numerous farms and mines. Throughout those days, Darwin found excavations left by entrepreneurs, successful and otherwise, who had sought wealth in the earth's depths. Their diggings pocked the country like holes in Swiss cheese: "The rage for mining has left scarcely a spot in Chili unexamined, even to the regions of eternal snow." Or as Milton had lamented, such men had "Rifled the bowels of their mother Earth / For treasures better hid."

Near Cerro la Campana's summit, for instance, Darwin had inspected an empty pit where a prospector had hoped to find gold. Days later, he visited a copper mine overseen by Humphrey Bunster, an émigré from Cornwall, England. Having grown up during England's Industrial Revolution's early years, Darwin was appalled by the miner's "shrewd but ignorant" methods. In his mine and others in the region, the Cornishman explained, laborers removed water from them by hauling it up mineshafts to the surface, in skins carried on their backs.

Agricultural conditions likewise appalled Darwin. "Poverty is very common with all the labouring classes." Unmindful of or failing to acknowledge the labor practices and land tutelage system that had produced much of his own family's wealth, he condemned Chile's exploitation of workers: "This must be chiefly owing to the miserable feudal-like system by which the land is tilled," he inveighed.

> The land-owner gives so much land to a man, which he may cultivate & build on, & in return has his services (or a proxy) for every day for his life gratis. Till a father has a grown up son to pay his rent by his labor, of course there is no one to take care of the patch of ground. Hence poverty is very common with all the labouring classes.

On August 27, the party reached Santiago. There, joined by his Valparaiso housemate Richard Corfield, Darwin enjoyed a week "comfortably established at an English Hotel." Afterwards, the travelers spent another several weeks wandering the Chilean countryside that lay between Santiago and Valparaiso—eventually, on October 27, returning to Valparaiso. But as those final miles slipped away, little did Darwin know that—similar to those forces deep in the planet that, by his reckoning, had "upheaved" the Andes—so too were unseen forces about to up-end his personal world.

27

"STRANGE PROCEEDINGS
ABOARD THE *BEAGLE*"

During the final days of his return trip to Valparaiso, a razor-sharp stomach pain ambushed Darwin, an agony soon compounded by fever. When the malady first struck days earlier, he had attributed it to some "Chichi a very weak, sour new made wine" consumed in mid-September while visiting a gold-mine near central Chile's town of Rancagua. Afterward, he remained there with a "Mr Nixon, an American gentleman," the mine's operator, for two days until the discomfort lifted.

Assuming his troubles over, Darwin had resumed his journey's final stretch. But whatever the ailment's origins, he collapsed on September 27, 1834, soon after reaching the home of his Valparaiso host Richard Corfield.

The *Beagle*'s assistant surgeon Benjamin Bynoe, summoned to the house, administered calomel (mercurous chloride) to break the fever. Initially, the medicine seemed "to put me right again." But enfeebled, Darwin remained bedridden for four weeks, into October's waning days. "It was a grievous loss of time, as I had hoped to have collected many animals." A milestone, the episode marked the only serious illness ever yet suffered by the now twenty-five-year-old young man.

Darwin and Bynoe eventually abandoned their speculation that tainted wine had caused Darwin's illness. Six months later, however, without specifying when, he recalled having been bitten on an earlier occasion by a Benchuca (*Vinchuca* in Spanish) bug—*Triatoma infestans*, an insect that still bedevils South America. The insect's feces, we now know, carries Chagas's disease, a tropical parasitical malady discovered in the early twentieth century whose symptoms comport with Darwin's account of his illness in Chile. Whatever his ailment's origins, and many experts now believe it was Chagas's disease, its symptoms, or those like them, would plague him for the rest of his life.*

While bedridden in autumn 1834, Darwin indulged his growing home-sickness. Although missing Shrewsbury, there remained places in South America that he longed to visit, particularly geological destinations. And over those weeks—reviving an idea he had broached to Henslow in June 1833—he refined his "scheme": Over the coming summer, after resigning from the *Beagle*, he would, as he explained to Catherine Darwin, "examine the Cordilleras of Chili . . . & in the winter go from Port to Port on the coast of Peru to Lima returning this time next year [in 1835] to Valparaiso." From there, he would "cross the Cordilleras to B. Ayres & take [a] ship to England."

But Darwin soon abandoned thoughts of leaving the expedition, if indeed those contemplations were ever anything more than the fever-stoked musings of a young man a long way from home. Moreover, he was soon touched to learn that, in deference to the *Beagle*'s naturalist, FitzRoy had postponed the ship's scheduled November 10 departure from Valparaiso.

Also on Darwin's mind during those days were reports reaching him of "some strange proceedings on board the Beagle." Actually, the reports concerning FitzRoy originated more from ashore than from the ship. The captain, after all, had, by then, found lodgings in the city. Recalled FitzRoy:

---

* In *Journal and Remarks*, Darwin, typifying the reticence that often elides references in that work to personal matters, encapsulates his illness and recovery in a single sentence whose action commences on September 19, 1834: "During the day I felt very unwell, and from that time till the end of October did not recover."

As I proposed to remain at Valparaiso during the winter months, Messrs. Stokes, King, Usborne, and myself, whose occupation would be sedentary and would require room, as well as more light and quiet than we could always have on board, took up our quarters on shore; while those on board attended to the refit and provisioning of our vessels.

The "strange proceedings" that worried Darwin issued from troubles afflicting FitzRoy that fall of 1834—most of which, truth be known, arose from his own decisions. Using his own funds, FitzRoy, in March 1833, had purchased the *Unicorn* (later renamed the *Adventure*), the schooner he deemed necessary to complete the expedition's tasks. Likewise, in the months ahead, once again using his own funds, he had paid to refit and reprovision that ship, and to recruit twenty additional seamen for its complement. All along, FitzRoy assumed, the Admiralty would eventually reimburse his expenditures.

In late 1834, however, a letter reached him that dashed those expectations. In his *Narrative*, FitzRoy recalled his devastation upon learning of the Admirality's denial of the reimbursements: "I was made to feel and endure a bitter disappointment; the mortification it caused preyed deeply." Moreover, "I saw that all my cherished hopes of examining many groups of islands in the Pacific, besides making a complete survey of the Chilian and Peruvian shores, must utterly fail." Sadly, over the coming days—though not a member of the *Adventure*'s crew but, in a related consequence, numbering among those discharged from the *Beagle* for "want of room"—was artist Conrad Martens.

In his *Narrative*, FitzRoy made no effort to understate the hurt caused by the Admiralty's rebuke. Even so, his account left much unsaid. According to Darwin, FitzRoy, devastated by the Admiralty's letter and, over those weeks, ill-tempered, depressed, and emotionally spent, convinced himself that the *Beagle* was falling short of its objectives. Notably, he believed, the ship had failed to adequately survey Tierra del Fuego.

Accordingly, FitzRoy resolved, the ship in the coming months *must* return to those waters. To compensate for the extra sailing time expended and avoid additional costs for the Admiralty, the *Beagle* would forgo its planned circumnavigation—the voyage's remaining leg, through the Pacific and Indian oceans. Instead, backtracking, they would return to England via the Atlantic, the most direct route.

In October, a dejected Darwin, resigned to returning to the bottom of the world, poured out his disappointments to Caroline Darwin. "I suspect we shall pay T del Fuego another visit," he lamented. "But of this good Lord deliver us: it is kept very secret, lest the men should desert; every one so hates the confounded country. Our voyage sounded much more delightful in the instructions, than it really is." Instead of a global circumnavigation, "in fact it is a survey of S. America."

FitzRoy's revised plans, soon circulated aboard the *Beagle*, sparked the shipboard rancor Darwin predicted. The captain, in turn, increasingly dejected, announced his resignation from the ship, turning over his captaincy to John Wickham. Darwin, meanwhile, increasingly feared that, like Captain Stokes, FitzRoy might take his own life. To Catherine Darwin, Charles described the captain's state of mind and what he viewed as his ill-treatment by Britain's Whig government:

> The cold manner the Admiralty (solely I believe because he is a Tory) have treated him, & a thousand other &c &c has made him very thin & unwell. This was accompanied by a morbid depression of spirits, & a loss of all decision & resolution The Captain was afraid that his mind was becoming deranged (being aware of his heredetary predisposition).

By early November, FitzRoy, to the crew's relief, had rescinded his resignation, an act never actually communicated to the Admiralty. Moreover, eventually convinced by the ship's officers that the *Beagle* was accomplishing its assigned tasks, FitzRoy canceled the return to Tierra del Fuego and reinstituted the global circumnavigation. Instead of returning to Tierra del Fuego, the *Beagle* would conduct a thorough survey of South America's Pacific coast, beginning with the Chiloé Archipelago.

Before leaving Valparaiso for Chiloé, however, FitzRoy and Darwin fell into one of their rare quarrels—this time, as Darwin recalled, over his alleged boorishness.

Poor FitzRoy was sadly overworked and in very low spirits; he complained bitterly to me that he must give a great party to all the inhabitants of the place. I remonstrated and said I could see no such necessity on his part under the circumstances. He then burst out into a fury, declaring that I was the sort of man who would receive any favours and make no return. I got up and left the cabin without saying a word.

When the argument occurred, Darwin was still living at Richard Corfield's house. But days later, when, before sailing, he returned to his shipboard quarters, he was "received by the Captain as cordially as ever, for the storm had by this time quite blown over." In Darwin's telling of the incident in his *Autobiography*, however, he gave John Wickham the last word: "The first Lieutenant, however, said to me, 'Confound you, philosopher, I wish you would not quarrel with the Skipper; the day you left the ship I was dead-tired (the ship was refitting) and he kept me walking the deck till midnight abusing you all the time.'"

On November 10, the *Beagle*, sailing alone but now without its former auxiliary ship, weighed anchor from Valparaiso, again bound for the Chiloé Archipelago.

28

"THE GREATEST PHENOMENA
TO WHICH THIS WORLD IS SUBJECT"

"A Rock, A River, A Tree
Hosts to species long since departed,
Marked the mastodon,
The dinosaur, who left dried tokens
Of their sojourn here
On our planet floor,
Any broad alarm of their hastening doom
Is lost in the gloom of dust and ages."
　　　　　　—Maya Angelou, "On the Pulse of Morning"

On November 21, 1834, HMS *Beagle* sailed into the harbor of San Carlos, capital of the Chiloé Archipelago, on the island of Chiloé. Over the coming weeks, Captain FitzRoy, determined to thoroughly survey Chile's southern coast, threw himself, the *Beagle*, and parties he dispatched in open boats, into the labors of accomplishing that task.

The elongated islands belonged to a largely submerged coastal range stretching along Chile's southern coast. And, from the main island of Chiloé at the chain's northern end, to Guafo Island at its southern extremity, the *Beagle*'s men spent the next six weeks surveying the archipelago's coast and harbors.

For Darwin, recovered from illness and freshly energized by the Chiloé survey, the *Beagle*'s return to the islands commenced a richly productive period. During those weeks, he traveled about the archipelago aboard both the *Beagle* and its open boats. But, not infrequently, he also, often on horseback, struck out on his own, gathering specimens from the shorelines and interiors of the chain's myriad islands.

Not until 1826, eight years after the rest of Chile won its independence, had the Chiloé Archipelago become part of the Chilean Republic. Thus, when the *Beagle*, in 1834, visited the islands, Spanish governance there lingered as a fresh memory. To Darwin, it seemed that many islanders—particularly Natives—were already weary of Santiago's rule and a growing presence of white settlers. Some would have even welcomed a return of the old regime. "In several places, the inhabitants were much astonished at the appearance of the English vessels [the *Beagle* and its open boats] "& hoped & believed it was the forerunners of a Spanish fleet coming to recover the Island from the patriot Government of Chili."

Similarly, Darwin recalled a January 25 exchange on Chiloé Island:

> We soon ingratiated ourselves by presents of cigars & matte: a lump of white sugar was divided between all present & tasted with the greatest curiosity. The Indians ended all their complaints by saying "& it is only because we are poor Indians & know nothing, but it was not so when we had a King" I really think a boats crew with the Spanish flag might take the island of Chiloe.

Predicaments familiar from books, fictional and historical, also animated Darwin's thoughts. No evidence has come to light that Darwin, in 1834, had read Daniel Defoe's 1719 novel *The Life and Strange Surprising Adventures of Robinson Crusoe*. But, based on references he made to Crusoe during the *Beagle* voyage, he was, at the least, aware of that celebrated book. Likewise, he was certainly aware of the novel's inspiration—Alexander Selkirk, a Scottish privateer and Royal Navy officer who was marooned for four years on an otherwise uninhabited Chilean island.

Bringing both tales closer to mind, FitzRoy no doubt told Darwin of his visit—in February 1830, during his first South American survey expedition—to the island where Selkirk had been marooned.* No doubt, too, both men's thoughts turned toward Selkirk and Crusoe when the *Beagle*'s men, in December 1834, anchored in a remote Chiloé harbor, spotted a man ashore waving a shirt.

A boat sent from the *Beagle* soon returned with two men. Both belonged to what had been a group of six sailors, all former crewmen of the *Frances Henrietta*, a whaler out of New Bedford, Massachusetts. The sailors said they had fled their ship due to "bad treatment." Carrying a week's worth of provisions and seventy miles from the nearest land, the two had escaped in one of their ship's open boats. As Darwin recounted,

> The boat on their first landing had been dashed into pieces. This happened 15 months ago; since which time the poor wretches have been wandering up & down the coast, without knowing which way to go or where they were (they knew nothing of Chiloe). . . . They were now all together & the boat subsequently brought off three more. One man had fallen from a cliff & perished. I never saw such anxiety as was pictured in the mens faces to get into the boat. Before she landed, they were nearly jumping into the water. They were in good condition, having plenty of seals-flesh which together with shell-fish had entirely supported them.

While presumably the *Beagle* provided the castaways passage to a hospitable berth, neither Darwin nor FitzRoy disclosed the tale's denouement.

Darwin's diary entries also remind us that his and the lives of the *Beagle*'s other men included social interactions with members of the local

---

* The specific island, in Chile's Juan Fernández archipelago, on which Selkirk was marooned, formerly called *Más a Tierra* ("closer to land"), today bears the name Robinson Crusoe Island.

populations in the places through which they passed. And, that those relations likely included sexual interactions—intimacies unlikely to be explicitly recorded in writings being shared with Darwin's sisters or, later, a public audience. In Valdivia harbor, in late February 1825, for instance, Darwin records "an unusual degree of gaiety on board."

> The Intendente paid us a visit one day & brought a whole boat full of ladies: bad weather compelled them to stay all night, a sore plague both to us & them. They in return gave a ball, which was attended by nearly all on board. Those who went returned exceedingly well pleased with the people of Valdivia. The Signoritas are pronounced very charming; & what is still more surprising, they have not forgotten how to blush, an art which is at present quite unknown in Chiloe.

Natural history, however, particularly geology, remained the focus of Darwin's attentions. The Chiloé survey completed, the *Beagle*, on February 3, weighed anchors from San Carlos, bound for southern Chile's port of Valdivia. During the *Beagle*'s February 8–21 anchorage there, Darwin made extended excursions into the surrounding area.

Beyond collecting opportunities accorded by the Chiloé Archipelago and Valdivia, both places also allowed Darwin to observe natural phenomena about which he had read but never witnessed. Indeed, in a single day, November 26, while traveling south down Chiloé Island's east coast, for the first time in his life, he saw, albeit from afar, three steam-billowing volcanoes,

> The Volcano of Osorno was spouting out volumes of smokes; this most beautiful mountain, formed like a perfect cone & white with snow, stands out in front of the Cordillera. Another great Volcano, with a saddle shaped summit, also emitted from its immense crater little jets of steam or white smoke. Subsequently we saw the lofty peaked Corcobado, well

deserving the name of "el famoso Corcovado."* Thus we saw at one point of view three great active Volcanoes, each of which had an elevation of about seven thousand feet.

The following January 19 (1835), he witnessed, from the *Beagle*'s deck, a full-blown Osorno eruption, "a very magnificent sight." Peering into a spyglass, he was dazzled by a "great red glare of light, dark objects in a constant succession . . . thrown up" and thence cascading down the volcano's slopes.

Similarly eye-opening, six weeks earlier, on December 2, on the Chiloé Archipelago's Lemuy Island, Darwin had seen his first petrified forest: Among its treasures, "I found in the yellow sandstone a great trunk (structure beautifully clear) throwing off branches: main stem much thicker than my body & standing out from weathering 2 feet."

On February 20, 1835, fatigued while hiking with an unnamed "servant" (likely Covington) outside of Valdivia, Darwin decided to lie down on the forest's floor. A violent shaking, however, soon interrupted his rest. At Richard Corfield's house in Valparaiso, the naturalist had experienced a similar tremor. But this was more severe.

> It came on suddenly & lasted two minutes (but appeared much longer). The rocking was most sensible; the undulation appeared both to me & my servant to travel from due East. There was no difficulty in standing upright; but the motion made me giddy. I can compare it to skating on very thin ice or to the motion of a ship in a little cross ripple.

But, Darwin recalled, the tremor's force notwithstanding, he "saw no consequence from it." And later that day when the two men returned to Valdivia, they found a city with most of its buildings intact but with the earthquake's violence registered in its residents' faces.

---

* Not to be confused with the Brazilian mountain of the same name.

All the houses being built of wood, none actually fell & but few were injured. Every one expected to see the Church a heap of ruins. The houses were shaken violently & creaked much, the nails being partially drawn. I feel sure it is these accompaniments & the horror pictured in the faces of all the inhabitants, which communicates the dread that every one feels who has thus seen as well as felt an earthquake.

On February 22, sailing north, the *Beagle* departed Valdivia, bound for central Chile's port of Concepción. On March 4, as the ship neared its destination, FitzRoy landed Darwin on Quiriquina Island, close to Concepción. There, from a resident, he learned of local destruction from the February 20 temblor—"that not a house in Concepcion or Talcahuano (the port) was standing, that seventy villages were destroyed, & that a great wave had almost washed away the ruins of Talcuhano."

Later that day, while exploring Quiriquina's shoreline, he noticed that the earthquake had affected more than houses and the built environment: rocks and marine shellfish attached to them—including "a slab six feet by three square & about two thick"—"had been cast high up on the beach." Indeed, "the Island . . . itself showed the effects of the Earthquake, as plainly as the beach did that of the consequent great wave."

Marking a personal intellectual milestone over those days, Darwin, historian Peter J. Bowler observed, had witnessed firsthand, evidence of phenomena that a thinker he greatly admired, breaking with that day's conventional wisdom, had long recognized: "Obviously Lyell was right: earthquakes not only shook the land, but they also raised or lowered it to a significant degree. Over a period of time a series of such movements would produce large-scale effects, such as the building of a mountain range."

The *Beagle* soon sailed on to Concepción, also devastated by the earthquake. There, Darwin spent March 5 and 6 inspecting the city's ruins.

To any person who had formerly known them it must be still more so; for the ruins are so confused & mingled & the scene has so little the air of an habitable place that it is difficult to understand how great the damage has been. Many compared the ruins to those of Ephesus or the drawings of Palmyra & other [Middle] Eastern towns; certainly there is the same impossibility of imagining their former appearance & condition. In Concepcion each house or row of houses stood by itself a heap or line of ruins.

⁘

The frontispiece of volume I of Charles Lyell's *Principles of Geology* had depicted three ancient columns, the ruins of a Roman temple in the harbor of Naples, Italy. Bands of discoloration, from periods of submergence in, and reemergence from, the surrounding waters, stain the columns. The engraving, implicitly rebuking "Mosaic geology," attested to Lyell's conviction that landforms are created not suddenly in the distant past, but incrementally, over time, by processes still continuing, still observable.

For three years, Darwin, by then twenty-six, had read Lyell. Enthralled by his ideas, from Jago to the Andes, he had examined fossils, other rocks, and geological formations that he inferred as evidence of processes described by the geologist. And so it was even more astounding to witness firsthand, in all their sublime terror, acts of violence associated with those processes:

> It is a bitter & humiliating thing to see works which have cost men so much time & labour overthrown in one minute; yet compassion for the inhabitants is almost instantly forgotten by the interest excited in finding that state of things produced at a moment of time which one is accustomed to attribute to a succession of ages. To my mind since leaving England we have scarcely beheld any one other sight so deeply interesting. The Earthquake & Volcano are parts of one of the greatest phenomena to which this world is subject.

⁘

By March 7, 1835, his geological worldview freshly shaken, Charles Darwin, back aboard the *Beagle*, was again bound for Valparaiso.

FIGURES 1 AND 2: We have scores of images of the older Charles Darwin (1809–82), many of them photographs, but only two widely-known portraits, neither photographs, of him before age thirty. The earliest (left), a chalk portrait drawn at age six, depicts him posed with his younger sister, Emily Catherine (1810–66). The second (below) a watercolor and chalk portrait captures the then still cherubic-looking young man in his late twenties.

FIGURE 3: The Mount, Charles Darwin's childhood home, in Shropshire, England's market-town of Shrewsbury, where he was born on February 12, 1809, the same day on which Abraham Lincoln also first saw the light of day.

FIGURE 4: Charles Darwin's father Robert Waring Darwin (1766–1848), a prominent physician and investor, depicted above in his early forties. He was a son of author Erasmus Darwin and his first wife Mary Howard.

Figure 5 (ABOVE LEFT): Susannah "Sukey" Wedgwood Darwin (1765–1817), Charles Darwin's mother, died when he was eight years old, leaving him with vague memories of her. Susannah was one of eight of children born to pottery industrialist Josiah and his wife Sarah—*née* Wedgwood—a third cousin. She married Robert Darwin in 1796, and the couple eventually had six children, of whom Charles was the fifth born. Figure 6 (ABOVE RIGHT): Family patriarch, physician and author Erasmus Darwin (1731–1802) ranked as a prominent intellectual in eighteenth-century England, whose views on politics and religion often sparked controversy. A free-thinker, Erasmus was a twice-married libertine who fathered at least fourteen children, several with unmarried women. He died before Charles was born.

Figure 7 (RIGHT): Industrialist, philanthropist and family patriarch Josiah Wedgwood (1730–95) founded the Wedgwood Company. The linkage of the Darwin and Wedgwood families originated in a personal friendship that grew into a business relationship between Josiah Wedgwood Sr. and author Erasmus Darwin. The Wedgwood firm pioneered modern manufacturing and marketing techniques and helped spark Britain's industrial revolution.

FIGURE 8: Complying with his father's wishes Charles, in fall 1825, enrolled at the University of Edinburgh to study medicine. By, late 1827, however, his squeamishness at the sight of blood had led him to withdraw from the school.

FIGURE 9: The University of Cambridge's Christ College, where Charles was a student from January 1828 until June 1831. He eventually earned a Bachelor of Arts degree—one of the sort taken by aspirants to the Church of England's priesthood.

FIGURE 10: A cartoon by Darwin's college friend Albert Way whimsically caricatures the future naturalist's obsession with collecting beetles, a fad that swept England during his time at Cambridge. It was beetling that, in 1829, first landed Charles Darwin's name in a scientific publication.

FIGURE 11: John Steven Henslow (1796–1861). A botanist, geologist, and Anglican minister, the Cambridge professor became Darwin's first mentor during the naturalist's student days. In August 1831, Henslow helped secure the invitation that placed Darwin aboard the *Beagle*.

FIGURE 12: Geologist and Cambridge Adam Sedgwick (1785–1873). In August 1831, in a formative experience for then twenty-two year old Darwin, he accompanied the forty-six year old Sedgwick on a surveying field-trip in the Welsh mountains.

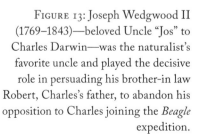

FIGURE 13: Joseph Wedgwood II (1769–1843)—beloved Uncle "Jos" to Charles Darwin—was the naturalist's favorite uncle and played the decisive role in persuading his brother-in law Robert, Charles's father, to abandon his opposition to Charles joining the *Beagle* expedition.

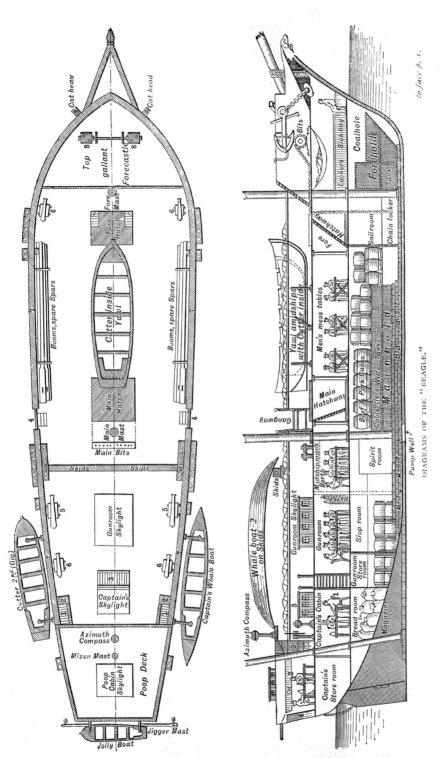

DIAGRAMS OF THE "BEAGLE."

FIGURE 14: Diagram of HMS *Beagle* that first appeared in an 1890 edition of the work now known as *The Voyage of the Beagle*. The diagram is based on drawings by Darwin's friend and shipmate Philip Gidley King (1817–1904).

FIGURE 15: Robert FitzRoy (1805–1865), HMS *Beagle*'s captain, was twenty-six years old—four years older than Darwin—when his ship, in December 1831, departed on its five-year global expedition to survey various coasts and ports around the world.

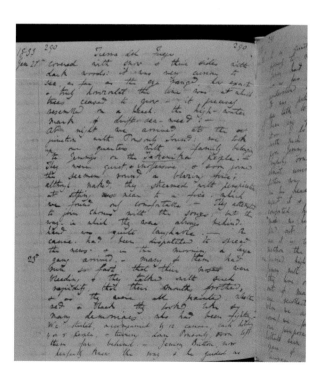

FIGURE 16: In the above January 22, 1833 entry from Darwin's *Beagle* diary, he describes an evening he and other *Beagle* crewmen spent around a fire with a group of Fuegians. In ways that he could not have anticipated, the chronicle would play a major role in establishing his later career as a writer.

FIGURE 17: By February 1832, the *Beagle* was approaching the Brazilian coast. Five days after Charles's twenty-third birthday, on February 17, the ship crossed the Equator. To mark that passage, un-initiated sailors, those new to the crossing, traditionally submit to an unpleasant ritual: costumed "Neptunes" using a gruesome concoction—the *Beagle*'s recipe was tar and paint—shave and wash out the mouths of the hapless novitiates. Accordingly, at nine o'clock that morning, Darwin, with dread, faced the ritual that he had anticipated for the past four months.

Figure 18 (above): "Brazilian rain-forest," an 1819 line-drawing by French artist by Charles Othon Frédéric Jean-Baptiste de Clarac. For Darwin, who was familiar with nature scenes created by Clarac and other artists, his encounters with Brazilian forests often seemed a case of life imitating art. Describing such untamed nature, he wrote in an April 8, 1832 diary entry: "The colours were intense & the prevailing tint a dark blue, the sky & calm waters of the bay vied with each other in splendor. After passing through some cultivated country we entered a Forest, which in the grandeur of all its parts could not be exceeded. As the gleams of sunshine penetrate the entangled mass, I was forcibly reminded of the two French engravings after the drawings of Maurice Rugendas & Le Compte de Cla[r]ac." Figure 19 (below): At the tiny hamlet of Botafogo on the bay of the same name, near Rio de Janerio but now part of that sprawling metropolis, Charles Darwin and the *Beagle*'s artist Augustus Earle spent May and June of 1832 living in a rented cottage.

FIGURE 20 (LEFT): On May 25, 1832, Darwin made the first of two climbs to the top of Rio de Janeiro's famed Corcovado. Long before the 1920s when Rio's famous 98-foot high Christ the Redeemer statue was erected atop the 2,330-foot mountain, the elevation ranked as an internationally famous tourist destination. "We soon gained the peak & beheld that view, which perhaps excepting those in Europe, is the most celebrated in the world." FIGURE 21 (BELOW): An engraving that appeared in 1839, in the four-volume account of the two expeditions involving HMS *Beagle* depicts the three kidnapped Fuegians that the second expedition repatriated to Tierra del Fuego and the tribal woman that the man the crew called Jemmy Button later took for his wife.

FIGURE 22 (LEFT): An 1843 portrait of Argentine general Juan Manuel de Rosas (1793–1877) depicts him amid tributes to his military and political triumphs. A classic Latin American caudillo, Rosas, during Darwin travels in Argentina, arranged safe passage for the naturalist through otherwise dangerous realms. FIGURE 23 (BELOW): "As our boats became visible to the natives, who were eagerly paddling towards the cove from every direction, hoarse shouts arose, and, echoed about by the cliffs, seemed to be a continual cheer. In a very short time there were thirty or forty canoes in our train, each full of natives, each with a column of blue smoke rising from the fire amidships, and almost all the men in them shouting at the full power of their deep sonorous voices."—Captain Robert FitizRoy describing January 23, 1833 approach of HMS *Beagle*'s three whale-boats to the Wulaia settlement, on Navarino Island. Of the three Fuegians aboard the *Beagle*, only Jemmy Button hailed from Wulaia. FitzRoy, however, decided to leave all three there.

Figure 24 (above): "In most of the coves there were wigwams; some of them had been recently inhabited. The wigwam or Fuegian house is in shape like a cock of hay, about 4 feet high & circular; it can only be the work of an hour, being merely formed of a few branches & imperfectly thatched with grass, rushes &c."—Charles Darwin, *Beagle* diary, Tierra del Fuego, December 1832. Figure 25 (below): On December 23, 1833, the *Beagle*, to celebrate the coming holidays, anchored at southern Patagonia's Port Desire (today's Puerto Deseado), six-hundred miles north of Cape Horn. "I thought I had seen some desart looking country near B[ahía] Blanca," Darwin wrote in his diary, "but the land in this neighbourhead so far exceeds it in sterility, that this alone deserves the name of a desart."

FIGURE 26 (ABOVE): In mid-April 1834, upon the *Beagle*' arrival at the mouth of southern Patagonia's Rio Santa Cruz, Captain FitzRoy anchored the ship ashore at high tide. After the tides rolled
out, a team of sailors successfully repaired the ship's damaged cooper-bottom, a process shipboard
artist Conrad Martens memorialized in a drawing later rendered as a detailed engraving. FIGURE 27
(BELOW): On April 18, 1834, having selected twenty-four men, including Darwin, Captain FitzRoy,
deploying the *Beagle*'s three whaleboats, set off from the mouth of southern Patagonia's Rio Santa
Cruz, intending to ascend and explore the river to its Andes headwaters. On May 4, however, as the
river's grade grew increasingly steep, and the surrounding country (pictured below in "Basalt Glen")
grew increasingly desolate, FitzRoy ordered the ascent abandoned. Before turning back, however,
Darwin glimpsed the Andes. "At the furthest point we were about 140 miles from the Atlantic, &
60 from the nearest inlet of the Pacific."

FIGURE 28 (ABOVE): In 1834, while exploring the Andes, Darwin developed lofty theories concerning the origins of the range—the world's longest: "Who can avoid admiring the wonderful force which has upheaved these mountains, & even more so the countless ages which it must have required to have broken through, removed & levelled whole masses of them?" FIGURE 29 (BELOW): On March 30, 1835, at 7,000 feet, at Uspallata Pass in the Andes, Darwin stumbled upon a petrified forest. "I saw the spot where a cluster of fine trees had once waved their branches on the shores of the Atlantic, when that ocean (now driven back 700 miles) approached the base of the Andes." Alas, souvenir-hunters have chipped away all but the bases of most of the petrified trees which enchanted Darwin.

FIGURE 30: Visiting the city of Concepcion, Chile, after the earthquake of February 20, 1835, Darwin was taken aback by the scene: "The ruins are so confused & mingled & the scene has so little the air of an habitable place that it is difficult to understand how great the damage has been. Many compared the ruins to those of Ephesus or the drawings of Palmyra & other [Middle] Eastern towns."—Charles Darwin, March 5, 1835.

FIGURE 31 (LEFT): In fall 1835, HMS *Beagle* spent about five weeks in the Galápagos Islands, a name assumed to be a plural adaption of *galapago*, an old Spanish word for tortoise. While there, Darwin noticed its abundant population of the reptiles. But he later acknowledged that he only learned of the animals' variability from island to island after being told of them by Nicholas Lawson, Ecuador's acting governor for the archipelagos.

FIGURE 32: An early nineteenth-century view of Sydney, capital of the British colony of New South Wales, where the *Beagle* arrived on January 12, 1836. Darwin savored his return to an English-speaking society. By the 29th, however, having also visited the colony's interior, disenchantment had set in: "On the whole I do not like new South Wales: it is without doubt an admirable place to accumulate pounds & shillings; but Heaven forfend that ever I should live [here]."

FIGURE 33 (RIGHT): Emma Wedgwood Darwin (1808–1896) married Charles on January 29, 1839. She was thirty, he was twenty-nine. The couple eventually had ten children, seven of whom survived into adulthood. The well-read, musically-gifted grand-daughter of pottery industrialist Josiah Wedgwood, Emma was also a first cousin of her husband. Theirs was the second generation of Darwin-Wedgwood marriages.

FIGURE 34 AND 35: The Darwin family's Down House, as depicted in a wood-engraving. Soon after their January 1839 wedding, Charles and Emma settled into a house in London at 12 Upper Gower Street that Charles had rented the previous November. Increasingly perturbed by the city's noise and coal-smoke, however, they soon decided they preferred a rural life. Thus, in the summer of 1842, with a loan from his father, he purchased the house fourteen miles southeast of London, near the village of Down (now Downe), in the county of Kent. That September, the Darwins moved into the handsome dwelling they soon called Down House. In the coming decades, the couple commissioned extensive refurbishments and expansions at the property. Eventually, Down House became a working farm that provided much of the family's food. It also housed the 1,500 titles that comprised Charles' personal library (shown below).

FIGURE 36: Charles' second major mentor, Scottish geologist Charles Lyell (1797–1875). Lyell's three-volume *Principles of Geology*, published between 1830 and 1833; dramatically influenced the young naturalist. He avidly read Lyell's works during his *Beagle* travels and, after his return to England, the geologist brought him into Britain's most elite scientific circles.

FIGURE 37: The frontispiece of Charles Lyell's *Principles of Geology* (1830) depicts three ancient columns, the ruins of a Roman temple along the Italian coast, just north of Pazzuoli. Bands of discoloration, from periods of submergence in, and reemergence from, the surrounding waters, stain the columns. The engraving, implicitly rebuking "Mosaic geology," attests to Lyell's conviction that landforms are created not suddenly in the distant past, but incrementally, over time, by processes still continuing, still observable.

FIGURE 38: French naturalist Jean-Baptiste Lamarck (1744–1829) believed that physical changes in individual species, including use of particular organs or limbs, during their lifetime could be inherited by offspring. He numbered among the first intellectuals to apply the term evolution to changes over time in species.

FIGURE 39: English zoologist, botanist, and paleontologist Richard Owen (1804–92) is now best remembered for, in 1842, allegedly coining the term "dinosaur," from the Greek *deinos* for terrible, *sauros* for lizard. But during his long career, he also played the role of both ally and detractor of Charles Darwin. During and after the *Beagle* expedition, Owen, at the request of Darwin's mentor John Henslow identified several important fossils Darwin unearthed in South America.

FIGURE 40: Naturalist Alfred Russel Wallace (1823–1913) then in his early forties, and photographed shortly after his return to England in 1862, following eight years in the Malay archipelago. Based on his research there, Wallace in 1855, had published an article in *Annals and Magazine of Natural History* on the geologic and geographic distribution of fossil and living species. After reading the article, Charles Lyell warned Darwin that Wallace seemed to be working on a theory of species transmutation similar to that on which Darwin was by then writing an article but at a desultory pace—and urged Darwin to complete his article.

FIGURE 41: Typical of popular-culture lampoons of the naturalist during his later years, an 1874 advertisement for a London newspaper depicts him as, and with, an ape. Darwin owned a copy of this particular cartoon.

FIGURE 42: At Down House, Charles Darwin, defying increasingly poor health, eventually pro-duced over twenty published works. In 1866, following a particularly aggravated bout of illness, he re-emerged into public life with a freshly grown beard—the bushy white Old Testament patriarch's beard with which posterity came to associate him. Four years before Charles' death, his son Leonard captured him in this 1878 photograph.

29

ADVENTURES ON THE
ANDES' ATLANTIC COAST

"I am become a zealous disciple of Mr Lyells views, as
known in his admirable book. Geologizing in S. America,
I am tempted to carry parts to a greater extent, even than
he does. Geology is a capital science to begin, as it requires
nothing but a little reading, thinking & hammering."
                    —Charles Darwin to W. D. Fox, August 1835

The replacement of an anchor, lost in February 1835, en route to
Concepción, had prompted Captain FitzRoy's order for the *Beagle's*
return to Valparaiso. After leaving Concepción on March 7, the
ship reached Valparaiso four days later; the following day, the twelfth,
Darwin returned to the home of his friend Richard Corfield.

Adopting elements of the itinerary he pondered when he was considering resigning from the *Beagle*, Darwin, by then, had decided to return
to Chile's mountains, in this case the Andes. Notably, he hoped to get to
Portillo Pass, a storied corridor linking Chile's inland capital of Santiago
to the Argentine town of Mendoza, east of the Andes.

On March 14, he set off for Santiago. There, the next day, he called
on the prominent English-born author, miner, and botanist Alexander
Caldcleugh. Darwin had met Caldcleugh the previous August during his

first visit to Santiago. And now, in the two men's latest encounter, the seasoned South American traveler helped Darwin plan a loop through the Andes and otherwise assisted in final preparations for his trip. Darwin had already rehired Mariano Gonzalez, his guide on his first venture into Chile's high country. He also engaged two muleteers with a team of ten mules. Finally, in Santiago, calling on the Chilean republic's president, José Joaquín Prieto Vial, Darwin obtained a passport to smooth their passage through the country.

Leaving Santiago on March 18, the party spent that day and most of the next crossing the lush Maipo River valley. "Six of the mules were for riding & four for Cargoes; each taking turn[s] about." The Maipo's headwaters lay deep in the Andes and the river's 250-mile course to the Pacific passed south of Santiago.

Darwin reveled in the valley's sun-dappled agricultural bounty, in his mind, an Edenic, vastly expanded, incarnation of the insular botanic world fondly recalled from his family's greenhouse at The Mount: "The numerous cottages are surrounded with Grapes, Apples, Nectarines & Peaches; the boughs of the latter were bending & breaking with the weight of the beautiful ripe fruit." Later that day, the party reached a customs station, where "our boxes were examined." There was, after all, much to inspect: "We carried a good deal of food, in case of being snowed up, as the season was rather late for passing by the Portillo."

The inspection passed quickly, a welcome augury. "The officers were very civil, partly owing to my carrying a strong passport from the President of Chili," Darwin noted. "But I must express my admiration of the politeness of every Chileno. In this instance the contrast is strong with the same class of officers in England." Even so, by his lights, the officers performed a task rendered superfluous by geography. "The frontier of Chili is better guarded by the Cordilleras than by so much sea; the mountains on each side of the few narrow valleys where there are Customhouses, are far too steep & high for any beast of burden to pass over."

The party lodged at a cottage that night. By late afternoon the next day, however, as their increasingly twisting road rose into higher country, human dwellings had disappeared. The Maipo Valley's namesake river, meanwhile, recently wide and cloaked in pastoral pleasures, had become

a "great mountain torrent [rather] than a river": "The fall is very great, &
the water the color of mud; the roar is very like that of Sea, as it rushes
amongst the great rounded fragments. Amidst the din, the noise of the
stones rattling one over the other is most distinctly audible."

By March 21, having left the Andes' foothills, they were approaching
the Continental Divide and its intimidating elevations. "We began our
march early in the day," Darwin wrote. "Untill now our road had been
good & the ascent steady but very gradual; now commenced the steep
zigzag track." As they climbed, "the wind . . . was violent & very cold."

Reaching the ridge's crest, Darwin, looking back over the country
through which they had passed, savored the "glorious" view: "The atmosphere so resplendently clear, the sky an intense blue, the profound valleys." The contrast between the Andes' picturesque snowy heights and
what Darwin read as evidence of their violent origins likewise struck
him: "the wild broken forms, the heaps of ruins piled up during the
lapse of ages, the bright colored rocks." That contrast, "produced a scene
I never could have imagined." Except for a few condors circling the high,
icebound peaks, the mountain-scape before him—the entire "inanimate
mass"—lay barren of plants and animals. "I felt glad I was by myself, it
was like watching a thunderstorm, or hearing in the full Orchestra a
Chorus of the Messiah."

On March 28, the party stopped for a day's rest in the Argentine town
of Mendoza ("From the number of houses it was almost one straggling
village; the whole is celebrated for its fruit."). In a trek abounding in
revelatory pleasures, however, none rivaled the delight Darwin experienced two days later.

At 7,000 feet—west of Mendoza at Uspallata Pass—he stumbled
upon a petrified forest. "It required little geological practice to interpret
the marvellous story, which this scene at once unfolded; though I confess

I was at first so much astonished that I could scarcely believe the plainest evidence of it."*

Later geologists, emboldened successively by theories of continental drift and plate tectonics, would routinely, like chess players pushing chess pieces across a chessboard, postulate the sinking, rising, and colliding of continental landmasses. By contrast, geologists of Darwin's era, Charles Lyell excepted, seldom indulged such expansive speculations.

Even so, Darwin, in 1835, was already presciently developing his own theory concerning the origins of both the Andes and South America. More particularly, after examining rocks and geological formations across the continent, he theorized that the Atlantic Ocean once stretched across what is now Patagonia and the contiguous plains to its north, to the Andes' present eastern flanks. Those flanks, he theorized, once belonged to a low-lying coastal plain. And over time, still active geological forces had lifted those once low-lying plains to higher elevations.

Darwin's inventory of earth-shaping surface forces included volcanoes, earthquakes, and erosional actions. Like that era's other geologists, however, not until the 1840s when Swiss-born American geologist Louis Agassiz published his work, did Darwin—and for that matter, Lyell—recognize the powerful role of glaciers in sculpting the earth's surfaces.**

Nonetheless, the scene that Darwin, on March 30, 1835, beheld at Uspallata Pass did stagger him. An abstraction, after all, is one thing, dramatic

---

*   The scene of Darwin's Uspallata Pass epiphany today lies in Chile's Bosque (Forest) de Darwin en Los Paramillos. Alas, however, souvenir-hunters have chipped away all but the bases of most of the petrified trees which enchanted Darwin. Some specimens from the site, however, can be found in the Cornelio Moyano Natural and Anthropological Science Museum, in Mendoza, Argentina.

** In a tantalizing historical what-if, geologists speculate that, had the *Beagle*'s Rio Santa Cruz exploring party, in May 1834, instead of turning back, continued upstream another few miles, they would have reached the glacier-created Lago Argentino whence Rio Santa Cruz's waters flow. There, many geologists believe, gravel deposited by glaciers and other evidence of glaciation are so compelling that Darwin would have scooped Agassiz by a decade in recognizing the often key role of glaciers in sculpting the earth's landscapes.

physical evidence, quite another: "I saw the spot where a cluster of fine trees had once waved their branches on the shores of the Atlantic, when that ocean (now driven back 700 miles) approached the base of the Andes."

> I saw that they had sprung from a volcanic soil which had been raised above the level of the sea, and that this dry land, with its upright trees, had subsequently been let down to the depths of the ocean. There it was covered by sedimentary matter, and this again by enormous streams of submarine lava—one such mass alone attaining the thickness of a thousand feet; and these deluges of melted stone and aqueous deposits had been five times spread out alternately. The ocean which received such masses must have been deep; but again the subterranean forces exerted their power, and I now beheld the bed of that sea forming a chain of mountains more than seven thousand feet in altitude.

Throughout the nineteenth century, most Indigenous peoples of today's continental United States faced near decimation or else were dispossessed of traditional lands and shunted into increasingly shrinking enclaves west of the Mississippi River. In South America, by contrast, Native peoples—despite persecutions, depredations, and continuing subordination by descendants of the continent's Iberian colonizers—remained, in many instances, active presences in its mainstream daily life.

In North America, after all, Britain's colonial overseers had generally dispatched families to people their overseas empire. By contrast, men—conquistadors, government officials, and missionaries—comprised most of the early Iberian people who came to the New World. And many among the conquistadors and government officials subsequently had relations with Indigenous women (among the latter some willingly, some against their will), unions that resulted in the mestizos who today comprise much of the continent's population.

From readings of, among others, the eighteenth century Spanish explorer and scientist Antonio de Ulloa, Darwin was familiar with the history of the Andes and its storied Inca empire. But seldom do his travel writings record his encounters with ruins left by the Incas or other pre-Columbian cultures. However, in a conspicuous exception to that tendency, he does write of a visit to the ruins of an Inca settlement along the southern flank of the Inca's empire, a monarchy that once dominated the Andes. On April 4, days after stumbling upon the petrified forest, Darwin, while returning to Santiago, passed through the ruins of the Inca settlement of Tambillos. While he had visited other Inca ruins, the Tambillos site seemed "the most perfect" he had seen:

> Small square rooms were there huddled together, but placed in distinct groups. Some of the doorways were yet standing: they were formed by a cross slab of stone, but only raised about three feet high. . . . These houses, when perfect, must have been capable of containing a considerable number of persons. Tradition says, they were used as halting-places for the Incas, when they crossed these mountains.

Indeed, since Darwin's passage through Tambillos, archeologists have excavated three of the Inca staging posts he inspected, as well as remnants of the paved road that, covering over 25,000 miles, once bound together the far-flung Inca empire.

On April 17, Darwin returned to Valparaiso. And by the twenty-third, the *Beagle,* having completed its southern Chile surveys, was passing Valparaiso on its now northerly course. And by prior agreement, it dispatched a boat ashore that day for Darwin. Afterward, Darwin and FitzRoy, conversing aboard the *Beagle,* agreed that the naturalist, now planning a final trek into South America's interior, would meet the ship at northern Chile's Puerto Copiapó, now called Puerto Viejo ("Old Port"), in those days the main entrepot for the nearby mining town of Copiapó.

Interestingly, attesting to the power of repeated rumors, Darwin, while ashore in Valparaiso during those weeks when the *Beagle* was away, heard multiple allegations concerning the English ship's true purposes. The suspicions arose, in part, from FitzRoy's frequent unwillingness to purchase goods from local merchants:

> All the inhabitants were convinced she was a Smuggler, they complained of the entire want of confidence the Captain showed in not coming to any terms; each man thought his neighbour was in [on] the secret. I had even difficulty in unde- ceiving them. By the way, this anecdote about the smuggling shows how little even the upper classes in these countries understand the wide distinction of manners. A person who could possibly mistake Capt. FitzRoy for a smuggler, would never perceive any difference between a Lord Chesterfield & his valet.

On April 27—again traveling with Mariano Gonzalez, this time with four horses and two mules—Darwin embarked for Chile's northern coast. "I set out on a journey to Coquimbo, from thence through Guasco [now called Huasco] to [Puerto] Copiapo, where Capt. FitzRoy offered to call for me. The distance in a straight line is only 420 maritime miles [485 miles], but as I travelled I found the journey a very long one."

Over the coming weeks, the two passed scenes by now familiar to Darwin, including mines, mountains, and lush valleys. On May 17, in the town of Coquimbo, he experienced another earthquake, albeit of moderate force. Three days earlier, not far from Coquimbo, at the port of Herradura, he had a coincidental intersection with the *Beagle*. "All hands were living on shore under tents; the ship undergoing a thorough refit before the long passage of the Pacifick." He spent the night of May 15 aboard the ship; and the next day "hired with Capt. FitzRoy lodgings in the city of Coquimbo, which is distant 11 miles from the Beagles anchorage." Coquimbo was, Darwin added, "like the other towns in the North of Chili, it depends, but in a less degree, for its support on the mines."

Over the next two weeks in Coquimbo, as the captain awaited the *Beagle*'s refitting, Darwin and FitzRoy resided in their shared quarters. And from Coquimbo, during those days, Darwin made brief excursions in the area to examine mines or geological formations.

By June 2, the refitted *Beagle* was scheduled to sail in three days. Darwin and Gonzalez, meanwhile, bound for the port of Huasco to the north and joined by a second hired guide, left Coquimbo. After reaching Huasco, they passed through Carrizal and northern Chile's other coastal towns. En route, the travelers found themselves on increasingly arid landscapes, eventually in the northern extremities of what Darwin correctly recognized as the "real desert of Atacama."

The Atacama, a six-hundred-mile-long strip west of the Andes possessed of a Mars-like topography, ranks as the world's driest nonpolar desert and had long fascinated naturalists: Observed Darwin, "The whole country from the coast to the Cordillera is a desert & uninhabited." On June 3, in the coastal town of Carrizal, the party found "a few cottages, some brackish water & a trace of cultivation"; and "with difficulty . . . purchased a little corn & straw for the Horses."

At noon, on July 5, following four more weeks of northerly travels, the party reached Puerto Copiapó—by Darwin's lights, "a miserable little assemblage of a few houses, situated at the foot of some sterile plains & hills." Even so, on the harbor's beach, he soon found, "large piles of merchandize & the little place had an air of bustle & activity." More importantly, "I found the *Beagle* had arrived on the 3rd."

FitzRoy, however, was not aboard the ship. Weeks earlier, the captain, while passing through Valparaiso, had learned that a British ship, HMS *Challenger*, had been shipwrecked. Its crew had been left stranded at a site south of Valparaiso. Immediately, he had volunteered to pilot another British ship, HMS *Blonde* on a mission to rescue the ship's survivors. Thus, the latest plans called for FitzRoy, sailing aboard the *Blonde*, to meet the *Beagle* in Lima, Peru, in early September.

The postponement of his reunion with FitzRoy disappointed Darwin. Even so, with Lieutenant Wickham installed as the *Beagle*'s acting captain, "I felt very glad to be again on board." Hours later, "In the evening I gave my adios with a hearty goodwill to my companion, Mariano Gonzalez, with whom I had ridden so many leagues in Chili."

The *Beagle* sailed the next day; "On the 10th we crossed the Tropic of Capricorn: on the 12th in the evening came to an anchor at the port of Iquique." The next day, Darwin headed inland to visit a saltpeter mine whose owner welcomed him and offered lodging for the night. But it was the road from Iquique to the mine and the surrounding countryside that left the deepest impression on the naturalist.

"The road was strewed over with the bones and skins of dead Mules & Jackasses: what travellers have rather strongly written about the numbers in the Cordillera passes, is here actually verifyed." Indeed, "excepting the Vulture . . . which feeds on the Carcasses, I saw neither bird, quadruped, reptile, or insect. Excepting . . . [for some lichens], I saw not one plant."

Two days after arriving at Iquique, the *Beagle*, on July 14, weighed anchors. Five days and 750 northerly miles later, it reached the Peruvian harbor town of Callao, seven miles from Lima, Peru's (then smaller and inland) capital city.* The place that later became the city of Lima and capital of the Viceroyalty of Peru had served as the base of operations for Spanish explorer and conquistador Francisco Pizarro. In 1532, Pizarro commenced what became the Spanish conquest of Peru, a realm formerly at the heart of the vast Inca empire.

From its Pacific coast, Peru stretched westward over arid coastal plains to the Andes. To that range's southeast, the country descended into the tropical Amazon basin rainforest. Ecuador and Colombia bordered Peru's north, Brazil its east, Bolivia its southeast, and Argentina its south.

Peru had won its independence from Spain in 1826, but a decade later political turbulence still plagued the country. At Callao, FitzRoy intended to reprovision the *Beagle* and otherwise prepare for its voyage west across the Pacific. In the meantime, because of the turmoil gripping Lima and much of Peru, officers and crew were advised to not stray far

---

* Darwin's admiration of Alexander von Humboldt notwithstanding, Lima was the only place in South America visited by both men.

from the vessel. Weeks later, to Susan Darwin, Charles complained, "I have scarcely stirred out of the Ship for the last fortnight: the country is in such a miserable state of misgovernment, that nothing can exceed it. The President is daily shooting & murdering anyone who disobeys his orders."

Warnings aside, during the *Beagle*'s two-week Peruvian anchorage, Darwin, leaving Callao, did spend five days lodging in nearby Lima—time enough to take his measure of Peru's capital and its municipal population, then approaching 55,000. "There is little air of business," he noted— "few Carriages, carts or even Cargo-Mules in the streets." Many houses showed plastered woodwork, evidence of earthquake damage. Even so, "some of the old-houses now used by several families are immensely large & would rival . . . the most magnificent in London."

With no paramour awaiting his return to England, Darwin also took notice of Lima's ladies, including those donning the *tapada*, a distinctive, black silk veil fastened at the waist and worn over the head and shoulders by many of the city's elite women. Tapadas left only a tiny triangular space for one eye to see out. "But that one eye," he noted, "is so black & brilliant & has such powers of motion & expression, that its effect is very powerful." In conjunction with the tapada, the women wore a saya, a skirt fitted tightly at the waist and raised to display feet and ankles. "The close elastic gown fits the figure closely & obliges the ladies to walk with small steps which they do very elegantly & display very white silk stockings & very pretty feet."

Mostly, however, Darwin used his time in Peru to catch up on his diary and letters to correspondents, including Susan Darwin. He asked that she alert their "father that I have drawn a 50£ bill *instead of* 30£ . . . So that this must be notified to the Banker, otherwise he will be surprised at seeing the 50£. Our prolonged stay in this place, has caused me to draw for the extra money."

Lightheartedly, Charles added, he was not alone among his shipmates in incurring unforeseen expenses. FitzRoy, unchastened by his last rebuke by the Admiralty for unauthorized spending, had recently leased another vessel—*La Constitución*, a small schooner (returned by May 1836).

> The Captain discovered in Lima some old charts & Papers, which he thinks of considerable importance. Two of the Midshipmen, Ms. Usborne & Forsyth are to be left behind to survey in a small Schooner, the coast of Peru; afterwards they will return in a Merchant man to England.

To Caroline Darwin, Charles vented his weariness of foreign climes. "The very little I have seen of this country, I do not like," he complained. "The weather, now in the winter season is constantly cloudy & misty, & although it never rains; there is an abundance, of what the people are pleased to call Peruvian dew, but what in fact is a fine drizzle."

Even the anticipation of calls at storied South Pacific ports failed to rejuvenate his jaded spirits. "With respect to Otaheite"—Tahiti— "that *fallen* paradise, I do not believe there will be much to see. In short nothing will be very well worth seeing, during the remainder of this voyage, excepting the last & glorious view of the shores of England."

Caroline's younger brother did, however, admit to looking forward to one upcoming anchorage: "I am very anxious for the Galapagos Islands," he wrote. "I think both the Geology & Zoology cannot fail to be very interesting." Even so, to cousin William Fox, Charles allowed that the latter discipline's pursuit necessitated some brushing up: "For the last months I have been shamefully negligent of all branches of Zoology; I hope to make up a little in the Pacifick." Nonetheless, "I look forward to the Galapagos, with more interest than any other part of the voyage. They abound with active Volcanoes & I should hope contain Tertiary"—66 to 2.2-million years old—"strata."

On September 7, 1835, leaving Callao, the *Beagle* struck out for the Galápagos.

30

GALÁPAGOS

//

On September 15, 1835, eight days and 1,200 miles after the *Beagle* weighed anchor from Peru, the Galápagos archipelago moved into view. Darwin had hoped for warmer days, but the overcast skies of his ship's last anchorage seemed to follow him to these ostensibly newer climes.

"The weather, now & during the passage, has continued as on the coast of Peru, a steady, gentle breeze of wind & gloomy sky." Sailing closer to the archipelago, the men spent the day surveying Chatham Island, along the chain's eastern edge.*

The following day, the *Beagle* ran close to Hood Island (today's Isla Española). There, officers and crew launched one of the whaleboats, crewed with a small party for survey work. Hours later that evening, Darwin recorded, "the Yawl was also sent away on a surveying cruize of some length." On the seventeenth, two days after reaching the archipelago, the *Beagle* anchored in St. Stephens harbor (today's Bahía Stephens), on Chatham Island. "We found there," wrote Darwin, "an American Whaler [that] . . . we previously had seen . . . at Hoods Island."

---

* Reflecting the Galápagos' reorientation away from its former British identity, already fading during Darwin's visit, Chatham Island—today's Isla San Cristóbal—and the archipelago's other islands today carry Spanish names that bear no relation to their past Anglo appellations. The name of the archipelago is assumed to be a plural adaption of *galápago*, an old Spanish word for tortoise.

Sixteen principal islands comprised the Galápagos archipelago. North to south, straddling the Equator, the chain spread over 140 miles. Although separated by deep oceanic channels, the islands, in many cases, lay in sight of one another. Inconclusive evidence suggests early, albeit intermittent, pre-Columbian-era habitation of the archipelago by Indigenous peoples. More certain records attest to Spanish and English seamen touching there in the sixteenth and seventeenth centuries. Still later, the archipelago became successively a hideout for pirates and a stopover for whaling and sealing ships. Reflecting that outlaw pedigree, the islands appeared on early maps as Isla Encantadas—"enchanted"—in the sense of the accursed. In 1832, the Republic of Ecuador, founded two years earlier and six-hundred miles distant, laid claim to the islands.

Darwin longed to examine the Galápagos' flora, fauna, and geology. But, like the Falklands, it was the islands' importance as a stopover for whaling and sealing ships that had led the Admiralty to include them—conditionally, seemingly almost an afterthought—in FitzRoy's instructions: "If he should reach Guayaquil [Ecuador], or even Callao [Chile], it would be desirable he should run for the Galapagos, and, if the season permits, survey that knot of islands." Even so, the Admiralty's bland directive aside, Darwin, gazing that day from the *Beagle*'s poop-deck into St. Stephens harbor, liked what he saw.

> The Bay swarmed with animals; Fish, Shark & Turtles were popping their heads up in all parts. Fishing lines were soon put overboard & great numbers of fine fish 2 & even 3 ft long were caught. This sport makes all hands very merry; loud laughter & the heavy flapping of the fish are heard on every side.

A visit ashore after dinner deepened his first-blush enchantment: "These islands appear paradises for the whole family of Reptiles." Darwin saw no tortoises that day, but what he soon heard intrigued him. "Besides three kinds of Turtles, the Tortoise is so abundant; that [a] single Ship's company here caught from 500–800 in a short time." But even without spotting any tortoises over those hours, there was much he did see:

The black Lava rocks on the beach are frequented by large (2–3 ft) most disgusting, clumsy Lizards. They are as black as the porous rocks over which they crawl & seek their prey from the Sea. Somebody calls them "imps of darkness." They assuredly well become the land they inhabit. When on shore I proceeded to botanize & obtained 10 different flowers; but such insignificant, ugly little flowers, as would better become an Arctic, than a Tropical country.

To be sure, Chatham Island's geology and natural diversity (particularly, its abundance of fish, reptiles, and birds) engrossed Darwin—albeit often in a dark sense. (Call it Tropical gothic—"imps of darkness" and the like.) The birds' seeming lack of fear of human beings particularly snagged his attention. "The birds are Strangers to Man & think him as innocent as their countrymen the huge Tortoises," he noted. "Little birds within 3 & four feet, quietly hopped about the Bushes & were not frightened by stones being thrown at them. Mr King killed one with his hat & I pushed off a branch with the end of my gun a large Hawk."

The following day, the eighteenth, the *Beagle*'s anchorage was moved, and Darwin explored Chatham's interior. "We ascended the broken remains of a low but broard crater," he wrote, fascinated by the evident role of oceanic volcanoes in sculpting the island's landscape.

The Volcano had been sub-marine. The strata which dipped away on all sides were composed of hard Sandstones composed of Volcanic dust. A few leagues to the North a broken country was studded with small black cones; the ancient chimneys for the subterranean melted fluids.

Over the coming days, as Darwin, accompanied by Syms Covington, continued to explore Chatham, the island's dormant volcanoes stoked his imagination. On September 21, from a single spot, he recalled, "I counted 60 of these truncated hillocks, which are only from 50 to 100 ft above the plain of Lava." The cones appeared otherworldly but evoked a well-worn memory, "the Iron furnaces near Wolverhampton," England.

Inevitably moving closer for a better look, Darwin, like Professor Liden-brock in Jules Verne's *Journey to the Center of the Earth*, grew fixated on the apertures' Dantean depths:

> The craters are all entirely inert; consisting indeed of nothing more than a ring of cinders. There are large circular pits, from 30 to 80 ft deep; which might be mistaken for Craters, but are in reality formed by the subsidence of the roofs of great caverns, which probably were produced by a volume of gaz at the time when the Lava was liquid. The scene was to me novel & full of interest; it is always delightful to behold anything which has been long familiar, but only by description.

Later that day, the twenty-first, two large tortoises ("circumference of shell about 7 ft.") caught his attention: "One was eating a Cactus & then quietly walked away. The other gave a deep & loud hiss & then drew back his head. They were so heavy, I could scarcely lift them off the ground." Indeed, the island's volcanic topography combined with the sheer strange-ness (to Darwin's eyes) of its tortoises and other fauna and flora inspired in his diary some distinctly un-Lyellian language: "Surrounded by the black Lava, the leafless shrubs & large Cacti, they appeared most old-fashioned antediluvian animals; or rather inhabitants of some other planet."

That night, Darwin and Covington slept soundly on the beach. Even better, with the following morning's sunrise, the Galápagos delivered the bright, searing heat for which he had pined.* "This day was glowing hot, & was the first when our closeness to the Equator was very sensible." Later that day, lugging their latest haul of "new plants, birds, shells & insects," the two returned to the *Beagle*.

---

* While geographically in the tropics, the chain, due to other factors, including cold oceanic currents, does not have a tropical climate.

By September 23, the *Beagle*, had moved to Charles Island (today's Isla Floreana). A whaler lay anchored nearby; and, by coincidence, the *Beagle* had just arrived when Nicholas Lawson, the archipelago's acting governor, arrived to visit one of the whaling ships in the harbor. Afterward, Lawson came aboard the *Beagle*.

Then in his mid-forties, Lawson was born Nicolai Lossius, in Norway. In his adolescence, he sailed on a British ship to Brazil and the Mediterranean, and later found his way to Philadelphia, and, in time, China. In 1812, he became a US citizen. A year later, he was in New Brunswick, Canada, where he became a merchant and shipbuilder. After those businesses collapsed, he eventually, in 1820, became a Chilean navy officer and married the daughter of a prominent Chilean family. Stints in Valdivia and Valparaiso followed. Still later—inadvertently fulfilling the elusive dream of Don Quixote's hapless Sancho Panza of obtaining an insular (island) governorship—Lawson landed in the Pacific as the Galápagos' governor.

On September 23, 1835, after boarding the *Beagle*, Lawson invited Darwin, FitzRoy, and others from the ship into his home in Charles Island's lone settlement. The hamlet, Darwin wrote, sat "nearly in the centre of the Island, about 4 &½ miles inland, & elevated perhaps 1000 ft above the sea." It consisted of only a few dwellings, all "very simple" and "built of poles & thatched with grass." Nearby was a small penal colony managed by Lawson.

> The inhabitants are in number 200–300: nearly all are people of color & banished for Political crimes from the State of the Equator (Quito & Guyaquil &c) to which this Archipelago belongs. It appears the people are far from contented; they complain, here as in Chiloe, of the deficiency of money . . . Part of their time is employed in hunting the wild pigs & goats with which the woods abound; from the climate, agriculture requires but a small portion. The main article however of animal food is the Terrapin or Tortoise.

From Lawson and others, Darwin learned how the islanders came to lead "a sort of Robinson Crusoe life," in their case, dependent on the island's tortoises. For that era's sailing vessels, tortoises constituted a prized source of protein-rich nourishment. They were large but, requiring little food and water, able to survive sustained periods, even months, between ports of call.

> Mr Lawson reccollect having seen a Terrapin which 6 men could scarcely lift & two could not turn over on its back. These immense creatures must be very old, in the year 1830 one was caught (which required 6 men to lift it into the boat) which had various dates carved on its shells; one was 1786. The only reason why it was not at that time carried away must have been, that it was too big for two men to manage. The Whalers always send away their men in pairs to hunt.

Underscoring the animals' prized status among sailors, Lawson recalled that, years earlier, crewmen from a visiting frigate captured and "brought down to the Beach in a single day more than 200" tortoises. Afterward, tortoises grew scarce; and Lawson feared the island would never recover from the frigate's depletion of the animals. Noted Darwin, "Mr Lawson thinks there is yet left sufficient for 20 years."

———

Darwin's most productive collecting in the Galápagos occurred during his visit's waning days. On October 8, as the *Beagle* was preparing to survey other parts of the archipelago; and, on Chatham Island, acquire fresh water for its imminent Pacific crossing. And on that same day, FitzRoy landed Darwin, Benjamin Bynoe, and three other crewmen on James (today's Santiago) Island.

There, particularly in the island's interior, for nine days—until the seventeenth—Darwin, assisted by *Beagle* shipmates, gathered a bounteous assemblage of flora, fauna, and rocks. "We all were busily employed during these days in collecting all sorts of Specimens." Their gatherings included ferns, birds, and epiphytes (plants that grow on other plants but live on moisture and nutrients from surrounding air and rain). Collected birds included two species of mockingbirds, along with the smaller birds, thirteen species spread over four genera, now known as Darwin's finches (*Geospizinae*), destined to be linked by posterity to his stay on the islands.

On James Island, wrote Darwin, kismet smiled upon the visitors. "We found on the Isld a party of men sent by Mr Lawson from Charles Isd to salt fish & Tortoise meat (& procure oil from the latter)." Over the coming days, "We employed these men to bring us sufficient [fresh water] for our daily consumption." On October 9, after hiring a local guide, the *Beagle* party ascended to the high country of the island's interior. "Our walk was a long one. . . At about six miles distance & an elevation of perhaps 2000 ft the country begins to show a green color."

> Here there are a couple of hovels where the men reside. Lower down, the land is like that of Chatham Isd, very dry & the trees nearly leafless. I noticed however that those of the same species attained a much greater size here than in any other part. The Vegetation here deserved the title of a Wood: the trees were however far from tall & their branches low & crooked. About 2 miles from the Hovels & probably at an additional 1000 ft elevation, the Springs are situated. They are very trifling ones, but the water good & deliciously cold. They afford the only watering places as yet discovered in the interior.

As the men came upon other fresh water sources, their frequency of encounters with James Island's tortoises increased. "The tortoise when it can procure it, drinks great quantities of water," Darwin observed. "Hence these animals swarm in the neighbourhead of the Springs." The reptiles' gargantuan scale amazed him: "The average size of the full-grown ones is nearly a yard long in its back shell." So too their strength: "They are so strong as easily to carry me, & too heavy to lift from the ground." And likewise, their speed: "I think they march at the rate 360 yards in an hour; perhaps four miles in the 24 [hours]."

In the pathway many are travelling to the water & others returning, having drunk their fill. The effect is very comical in seeing these huge creatures with outstreched neck so deliberately pacing onwards. . . . When they arrive at the Spring, they bury their heads *above* the eyes in the muddy water & greedily suck in great mouthfulls, *quite regardless* of lookers on.

The Galápagos exceeded Darwin's expectations. Even so, the *Beagle*'s five-week stay there has left widely held misconceptions concerning the actual time he spent exploring the archipelago. Moreover, a careful examination of his diary indicates that he saw less of the Galápagos and visited fewer of its islands than commonly assumed.

To be sure, the *Beagle* spent five weeks in the archipelago's waters. But, as geographer Patrick Armstrong has observed,

Darwin spent only nineteen days, in some cases, only in part (and in a few instances, only for a period of an hour or two), on land in the Galapagos archipelago. The remainder of the 40 or so days he was aboard the *Beagle*, as she made her way from island to island engaged in hydrographic survey work.

Moreover, according to Armstrong, Darwin seems to have landed on only four islands during his entire stay, though he would have had a good view from the ship of another eight islands.

Darwin's diary, his Galápagos field notes, and letters written shortly after his visit teem with sharp observations on a wide range of topics, from volcanic geology to giant tortoises, birds to marine iguanas. He also speculated about which "centre of creation" the islands' various species originated—the latter, a term used by Lyell and other geologists that posited multiple, often continental, realms in which the Creator had initiated new species.

I industriously collected all the animals, plants, insects & reptiles from this Island. It will be very interesting to find from future comparison to what district or "centre of creation" the organized beings of this archipelago must be attached.

Equally revealing of Darwin's state of mind when he visited the islands is the absence of specific assumptions with which he later came to be associated. Indeed, that silence, one could argue, constitutes the scientific equivalent of Sherlock Holmes's famed "dog that didn't bark," a conspicuous absence that, in this case, would seem to debunk by now widely held assumptions concerning Darwin's activities in the Galápagos.

Particularly telling, in none of Darwin's contemporary Galápagos writings, those produced during or soon after his stay there, does he undercut or rebuke his earlier expressed beliefs concerning the immutability of species—or, more specifically, the creationist beliefs he derived from William Paley's *Natural Theology*.

Over the coming years, Darwin's thoughts concerning mockingbirds, finches, and tortoises of the Galápagos, and their variability from island to island, would lead him to reformulate many past assumptions. And, to be sure, his Galápagos field notes do include references to mockingbirds collected in the archipelago—species that, he noted, closely resembled the Chilean mockingbird (*Mimus thenca*) he had observed on the mainland:

> These birds are closely allied in appearance to the Thenca of Chile or Callandra of la Plata. . . . I have specimens from four of the larger Islands; . . .The specimens from Chatham & Albermarle Isd appear to be the same; but the other two are different.

But none of Darwin's writings from the archipelago refer to the famous group of passerine species, a broad order of songbirds, that later bore his name. Indeed, his diary's coverage of his Galápagos visit contains only one reference, and a passing one at that, to *any* sort of finch.

In his diary's October 1 entry, Darwin recounts a search by him and others for freshwater sources on Albemarle (now Isabela) Island. With 1,792 square miles, occupying an area roughly that of the US state of Delaware, Albemarle is the largest of the Galápagos' islands. There, the men found a series of sandstone pits that, from a distance, appeared promising. Closer inspection, however, revealed another reality. "To our disappointment the little pits in the Sandstone contained scarcely a Gallon & that not good. It was however sufficient to draw together all the little birds in the country. Doves & Finches swarmed round its margin."

During his visit, Darwin did collect finch specimens that eventually found their way to England. But comingling the finch specimens during those weeks in the Galápagos, he apparently failed to record on their respective labels the specific island on which each had been killed. As a consequence, not until 1837, after his return to England and the birds' inspection by zoologist John Gould, did he learn of the variations among them.

A similar oversight attended Darwin's observations of the archipelago's tortoises. For all his attention to their habits and habitats, he later acknowledged, he only learned of the animals' variability from island to island after Nicholas Lawson informed him of them; and only later, after leaving the islands, did he appreciate the significance of those variances. As Darwin, in 1845, recounted,

> My attention was first called to this fact by the Vice-Governor [sic], Mr. Lawson, declaring that the tortoises differed from the different islands, and that he could with certainty tell from which island any one was brought. I did not for some time pay sufficient attention to this statement, and I had already partially mingled together the collections from two of the islands. I never dreamed that islands, about fifty or sixty miles apart, and most of them in sight of each other, formed of precisely the same rocks, placed under a quite similar climate, rising to a nearly equal height, would have been differently tenanted.

To wit, even after Lawson alerted Darwin to differences among the Galápagos' tortoises, he remained insufficiently interested to systematically collect them. Aside from a juvenile tortoise that he caught and brought aboard the ship as a pet, his primary engagement with the reptiles was, like his shipmates, eating them, both in the Galápagos and in the coming weeks aboard the ship. Though the *Beagle* left the archipelago with more than thirty live adult tortoises, after being eaten by the ship's men, their shells were tossed overboard. Only after Darwin's return to England did French zoologist Gabriel Bibron—who had earlier inspected Galápagos tortoise specimens in Paris's natural history museum—confirm for Darwin Lawson's observation concerning their island-to-island variances.

No letters Darwin wrote while on the islands are known to exist. In a December 1835 letter from Sydney, Australia, to Caroline Darwin, he does allude to "my last letter . . . written from the Galapagos." But that missive has gone missing. However, another letter—one, for present purposes, likely more telling than the lost dispatch—does exist. Written from Sydney in January 1836, the letter's recipient was Darwin's mentor John Stevens Henslow. It had been five months since his last letter to Henslow; and updating the Cambridge professor on his latest activities, Darwin spent 208 words of the 950-word missive recounting his Galápagos visit:

> I last wrote to you from Lima, since which time I have done disgracefully little in Nat: History; or rather I should say since the Galapagos Islands, where I worked hard. Amongst other things, I collected every plant, which I could see in flower, & as it was the flowering season I hope my collection may be of some interest to you. I shall be very curious to know whether the Flora belongs to America, or is peculiar. I paid also much attention to the Birds, which I suspect are very curious. The Geology to me personally was very instructive & amusing; Craters of all sizes & forms, were studded about in every direction; some were s(uch) tiny ones, that they might be called quite Specim(en) Craters. There were however a few facts of interest, with respect of layers of Mud or Volcanic Sandstone, which must have flowed liked streams of Lava.

> Likewise respecting some grand fields of Trachytic Lava. The Trachyte contained large Crystals of glassy fractured Feldspar & the streams were naked, bare & the surface rough, as if they had flowed a week before. I was glad to examine a kind of Lava, which I believe in recent days has not in Europe been erupted.

Darwin's account of his work in the archipelago—self-assured, detailed, tonally matter-of-fact—reflected a growing self-confidence. But, alas, they were hardly the words of a protégé recording a eureka moment to a mentor thousands of miles away.

The German zoologist Otto Zacharias holds the distinction of being the only person known to have asked Charles Darwin whether he was an evolutionist during his *Beagle* travels; and the answer Zacharias received from him, in 1877, while acknowledging "vague doubts" concerning that day's conventional wisdom on such matters, was frank, straightforward, and made no mention of the Galápagos or its finches.

> When I was on board the Beagle, I believed in the permanence of Species, but, as far as I can remember, vague doubts occasionally flitted across my mind. On my return home in the autumn of 1836, I immediately began to prepare my journal for publication, and then saw, how many facts indicated the common descent of species, so that in July 1837 I opened a note book to record any facts which might bear on the question. But I did not become convinced that species were mutable until, I think, two or three years had elapsed.

Moreover, as Darwin scholar and historian of science John van Wyhe has observed, "After Darwin died in April 1882 a torrent of obituaries appeared." But a lengthy search by van Wyhe of those death notices turned up "not a single mention of the Galápagos finches and more often than not, never even mention the Galápagos Islands." Furthermore, wrote van Wyhe, "most accounts of the origins of Darwin's theory in the fifty years after his death never mention the Galápagos at all or attribute no particular significance to his visit there as compared to South America."

Indeed, in *On the Origin of Species*'s opening sentence, Darwin assigns no special role to the Galápagos and identifies the South American *continent* as the primary inspiration for his theory: "When on board H.M.S. *Beagle*, as naturalist, I was much struck with certain facts in the distribution of the inhabitants of South America, and in the geological relations of the present to the past inhabitants of that continent."

Whence then the origin of the storied association between the Galápagos, its finches, and Darwin's famous theory? To be clear, Charles Darwin himself, in a backdated 1837 entry in a personal journal that he began keeping in 1838, referenced the "character of S. American fossils—& species on Galapagos Archipelago" and noted, "These facts origin (especially latter) of all my views." More broadly, John Van Wyhe traced the mystique to an 1888 entry that Charles's son and biographer, botanist Francis Darwin, wrote for Britain's *Dictionary of National Biography*: "And above all," Francis wrote in the entry, his father, "came back [from the voyage of the *Beagle*] full of the thoughts on evolution impressed on him by South American fossils, by Galapagos birds, and by the general knowledge of the complex interdependence of all living things gained in his wanderings."

Curiously, van Wyhe noted, in Francis Darwin's 1880 *Life and Letters* of *Charles Darwin*, he "did not stress" any special role of the Galápagos in the formulation of his father's famous theory. Even so, in the coming years, up until his death in 1925, Francis Darwin continued to assert a linkage between the islands and his father's theory. As a consequence, observed van Wyhe,

> Between 1909 and the 1930s accounts of [Charles] Darwin remained much the same though now the Galapagos were mentioned in a much higher percentage of accounts of Darwin than before. In about a quarter of the publications in these years he was said to have uncovered evolution in the islands, though more often evolution was derived from Galapagos evidence later on. And still there were numerous accounts of Darwin in which the Galapagos were never mentioned at all.

Moreover, as the Galápagos increasingly became, in the public imagination, the site of Charles Darwin's alleged road-to-Damascus-conversion to evolutionary theory, that association, in 1935—the centennial of his visit to the islands—received an important ratification. Among those flocking to the archipelago that year was a group of pilgrims self-designated as the "Darwin Memorial Expedition." Led by American author and explorer Victor von Hagen, the group unveiled, on San Cristóbal Island, a monument inscribed with a text by Leonard Darwin, Charles's (then still living) last surviving son:

> Charles Darwin landed on the Galapagos islands in 1835 and his studies of the distribution of animals and plants thereon led him for the first time to consider the problem of organic evolution. Thus was started that revolution in thought on this subject which has since taken place.

Later that year, a British Association for the Advancement of Science meeting included a session that invited papers devoted to the "Centenary of the landing of Darwin on the Galapagos Islands, and of the birth of the hypothesis of the 'Origin of species.'"

"Now, for the first time," wrote van Wyhe, "Darwin was widely represented as discovering evolution on the Galapagos. The title of this section alone was reproduced in newspapers and journals throughout the world."

In October 1835, preparing for the *Beagle*'s lunge across the broad Pacific, Captain FitzRoy reprovisioned his ship with vegetables, pigs, and more than thirty tortoises captured on Chatham Island. And on the twentieth, with a single-sentence in his diary, twenty-five-year-old Charles Darwin memorialized the conclusion of his Galápagos adventures: "After having surveyed these [islands] the Ships head was put towards Otaheite [Tahiti] & we commenced our long passage of 3200 miles."

31

WEST OF THE
ONE-HUNDRED-EIGHTIETH MERIDIAN

A fter the *Beagle* left the Galápagos on October 20, 1835, trade winds over the next three weeks scudded the ship 3,200 southwesterly miles toward the South Seas Islands—thus far, the expedition's longest sustained passage. Darwin spent many of those days immersed in books about those islands. Speculation concerning the influence of Anglican missionaries there captivated him; likewise, theories that identified Polynesians as ancestors worshipped by Native peoples in Chile also fascinated him.

On November 9, the survey ship approached Polynesia's "low islands." Scattered along the archipelago's eastern and northeastern edges, the lush beach-fringed specks lay on accretions of coral. Darwin found the first of the islands unbeguiling: "The insignificant patch of land bears no proportion & seems an intruder on the domain of the wide all-powerful ocean."

Six days later as the *Beagle*, sailing westward, approached Tahiti, several officers, performing a usual navigational task, brought out a sextant to "shoot" the sun, to determine the *Beagle's* latitudinal position. Afterward, checking one of the ship's chronometers and consulting a book of mathematical tables, they calculated its longitudinal position. It was a simple ritual, one performed hundreds of times during the expedition. On this particular morning, however, noting their navigational position, they calculated they had passed across the 180° line of longitude, and therefore into a new calendar day: "our Sunday but their Monday."*

Still later that morning, November 15, as the *Beagle*'s men gazed upon Tahiti, Darwin exulted in "the wildest & most precipitous peaks which can be well imagined."

> As soon as we got to an anchor . . . we were surrounded by canoes. This was our Sunday but their Monday; if the case had been reversed we should not have received a single visit, for the injunction not to launch a canoe on the Sabbath is rigidly obeyed. After dinner we landed to enjoy all the delights of the first impressions produced by a new country & that country the charming Tahiti. Crowds of men, women & children . . . receive[d] us with laughing merry faces.

Among those welcoming the mariners was a "Mr. Wilson," a locally prominent missionary who invited several *Beagle* shipmates, including Darwin, to his house for tea. Afterward, on at least one occasion, "I hired a canoe & men to take me on the reef." More generally during their stay, disappearing for days at a time, Darwin explored the island's reefs, lowlands, and extinct-volcanic heights.

Even so, compared to other islands he visited, Darwin adjudged Tahiti's wildlife wanting in what a later age would call biodiversity: "It must not . . . be supposed that these woods at all equalled the forests of Brazil. In an island, that vast number of productions which characterize a continent cannot be expected to occur."

He reveled, meanwhile, in Tahiti's botanic delicacies, wild and cultivated, including oranges, bananas, coconuts, bread fruit trees, yams, sweet potatoes, sugarcane, and pineapples. "The whole of this land is covered by

---

* Well before 1884, when a conference of the world's nations formally established the International Dateline, mariners had adopted Latitude 180° as the line of demarcation between calendar dates.

a most beautiful orchard of Tropical plants." Indeed, a sampling of foods served to Darwin on November 17, after one of his interior excursions, typified the local fare and his ardor for it.

> When I descended in the evening from the mountain, a man whom I had pleased with a trifling gift met me bringing with him hot roasted Bananas, a pineapple & Cocoa Nuts. I do not know anything more delicious than the milk of a young Cocoa Nut, after walking under a burning sun. The pineapples here are also of such excellence as to be better than those reared in England & this I believe to be the last & highest compliment which can be paid to a fruit or indeed anything else.

Tahiti's natives—and what Darwin concluded was evidence of what he saw as Christianity's uplifting impact on the Indigenous population—likewise impressed him.

> In nothing have I been so much pleased as with the inhabit-ants. There is a mildness in the expression of their faces, which at once banishes the idea of a savage, & an intelligence which shows they are advancing in civilization. No doubt their dress is incongruous, as yet no settled costume having taken the place of the ancient one.

Darwin, by then having met at least two other missionaries, was revising a former opinion, shaped by recent readings, of the alleged deleterious impact of Christian proselytizing on the island. Earlier he had believed, "Tahitians had become a gloomy race & lived in fear of the Missionaries." But now, "of the latter feeling I saw no trace." Indeed, "instead of discontent," he saw "so many merry, happy faces."

As the ship's Tahitian anchorage neared its conclusion, FitzRoy acceded to a request from the Royal Navy's commodore at Lima and sought to address some unfinished official business with the government of the Society Islands (part of today's French Polynesia). Several years earlier, inhabitants plundered a British merchant ship docked in Tahiti, after which the British government had demanded $3,000 in compensation. But the indemnity had gone unpaid, and the commodore in Lima thus asked FitzRoy to rectify the matter.

Recounted Darwin, "Capt. FitzRoy asked for an interview with the [Society Islands'] Queen [Pomare Vahine]. For this purpose a Parliament was held where all the principal chiefs of the Island & the Queen were assembled." Soon thereafter, "the chiefs & people resolved to subscribe & complete the sum which was wanting."

The meeting, conducted with mutual cordiality, lasted several hours; and, before its adjournment, FitzRoy invited Queen Pomare to visit the *Beagle* the following evening. She accepted; and November 25 thus found the *Beagle* bedecked in flags, with songs and fireworks adding to the celebratory atmosphere:

> With her came most of the chiefs: the behaviour of all was very proper; they begged for nothing & appeared much grati- fied by the presents which were given them. The Queen is an awkquard large woman, without any beauty, gracefulness or dignity of manners. She appears to have only one royal attribute, viz a perfect immoveability of expression (& that generally rather a sulky one) under all circumstances. . . . The Royal party did not leave us till past midnight: they all appeared well contented with their visit.

The following evening the *Beagle* sailed for New Zealand.

The passage to New Zealand took three weeks. When not seasick, Darwin spent most days writing—gathering his thoughts in work on sustained essays on the geological origins of South America and the formation of "coral islands"—atolls.

On December 21, his first impression of the harbor of Paihia, on the east coast of New Zealand's North Island, summoned memories of the Chilean coast, south of Concepción: "the landscape" was "not a very bright green"; and appeared "hilly . . . with a smooth outline." Entering the harbor, the *Beagle*'s men found three whaling ships at anchor, scattered square-framed houses along the waterfront, and an "air of extreme quietness." Noted Darwin, "Only one single canoe came alongside; this & the whole scene afforded a remarkable & not very pleasing contrast to our joyful boisterous welcome at Tahiti."

Two main landmasses, North Island and South Island, along with numerous smaller islands, comprised the then nominally independent archipelago of New Zealand. And, after arriving at Paihia on the twenty-first and over the next five days of the *Beagle*'s call there, Darwin made time for collecting. He gathered specimens during the day; and devoted evenings to preserving, labeling, and describing in his notes his collected rocks, insects, birds, and shells. He also over those days enjoyed the company of local English colonists. But it was the local Indigenous population who, bringing out the scold in Darwin, snared his attentions. New Zealand's indigenous Maori (a term not then in usage) belonged to the same Polynesian culture that dominated Tahiti. Even so, unlike Tahiti's Natives, North Island's Maori population appalled the naturalist.

His contempt began with their houses. In contrast to the tidy white-washed, flower-garden-adorned houses of the English colonists, "All the native hovels which I have seen, have nearly the same form & dimensions & all agree in being filthily dirty. They resemble a cow shed with one end open; but having a partition a little way within, with a square hole in it, which cuts off a part & makes a small gloomy chamber."

But the Maori's houses soon proved the least of Darwin's concerns. Over the coming days, as he explored Paihia and other parts of North Island, rural and otherwise, his English presumptions of cultural superiority grew more pronounced. "Looking at the [Native] New Zealander, one naturally compares him with the Tahitian; both belonging to the same family of mankind. The comparison however tells heavily against the New Zealander. He may perhaps be superior in energy, but in every other respect his character is of a much lower order."[*]

Over those days, Darwin grew convinced that without continued English influence in New Zealand, both missionary work and colonization, Maori culture, which he associated with cannibalism, would prevail.

> I should think in no part of the world a more war-like race of inhabitants could be found than the New Zealanders. Their conduct in first seeing a Ship, as described by Capt. Cook, strongly illustrates this. The act of throwing volleys of stones at so great & novel an object as a ship & their defiance of "come on shore & we will kill & eat you all" shows uncommon boldness. This warlike spirit is evident in many of their customs & smallest actions. If a New Zealander is struck, although but in joke, the blow must be returned.

Providing no details, Darwin claimed to have witnessed "an instance" of such Maori behavior during an interaction "with one of our officers." For the most part, however, his antipathy toward the Maori apparently derived from prior readings, particularly explorer James Cook's journals, and from conversations with English colonists and missionaries whom he met on North Island.

Adding to Darwin's zeal to defend New Zealand's missionaries were his resentments over an unflattering portrait of their numbers published by his former shipmate, artist Augustus Earle. In 1827, for nine months, Earle had lived on North Island with a Maori woman; five years later, he published a memoir of that period which, while respectful of the Maori, cast missionaries as deficient in education, character, and moral character. Evoking Darwin's wrath, Earle had written,

---

[*] FitzRoy, for his part, while sharing many of Darwin's views of the Maori, nonetheless envisioned a day when, aided by "the strong but humane arm of a powerful European government," they might "see the wonderful effects of a changed system." In 1840, the archipelago became a British colony; and, from 1843 to 1845, FitzRoy served as its second governor, albeit with limited success.

I found that the greater part of them were hardy mechanics
(not well-educated clergymen). . . . In New Zealand, the
"mechanic" missionary only carries on his trade till he has
every comfort around him—his house finished, his garden
fenced, and a strong stockade enclosing all, to keep off the
"pagan" savages. This done, then commences the easy task
of preaching. They collect a few ragged urchins of natives,
whom they teach to read and write their own language—the
English tongue being forbidden; and when these children
return to their families, they are despised by them, as being
effeminate and useless.

Earle's book, already read by Darwin, numbered among the volumes
in the *Beagle* library. Adding to the naturalist's outrage was his experience three years earlier of sharing the Botafogo cottage with Earle, an
experience that gave Darwin a dark view of the artist's personal morality.
Thus, when Darwin arrived on North Island, he required no persuasion
to commiserate with the local missionaries' still raw indignation over
Earle's unflattering portrait of them.

For proof of the missionaries' beneficence, Darwin believed, one need
look no further than the young Maori women he encountered on a farm
run by English colonists: "A more decided & pleasing change was manifest in the young women who acted as servants within the houses; their
clean tidy & healthy appearance, like that of dairy maids in England."
Indeed, the women "formed a wonderful contrast with the women of the
filthy [Maori] hovels" he had seen elsewhere on North Island.

In his Christmas Day 1835 diary entry, Darwin strained to put a positive gloss on his New Zealand visit: "We attended Divine Service in the
Chapel of Pahia; part of the Service was read in English & part in
the New Zealand language. As far as I was able to understand, the
greatest proportion of the population in this northern part of the island
profess Christianity. It is curious that even the religion of those who do

not, is altered & is now partly Christian, partly Heathen. Moreover, so excellent is the Christian faith, that the outward conduct of the believers is said most decidedly to have been improved by its doctrines, which are to a certain extent generally known."

Mere days later, however, as the *Beagle* prepared to leave New Zealand, Darwin, for reasons unrecorded in his diary, had abandoned his sanguinity. "New Zealand," he wrote, "is not a pleasant place; amongst the natives there is absent that charming simplicity which is found at Tahiti; & of the English the greater part"—missionaries presumably included—"are the very refuse of Society."

Journal and Remarks, published four years later, however, contained a passage that, at least in part, seemed to reveal the origins of Darwin's apparent ambivalence toward New Zealand. More broadly, the passage (absent his disparagement of New Zealand's English) offered a sort of Rosetta stone, translating his views—starting with the Fuegians and other Indigenous peoples—on nature, politics, and culture: "The perfect equality," he wrote, "among the individuals composing these tribes [of Tierra del Fuego], must for a long time retard their civilization."

As we see those animals, whose instinct compels them to live in society and obey a chief, are most capable of improvement, so is it with the races of mankind. Whether we look at it as a cause or a consequence, the more civilized always have the most artificial governments. For instance, the inhabitants of Otaheite [Tahiti] who, when first discovered, were governed by hereditary kings, had arrived at a far higher grade than another branch of the same people, the New Zealanders, who although benefited by being compelled to turn their attention to agriculture, were republicans in the most absolute sense. In Tierra del Fuego, until some chief shall arise with power sufficient to secure any acquired advantages, such as the domesticated animals or other valuable presents, it seems scarcely possible that the political state of the country can be improved. At present, even a piece of cloth is torn into shreds and distributed; and no one individual becomes richer than another. On the other hand, it is difficult to understand how a chief can arise till there is property of some sort by which he might manifest and still increase his authority.

Moreover, to Darwin, as he also wrote in *Journal and Remarks*, the Maori's future was already written in the stars: "It was melancholy at New Zealand to hear the fine energetic natives saying, they knew the land was doomed to pass from their children."

On December 30, 1835, the *Beagle* concluded its New Zealand stay. "In the afternoon we stood out of the Bay of Islands on our course to Sydney," Darwin noted. But if the naturalist left New Zealand with reservations about its English ("the very refuse of Society") and Indigenous populations, he also left knowing the *Beagle* had added to that former cohort: At his own request, Richard Matthews, the failed missionary to the Fuegians, had been left on North Island to live with his missionary brother Joseph Matthews.

32

ANTIPODES

T he passage to Australia took two weeks; and as the *Beagle*, on January 12, 1836, entered Sydney Cove, Darwin, after gloomy New Zealand, like some nautical Lazarus risen from the dead, reveled in the sight: "beautiful Villas & nice Cottages were here & there scattered along the beach." Beyond those, in "the distance large stone houses, two or three stories high, & Windmills standing on the edge of a bank, pointed out to us the neighbourhead of the Capital of Australian civilization."

At Sydney, Darwin, soon ashore, found a waterfront crowded with warehouses and ships. And away from the docks, he discovered a teeming city of 23,000 in which his own tongue—and, however nominally, his own distant king—reigned supreme:

> In the evening I walked through the town & returned full of
> admiration at the whole scene. It is a most magnificent testimony
> to the power of the British nation: here, in a less promising
> country, scores of years have effected many times more than
> centuries in South America. My first feeling was to congratulate
> myself that I was born an Englishman: Upon seeing more of
> the town on other days, perhaps it fell a little in my estima-
> tion; but yet it is a good town; the streets are regular, broad,

clean & kept in excellent order; the houses are of a good size & the Shops well furnished. It may be faithfully compared to the large suburbs which stretch out from London & a few other great towns: but not even near London or Birmingham is there an aspect of such rapid growth; the number of large houses just finished & others building is truly surprising.

For privileged young Englishmen of Darwin's generation, Australia held a unique claim on the imagination; and for him those interests extended beyond natural history. "Before arriving here the three things which interested me most were—the state of society amongst the higher classes, the condition of the convicts, and the degree of attraction sufficient to induce persons to emigrate," he wrote in *Journal and Remarks*.

Notwithstanding the political reforms and industrialism reshaping Britain during Darwin's early years, the Australian colony of New South Wales and its Sydney capital, abounding in convicts cum arrivistes, confounded his notion of a well-ordered society. More specifically, he believed that tensions between "emancipists" and "free settlers" warped life in the colony, the former having been brought there as convicts but having since then received full or conditional pardons for their crimes.

There is much jealousy between the children of the emancipists and the free settlers; the former being pleased to consider honest men as interlopers. The whole population, poor and rich, are bent on acquiring wealth; amongst the higher orders wool and sheep-grazing form the constant subject of conversation. The very low ebb of literature is strongly marked by the emptiness of the booksellers' shops.

On January 16, pining to see the colony's backcountry, Darwin, with a hired guide, set off for the town of Bathurst. On the western side of the north-to-south running Blue Mountains range, Bathurst lay 125 miles northwest of Sydney. New South Wales traced its origins to a British penal colony established in 1788; and, traveling by coach from Sydney to Bathurst, Darwin was impressed with the roads built by forced labor brigades.

> The roads were excellent & made on the Macadam principle, whinstone being brought from the distance of several miles for this purpose; nor had turnpikes been forgotten. The road appeared much frequented by all sorts of carriages. I met two Stage Coaches. In all these respects there was a most close resemblance to England.

Less reassuring were two other fixtures of the landscape. "Perhaps," Darwin reflected, "the number of Ale-houses was here in excess." More disconcerting were the ubiquitous convicts, dressed in yellow and grey prisoner garb, many shackled in leg-irons, that his carriage passed. "The Iron gangs, or parties of convicts, who have committed some trifling offence in this country, appeared the least like England."

Late one afternoon, spotting a party of spear-bearing "Aboriginal Blacks," Darwin, for a shilling, purchased a weapons demonstration. Of the "partly clothed" men, "several" of whom "could speak a little English," he recalled in his diary, "They were easily detained & they threw their spears for my amusement . . . [their] countenances were good-humoured & pleasant & they appeared far from such utterly degraded beings as usually represented."

> In their own arts they are admirable; a cap being fixed at thirty yards distance, they transfixed it with the spear delivered by the throwing stick, with the rapidity of an arrow from the bow of a practised Archer; in tracking animals & men they show most wonderful sagacity & I heard many of their remarks, which manifested considerable acuteness. They will not how-ever cultivate the ground, or even take the trouble of keeping flocks of sheep which have been offered them; or build houses & remain stationary. Never the less, they appear to me to stand some few degrees higher in civilization, or more correctly a few lower in barbarism, than the Fuegians.

Although the Indigenous Australians intrigued Darwin, the Blue Mountains proved disappointing.

> I had expected to see a bold chain crossing the country; instead of this a sloping plain presents merely an inconsiderable front to the low country. From this first slope, the view of the extensive woodland towards the coast was interesting, & the trees grew bold & lofty; but when once on the sandstone platform, the scenery became exceedingly monotomous.

Similarly, the Bathurst settlement projected "a singular & not very inviting appearance; groups of small houses, & a few large ones, are scattered rather thickly over two or three miles of a bare country which is divided into numerous fields by lines of rails."

Darwin's quest to observe the colony's flora and fauna proved likewise unrewarding. From a giant sheep ranch that he visited in mid-January, he set off with the operation's foreman on a kangaroo hunt. Mounted, they used greyhounds to track their quarry. But overhunting and fires had already, in 1836, severely reduced the marsupials' numbers. "In the whole country I scarcely saw a place without the marks of fire."

Dusk found the two men walking along a chain of ponds teeming with platypus. "They were diving & playing about the surface of the water; but showed very little of their bodies, so that they might easily have been mistaken for many water rats." Darwin's companion killed one of the creatures, permitting the naturalist a close-up view of the semi-aquatic mammal: "Certainly it is a most extraordinary animal; the stuffed specimens do not give at all a good idea of the recent appearance of the head & beak; the latter becoming hard & contracted."

En route back to Sydney, Darwin visited Captain Phillip Parker King, commander of the first survey with which the *Beagle* was associated. King, whose father had been governor of New South Wales, was, that year, living on his 4,000-acre farm, at Dunheved, west of Sydney (today part of the St. Marys suburb). There, Darwin also reunited with Captain King's eldest son Philip Gidley King, the *Beagle*'s former midshipman who had accompanied Darwin on several overland excursions. The younger King had resigned from the *Beagle* in Sydney.

Days later in Sydney, Darwin reunited with another former shipmate, artist Conrad Martens, who after being discharged from the *Beagle* in Valparaiso had returned to Australia. From Martens, Darwin purchased two watercolors—one of the *Beagle* undergoing repairs at Rio Santa Cruz, the other of the ship in Tierra del Fuego's Beagle Channel.

By January 27, back in Sydney, Darwin's ardor for Britain's distant New South Wales colony had waned. Much of his disenchantment turned on what he saw as an unbridgeable chasm between free settlers and emancipists. To Henslow, he expressed his worries that the free settlers would forever fear the emancipists with whom they shared their streets and shops: "On the whole I do not like new South Wales: it is without doubt an admirable place to accumulate pounds & shillings; but Heaven forfend that ever I should live, where every other man is sure to be somewhere between a petty rogue & bloodthirsty villain."

The *Beagle* sailed from Sydney on January 30. But a similar trajectory, from ardor to disillusionment, characterized Darwin's reaction to the ship's next anchorage—an eleven-day stay, February 5–16, at the Australian port of Hobart Town, another town begun as a British penal colony, in the freshly renamed colony of Tasmania. The area's farms impressed Darwin, and his collecting went well—particularly of "lamp-shells" (brachiopods), flatworms, and insects (119 species). Indeed, he spent his birthday, his twenty-seventh, hunting snakes and skinks. And—a day earlier, on February 11—as recalled in his diary, he climbed Mt. Wellington (4,170 feet) that rises over Hobart Town:

> I took with me . . . a guide, but he was a stupid fellow & led
> me up by the South or wet side. Here the vegetation was
> very luxuriant & from the number of dead trees & branches,

the labor of ascent was almost as great as in T. del Fuego or
Chiloe. It cost us five & a half hours of hard climbing before
we reached the summit.

In Hobart Town, Darwin's diary records, prominent and cultivated
residents feted him in their homes, among them the colony's surveyor-
general George Frankland. "He took me two very pleasant rides & I
passed at his house the most agreeable evening since leaving England."

> There appears to be a good deal of Society here: I heard of a Fancy
> Ball, at which 113 were present in costumes! I suspect also the
> Society is much pleasanter than that of Sydney. They enjoy an
> advantage in there being no wealthy Convicts. If I was obliged
> to emigrate I certainly should prefer this place: the climate &
> aspect of the country almost alone would determine me. The
> Colony moreover is well governed; in this convict population,
> there certainly is not *more*, if not *less*, crimes, than in England.

Even so, beneath Tasmania's prosperity and refinements, Darwin,
as in Sydney, suspected darker forces behind the outward gaiety. His
host, surveyor-general Frankland, for instance, had arranged land grants
for thousands of English settlers. But, as Darwin wrote in *Journal and
Remarks*, he also knew that those lands had been since cleared for agriculture at the expense of the colony's Aboriginal peoples.

> Hobart Town, from the census of this year, contained 13,826
> inhabitants, and the whole of Tasmania 36,505. All the
> aborigines [210, when Darwin visited] have been removed to
> an island in Bass's Straits, so that Van Diemen's Land* enjoys
> the great advantage of being free from a native population.
> This most cruel step seems to have been quite unavoidable, as
> the only means of stopping a fearful succession of robberies,
> burnings, and murders, committed by the blacks; but which

---

* Van Diemen's Land was the older British name for Tasmania.

sooner or later must have ended in their utter destruction. I fear there is no doubt that this train of evil and its consequences, originated in the infamous conduct of some of our countrymen. Thirty years is a short period, in which to have banished the last aboriginal from his native island, and that island nearly as large as Ireland. I do not know a more striking instance of the comparative rate of increase of a civilized over a savage people.

On February 17, the *Beagle* sailed from Hobart Town. Over the days ahead, the ship's westward course would bring its men into the Indian Ocean. But for those weary and homesick souls, now having been at sea for four years, a single longing preoccupied their days—their return to England. As Darwin lamented to Henslow, "Certainly I never was intended for a traveller; my thoughts are always rambling over past or future scenes; I cannot enjoy the present happiness, for anticipating the future; which is about as foolish as the dog who dropt the real bone for its' shadow."

33

"'ROUND THE WORLD,
LIKE A FLYING DUTCHMAN"

//

"We shall go 'round the world, like a Flying Dutchman."
—Charles Darwin to Susan Darwin,
September 3, 1835

E ighteen days after leaving Hobart Town, the *Beagle*, on March 6, of that leap year 1836, anchored in King George Sound, on Western Australia's south coast. There, as surveys were conducted, Darwin explored the sound's namesake colony and hills and valleys, outings he found less than edifying: "We staid there eight days & I do not remember since leaving England having passed a more dull, uninteresting time."

Thirty to forty "small whitewashed cottages" comprised the King George settlement (today's Albany, Western Australia). "The inhabitants live on salted meat & of course have no fresh meat or vegetables to sell; they do not even take the trouble to catch the fish with which the bay abounds."

The colonists, in Darwin's view, were successfully drawing on a labor source otherwise untapped by English-speaking people he had observed elsewhere in Australia. The local aborigines "are quite willing to work &

to make themselves very useful; in this respect they are very different from those in the other Australian colonies." Ironically, however, given his abolitionist sympathies and recent criticism of New South Wales society, Darwin added, "Whether" King George "will ever be able to compete with the Colonies which possess the cheap labor of convicts, time alone will show."

On March 14, when the *Beagle* weighed anchored from King George Sound, as that day's diary entry attested, Darwin's cynicism regarding Australia in general remained undiminished: "Farewell Australia, you are a rising infant & doubtless some day will reign a great princess in the South; but you are too great & ambitious for affection, yet not great enough for respect; I leave your shores without sorrow or regret."

Except for the "thick & tempestuous" weather through which the *Beagle* passed on the final four of the next eighteen days of sailing, the passage to its next destination, the Keeling Islands, went smoothly.*

Francis Beaufort's November 1831 instructions requested that, during the *Beagle*'s return voyage, "if circumstances are favourable, she might look at the Keeling Islands, and settle their position." Situated in the eastern Indian Ocean, 2,300 miles off Australia's west coast, were the Keelings, which consisted of two atolls (5½ square miles) made up of twenty-seven islands. Though small, the atolls (a word not then in use), due to their location in an important shipping lane, held a disproportionate importance to British maritime interests. Thus, instructed Beaufort, if the *Beagle*'s schedule permitted, "an exact geological map of the whole island should be constructed," as well as "a rigorous soundings of its edges."

But Beaufort also made clear that the Admiralty's interest in the Keelings extended to the nature of atolls in general: "A modern and very

---

* The Keelings are today an external territory of Australia, officially known as the "Cocos (Keeling) Islands."

plausible theory has been put forward, that these wonderful formations, instead of ascending from the bottom of the sea, have been raised from the summits of extinct volcanoes; and therefore the nature of the bottom at each of these soundings should be noted, and every means exerted that ingenuity can devise of discovering at what depth the coral formation begins, and of what materials the substratum on which it rests is composed."

By coincidence, as the Keelings appeared before the *Beagle*'s bow, Darwin's interest in reefs was approaching fever level. He had observed coral (if not initially, actual reefs) in, among other places, the Water of Leith's tidal pools near Edinburgh, Jago's shoreline, and the Abrolhos archipelago. And in Tahiti he had extensively explored the island's coral reefs. His enthusiasm for the pastel-colored polyps had surged two summers earlier in the Andes, while pondering the South American continent's marine origins. "No other work of mine," he reflected in his *Autobiography*, "was begun in so deductive a spirit as this; for the whole theory was thought out on the west coast of S. America before I had seen a true coral reef. I had therefore only to verify and extend my views by a careful examination of living reefs."

Moreover, as geologist Rob Wesson observed, in the study of coral reefs, Darwin saw an opportunity to extend the theoretical vision of an increasingly esteemed influence. "In his mind's eye he saw South America—and especially the Andes—clearly rising above the level of the sea. With the ever-present influence of Lyell, it began to occur to him that a wonderful test of these ideas would be a complementary proof that the bottom of the ocean was sinking. Coral reefs might provide that proof."

In the Keelings, Darwin reveled in being allowed a close-up inspection of a reef that, he noted, "with the exception of one small gateway" encircled an entire island. More broadly, while in the Keelings, literally immersing himself in the ship's survey work, he spent entire days crisscrossing atolls and wading up to his waist in lagoons and along shorelines. Increasing his pleasures was the peerless scenery: "Coral are seen through the emerald green water." Cloudless skies and white Cocoa-nut tree-fringed beaches completed the tableau. "It is impossible not to admire the great elegant manner in which the young & full grown Cocoa-nut trees, without destroying each others symmetry, mingle together into one wood: the beach of glittering white Calcareous sand, forms the border to these fairy spots."

Before and during much of the voyage, geology more than biology had engaged Darwin's attentions. Should he pursue a career as a naturalist, after all, he expected to earn his reputation as a geologist. But, during the *Beagle* voyage, Darwin's shipmates' attentions to the Anthozoa class of marine invertebrates deepened his own interest in biology.

Eventually, he even challenged Charles Lyell's view, expressed in the second volume of *Principles of Geology*, of atolls as "nothing more than the crests of submarine volcanoes, having the rims and bottoms of their craters overgrown by corals." By contrast, Darwin's theory, eventually published in 1842, his first monograph, argued that atolls were formed by the upward growth of coral as the sea floor sank, thus allowing the organisms to continue living in shallow water as the ocean's surrounding waters rose. Indeed, during the 1950s, drilling in a Pacific Ocean atoll confirmed his theory.

As Darwin soon learned, a small ethnically Malay settlement lived in the Keelings. Exploring the island's beaches and interior jungles, he also took note of its seabirds, several species of (ubiquitous) hermit crabs, and coconut trees—the latter "so numerous as at first to appear the only tree, there are five or six other kinds. One called the Cabbage tree, grows to a great bulk in proportion to its height, & has an irregular figure; its wood being very soft."

But, like other islands he had visited, "the number of native plants is exceedingly limited; I suppose it does not exceed a dozen." Moreover, "In such a loose, dry, stony soil, nothing but the climate of the intertropical regions could produce a vigorous vegetation." Even so, testament to his ardor for the reefs, as the *Beagle*'s anchorage in the Keelings drew to a close, Darwin, in his diary, memorialized his visit with words that evoked poet William Blake's admonition, "to see a World in a Grain of Sand."

> I am glad we have visited these Islands; such formations surely rank high amongst the wonderful objects of this world. It is not a wonder which at first strikes the eye of the body, but rather after reflection, the eye of reason. We feel surprised when travellers relate accounts of the vast piles & extent of some ancient ruins; but how insignificant are the greatest of them, when compared to the matter here accumulated by various small animals. Throughout the whole group of Islands, every single atom, even from the most minute particle to large fragments of rocks, bear the stamp of once having been subjected to the power of organic arrangement.

On April 12—freshly reprovisioned with water, fish, coconuts, and turtles (the latter to replace the dwindling supply from the Galápagos)—HMS *Beagle* departed the Keeling Islands. With Britain's Indian Ocean island colony of Mauritius as their next port, Darwin, when not seasick, devoted much of the next seventeen days to work on his essay on atolls. "Whilst we are at sea, & the weather is fine, my time passes smoothly, because I am very busy," he wrote to Caroline Darwin. His newest writing project, he added, presented challenges unlike those encountered in his correspondence and diary:

> My occupation consists in rearranging old geological notes: the rearranging generally consists in totally rewriting them. I am just now beginning to discover the difficulty of expressing one's ideas on paper. As long as it consists solely of description it is pretty easy; but where reasoning comes into play, to make a proper connection, a clearness & a moderate fluency, is to me, as I have said, a difficulty of which I had no idea.

Over the coming years, Darwin worked to hone writing skills—exemplified in his first scientific monograph *The Structure and Distribution of Coral Reefs* (1842)—capable of expressing complex theories clearly and persuasively. Vital to that process was a door that opened for him as a writer during that spring 1836 passage from the Keelings to Mauritius.

Going back to the *Beagle*'s early 1832 stop at Jago, Darwin had resolved to write a book on the geology of South America. And though for four years he had made copious notes on the topic, he had yet to commence the book's writing. Truth be known, he still harbored insecurities about his writing talents and even his insights as an aspiring geologist. To Caroline, he confessed to dreading the day when his mentor was called upon to judge both:

> I assure you I look forward with no little anxiety to the time when Henslow, putting on a grave face, shall decide on the merits of my notes. If he shakes his head in a disapproving manner: I shall then know that I had better at once give up science, for science will have given up me. For I have worked with every grain of energy I possess.

FitzRoy, meanwhile, throughout the voyage, had been writing what he envisioned as the sole published account of the expedition—a project that Charles, as he confided to Caroline, viewed with ambivalence. "I sometimes fear his 'Book' will be rather diffuse, but in most other respects it certainly will be good: his style is very simple & excellent."

But as the *Beagle* neared Mauritius, FitzRoy, having read parts of Darwin's diary—his "journal"—surprised him, as he soon wrote to Caroline Darwin, with a proposition:

> He has proposed to me, to join him in publishing the account, that is, for him to have the disposal & arranging of my journal & to mingle it with his own. Of course I have said I am perfectly willing, if he wants materials; or thinks the chit-chat details of my journal are any ways worth publishing. He has read over the part I have on board, & likes it. I shall be anxious

to hear your opinions, for it is a most dangerous task, in these days, to publish accounts of parts of the world which have so frequently been visited. It is a rare piece of good fortune for me, that of the many errant (in ships) Naturalists, there have been few or rather no geologists. I shall enter the field unopposed.

By FitzRoy's proffered terms, Charles's words would be subordinate to the Captain's; moreover, FitzRoy would have editorial control over the book. Even so, without giving a firm answer, Charles was flattered.

Perhaps he did have a future as a naturalist and writer.

Darwin, meanwhile, knew his *Beagle* years were drawing to a close. He also knew the voyage's conclusion would cast him into a life starkly different than the one he left behind five years earlier. But what sort of life would he create for himself? If only through his letters' conspicuous lack of enthusiasm on the subject, friends and family members tacitly assumed that his post-voyage plans no longer included the ministry.

Weeks earlier, without knowing how or under what circumstances, Darwin had resolved to devote the rest of his life to natural history. "Leaving America," he wrote to William Fox, "all connected & therefore interesting, series of observations have come to an end. I look forward with a comical mixture of dread & satisfaction to the amount of work, which remains for me in England." Beyond that, his horizons now reached beyond Shropshire: "I suppose my chief (place) of residence will at first be Cambridge & then London."

Even so, Darwin also made clear, he was returning to England with a deeper appreciation for home and hearth: "I am sure, if a long voyage may have some injurious tendencies to a person's character, it has the one good one of teaching him to appreciate & dearly love his friends & relations."

Meanwhile, as Darwin anticipated the *Beagle*'s stop at the French-speaking island of Mauritius, with its aura of romance, he grew self-conscious about an absence in his life—of a paramour and, for the longer future, a spouse with whom to establish a family. "Imagine," he wrote to Fox, "what a fine opportunity for writing love letters. Oh that I had a sweet Virginia to send an inspired Epistle to. A person not in love will have no right to wander amongst the glowing bewitching scenes."

Darwin's biographer Janet Browne aptly perceived in such reflections evidence of the naturalist's reassessment of past habits and his grappling for new values, ranging from his eventual renunciation of hunting to a newfound appreciation of reading and the life of the mind: "All these finer emotions signified something of Darwin's imperceptible shift into being a different kind of man—a man deliberately leaving behind the rough naval life as he gradually neared his home country, deliberately prepared to allow his more sensitive feelings to take over."

On April 29, when the *Beagle* anchored at Mauritius, the island's beauty immediately enthralled Darwin: "The whole island, with its sloping border & central mountains, was adorned with an air of perfect elegance." The following day, he toured the French-speaking harbor town of Port Louis. The former French colony had fallen to British forces in 1810 during the Napoleonic Wars. And, as Darwin explored the city of 20,000, he savored its handsome streets and amenities: "Since leaving England I have not spent so idle & dissipated a time. I dined out almost every day in the week. All would have been very delightful, if it had been possible to have banished the remembrance of England."

Moreover, with England growing closer, he savored cafés and other greatly missed amenities. "There is a very pretty little theatre, in which operas are excellently performed, & are much preferred by the inhabitants to common plays," he rejoiced to his diary. "We were also surprised at seeing large booksellers shops with well stored shelves: music & reading bespeak our approach to the old world of civilization, for in truth both Australia & America may be considered as New Worlds."

Venturing away from Port Louis, Darwin climbed Mauritius's thumb-like mountain Le Pouce (2,664 feet), which provided, "an excellent view over this great mass of volcanic matter." Joined by John Lort Stokes, the

Beagle's assistant surveyor, he spent several days as a guest of the island's surveyor-general John Augustus Lloyd, renowned then for conducting, for Colombia's president Simón Bolívar, a survey of the Panamanian isthmus for a never-built canal.

On May 5, Darwin recalled, "Capt. Lloyd took us to the Rivière Noire which is several miles to the southward, in order that I might examine some rocks of elevated coral." Later, after Darwin learned that Lloyd owned an elephant and asked if he might ride it, his host graciously complied, arranging an outing for both guests. "He sent it half way on the road, that we might enjoy a ride in true Indian fashion."

On the evening of May 9, the *Beagle*, bound for Cape Town, sailed from Port Louis. Darwin had enjoyed Mauritius but was discomfited by his realization that many of his pleasures there owed to the triumphs of successive colonial overseers—Portuguese, Dutch, French and British—over native peoples. It also dawned on him that still other islanders were not there by choice, and they too had suffered: "Convicts from India are banished here for life; of them at present there are about 800 who are employed in various public works. Before seeing these people I had no idea that the inhabitants of India were such noble looking men."

Such inequities, he grudgingly conceded, left many islanders reduced to lives of constant want: "Pleasant as the society appeared to us, it was manifest even during our short visit that no small portion of jealousy, envy & hatred was common here, as in most other small societies."

Two weeks later, on the evening of May 31, the *Beagle* anchored in Simon's Bay, in Britain's Cape Colony, a lonesome port with "about a couple of hundred square whitewashed houses." To Darwin, the scene offered "a cheerless aspect to the stranger." The following morning, "There being nothing worth seeing here, I procured a gig & set out for the Cape town, which is 22 miles distant."

Reaching Cape Town after nightfall, Darwin after a "good deal of difficulty" (barely) found lodging. "There is only one good hotel, so that all strangers live in boarding houses a very uncomfortable fashion to which I was obliged to conform." Morning, however, rendered Cape Town more to his liking, a domain "laid out with the rectangular precision of a Spanish city." Its streets were "in good order & macadamized," some lined with "rows of trees on each side," houses "white-washed & look[ing] clean."

After centuries under Dutch governance, the Cape Colony, in 1814, following the Napoleonic Wars, had become a British possession. Darwin took pride in his country's overseas empire; and reflecting on the British colonies recently visited by the *Beagle*, his patriotic impulses swelled.

> All the fragments of the civilized world, which we have visited in the southern hemisphere, all appear to be flourishing; little embryo Englands are hatching in all parts. The Cape Colony, although possessing but a moderately fertile country, appears in a very prosperous condition.

Even in Cape Town, the capital of a recently acquired colony, "there is," he noted, "scarcely a resident . . . excepting among the lowest order, who does not speak some English; in this facility in becoming Anglefied, there appears to exist a wide difference between this colony & that of Mauritius."

For all that, however, Cape Town's inhabitants soon disabused Darwin of all illusions concerning Britain's popularity in the former Dutch colony. For instance, "In the country universally there is one price for a Dutchman, & another & much higher one, for an Englishman." He likewise acknowledged that most of this distant realm of the British Empire would remain unseen by him, beginning with the diversity of its peoples.

In Cape town it is said the present number of inhabitants is about 15,000, and in the whole colony, including coloured people, 200,000. Many different nations are here mingled together; the Europæans consist of Dutch, French & English, & scattered people from other parts. The Malays, descendants of slaves brought from the East Indian archipelago, form a large body; they appear a fine set of men; they can always be distinguished by conical hats, like the roof of a circular thatched cottage, or by a red handkerchief on their heads. The number of negroes is not very great, & the Hottentots, the ill treated aboriginals of the country, are, I should think, in a still smaller proportion.

In Cape Town, Darwin did have the good fortune to meet an author-scientist, a personal hero whose work, introduced to him by Henslow, he had admired for the past five years. Astronomer Sir John Herschel had moved to Cape Town two years earlier to study the stars of the Southern Hemisphere. And days after arriving, Darwin and FitzRoy had dinner in Herschel's home.

Writing to Henslow, Darwin recounted that, while he found Herschel's manners "rather awful," the astronomer was nonetheless "good natured." Among subjects discussed that evening was Herschel's views on volcanoes, earthquakes, and the formation of continents—all topics about which, the astronomer added, Herschel had recently written to Charles Lyell.

Whether Darwin summoned the boldness to share his own theory on the formation of South America with the eminent Herschel remains unclear. He did, however, soon receive news that boosted his fledgling confidence. From Catherine Darwin, he learned that Henslow, without Charles's knowledge, had edited extracts concerning South American geology from his recent letters, and cobbled them into an academic paper. Moreover, Henslow had read the paper at a November 1835 meeting of the Cambridge Philosophical Society;

and arranged for it to be printed in a thirty-one-page booklet for limited distribution.

Though not yet returned to England, Charles was already winning a place at the table among Britain's leading naturalists. Even so, to Catherine, he fretted over the circumstances of his first published work: "I have always written to Henslow in the same careless manner as to you; & to print what has been written without care & accuracy, is indeed playing with edge tools. But as the Spaniard says, 'No hay remedio'—Nothing to be done."

Weeks later, however, recovered from that concern, a newly emboldened Darwin, writing to Henslow, made a brazen request:

> I am going to ask you to do me a favor. I am very anxious to belong to the Geolog: Society. I do not know, but I suppose, it is necessary to be proposed some time before being balloted for, if such is the case, would you be good enough to take the proper preparatory steps. Professor Sedgwick very kindly offered to propose me, before leaving England: if he should happen to be in London, I daresay he would yet do so.

Before leaving Cape Town, FitzRoy, in what was becoming for him a de rigueur occurrence at recent anchorages, became embroiled in a dispute concerning missionaries. For the Captain, after all, the since abandoned mission in Tierra del Fuego had numbered among this voyage's original objectives; and in Tahiti and New Zealand, he—and Darwin—had both been ensnared in missionary-related kerfuffles. And after hearing of criticism of missionaries in the Cape Colony, the devout FitzRoy had little trouble enlisting (the however less devout) Darwin into their defense.

The *Beagle* sailed from the Cape Colony on June 18. Over the coming days, the two men wrote an article defending Christian missionaries that FitzRoy had promised to the *South African Christian Recorder*. In "A letter Containing Remarks on the Moral State of Tahiti, New Zealand, &c."—published that September, the authors, one a high Tory, the other a reformist Whig, seeking to vindicate the missionary ethos, extolled what they described as the moral progress of FitzRoy's abducted Fuegians during their stay in England:

> Surely, if three years sufficed to change the natures of such cannibal wretches as Fuegians, and transform them into well behaved, civilized people, who were very much liked by their English friends, there is some cause for thinking that a savage is not irreclaimable, until advanced in life; however repugnant to our ideas have been his early habits.

The article was Darwin's first intended publication and the first published work produced by the second *Beagle* expedition.

Back at sea, meanwhile, as the voyage approached its conclusion, Darwin increasingly reviewed his notes and catalogs, rechecking to ensure that all specimens had been assigned numbers and were adequately described. On June 29, the *Beagle*, sailing northward, passed, for the sixth & last time, the Tropic of Capricorn. The following day, it anchored off yet another lonely outpost of the British Empire, windswept St. Helena island, the rocky promontory where, between 1815 and 1821, a broken Napoleon Bonaparte spent his final years.

"I am at present living in a small house (amongst the clouds) in the centre of the Isld. & within stone's throw of Napoleon's tomb," Darwin wrote to Henslow. "It is blowing a gale of wind, with heavy rain, & wretchedly cold: if Napoleon's ghost haunts his dreary place of confinement, this would be a most excellent night for such wandering Spirits." But when the storm ceased, freeing Darwin to leave the ship, the island's flora proved disappointing. Dominating its rocky surfaces, replacing natives species were Scotch firs, weeping willows, blackberry bushes, and other species introduced from England.

On July 14, the *Beagle* sailed from St. Helena; five days later, it reached its next anchorage, Ascension Island, yet another British imperial outpost of volcanic pedigree. On Ascension, during the ship's five-day stay, Darwin received and sent off more mail, and otherwise explored the island.

On the twenty-third, however, a surprise jolted the *Beagle*'s shipmates. The perfectionist FitzRoy, they learned, had concluded that the completion of the ship's survey required rechecking a longitudinal measurement taken in Bahia (today's Salvador), Brazil. Thus, he had decided to return to that port, a decision Darwin laconically summarized in his diary: "the Ships head was directed in W.S.W. course a sore discomfiture & surprise to those on board who were most anxious to reach England. I did not think again to see the coast of S. America; but I am glad our fate has directed us to Bahia in Brazil."

The *Beagle* reached Bahia on August 1. For Darwin, the visit marked a welcome return to a place that had numbered, at least initially, among his favorite anchorages of the expedition. "We staid here four days, in which time I took several long walks. I was glad to find my enjoyment of tropical scenery, from the loss of novelty, had not decreased even in the slightest degree."

On August 6, the *Beagle* sailed from Bahia. Over the next two months, en route to England, the ship stopped briefly at Pernambuco, Brazil; crossed the Equator (on August 21), and made anchorages successively at his beloved "Jago" (Santiago Island), in the Cape Verde Island; and at Terceira, in the Azores. To Susan, Charles—longing for the familiarity of native soil, his renewed pleasures at Bahia notwithstanding—declared himself finally immune to the enchantments of tropical landscapes. "I can now walk soberly through a Brazilian forest . . . it is exquisitely beautiful, but now, instead of seeking for splendid contrasts; I compare the stately Mango trees with the Horse Chesnuts of England."

Even so, on October 2, 1836, when the *Beagle* anchored at the English port of Falmouth, the moment, memorialized in Charles diary, proved anticlimactic: "To my surprise and shame I confess the first sight of the shores of England inspired me with no warmer feelings, than if it had been a miserable Portuguese settlement. The same night (and a dreadfully stormy one it was) I started by the Mail for Shrewsbury."

After Darwin departed the ship at Falmouth, the *Beagle* continued on to Plymouth; and from Shrewsbury, on October 6, he wrote to FitzRoy:

> I arrived here yesterday morning at Breakfast time, & thank God, found all my dear good sisters & father quite well. My father appears more cheerful and very little older than when I left. My sisters assure me I do not look the least different, & I am able to return the compliment. Indeed all England appears changed, excepting the good old Town of Shrewsbury & its inhabitants, which for all I can see to the contrary may go on as they now are to Doomsday. I wish with all my heart, I was writing to you, amongst your friends instead of at that horrid Plymouth. But the day will soon come and you will be as happy as I now am. I do assure you I am a very great man at home. The five years voyage has certainly raised me a hundred percent. I fear such greatness must experience a fall.
>
> I am thoroughly ashamed of myself, in what a dead and half alive state, I spent the few last days on board, my only excuse is, that certainly I was not quite well. The first day in the mail tired me but as I drew nearer to Shrewsbury everything looked more beautiful & cheerful. In passing Gloucestershire & Worcestershire I wished much for you to admire the fields woods & orchards. The stupid people on the coach did not seem to think the fields one bit greener than usual but I am sure, we should have thoroughly agreed, that the wide world does not contain so happy a prospect as the rich cultivated land of England.
>
> I hope you will not forget to send me a note telling me how you go on. I do indeed hope all your vexations and trouble with respect to our voyage which we now *know* has an end, have come to a close. If you do not receive much satisfaction for all the mental and bodily energy, you have expended in His Majesty's Service, you will be most hardly treated. I put my radical sisters into an uproar at some of the *prudent* (if they were not *honest* whigs, I *would* say shabby), proceedings

of our Government. By the way I must tell you for the honor &
glory of the family, that my father has a large engraving of
King George the IV. put up in his sitting Room. But I am
no renegade, and by the time we meet, my politics will be as
firmly fixed and as wisely founded as ever they were.

I thought when I began this letter I would convince you
what a steady & sober frame of mind I was in. But I find
I am writing most precious nonsense. Two or three of our
labourers yesterday immediately set to work, and got most
excessively drunk in honor of the arrival of Master Charles.
Who then shall gainsay if Master Charles himself chooses to
make himself a fool.

Good bye. God bless you. I hope you are as happy, but
much wiser than your most sincere but unworthy Philos.
Chas. Darwin.

PART VI

GREAT BRITAIN, 1836–1882

"I dream the sea, that sea, surrounding me,
And from the dream I'm rescued by the bells
Of God, which bless and sanctify the mornings
Of these domesticated English fields.
For years I suffered, looking at eternal
Images of infinity and solitude,
Which have become that story I repeat . . ."
                    —Jorge Luis Borges, "Alexander Selkirk"

34

ODYSSEUS RETURNED

"Owning everything,
I have nowhere to go."
—Leonard Cohen, "Owning Everything"

Much had changed in the England to which, in October 1836, twenty-seven-year-old Charles Darwin, after five years abroad, returned. Culminating a landmark struggle, the Whigs' Great Reform Act of 1832 had broadened the franchise in England and Wales, and also reduced an inequity in apportioning Parliamentary seats that had favored rural over urban areas in the House of Commons.

But even as reformers nibbled away at Britain's vestigial feudalism, an ascendant industrial capitalism of banks, factories, and railroads, widening Dickensian inequities, continued to alter the country. Simultaneously, for Britain, newly acquired territories and markets in India, Latin America, and Asia—filling the gap left by the late eighteenth century loss of its North American colonies—were creating a refurbished overseas empire.

Meanwhile, in 1836, the year of Darwin's return, Britain's seventeen-year-old heir presumptive awaited her birthday the following year to ascend the throne as Queen Victoria.

As for Charles, those greeting him upon his return noticed a few new lines in his face; that he spoke with a new confidence; and, reported Caroline Darwin, was "looking very thin." In Shrewsbury, Charles, in turn, immediately noticed the changes those five years had wrought upon his family: His father Robert, in poor health when Charles last saw him, was now, at seventy, in worse condition, gout-ridden, often short of breath, and even more obese. A son-in-law, Henry Parker, the husband of Dr. Darwin's oldest daughter Marianne, had largely taken over the elder Darwin's medical practice. (Robert Darwin would die in 1848.) As for Charles's three sisters who still lived at The Mount—Catherine, twenty-six; Caroline, thirty-six; and Susan, thirty-three—all three already appeared matronly or headed in that direction.

Charles soon wearied of Shrewsbury's insularity. Likewise, eager to resume his naturalist work, he resented intrusions upon his time by social calls, encouraged by his family, on various townspeople. "My time was most grievously destroyed by visits to stupid people, who neither cared for me, nor I for them," he complained to William Fox.

In December, Charles moved back to Cambridge. There, with stocks and an allowance of about £400 a year from his father and assisted by Syms Covington (still in Charles's employ), he commenced the unpacking and study of his specimens.

To accommodate himself, his specimens, and Covington, Darwin rented a house (still standing) on Cambridge's Fitzwilliam Street. In large part, a desire to reduce interruptions by family members and friends occasioned the move to Cambridge. But once there, Darwin's growing social life, much of it centered around the Henslow family, eventually resulted in another move, to London, in March 1837.

There, with Covington, he took lodgings at 36 Great Marlborough Street, not far from his brother Erasmus's rooms. The move, however, put no damper on Charles's social life. He soon became an habitual attendee of soirees his brother Erasmus hosted, gatherings with the Wedgwood cousins, and London luminaries such as actress Fanny Kemble and writers Harriet Martineau and Thomas Carlyle. Erasmus never married; in faltering health during his later years, he died at age seventy-six in September 1881.

Charles Darwin, meanwhile—his professional reputation, thanks to Henslow, established before the *Beagle*'s return—built upon his growing prominence. On October 29, 1836, weeks after returning from the voyage, he finally met and immediately befriended Charles Lyell. Indeed, after moving to London, in addition to evenings spent under Erasmus's roof, Charles regularly attended dinners hosted by Lyell and his wife, Mary Horner Lyell, herself a formidable geologist. But, in hours and depth, the relationship between the two men soon transcended polite socializing. As Darwin later recalled, "I saw more of Lyell than of any other man both before and after my marriage."

Further accelerating Lyell's role as Darwin's new mentor, Henslow, in 1833 and 1837, accepted clerical posts that increasingly kept him away from Cambridge. Meanwhile, as the Darwin-Lyell friendship flourished, Lyell, then concluding a turn as president of the Geological Society of London, advised the younger man to stay focused on his own projects. Resist invitations, he advised, that squander time through commitments to scientific societies or otherwise entangle him in institutional responsibilities. ("Tell no one I gave you this advice.")

Through Lyell and others, Darwin, expanding his professional network, befriended other naturalists willing to evaluate his specimens. Their numbers included ornithologist John Gould of the London Zoological Society's museum, zoologist Thomas Brown of King's College, the Rev. William Buckland of Oxford University, zoologist, botanist, and explorer Joseph Dalton Hooker (recently returned from an expedition that brought him to Antarctic regions), and paleontologist and zoologist Richard Owen of London's Royal College of Surgeons.

Owen, five years older than Darwin, was a rising star in London's scientific world. The two men's relationship would later sour. But when Darwin returned from his *Beagle* travels, they shared a warm rapport. Darwin welcomed Owen's advice that he not deposit his specimens with the British Museum, already by then teeming with collections. There, Owen warned, Darwin risked having his collections languish in the building's basement—better to find another, even if less prestigious, museum for the specimens.

Writing to William Fox, Darwin expressed gratitude to the "Dons in science": "I find there are plenty who will undertake the description of whole tribes of animals, of which I know nothing." Unsurprisingly, however, as the experts' reports drifted back to Darwin, he often found their findings humbling—revealing mistakes in labeling or overlooked details concerning the specimens. In several instances, labeling errors had resulted from his adjudging specimens of different species to be of the same species. In some cases, such as his encounter with a botanist in the Linnean Society library, he faced downright embarrassment:

> I felt very foolish, when [he] remarked on the beautiful appearance of some plant with an astounding long name, and asked me about its habitation. Some one else seemed quite surprised that I knew nothing about a Carex [a genus of more than 2,000 grassy plants in the *Cyperaceae* family] from I do not know where. I was at last forced to plead most entire innocence, and that I knew no more about the plants which I had collected than the man in the moon.

As Darwin's web of associates grew, so too did his professional visibility. In January 1837, making his first appearance before a scientific society, he read his paper "Elevation on the coast of Chili" to the Geological Society in London. Moreover, between, 1838 and 1840, he was inducted into three of Britain's most prestigious learned societies—the Athenaeum, the Royal Society, and the Council of the Royal Geographical Society.

Meanwhile, as experts inspected his gathered specimens, Darwin turned to another pressing matter, his contribution, if he was to make one, to the published account of the *Beagle* expedition. FitzRoy, in spring 1836, had invited him to contribute to the project. But since returning to England, Charles, encouraged by his sisters, had balked at FitzRoy's terms, which called for extracts from Charles's diary to be incorporated into FitzRoy's account of the expedition.

Flummoxed, Charles, in late 1836, called on Henry Holland, a second cousin and high-society physician but also an admired travel writer. Holland read a few pages of the diary but, leaving its author crestfallen, offered no encouragement. To Caroline Darwin, Charles lamented, "Dr Holland looked over a few pages, and evidently thought that it would not be worth while to publish it alone." Discouraged, he confessed, "I am becoming rather inclined to the plan of mixing up long passages with Capt FitzRoy."

In Shropshire and Maer, however, Holland's rebuff steeled the Darwin-Wedgwood cabal's support for Charles. And, as family members joined the fray, it became clear that their displeasure extended to both Holland and the idea of *any* joint authorship by Charles with FitzRoy. Typifying the rancor, Charles's first cousin Emma Wedgwood sent the manuscript to her sister-in-law Fanny Wedgwood (not to be confused with Charles's late cousin of the same name, deceased since 1832) and Fanny's spouse (Emma's brother) Hensleigh Wedgwood, a barrister and prominent philologist and etymologist. Soliciting the couple's thoughts, Emma, in an accompanying letter, wrote to her sister-in-law,

> Catherine tells me they are very anxious to have your and Hensleigh's real opinion of Charles's journal. I am convinced Dr Holland is mistaken if he thinks it not worth publishing. I don't believe he is any judge as to what is amusing or interesting. Cath. does not approve of its being mixed up with Capt. Fitz-Roy's, and wants it to be put altogether by itself in an Appendix.

The couple, in turn, forwarded the manuscript to Erasmus Darwin. Days later, writing to Charles, Hensleigh Wedgwood praised his writings and disparaged Dr. Holland as an arbiter of literary stylings. "If Dr Holland read your journey from the Rio Negro & thought it would not do for publication it only affects my opinion of his taste & not the least in the world the merits of the thing itself." Mostly, however, Hensleigh praised the diary's passion and clarity:

> It is difficult to discriminate how much of the interest we felt in it belongs to yourself, from what it would have possessed if it had been written by an indifferent person. . . . I am not in general a good reader of travels, but I found no part of yours tedious. We read a great deal of it aloud too, which is a more severe test. . . . I was especially interested with your account of

Otaheite [Tahiti] & New Zealand. I think that of . . . [Australia] to which you called my attention is well worth insertion. In short there is more variety and a greater number of interesting portions than in 99.100ths of the travels that are published I should not have the least doubt of it's success.

Hensleigh furthermore opposed comingling Charles's writings with FitzRoy's. "I think the less it is mixed up with the Captains the better."

As it turned out, Charles and his allies' concerns were for naught. In late December, FitzRoy, while in London seeking editorial guidance, called on prominent naturalist William John Broderip; and, as FitzRoy soon wrote to Darwin, "He recommended a joint publication." Moreover, accepting Broderip's counsel, FitzRoy soon shared with Darwin his own latest thoughts concerning the project: "One volume might be for [Captain Phillip Parker] King, another for you and a third for me." As for business arrangements, FitzRoy's proposal was straightforward: "The *profits* if *any*, to be divided into three equal portions. What think you of such a plan?"

Darwin accepted FitzRoy's latest terms. But as he began adapting his diary, he soon felt burdened by the arrangement's restrictions. Moreover, Charles had sailed on the *Beagle* as a civilian; and both King and FitzRoy were aware of a Royal Navy tradition, described by Charles in a letter to a friend, that a ship's captain enjoyed "a right to the first use of all the papers belonging to the officers on board." And while FitzRoy apparently never (explicitly) invoked that protocol, it hovered over their collaboration.

To his family's disappointment, Charles also had agreed that his narrative would be considerably shorter than the diary he had written. A cousin, passing along her concerns via his sisters Catherine and Caroline, thus worried,

I hope Charles will rather risk a little repetition, than leave out too much of his Journal, especially about the *people*, which is always a more interesting subject than the *place*. What he says is sure to be said in so different a way from the Captain, that it is sure not to have the effect of repetition; and if he cuts up too much, he might make his Journal dryer.

Furthermore, airing their own worries, Catherine and Sarah added, they were "very sorry to hear that it only promises to be half the size of the old one; a vast deal must have been left out, and I am sure a great deal we thought very interesting."

But the diary's transformation into a published book entailed more than reducing its length. On a brighter note, the process also allowed Charles to polish sentences, correct errors, and supplement his original writings with even more information culled from the thirteen small pocket-size field notebooks he filled during the expedition.

Less edifying were editorial changes that diminished the diary's drama, candor, and topical breadth. Notably, he felt obliged to abandon the diary's strictly chronological organization and reconfigure his narrative into chapters organized by place. To wit, places like Tierra del Fuego and the Falklands to which the *Beagle* made multiple visits were presented in single chapters. More lamentably, Darwin, in his new account of his *Beagle* travels, deferring to FitzRoy, eliminated all but cursory references to the three Fuegians aboard the ship. His treatment of the party's first visit, in 1833, to Jemmy Button's Wulaia typified the extreme concision: "We staid there five days. Captain FitzRoy has given an account of all the interesting events which there happened."

Beyond that, Darwin's reconfigured narrative, emphasizing natural history, left out most of the diary's observations on personal matters, politics, cities, slavery, as well as, for obvious reasons, disparagements of shipmates. And though the materials garnered from Darwin's field notebooks swelled the final manuscript to a length of 223,000 words, the compression of his diary eliminated about half of that latter work's 182,000 words.

FitzRoy, upon reviewing the final manuscript, nonetheless chastised its author for insufficiently recognizing the *Beagle*'s crew, an oversight that Darwin subsequently corrected in the volume's preface. To William Fox, he described the changes:

> I am to have the third volume, in which I intend giving a kind of journal of a naturalist, not following however always the order of time, but rather the order of position. The habits of animals will occupy a large portion, sketches of the geology,

the appearance of the country, and personal details will make the hodge-podge complete.

Throughout the editing, meanwhile, Henslow remained Darwin's closest confidant. In August 1837, he sent Henslow the work's first proofs. And, three months later, while thanking his mentor, Darwin could not resist expressing his amazement at his own name's acquisition of a new professional title.

If I live till I am eighty years old I shall not cease to marvel at finding myself an author: in the summer, before I started, if anyone had told me I should have been an angel by this time, I should have thought it an equal improbability. This marvellous transformation is all owing to you.

When FitzRoy's project appeared, in August 1839, under the imprint of London publisher Henry Colburn, its three volumes bore the title *Narrative of the Surveying Voyages of His Majesty's Ships Adventure and Beagle between the Years 1826 and 1836, describing their Examination of the southern Shores of South America, and the Beagle's Circumnavigation of the Globe.* King and FitzRoy's *Narrative* (the latter with an appendix) appeared respectively as Volumes One and Two. Darwin's contribution to the work—subtitled *Journal and Remarks, 1832–1836* appeared as volume III. To illustrate the set, FitzRoy commissioned a set of engravings of places the *Beagle* visited. Based on watercolors produced by Augustus Earle and Conrad Martens, they appeared in volumes I and II of the set. Darwin's volume contained no illustrations.

All three volumes received a welcoming reception. In popularity, however, Darwin's narrative eclipsed the other two volumes, an outcome that accelerated deteriorating relations between Darwin and FitzRoy. Foreshadowing their eventual permanent rift, the two, in the first month after the *Beagle*'s return, saw each other on but one occasion, for tea, when

Darwin called on FitzRoy to meet the former Mary Henrietta O'Brien, now Mrs. FitzRoy. To Darwin's surprise, FitzRoy had married the pious young woman weeks after returning to England. The couple, as it turned out, were already engaged when the *Beagle* departed England but not once during the cruise did FitzRoy mention the engagement to Darwin.

During the *Beagle*'s voyage, Darwin's and FitzRoy, their divergent political and religious views notwithstanding, had found common ground on scientific matters. In his book on the voyage, however, FitzRoy, straying from past reticence, sought to reconcile geology and Biblical accounts of creation. To Caroline Darwin, Charles predicted, "You will be amused with FitzRoy's Deluge Chapter," adding that Charles Lyell "says it beats all the other nonsense he has ever read on the subject."

In 1839, soon after its first printing, Colburn reissued Darwin's book with a slightly tweaked title; second and third printings followed in 1840. And in 1845—after London publisher John Murray, for £150, purchased the work's copyright—Darwin's narrative appeared in a revised edition with a dozen illustrations. Although Charles would draw on his father's wealth for the rest of his life, the sales and reviews garnered by *Journal and Remarks* did nonetheless establish him as a successful author.

For Charles, his *Beagle* narrative, which has never gone out of print, remained a special book: "The success of this my first literary child always tickles my vanity more than that of any of my other works." He was particularly gratified when his idol Alexander von Humboldt, to whom he sent a first edition, responded with effusive praise. In a letter, the Prussian-born explorer lauded the narrative as "the fruits of his noble and courageous expedition," and predicted for its author "a great career" ahead.

During the journey chronicled in Darwin's book, he spent three-fifths of five-years of travels on land—three years and three months on terra firma versus a total 535 days on water. And while his narrative of those years appeared under several titles during its early printings, it was the title, however misleading, under which it appeared in 1905, decades after its author's death, that later readers came to cherish the work—*The Voyage of the* Beagle.

During those years, as Darwin prepared and published his account of his *Beagle* travels, HMS *Beagle* had already returned to sea. For its third and longest survey expedition, it sailed from England in June 1837 and returned in 1843. John Wickham, the first lieutenant on the *Beagle*'s second expedition, commanded the voyage. And like the second expedition, the ship's third survey—albeit focused on Australia's ports—circumnavigated the globe. Along the way, Wickham named a harbor, Port Darwin, on north Australia's coast, for his friend. Upon its return, HMS *Beagle* was ignominiously refitted as a "static" (assigned to a fixed position) coast guard ship—becoming the *Beagle Watch Vessel*, to monitor would be smugglers in various coastal and river locations around Britain. By 1870, it had been sold to a private firm and broken up.

Upon his return to England in 1836, Charles, though overwhelmed with work, still longed for a wife. Speculation in his circles focused on a handful of young Shropshire women as spousal candidates. Thus, few were surprised to learn, in November 1838, that, in a betrothal approved by his father and encouraged by his sisters, thirty-year-old Emma Wedgwood had accepted a marriage proposal from her twenty-nine-year-old first cousin. Theirs would be the second generation of Darwin-Wedgwood marriage. Even so, for Charles, speculations concerning the possible dangers of first-cousin marriages remained a nagging question for the rest of his life.

Emma, the youngest of Josiah Wedgwood II's eight children, had grown up socializing with all of her Darwin cousins. Notably, in 1828, she and Charles shared time together in Paris, when Charles and his sister Caroline accompanied their Uncle Jos there to collect Emma and her sister Fanny. More recently, the two saw one another frequently in the home of Emma's brother Hensleigh, by then a neighbor of Erasmus Darwin on London's Marlborough Street. And, finally, the two grew still closer during the travails associated with the publication of Charles's *Beagle* narrative.

For all that, Emma's social life had grown limited by duties associated with caring for her by then bedridden mother who had suffered a stroke several years earlier. And Charles's calculations for what he wanted in a spouse were more hard-headed than romantic. Even so, Emma, with her long brown hair falling into ringlets alongside her face and gold spectacles balanced on her nose, remained an intelligent and attractive young woman. (She had declined four earlier marriage proposals.) Moreover, she was well-read, had lived abroad, (mainly in Paris, for three years, 1815–18), and knew French and Italian (and a little German); and, having studied in Paris (with Frédéric Chopin among her teachers), she was also a talented pianist.

Emma, however, was also a Unitarian whose religious views were more devout than those of Charles—a difference that led to advice that Robert Darwin offered his son:

> Before I was engaged to be married, my father advised me to conceal carefully my doubts, for he said that he had known extreme misery thus caused with married persons. Things went on pretty well until the wife or husband became out of health, and then some women suffered miserably by doubting about the salvation of their husbands, thus making them likewise to suffer.

Charles and Emma's wedding, on January 29, 1839, at St. Peter's Church, in Maer village, was conducted with Anglican rites modified to avoid offending Unitarian precepts. Afterward, the couple, due to the press of Charles's work, made a hasty exit for the train station. During the brief trip to London, Emma recalled, "We ate our sandwiches with grateful hearts for all the care that was taken of us, and the bottle of water was the greatest comfort."

But if Charles harbored expectations that Emma intended to surrender her religious faith, she soon disabused him of them. Until her death in 1896, at age eighty-eight, fourteen years after her husband's, she remained devoutly religious. In February 1839, weeks after their wedding, resolved to not passively acquiesce to her husband's religious doubts, Emma wrote Charles a letter whose 650 words constituted a sort of personal declaration of spiritual independence:

> The state of mind that I wish to preserve with respect to you, is to feel that while you are acting conscientiously & sincerely wishing, & trying to learn the truth, you cannot be wrong; but there are some reasons that force themselves upon me & prevent my being always able to give myself this comfort. I dare say you have often thought of them before, but I will write down what has been in my head, knowing that my own dearest will indulge me.

Emma then plunged to the heart of her concerns: "Your mind & time are full of the most interesting subjects & thoughts of the most absorbing kind, viz following up yr own discoveries." But, she added, those discoveries, "make it very difficult for you to avoid casting out as interruptions other sorts of thoughts which have no relation to what you are pursuing or to be able to give your whole attention to both sides of the question."

> It seems to me also that the line of your pursuits may have led you to view chiefly the difficulties on one side, & that you have not had time to consider & study the chain of difficulties on the other, but I believe you do not consider your opinion as formed. May not the habit in scientific pursuits of believing nothing till it is proved, influence your mind too much in other things which cannot be proved in the same way, & which if true are likely to be above our comprehension. I should say also that there is a danger in giving up revelation which does not exist on the other side, that is the fear of ingratitude in casting off what has been done for your benefit as well as for that of all the world & which ought to make you still more careful, perhaps even fearful lest you should not have taken all the pains you could to judge truly.

In closing, Emma made clear that she did not intend her letter as a starting point for further conversations—in fact, precisely the opposite: "I do not wish for any answer to all this. It is a satisfaction to me to write it & when I talk to you about it I cannot say exactly what I wish to say, & I know you will have patience, with your own dear wife."

> Don't think that it is not my affair & that it does not much signify to me. Every thing that concerns you concerns me & I should be most unhappy if I thought we did not belong to each other forever.

In London, Charles and Emma settled into the house at 12 Upper Gower Street they had selected and Charles had rented the previous November. (Syms Covington, having helped Charles with the move that November, soon left his employ and emigrated to Australia.) Charles and Emma eventually had ten children, seven of whom survived into adulthood. After the births of the first two, however (William, in 1839, and Anne, in 1841), the couple, increasingly perturbed by London's noise and coal-smoke, decided they preferred a rural life. And in the summer of 1842, with a loan from his father, Charles purchased a house fourteen miles southeast of London, near the village of Down (now Downe), in the county of Kent.

That September, the Darwins moved into the handsome dwelling they soon called Down House. In the coming decades, the couple commissioned extensive refurbishments and expansions of the property. Eventually becoming a working farm, the estate provided much of the family's food. Along the way, in 1866, following a particularly aggravated bout of illness, Charles reemerged into public life with a freshly grown beard—the bushy white Old Testament patriarch's beard with which posterity came to associate him.

35

"HERE, THEN, I HAD AT LAST GOT
A THEORY BY WHICH TO WORK"

"They got Charles Darwin trapped out there on Highway Five
Judge says to the High Sheriff,
'I want him dead or alive
Either one, I don't care'"
—Bob Dylan, "High Water (for Charley Patton)"

From October 1836, when Charles Darwin stepped off the *Beagle* at
Falmouth, to his and Emma's move, six years later, to Down House,
in Kent, he grappled with a particular conundrum from his world
travels. It lurked in myriad encounters, incidents, and specimens from those
journeys—from Punta Alta's *Megatherium* to Tierra del Fuego's Fuegians,
from Uspallata Pass's petrified forest to the Galápagos' tortoises. Moreover,
the mystery's topical breadth extended from the migration and extinction
of animals and plants to the nature of species and life itself.

From readings in Charles Lyell and investigations during his travels,
particularly in Argentina and Chile, Darwin had grown convinced
that, over time, landforms are reshaped in ways that Biblically-oriented
geologists could not explain. Given those assumptions, he increasingly
asked himself, why must animal and plant species be viewed as eternally

fixed if landforms were not? Wrote his biographer Janet Browne, "Did transmutation happen by jumps, one species suddenly changing into another? Or did a species split into two when geology and geography created unaccustomed barriers in the middle of a region?"

To record his thoughts, Charles, in July 1837, "opened" (began keeping) his notebook devoted to such speculations. Fearful of potential scandal, he pursued them secretly, albeit with a zeal that grew obsessive. The following September, meanwhile, he experienced an "uncomfortable palpitation of the heart." His doctor advised, "*strongly* to knock off all work and leave for the country." Charles left for Shropshire but, by October 21, was back in London.

In a nod to the book in which his grandfather Erasmus had expressed thoughts on similar topics, Charles had titled his notebook—"Notebook B" to Darwin scholars—"Zoonomia," the title of Erasmus's 1794 book. Unlike, Erasmus, however—or, for that matter, Jean-Baptiste Lamarck, who influenced Erasmus—Charles, like Lyell, refused to attribute the changes he contemplated to supernatural causes; nor, to the unfolding over time of any grand scheme.

Indeed, the adherence of Erasmus Darwin, Lamarck, and other early evolutionary theorists to what Charles considered a too brief geological timetable ultimately blunted their influence on him. By Charles's lights, such timetables, with or without resort to Biblical explanations, allotted insufficient time for evolution to unspool. Beyond that, those and other early evolutionary theorists never developed, to Charles's satisfaction, a plausible mechanism by which new traits were transmitted to offspring.

In the end, it was an essay by Anglican cleric Thomas Robert Malthus (1776–1834) that dislodged the intellectual boulder blocking Charles's path forward. Malthus was best known as an influential political economist and author of the 1798 "Essay on the Principle of Population" that Darwin read in September 1838. An ironclad law lay at that essay's grim heart: "Population, when unchecked, increases in a geometrical ratio. Subsistence increases only in an arithmetical ratio." In Malthus's formulation, Darwin found the non-supernatural mechanism for which he had been searching, a non-external cause that explained the "transmutation of species" that he increasingly pondered. Recalled Darwin in his *Autobiography*:

In [September] 1838, that is, [fourteen] months after I had begun
my systematic enquiry, I happened to read for amusement Malthus
on *Population*, and being well prepared to appreciate the struggle
for existence which everywhere goes on from long-continued
observation of the habits of animals and plants, it at once struck me
that under these circumstances favourable variations would tend
to be preserved, and unfavourable ones to be destroyed. The result
of this would be the formation of new species. Here, then, I had at
last got a theory by which to work; but I was so anxious to avoid
prejudice, that I determined not for some time to write even the
briefest sketch of it. In June 1842 I first allowed myself the satisfaction of writing a very brief abstract of my theory in pencil in
35 pages; and this was enlarged during the summer of 1844 into
one of 230 pages, which I had fairly copied out and still possess.

In late 1844, meanwhile, as Charles composed his essay, he worried
about repercussions against himself and his family were it ever published.
Even so, he refused to foreclose all prospects, however distant, of that
eventuality. Not only did he not destroy the essay's pages, to safeguard
their contents, he arranged for the local school master to copy them.
And, on July 5, he wrote Emma a letter, immediately hid away, that was
to be opened in the event of his "sudden death." "I have just finished my
sketch of my species theory," he wrote.

If, as I believe that my theory is true & if it be accepted even
by one competent judge, it will be a considerable step in science," he wrote. "I therefore write this, in case of my sudden
death, as my most solemn & last request, which I am sure you
will consider the same as if legally entered in my will, that
you will devote 400£ to its publication.

He asked Emma—with assistance from her brother Hensleigh Wedgwood if needed—to find a suitable editor for the essay. The editor, he
stipulated, should be paid £400, or if necessary, £500: "I wish that my

sketch be given to some competent person, with this sum to induce him to take trouble in its improvement & enlargement." Charles likewise asked Emma to assist the editor, as necessary, in "deciphering" his handwriting in any of his auxiliary notes.

As further inducement to whomever Emma recruited, "I give to him all my Books on Natural History, which are either scored or have references at end to the pages, begging him carefully to look over & consider such passages, as actually bearing or by possibility bearing on this subject."

Regarding the editor, Charles instructed, "Mr. Lyell would be the best if he would undertake it: I believe he wd find the work pleasant & he wd learn some facts new to him. As the Editor must be a geologist, as well as Naturalist." And, if Lyell declined, Charles asked Emma to approach other colleagues: naturalist Edward Forbes, botanist Joseph Dalton Hooker, botanist John Stevens Henslow, geologist and zoologist Edwin Strickland, and zoologist Richard Owen—albeit expressing doubt that Owen would undertake the project. (Owen had recently expressed ideas divergent from Darwin's.) And, should all of those alternate candidates decline the work, "I would request you to consult with Mr Lyell, or some other capable man, for some Editor, a geologist & naturalist."

The species transmutation sketch and letter of instructions to Emma safely stashed away, Darwin thus consigned the publication of his thoughts on a controversial topic to a purposely vague future. And if he needed a cautionary tale to vindicate his discretion, it arrived with the 1844 publication of *Vestiges of the Natural History of Creation*. Initially published anonymously, the work's author was later revealed to be Scottish publisher and geologist Robert Chambers. Addressing speculations similar to Darwin's, *Vestiges* won numerous admirers and critics. Some among the former, like Herbert Spencer, to Darwin's consternation, belonged to his own circle.

The resemblance of *Vestiges* to aspects of his own work irritated Darwin. But he was also discomfitted by the level of invective the book provoked. Writing in the *Edinburgh Review*, Adam Sedgwick castigated

Vestiges as issuing from a mind distorted by the "fetters of a rank and unbending materialism."

Over the next two decades, as Darwin's family responsibilities grew, so too did his medical ailments—many, according to scholars, likely linked to the affliction that struck him in Chile. But though the time he could devote to work each day declined, he continued his research and writing—producing books on topics such as coral reefs (1842), volcanic islands (1844), South American geology (1846), and barnacles (1851, 1854). Between 1838 and 1843, he also oversaw the publication of a five-volume series, *The Zoology of the Voyage of H.M.S. Beagle.* The work—which he edited, contributed extensive notes, and authored introductions to two volumes—eventually ran to 632 pages, with 166 engravings. Each volume focused on a particular subject with a main text authored by a relevant expert: Richard Owen on mammal fossils; George Robert Waterhouse on mammals; John Gould on birds; Leonard Jenyns on fish; and Thomas Bell on reptiles.

Throughout those years, meanwhile, Darwin also doggedly continued his work on the transmutation of species. At the crux of that theorized process lay a mechanism that he called "natural selection." Darwin's term applied Malthusian logic to organic life—postulating a mechanism, a winnowing, by which the weaker or ill-adpated of species, or varieties thereof, perish. Simultaneously, more robust (better adapted) organisms—figuratively "selected" by a process of elimination—survive to reproduce. Darwin analogized natural selection with another coinage—"artificial selection." In artificial selection, a breeder of plants or animals takes decisions to achieve set goals. Natural selection, by contrast, proceeds in the wild without external guidance.

Emblematic of Darwin's preoccupation with what, by the late 1850s, he was calling his "big Book," he failed to heed a warning from Charles Lyell in mid-1855 concerning Alfred Russel Wallace, a young English naturalist. Conducting research in the Malay Archipelago, Wallace recently had published an article in *Annals and Magazine of Natural History* on the geologic and geographic distribution of fossils and living species. Darwin read the article. As a courtesy, he afterwards wrote to Wallace, congratulating him and informing him that his article had even attracted the notice of the eminent Charles Lyell.*

Nonetheless, even as Lyell persisted in warning Darwin about Wallace's work and his theory's resemblance to Darwin's, his "Big book" remained unfinished. Writing to Joseph Hooker, in May 1856, Darwin noted, "I had good talk with Lyell about my species work, & he urges me strongly to publish something."

Given Darwin's foreknowledge of Wallace's research, the contents of another package that he later received from Wallace—in mid-1858, the exact date remains uncertain—should not have surprised him. But it did. The package contained a cordial letter from Wallace and a manuscript, a scientific paper entitled "'On the tendency of varieties to depart indefinitely from the original type."

A soon stunned Darwin read the paper—and eventually, in June 1858, he wrote to Lyell:

> Some year or so ago, you recommended me to read a paper by Wallace in the Annals, which had interested you & as I was writing to him, I knew this would please him much, so I told him. He has to day sent me the enclosed & asked me to forward it to you. It seems to me well worth reading. Your words have come true with a vengeance that I shd. be forestalled. You said this when I explained to you here very briefly my views of "Natural Selection" depending on the Struggle for existence. I never saw a more striking coincidence. if Wallace had my M.S. sketch written out in 1842 he could not have made a better short abstract! Even his terms now stand as Heads of my Chapters.

Moreover, adding to the wealthy, well-connected naturalist's discombobulation, Wallace, unlike most of Darwin's colleagues, possessed no

---

* Lyell, for his part, though professionally supportive of Darwin, rejected the idea of the transmutation of species until the early 1860s.

institutional affiliation, no cohort of influential supporters, no source of independent financial support. To make a living, he sold specimens that he collected to museums and private collectors.

In short, Wallace, lacking means and social position, was not a "gentleman."

The package from his rival prompted fears by Darwin of being denied first credit for his theory. But a tragedy at Down House soon eclipsed worries over Wallace's paper—the death by scarlet fever, on June 28, of the Darwins' infant son Charles Waring. Later, when sufficiently recovered to again think about Wallace's essay, Charles pondered ways to ensure that his years of research were not eclipsed by Wallace. But he was also determined to see, or to create the appearance, that Wallace had been treated fairly.

In the end, without Wallace's knowledge, Darwin, Lyell, and Hooker arranged for the publication of a paper, under *both* Darwin's and Wallace's names, in the *Transactions of the Linnean Society of London*, a journal edited by Hooker. The paper—consisting of extracts from both men's writings—was titled "On the Tendency of Species to form Varieties" and was presented at the society's July 1, 1858, meeting. Significantly, neither author was present for the reading.*

By that August—his conscience assuaged by an encouraging letter from Wallace—Darwin was busy writing what he intended as a proper formal exposition of his theory. Plans called for the "abstract" to appear in Hooker's *Linnean Society* journal. By early 1859, however, it was clear that, in length and style, the work had transcended the "abstract" genre.

Charles Darwin was writing a book.

---

* Not until 1862 did Wallace return from the Malay Archipelago to England.

36

"THE HIGHEST & MOST INTERESTING
PROBLEM FOR THE NATURALIST"

*O*n the Origin of Species by Means of Natural Selection, or the Pres- *ervation of Favoured Races in the Struggle for Life* was published on November 24, 1859. Its London publisher, John Murray, was gratified that advance orders exceeded the initial print run of 1,250 copies of the 502-page book. Those orders allowed Murray to later claim that the book "sold out" on its first day. While respectable, the book's initial sales relative to other books during those months—including novels and travel narratives selling in the thousands—were hardly phenomenal. Building on the book's promising initial sales, however, successive British editions of *Origin of Species* followed, as did American and other foreign printings and translations. More generally, as an anonymous essayist in London's *Saturday Review* suggested, the work's influence went "beyond the bounds of the study and lecture-room into the drawing-room and the public street."

In England, natural science experienced a vogue during the first half of the nineteenth century, with books on the topic occasionally outselling popular fiction. But while initial sales of *Origin of Species* were, relatively speaking, modest, the disproportionate attention and later sales that it garnered rested on factors beyond the public appetite for natural history. Nor did Darwin's reputation or even the merits of his ideas fully explain the book's impact. The idea of evolving species, if not their *transmutation,* after all, had been explored in published writings by other thinkers of, or still resonant to, that age—notably Jean Baptiste Lamarck, Erasmus Darwin, Robert Chambers, William Paley, and Edward Blyth.

However, unlike other authors exploring such matters, Darwin cast *Origin of Species* as a first-person narrative, in a voice that avoided specialized language. Moreover, he frankly conceded gaps and flaws in his argument. As historian John W. Burrow observed, though *Origin* was a "profoundly polemical work . . . Darwin was not in the position of a scientist who announces a theory confirmed by striking experiments."

Indeed, in *Origin's* introduction, Darwin disarmingly tipped off readers that the book's chapters would address "the most apparent and gravest difficulties" of his theory:

> namely, first, the difficulties of transitions, or in understanding how a simple being or a simple organ can be changed and perfected into a highly developed being or elaborately constructed organ; secondly, the subject of Instinct, or the mental powers of animals; thirdly, Hybridism, or the infertility of species and the fertility of varieties when intercrossed; and fourthly, the imperfection of the Geological Record.

In the wake of *The Origin of Species's* publication, Darwin, fifty years old when it appeared and facing long anticipated controversies, confined his defense of the book to his prodigious, private correspondence. Underscoring that predilection, on June 30, 1860, he did not attend a soon-to-be legendary debate at Oxford University that pitted his supporters, including biologist Thomas Huxley and botanist Joseph Dalton Hooker, against detractors such as cleric Samuel Wilberforce, zoologist Richard Owen, and even Robert FitzRoy.

Darwin's advocates that evening typified the formidable cohort coalescing in his defense. In addition to those at the debate, its numbers included botanist Asa Gray, zoologist Ernst Haeckel (in Germany), and Charles Lyell—albeit the latter, initially qualifying his support, declined to, in Lyell's words, "go the whole Orang." They and other Darwin allies spoke favorably of the book in public settings and wrote, or arranged for the appearance of, favorable reviews in literary and scientific journals then proliferating across Britain, Europe, and the United States. Beyond Wilberforce, Owen, and FitzRoy, Darwin's critics eventually included Swiss-born US geologist Louis Agassiz and astronomer John Herschel, whose work, once up a time, had "stirred" a young Darwin to aspire to contribute to "the noble structure of Natural Science."

By 1859 and *Origin's* publication, Darwin and FitzRoy had long ago drifted apart. Even so, Darwin knew that, since the *Beagle's* return, FitzRoy had been increasingly beset with declining health, financial woes, and professional reversals. And, on April 30, 1865, succumbing to the lifelong depression that had led him to invite Darwin aboard his ship, the *Beagle's* captain, at age fifty-nine, cut his throat with a straight razor. Afterward, Darwin wrote a check for £100 to ease his widow Mary's financial burdens.

"I was astounded at news about FitzRoy," he wrote to Hooker. "But I ought not to have been, for I remember once thinking it likely; poor fellow his mind was quite out of balance once during our voyage. I never knew in my life so mixed a character. Always much to love & I once loved him sincerely; but so bad a temper & so given to take offence, that I gradually quite lost my love & wished only to keep out of contact with him."

Neither the words "God" nor "evolution" appeared in *Origin of Species.* Nor did the book include a direct refutation of the idea of God. It did, however, make clear that its author saw no evidence of progress or divine direction at work in nature—only local adaptations by organisms to local conditions.

Likewise, *Origin of Species* did not explicitly specify how *Homo sapiens* fit into the book's enunciated theories. Indeed, it barely mentioned the Fuegians and other Indigenous peoples encountered during Darwin's *Beagle* travels. Truth be known, he had originally planned to include materials in the book that, reaching beyond discussions of animal and plant species, would have applied his transmutation of species theory to humankind as well.

But by 1857, deeming the subject too controversial, Darwin abandoned the temptation. "I think I shall avoid [the] whole subject," he lamented to Alfred Russel Wallace, adding that he found the topic fraught—"surrounded with problems." Wistfully, however, he expressed regret at having to avoid, for the time being, a topic that he considered "the highest & most interesting problem for the naturalist."

Not until 1871, in his two-volume work *Descent of Man, and Selection in Relation to Sex* did Darwin apply the word "evolution" to his theorizing concerning the fixity of species. And while the word "God" did appear in that work, it also avoided—as Darwin did throughout his public life—taking a position on the existence of a supreme being. In *Descent*, however, he did clearly state that he accorded monotheistic beliefs no more validity than other faiths dismissed in respectable circles:

> The same high mental faculties which first led man to believe in unseen spiritual agencies, then in fetishism, polytheism, and ultimately in monotheism, would infallibly lead him, as long as his reasoning powers remained poorly developed, to various strange superstitions and customs.

In *Descent*, Darwin also developed more fully his theory of "sexual selection," first proposed in the *Origin of Species*, that sought to explain how organisms seek out particular traits when choosing mating partners. He likewise gave voice to decades of pent-up reflections concerning the Fuegians* and humankind in general. Contrasts between the Fuegians and Europeans, he argued, represented differences of degree—not of kind.

For Darwin, the Victorian gentleman represented civilization's apex. But he did not view Indigenous peoples as racially inferior. "The Fuegians rank amongst the lowest barbarians," he avowed. "But I was continually struck with surprise how closely the three natives on board

---

* Following the original 1839 printing of Darwin's *Beagle* narrative, later editions of that work included more content on the Fuegians aboard the ship but those accounts remained cursory in scope.

H.M.S. *Beagle*, who had lived some years in England and could talk a little English, resembled us in disposition and in most of our mental faculties."

Indeed, *Descent of Man*'s final pages found its author—after four decades, still fixated on the Fuegians—in a cast of mind equally nostalgic and defiant:

> The main conclusion arrived at in this work, namely that man is descended from some lowly organized form, will, I regret to think, be highly distasteful to many persons. But there can hardly be a doubt that we are descended from barbarians. The astonishment which I felt on first seeing a party of Fuegians on a wild and broken shore will never be forgotten by me, for the reflection at once rushed into my mind—such were our ancestors. These men were absolutely naked and bedaubed with paint, their long hair was tangled, their mouths frothed with excitement, and their expression was wild, startled, and distrustful. They possessed hardly any arts, and like wild animals lived on what they could catch; they had no government, and were merciless to every one not of their own small tribe. He who has seen a savage in his native land will not feel much shame, if forced to acknowledge that the blood of some more humble creature flows in his veins. For my own part I would as soon be descended from . . . that old baboon, who, descending from the mountains, carried away in triumph his young comrade from a crowd of astonished dogs— as from a savage who delights to torture his enemies, offers up bloody sacrifices, practises infanticide without remorse, treats his wives like slaves, knows no decency, and is haunted by the grossest superstitions.
>
> Man may be excused for feeling some pride at having risen, though not through his own exertions, to the very summit of the organic scale; and the fact of his having thus risen, instead of having been aboriginally placed there, may give him hopes for a still higher destiny in the distant future. But we are not here concerned with hopes or fears, only with the truth as far as our reason allows us to discover it. I have

given the evidence to the best of my ability; and we must acknowledge, as it seems to me, that man with all his noble qualities, with sympathy which feels for the most debased, with benevolence which extends not only to other men but to the humblest living creature, with his god-like intellect which has penetrated into the movements and constitution of the solar system—with all these exalted powers—Man still bears in his bodily frame the indelible stamp of his lowly origin.

Like *Origin of Species*, *Descent of Man* bore witness in fundamental ways to Darwin's overseas travels. As he later affirmed in the *Autobiography*, "The voyage of the *Beagle* has been by far the most important event in my life and has determined my whole career."

After returning from those travels, Darwin settled into a half-century of research and writing, activities driven by a discipline undeterred by frequent ill health—fatigue, vomiting, retching, bowel irregularity, faintness, and dizziness. Darwin published six books before 1859's *Origin of Species*. Afterward, in addition to 1871's *Descent of Man*, he published books on myriad other topics: insects and the fertilizing of orchids (1862), climbing plants (1865), variations among domesticated animals and plants (1868), expressions of emotions in humankind and animals (1872), carnivorous plants (1875), cross- and self-fertilization among plants (1876), variations in flowers among plants of the same species (1877), powers of movement among plants (1880), and earthworms (1881).[*]

Providing the intellectual bedrock for all of Darwin's books, however, was his five years of *Beagle* travels. Indeed, those wanderings proved to be, literally, the Odyssey of his lifetime. The Ithacan traveler and namesake of Homer's epic, after all, reaching the end of his own celebrated wanderings—except for one more implied final adventure, to appease Poseidon—never left home again. Charles Darwin understood that longing for home: from the end of his *Beagle* voyage in 1836, until his death at age seventy-three, on April 19, 1882, he never again set foot outside of Britain.

---

[*]   Originally intended only for himself and his family, Darwin's autobiography was written in 1876 and published posthumously in 1887.

EPILOGUE
ADVICE FOR TRAVELERS

I n conclusion, it appears to me that nothing can be more improving to a young naturalist, than a journey in distant countries. It both sharpens and partly also allays that want and craving, which as Sir J. Herschel remarks, a man experiences, although every corporeal sense is fully satisfied. The excitement from the novelty of objects, and the chance of success stimulates him on to activity. Moreover, as a number of isolated facts soon become uninteresting, the habit of comparison leads to generalization; on the other hand, as the traveller stays but a short space of time in each place, his description must generally consist of mere sketches instead of detailed observation. Hence arises, as I have found to my cost, a constant tendency to fill up the wide gaps of knowledge by inaccurate & superficial hypotheses.

But I have too deeply enjoyed the voyage not to recommend to any naturalist to take all chances, and to start on travels by land if possible, if otherwise on a long voyage. He may feel assured he will meet with no difficulties or dangers (excepting in rare cases) nearly so bad as he before hand imagined. In a moral point of view, the effect ought to be, to teach him good humored patience, unselfishness, the habit of acting for himself, and of making the best of everything, or contentment: in short, he should partake of the characteristic qualities of the greater number of sailors. Traveling ought also to teach him to distrust others;

but at the same time he will discover how many truly good-natured people there are, with whom he never before had, nor ever again will have any further communication, yet who are ready to offer him the most disinterested assistance.

—Charles Darwin, *Beagle* diary,
October 1836

ACKNOWLEDGMENTS

Toward the end of Albert Camus's *The Plague*, the novel's narrator Dr. Rieux, expresses cautious optimism over what he perceives to be a small but noticeable return to pre-epidemic life in Oran, the coastal Algerian city that he calls home. "The change, no doubt, was slight," he observes. "Yet, however slight, it proved what a vast forward stride our townsfolk had made in the way of hope. And indeed it could be said that once the faintest stirring of hope became possible, the dominion of the plague was ended."

As I write these words, Atlanta, where I live, along with many places in the world, are experiencing similar ambivalences. Rarely going out, I spent 2020 largely confined to my home, devoting much of that time—seven days a week, for up to ten hours a day—to writing this book.

More recently, like others among my circle of friends, albeit still masked-up, I'm venturing out again. While, for me, indoor restaurants, concerts, and the like remain bridges too far, I am returning to familiar venues such as grocery stores, other retail outlets, and outdoor cafés. Even so, with continuing news reports of Covid and its variants, it seems, to my mind, increasingly doubtful that "the dominion of the plague" has truly ended.

But I do know that, whatever happens next, I'm grateful for this pandemic's heroes. Whether developing vaccines, caring for patients, driving buses and trucks, or working in grocery stores and other essential enterprises, they've kept the world's gears turning. Moreover, their dedication permitted fortunate souls like myself the luxury of working safely at home.

For kindly reading all or selected chapters of my manuscript and offering corrections and suggestions to improve it, I'm grateful to various scientists and scholars, as well as those I called on for their familiarity with places through which Darwin traveled; they include paleontologist Warren Douglas Allmon of Cornell University; geographer Patrick Armstrong of the University of Western Australia, Perth; historian Tony Badger of Cambridge University; neuroscientist Geert de Vries of Georgia State University, Atlanta; scientist and author Alvaro Fischer of Santiago, Chile; political commentator Josie Pagani of New Zealand's Kapiti Coast; from our shared graduate school and beers-at-Manuel's-Tavern days, historian of Argentina Gustavo Paz, now returned to Buenos Aires, at the Universidad Torcuato Di Tella; theologian Philip Reynolds of Emory University, recently retired to his beloved Yorkshire, England; physicians Katarina Tomas and Simon Parsons, now of Canmore, Alberta, Canada, formerly of, respectively, Melbourne, Australia and Launceston, Tasmania, Australia; geologist and author Rob Wesson of Evergreen, Colorado; and historian of Brazil Thom Whigham of the University of Georgia, Athens.

Among those listed above, three individuals kindly read the entire manuscript and provided the sort of constructive suggestions that are gold to any working author. Thus for generosity, extending above and beyond the call of duty, I owe singular gratitude to the aforementioned Warren Douglas Allmon, professor and director of the Paleontological Research Institution at Cornell University; Patrick Armstrong, adjunct professor of Geography at the University of Western Australia, and author of among other fine works, the indispensable *Darwin's Other Islands*; and geologist Rob Wesson, formerly of the US Geological Survey and more recently, author of the splendid *Darwin's First Theory*. For his early support and encouragement of this project, I also thank Richard White, professor of American history emeritus at Stanford University.

Beyond those individuals, *Odyssey* draws on the works of hundreds of other fine scholars and authors. Among those good souls, both living and deceased, I'm particularly indebted to Nora Barlow (a botanist and granddaughter of Charles Darwin); Janet Browne, Frederick Burkhardt, Peter

J. Bowler, Adrian Desmond, Nick Hazlewood, Richard Darwin Keynes (a physician and great-grandson of the naturalist), John Lynch, James Moore, Kees Rookmaaker, Alistair Sponsel, Keith Stewart Thomson, Rob Viens, and John van Wyhe.

I'm also grateful to the dedicated teams who operate two superb websites: the Darwin Correspondence Project, at the University of Cambridge; and the Darwin Online, at the National University of Singapore—the latter founded and directed by the aforementioned Professor van Wyhe. Both websites are invaluable to Darwin researchers under any circumstances, but appreciated all the more under pandemic circumstances. Special gratitude is owed Rosemary Clarkson of the Darwin Correspondence Project; and John van Wyhe, director of Darwin Online, who kindly fielded several questions stumping me during my research.

For the illustrations used in this book, I thank Down House, Kent, England; the Historic England Archive, Swindon, England; the Wellcome Collection Museum, London; the New York Public Library, the Cambridge University Library; the Grand Palais Museum, Paris; Art Resource, New York; Museo Histórico Nacional, Buenos Aires; the Fitz-William Museum, Cambridge; Wikimedia Commons; and John Huges of the Shropshire Wildlife Trust.

For other kindnesses and good cheer during trying times, I'm grateful to friends Tommy Archibald, Geert DeVries, Nancy Forger, Marysia Harbutt, Maria Jacobsen, Steve Johnson (who kindly read and offered suggestions for several early chapters), Elaine Longwater, Tim Ralston, Michael Robertson, Katie Wood, and Lyle York. I also thank my wonderful agent, Elise Capron of the Sandra Dijkstra Literary Agency in California; and my talented editor Jessica Case at Pegasus Books, in New York. I also thank associate editor Victoria Wenzel, copy editor Drew Wheeler, production manager Maria Fernandez, proofreader Mike Richards, and publicist Tim Thomas. I'm likewise indebted to designer Charles Brock for the luminous book jacket, and to Michael Siegel of Rutgers University for the elegant maps. For Kerouac quote-wrangling, I also thank Chris "Beat" Buxbaum, of Atlanta's beloved A Cappella Books. And while I'm at it, gratitude is due to my dear friend, geologist and environmentalist extraordinaire Dale Doremus, for all those hikes and backpacking trips in the mountains of Georgia and Wyoming many years ago—my first lessons in reading landscapes.

At home, I'm grateful to my wife Meta Larsson for her abiding love and support and her usual astute suggestions and insights concerning my work. For just over two years now, our life together has been enriched by the addition to our household of Meta's former student Lesly González Herrera of Jinotega, Nicaragua. Lesly, with her omnivorous appetite for learning, possesses a broad knowledge of Latin American culture and history. In innumerable ways, she has provided both help and good company during the writing of this book. More than that, Lesly has been an inspiration: With stalwart courage and rarely flagging good cheer, she, in her young years—finding her way alone, without resources or family, in a foreign land—has confronted more adversities than most face in a lifetime.

After arriving in Atlanta in February 2019 with a scholarship to study English in Georgia State University's Intensive English Program, Lesly completed ten weeks of classes. Afterward, when she did not appear at Atlanta's airport for her return flight, we learned that she had credible reasons to fear persecution, even violence, from Daniel Ortega's repressive government, if she returned to Nicaragua. Executing a plan long in the making, divulged only to family and a few friends, she applied for US political asylum.

Months later, after a series of temporary lodging arrangements, Lesly accepted our invitation to live with us. Her father, we knew by then, had been imprisoned and was being tortured, before Lesly's arrival in Atlanta, for publicly protesting Ortega's human rights abuses. Months later, as Ortega faced threats of new sanctions from the European Union, her father, after a year in prison, was released into house arrest, along with hundreds of other political prisoners.

But the family's ordeal was hardly over. Just outside their house, Lesly's parents and two younger siblings faced the menacing presence of twenty-four-hour surveillance by armed paramilitary thugs—fiends often given to homicidal tendencies.

We soon raised funds that enabled all four family members, in fall 2019, to slip out of Nicaragua to Meta's native Sweden. There, they are now safe and building new lives. Lesly, for her part, as I write this, is about to leave Atlanta to commence scholarship-supported studies at a New England college.

We're happy for, and proud of, Lesly. To my mind, she personifies Ernest Hemingway's definition of courage: "grace under pressure."*

Though we'll miss her daily presence, we trust that we'll see her often over the coming years. Beyond that, Lesly will remain in our hearts.

Tom Chaffin

Atlanta, August 2021

---

* "The change," Camus, *Plague* 272; "grace under pressure," Parker, "The Artist's Reward" [Hemingway profile], *New Yorker*, Nov. 30, 1929, 31.

IMAGE CREDITS

Figure 1 and 2. Chalk drawing by Ellen Sharples, 1816; Wellcome Collection; chalk and water-color by George Richmond, 1840; Down House, Kent, © Historic England Archive, Darwin Heirlooms Trust.

Figure 3: Photograph, John Hughes, 2014; Shropshire Wildlife Trust.

Figure 4: Engraving, by Thomas Lupton, 1839, after James Pardon; Wellcome Collection.

Figure 5: Miniature, watercolor on ivory by Peter Paillou the Younger; FitzWilliam Museum, Cambridge.

Figure 6; Portrait of Erasmus Darwin; New York Public Library.

Figure 7: Portrait of Josiah Wedgwood, after Sir J. Reynolds; Wellcome Collection.

Figure 8: 1820 drawing and engraving by J. and H. S. Storer; Wellcome Collection.

Figure 9: 1820 line-engraving by George Hollis, after John Chessell Buckler; Wellcome Collection.

Figure 10: Undated Cartoon by Albert Way; Reproduced by kind permission of the Syndics of Cambridge University Library

Figure 11: John Henslow lithograph by Thomas Herbert Maguire, 1835; Wellcome Collection.

Figure 12: Adam Sedgwick mezzotint by S. Cousins, 1833, after T. Phillips, 1832; Wellcome Collection.

Figure 13: Josiah Wedgwood II portrait by William Owen; Wikimedia Commons.

Figure 14: HMS *Beagle* diagrams; Wellcome Collection.

Figure 15: Robert FitzRoy lithograph 1835, after drawing by Philip Gidley King; Wellcome Collection.

Figure 16: *Beagle* diary page; © Historic England Archive.

Figure 17: "Crossing the Line," engraving by Thomas Landseer, from drawing by Augustus Earle, Wellcome Collection.

Figure 18: Line drawing "Brazil rain forest," by Frederic de Clarac, 1819; RMN-Grand Palais / Art Resource, NY.

Figure 19: Engraving from *Travels in South America, during the years 1819–20–20*, by Alexander Caldcleugh, New York Public Library.

Figure 20: "View of the Corcovado," engraving by Edward Francis Finden after Lady Maria Callcott, from *Journal of a voyage to Brazil, and residence there, during part of the years 1821, 1822, 1823*, pub. 1824 by Lady Maria Callcott, pub. 1824; New York Public Library.

Figure 21: Fuegians; Wellcome Collection.

Figure 22: 1843 portrait by Chilean-born Argentine artist Fernando García del Molino; Museo Histórico Nacional, Buenos Aires.

Figure 23: "Button Island, near Woolya," Thomas Landseer engraving, after drawing by Conrad Martens, from FitzRoy, *Proceedings of the Second Expedition, 1831–1836*, 1839; Welcome Collection.

Figure 24: "Fuegian Wigwam at Hope Harbor in the Magdalen Channel," engraving by S. Bell after drawing by Philip Parker King; Wellcome Collection.

Figure 25: "Bivouac at the Head of Port Desire Inlet," 1839 engraving after Conrad Martens drawing, from *Proceedings of the second expedition, 1831–1836*, by Robert Fitz-Roy, 1839; Wellcome Collection.

Figure 26: "Beagle laid ashore, River Santa Cruz," engraving by Thomas Landseer after drawing by Conrad Martens, from FitzRoy, *Proceedings of the Second Expedition, 1831– 1836*, 1839; Welcome Collection.

Figure 27: "Basalt Glen—River Santa Cruz," engraving after Conrad Martens; Wellcome Collection.

Figure 28: "Crossing the Cordillera on the 1st of June," aquatint from *Travels in South America during the years 1819, 1820, 1821*, by Alexander Caldcleugh, 1825; New York Public Library.

Figure 29: Uspallata Pass photograph circa 1870 – 1899; New York Public Library.

Figure 30: "Remains of the Cathedral at Concepcion Ruined by the Great Earthquake of 1835," engraving by S. Bull from drawing by John Clements Wickham, in *Proceedings of the Second Expedition, 1831–1836*, 1839; Wellcome Collection.

Figure 31: "Giant Tortoises of the Galapagos Island," from *The New Natural History*," by Richard Lydekker, circa 1901; New York Public Library.

Figure 32: Engraving from *A statistical, historical, and political description of the colony of New South Wales, and its dependent settlements in Van Diemen's Land*, by W.C. Wentworth, 1819; Library of New South Wales.

Figure 33: Emma Wedgwood Darwin, late 1830s watercolor portrait by George Richmond; Wikimedia Commons.

Figure 34 and 35: Down House exterior wood-engraving, by J. R. Brown; and photograph of library; both images courtesy Wellcome Collection.

Figure 36: Charles Lyell photograph by John Jabez Edwin Mayall: Wellcome Collection.

Figure 37: *Principles pf Geology* (1830) frontispiece, engraving, after drawing by John Izard Middleton; Wellcome Collection.

Figure 38: Jean-Baptiste Lamarck photogravure after C. Thévenin, 1801; Wellcome Collection.

Figure 39: Richard Owen photograph by Maull and Polyblank, about 1856; Wellcome Collection.

Figure 40: Alfred Russel Wallace, from *Alfred Russel Wallace letters and reminiscences*, Volume 1, James Marchant ed., 1916; Wellcome Collection.

Figure 41: "Charles Darwin as an ape holds up a mirror to another ape," color lithograph by Faustin Betbeder, 1874; Wellcome Collection.

Figure 42: Charles Darwin, photograph by Leonard Darwin, 1878; Wellcome Collection.

A NOTE ON SOURCES AND STYLE

Most of the documents that animate this work are primary sources—contemporary letters, diaries, publications, notebooks, and other writings. And while most of those materials are available in printed publications, while writing this book during the COVID pandemic, I've accessed many of them at two wonderful websites that constitute a scholar's dream—the Darwin Correspondence Project [DCP] and Darwin Online.

Based at the University of Cambridge, the Darwin Correspondence Project, offering more than 15,000 letters, contains expertly transcribed, astutely annotated correspondence between and among Charles's far-flung network of family, friends, and associates. Darwin Online, based at the University of Singapore, hosts a wealth of other published and unpublished documents that I've drawn upon—including successive editions of Charles's books, as well as his journals, notebooks, and other papers; and memoirs and diaries by his colleagues, relatives, and others who knew or influenced him; along with works by Darwin biographers and scholars.

Those seeking printed sources for materials quoted herein can readily locate or be guided to them through these two fine websites or by my own endnotes. My research has been further assisted by Kees Rookmaaker's invaluable "Darwin's itinerary on the voyage of the *Beagle*," found at Darwin Online.

In quoting transcribed manuscripts created by Charles Darwin, I've largely resisted the temptation to standardize punctuation, capitalization, and spelling—the latter so chronically bad on Charles's part that it became a topic of playful banter between him and his sister Susan.

When quoting, however, from letters, notebooks, and the diary that Charles produced during his *Beagle* travels, I have made one exception to the aforementioned policy. Charles frequently uses dashes, along with periods, to end his sentences. And, in the interest of preserving textual fluidity.—of avoiding an unnecessary distraction for readers.—I've removed most of those redundant, end-of-sentence dashes.

In other instances, in which Charles repeatedly employs a now obsolete place-name, I've provided, upon his first reference to that locale, its modern name. However, in subsequent references to the place, I've preserved his name for it; and, following his lead, used his term in my own references to the place.

Otherwise, when Charles or others, in passing mentions, use obsolete place-names, now obscure references, or hopelessly confusing spelling, I've inserted within brackets a clarifying reference. Similarly, in many cases, in which a significant place or geographic feature has differing names in English and Spanish or in other non-English languages, I've provided its English and non-English appellation upon the place's first appearance in the narrative.

Finally, in their respective original sources, Charles and others, when referring to various racial and ethnic groups, routinely employ terms now regarded as offensive, even hurtful. In the interest of fidelity to the historical record, however, I quote such terms herein verbatim as they appear in those original sources.

BIBLIOGRAPHY

PRIMARY SOURCES

[Anon.] "Professor Owen on the Origin of Species." *Saturday Review*, 9. May 5, 1860. 573–574.

Angelou, Maya. "On the Pulse of Morning." Poetry Foundation website.

Ashworth, J. H. "Charles Darwin as a Student in Edinburgh, 1825–1827." *Proceedings of the Royal Society of Edinburgh*. 1935. 55: 97–113.

Balzac, Honoré de. "The Wild Ass's Skin," short story in *Introduction to Comedy*. New York: President Publishing, 1920.

Blake, William. *The Portable Blake*. Alfred Kazin, ed. New York: Viking Press, 1971.

Borges, Jorge Luis. *Selected Poems*. New York: Penguin, 2000.

Butler, Samuel. *Evolution, Old and New, Or, The Theories of Buffon, Dr. Erasmus Darwin and Lamarck, as Compared with that of Charles Darwin*. London: David Bogie, 1882.

Bridges, Esteban Lucas. *Uttermost Part of the Earth*. New York: E.P. Dutton and Co., 1949.

Camus, Albert. *The Plague*. Stuart Gilbert, trans. New York: Vintage, 1991.

Cervantes, Miguel de. *Don Quixote*. Edith Grossman, trans. New York: HarperCollins, 2003.

Cohen, Leonard. *Selected Poems, 1956–1968*. New York: Viking, 1968.

Covington, Syms. *Journal of Syms Covington*. [Assistant to C. Darwin on Beagle Voyage]. Sydney: Australian Science Archives Project, 1998.

Darwin, Charles. *Autobiography*. New York: Harcourt, Brace, 1958.

Darwin, Charles, et al. *The Beagle Letters* [1831–1836]. Frederick Burkhardt, ed. Cambridge, UK: Cambridge University Press, 2008.

Darwin, Charles. *Charles Darwin and the Voyage of the* Beagle. Nora Barlow, ed. London: Pilot Press, 1945.

Darwin, Charles. *Charles Darwin's Beagle Diary*. R. D. Keynes, ed. Cambridge, UK: Cambridge University Press, 2001.

Darwin, Charles. *Charles Darwin's Letters: A Selection. 1825–1859*. F. Burckhardt, ed. Cambridge: Cambridge University Press, 2008.

Darwin, Charles. *Charles Darwin's Notebooks from the Voyage of the* Beagle. Gordon Chancellor and John van Wyhe, eds., with Kees Rookmaaker. Cambridge, UK: Cambridge University Press, 2009.

Darwin, Charles. *Charles Darwin's zoology notes & specimen lists from H.M.S. Beagle.* Richard Keynes, ed. Cambridge, UK: Cambridge University Press, 2000.

Darwin, Charles. "Darwin's Ornithological Notes." Nora Barlow, ed. *Bulletin of the British Museum (Natural History).* Historical Series 2, 1963. No. 7: 201–278.

Darwin, Charles. "Darwin's Insects: Charles Darwin's Entomological Notes." Kenneth G. V. Smith, ed. *Bulletin of the British Museum (Natural History)* Historical Series. Vol. 14(1): 1–143.

Darwin, Charles. "Darwin's Journal" (1809–81). John van Wyhe, ed. Darwin Online.

Darwin, Charles. *Descent of Man.* 2 Vols. London: John Murray, 1871.

Darwin, Charles. "Edinburgh Diary, for 1826." Transcribed and edited, John van Wyhe. Darwin Online.

Darwin, Charles. *The Expression of the Emotions in Man and Animals.* London: John Murray, 1872.

Darwin, Charles. *Extracts from Letters Addressed to Professor Henslow.* privately printed. Cambridge, UK: 1835.

Darwin, Charles. *Geological Diary.* Transcribed, Kees Rookmaaker *et al;* John van Wyhe, ed. [Darwin online].

Darwin, Charles. *Journal of the Geology and Natural History of the Various Countries Visited by H.M.S Beagle.* London: Henry Colburn, 1839.

Darwin, Charles. *Geological Observations on South America.* London: Smith Elder and Co., 1846.

Darwin, Charles. *On the Origin of Species by Means of Natural Selection,* London: Penguin, 1985.

Darwin, Emma. *A Century of Family Letters, 1792–1896.* Vol. 1. Henrietta Litchfield, ed. London: John Murray, 1915.

Darwin, Erasmus and Samuel Latham Mitchill. *Zoonomia; or the Laws of Organic Life.* Part One. London: Thomas & Andrews, 1809.

Darwin, Francis. *Life and Letters of Charles Darwin.* Vol. 1. London: John Murray, 1887.

Earle, Augustus. *A Narrative of a Nine Months' Residence in New Zealand in 1827, Together with a Journal of a Residence in Tristan D'Acunha.* London: Longman, Rees, 1830.

Earle, Augustus. *Sketches Illustrative of the Native Inhabitants and Islands of New Zealand.* Lithographed and published in London under the auspices of the New Zealand Association by Robert Martin, 1838.

Earle, Augustus. *Views in New South Wales, and Van Diemen's Land.* London: J. Cross, 1830.

Fitz-Roy, R. "Extracts from the Diary of an Attempt to Ascend the River Santa Cruz, in Patagonia, with the boats of his Majesty's sloop *Beagle* [1837]." *Journal of the Royal Geographical Society of London* 7. 1837. 114–126.

Fitz-Roy, Robert. *Proceedings of the Second Expedition 1831–1836, Under the Command of Robert M. Fitz-Roy, R.N.* London: Henry Colburn, 1839.

Fitz-Roy, Robert and Charles Darwin. "A Letter Containing Remarks on the Moral State of Tahiti, New Zealand, &c.," in *South African Christian Recorder,* Sept 4, 1836. Darwin Online.

FitzRoy, R., P. P. King, and Charles Darwin. *The Narrative of the Voyages of Adventure and Beagle 1826–1836.* Katharine Anderson, ed. 3 vols. and appendix. London: Pickering and Chatto, 2011.

Forsyth, Charles. "Midshipman Forsyth's Log from the voyage of HMS *Beagle*," Simon Keynes, ed. Darwin Online.

Goethe, Johann von Wolfgang. *The Essential Goethe.* Princeton, New Jersey: Princeton University Press, 2016.

Litchfield, Henrietta. "Recollections of Darwin's Beagle Voyage." Darwin Online.

Gilbert, W. S. *Plays and Poems.* New York: Random House, 1932.

Homer. *The Odyssey.* Robert Folger, trans. New York: Penguin, 1996.

Kerouac, Jack. *On the Road: The Original Scroll.* New York: Penguin, 2008

King, P. P. *Proceedings of the First Expedition 1826–30, Under the Command of Captain P. Parker King R. N., F. R. S.* London: Henry Colburn, 1838.

McCormick, Robert. "Diary"—in Steel, Emily. *He is No Loss: Robert McCormick and the Voyage of HMS Beagle.* London: British Society for the History of Science, 2011.

Malthus, Thomas. *Essay on the Principal of Population.* London: J. Johnson, 1798.

Martens, Conrad. "Journal of a voyage from England to Australia aboard HMS Beagle and HMS Hyacinth 1833–35." Michael K. Organ, transcription. Sydney, Australia: State Library of NSW Press, 1994.

Milton, John. "Paradise Lost" and "Paradise Regained" in *The Portable Milton.* Douglas Bush, ed. New York: Viking Press, 1973.

Neruda, Pablo. *Essential Selected Poems.* San Francisco: City Lights, 2004.

Paley, William. *Natural Theology, or Evidences of the Existence and Attributes of the Deity.* [orig. pub. 1802] Boston: Gould and Lincoln, 1853.

Parker, Dorothy. "The Artist's Reward." *New Yorker* 5. Nov. 30, 1929. 28–31.

Price, John. "Recollections of Darwin." Darwin Online.

Said, Edward. *Orientalism.* New York: Vintage, 1979.

Sulivan, Bartholomew James. *Life and Letters of the Late Admiral Sir Bartholomew James Sulivan, K.C.B., 1810–1890.* Henry Norton Sulivan, ed. London: John Murray, 1897.

Snow, W. Parker. "A Few Remarks on the Wild Tribes of Tierra del Fuego from Personal Observations." *Transactions of the Ethnological Society of London* 1 (1861): 261–267.

Whitman, Walt. *Poetry and Prose,* New York: Library of America, 1982.

Whitman, Walt. *With Walt Whitman in Camden.* Vol. 8, Walt Whitman Archive website.

Woodall, Edward. *Charles Darwin, A Paper Contributed to the Transactions of the Shropshire Archaeological Society.* London: Trubner and Co., 1884 or 1885.

Wordsworth, William. *Wordsworth: Poems.* New York: Everyman's Library, 1995.

SECONDARY SOURCES

———. Alumnos y docentes de la Universidad Nacional del Sur [Bahía Blanca, Argentina.] "Paseo virtual por la Fortaleza Protectora Argentina," July 3, 2012.

———.*Gaceta Marinera.* "A 124 años de la creación de la Base Naval Puerto Belgrano." n.d. Online.

Arana, Marie. *Silver, Sword, and Stone.* New York: Simon & Schuster, 2019.

Armitstead, Claire. "Unique Watercolour of Darwin on HMS *Beagle* Tipped to Fetch Upward of £50,000 at Auction." (London) *Guardian*, Nov. 25, 2015.

Armstrong, Patrick. "Charles Darwin's Image of the World: The Influence of Alexander von Humboldt on the Victorian Naturalist." *Beiträge Zur Regionalen Geographie* 49. 1999. 46–53.

Armstrong, Patrick. *Darwin's Luck: Chance and Fortune in the Life and Work of Charles Darwin*. London: Bloomsbury, 2009.

Armstrong, Patrick. *Darwin's Other Islands*. London: Bloomsbury Academic, 2004.

Armstrong, Patrick. *Under the Blue Vault of Heaven: A Study of Charles Darwin's Sojourn in the Cocos (Keeling) Islands*. Nedlands, Australia: Indian Ocean Centre for Peace Studies, 1991.

Beer, Gillian. *Darwin's Plots: Evolutionary Narrative in Darwin, George Eliot, and Nineteenth-Century Fiction*. Cambridge, UK: Cambridge University Press, 2009.

Bergad, Laird, *Comparative Histories of Slavery in Brazil, Cuba, and the United States*. Cambridge, UK: Cambridge University Press, 2007.

Birse, Ronald M. *Science at the University of Edinburgh, 1542–1993*. Edinburgh: University of Edinburgh, 1994.

Bowlby, John. *Charles Darwin: A New Life*. New York: W. W. Norton, 1992.

Bowler, Peter J. "The Changing Meaning of 'Evolution.'" *Journal of the History of Ideas* 36. Jan.–Mar. 1975. 95–114.

Bowler, Peter J. *Evolution: The History of an Idea*. Berkeley: University of California Press, 1989.

Browne, Janet. *Charles Darwin: A Biography, Vol. 1—Voyaging*. Princeton, N.J.: Princeton University Press, 1995.

Browne, Janet. *Charles Darwin: A Biography, Vol. 2, The Power of Place*. Princeton, N.J.: Princeton University Press, 2002.

Campbell, John. *In Darwin's Wake*. Dobbs Ferry, NY: Sheridan House, 1997.

Castro-Le-Fort, Eduardo. *Darwin en Chile (1832–1835): viaje de un naturalista alrededor del mundo*. Santiago, Chile: Editorial Universitaria, 1995.

Chaffin, Tom. *Fatal Glory: Narciso López and the First Clandestine U.S. War against Cuba*. Charlottesville: University Press of Virginia, 1996.

Chaffin, Tom. *Giant's Causeway: Frederick Douglass's Irish Odyssey and the Making of an American Visionary*. Charlottesville: University of Virginia Press, 2014.

Chaffin, Tom. *Pathfinder: John Charles Frémont and the Course of American Empire*. New York: Hill and Wang/Farrar, Straus and Giroux, 2002.

Chaffin, Tom. *Sea of Gray: The Around-the-World Odyssey of the Confederate Raider Shenandoah*. New York: Hill and Wang/Farrar, Straus and Giroux, 2006.

Clarkson, Rosemary, Darwin Correspondence Project. Emails to author, 2020–21.

Crockatt, Richard. "The Beagle's Pups: Small-boat Surveying Expeditions in South America." *Journal of Maritime Research* 20 (2018): 21–40.

De Paolo, Charles. *The Ethnography of Charles Darwin: A Study of His Writings on Aboriginal Peoples*. Jefferson, NC: McFarland & Co., 2010.

Desmond, Adrian and James Moore. *Darwin: The Life of a Tormented Evolutionist*. New York: Grand Central, 1992.

Desmond, Adrian and James Moore. *Darwin's Sacred Cause: How a Hatred of Slavery Shaped Darwin's Views on Human Evolution*. Boston: Houghton Mifflin Harcourt, 2009.

Estes, G., T. Grant, and P. Grant. "Darwin in the Galapagos. His Footsteps through the Archipelago." *Notes and Records of the Royal Society* 54 (2000): 343–368.

Freeman, R. B. "Bibliographical Introduction" [for *Journal of Researches, et al.*, Darwin Online].

Garretón, Juan Antonio. *Partes detallados de la expedición al desierto de Juan Manuel de Rosas en 1833*. Buenos Aires, Argentina: Editorial Universitaria de Buenos Aires, 1975.

Gribbin, John, and Mary Gribbin. *FitzRoy: The Remarkable Story of Darwin's Captain and the Invention of the Weather Forecast*. Scotts Valley, Calif.: Create Space, 1996.

Hackforth-Jones, Jocelyn. *Augustus Earle, Travel Artist: Paintings and Drawings in the Rex Nan Kivell Collection*. Canberra: National Library of Australia, 1980.

Hazlewood, Nick. *Savage: The Life and Times of Jemmy Button*. New York: Thomas Dunne, 2001.

Herbert, Sandra. *Charles Darwin, Geologist*. Ithaca, N.Y.: Cornell University Press, 2005.

Horenstein, Sidney. "Darwin's Busts and Public Evolutionary Outreach and Education." *Evolution: Education and Outreach* 4 (2011): 478–488.

Kelly, Andrew and Melanie Kelly, eds. *Darwin: For the Love of Science*. Essays. Bristol, UK: Bristol Community Development Partnership, 2009.

Kennedy, Maev. "Darwin's Lost Fossils, Including a Sloth the Size of a Car, to Be Made Public." (London) *Guardian*, April 6, 2018.

Keynes, Richard. *Fossils, Finches and Fuegians: Charles Darwin's Adventures and Discoveries on the "Beagle."* New York: HarperCollins, 2003.

Larson, Edward J. *Evolution's Workshop. God And Science On The Galapagos Islands*. New York: Basic Books, 2001.

Lynch, John. *Argentine Caudillo, Juan Manuel de Rosas*. Wilmington, Del.: Rowman & Littlefield, 2001.

McCalman, Iain. *Darwin's Armada: Four Voyages and the Battle for the Theory of Evolution*. New York: Norton, 2010.

McDonald, Patricia. *The Wandering Artist: Augustus Earle's Travels Round the World, 1820–29*. Canberra: National Library of Australia, 1996.

Marks, Richard Lee. *Three Men of the Beagle*. New York: Knopf, 1991.

Mayer, Ruth. "The Things of Civilization, the Matters of Empire: Representing Jemmy Button." *New Literary History* 39 n. 2. Spring 2008. 193–215.

Mulhern, Joseph Martin. "After 1833: British Entanglement with Brazilian Slavery," doctoral thesis, Durham University, 2018.

Mulholland, John. "Earthquakes, Tsunamis and a Naked Tribe." (London) *Guardian*, Jan. 11, 2015.

Murray-Oliver, Anthony. *Augustus Earle in New Zealand*. Christchurch, New Zealand: Whitcombe & Tombs, 1968.

Noyce, Diana. "Charles Darwin, the Gourmet Traveler." *Gastronomica* 12, No. 2 Summer 2012. 45–52.

Nichols, Peter. *Evolution's Captain: The Dark Fate of the Man Who Sailed Charles Darwin Around the World*. New York: HarperCollins, 2003.

Parodiz, Juan José. *Darwin in the New World*. Leiden, Holland: Brill, 1981.

Pearson, P. N. and C. J. Nicholas. "'Marks of Extreme Violence': Charles Darwin's Geological Observations at St Jago (São Tiago) Cape Verde Islands." *Special Publications*. Geological Society, London, Jan. 2007; 239–253.

Porter, Duncan M. "The Beagle Collector and His Collections," in *The Darwinian Heritage*. David Kohn, ed. Princeton, N.J.: Princeton University Press, 1985. 973–1019.

Porter, Duncan and Peter Graham. *Darwin's Sciences*. New York: John Wiley & Sons, 2015.

Quammen, David. *The Reluctant Mr. Darwin*. New York: Norton, 2007.

Roberts, Michael B. "Just before the Beagle: Charles Darwin's Fieldwork in Wales, Summer 1831." *Endeavour* 24, no. 1. April 2001. 33–37.

Robertson, John Parish, and William Parish Robertson. *Letters on Paraguay: Comprising an Account of a Four Years' Residence in that Republic, Under the Government of the Dictator Francia*. Vol. 1. London: William Clowes and Sons, 1838.

Robinson, Eugene. "Argentines Cheer Returning Hero 112 Years after His Death." *Washington Post*, Oct. 2, 1989.

Rock, David. *The British in Argentina: Commerce, Settlers and Power*. London: Palgrave, 2019.

Sæther, Steinar A. "Making Sense of a Minor Migrant Stream": 17–56, in *Expectations Unfulfilled: Norwegian Migrants in Latin America, 1820–1940*. Boston and Leiden, Netherlands: Brill, 2015.

Smith, Bernard. "Augustus Earle (1793–1838)." *Australian Dictionary of Biography*, 1966.

Smith, Bernard, *European Vision and the South Pacific, 1768–1850: A Study in the History of Art and Ideas*, Oxford, UK: Clarendon Press, 1960.

Sponsel, Alistair. *Darwin's Evolving Identity*. Chicago: University of Chicago Press, 2018.

Sponsel, Alistair. Interview. "New Books in Intellectual History" podcast. Feb. 14, 2020.

Stein, Stanley J. and Barbara H. Stein. *Colonial Heritage of Latin America: Essays on Economic Dependence in Perspective*. Oxford, UK: Oxford University Press, 1970.

Stoddart, David R. "Darwin, Lyell, and the Geological Significance of Coral Reefs." *British Journal for the History of Science* 9. 1976. 199–218.

Stone, James H. "Economic Plants Encountered on the Voyage of the *Beagle*." *Economic Botany* 16 no. 2. April–June 1962. 116–126.

Sulloway, F. J. "Darwin and his Finches: The Evolution of a Legend." *Journal of the History of Biology* 15. 1982. 1–53.

Taylor, James. *Voyage of the Beagle*. Annapolis, Md.: Naval Institute Press, 2008.

Thomson, Keith Stewart. "H.M.S. *Beagle*, 1820–1870." *American Scientist*, 63. 1975. 664–672.

Thomson, Keith Stewart. *H.M.S. Beagle: The Story of Darwin's Ship*. New York: W.W. Norton, 1995.

Viens, Rob. "Art of the Beagle, Conrad Martens, Part II." Beagle Project website, Dec. 17, 2013.

Viens, Rob. "Whalers on the Beagle." Beagle Project Website, August 18, 2012.

Wesson, Rob. *Darwin's First Theory: Exploring Darwin's Quest to Find a Theory of the Earth*. New York: Pegasus Books, 2017.

Williamson, Edwin. *Penguin History of Latin America*. rev. edition. New York: Penguin, 1992.

Wyhe, John van. *Charles Darwin in Cambridge: The Most Joyful Years*. Singapore: World Scientific Press, 2014.

Wyhe, John van. "The Evolution Revolution." *New Scientist*, July 16, 2016. 35–39.

Wyhe, John van. "Where Do Darwin's Finches Come From?" *The Evolutionary Review*, 3, 1 (2012): 185–195.

REFERENCE WORKS AND ONLINE RESOURCES AND MEDIA

The Beagle Project. Bellevue, Washington.

The Complete Review, New York.

Darwin Correspondence Project, University of Cambridge.

Darwin Online, National University of Singapore.

Darwin's Manuscripts, American Museum of Natural History, New York.

Bob Dylan website: bobdylan.com.

Freeman, R. B. 2007. *Charles Darwin: A Companion*. 2nd online edition. Compiled by Sue Asscher and edited by John van Wyhe.

Looking for Darwin (website of author Lloyd Spencer Davis, New Zealand).

National Portrait Gallery, London.

Poetry Foundation Website.

UNESCO World Heritage Centre, Paris. ["Historic Centre of Salvador de Bahía" article].

Rookmaaker, Kees. 2009. "Darwin's itinerary on the voyage of the Beagle" [Darwin Online].

Walt Whitman Archive website, Matt Cohen, Ed FOlsom, and Kenneth M. Price, editors

ENDNOTES

ABBREVIATIONS
CD, Charles Darwin
[CD] *Auto, Autobiography*
DCP, Darwin Correspondence Project
[CD] *Diary, Charles Darwin's Beagle Diary*
[CD] *Journal, Journal and Remarks* (unless otherwise indicated, the original 1839
      edition)

EPIGRAPH
p. ix   "I don't know," Whitman, *With Walt Whitman in Camden*, Vol 8, 454,
               Walt Whitman Archive website.

INTRODUCTION
p. xv   "There was nowhere," Kerouac, *On the Road: The Original Scroll*, 130.
p. xv   chalk portrait by Ellen Sharples, water-color portrait by George
               Richmond.
p. xv   "The voyage," Charles Darwin [hereafter CD], *Autobiography* [hereafter
               Auto], 76.
p. xvi   "Darwinian Man," Gilbert, *Plays and Poems*, 317.
p. xvi   "We staid," CD, *Journal and Remarks* [hereafter *Journal*], 241.
p. xviii   "Chit-chat details," CD to Susan Darwin, April 29, 1836, DCP.
p. xix   "Is not Cuvier," Balzac, "The Wild Ass's Skin," 74.
p. xix   "Sentences," CD, *Auto* 137; for lists of books read by Darwin, see "What
               Darwin Read," DCP; for Darwin and Eliot, see Beer, *Darwin's Plots*, and
               "George Eliot (Mary Ann Evans)" article, at DCP.
p. xxi   "I think that I am," CD, *Auto*, 140–141.
p. xxi   "The gods," Homer, *Odyssey*, 197.
p. xxi   "My mind has changed," CD, *Auto*, 138.
p. xxi   "I wholly lost," *ibid.*, 44.
p. xxi   "The Child," from "My Heart Leaps Up When I Behold," in Word-
               sworth, *Poems*, 13.

CHAPTER ONE

pp. 4–9   August 1832 scenes described, and unless otherwise cited, all quotations, from, CD, *Diary*, 73–87.

p. 4   "An El Dorado," CD, *Diary*, 151.

p. 5   *"cigarittos"* and "much mate," CD, *Journal*, 128.

p. 6   Adam's apple, CD, *Auto*, 19–20; also Browne, *Voyaging*, 254–58.

p. 7   "We philosophers," CD to Frederick Watkins, Aug. 18, 1832, Darwin Correspondence Project [hereafter DCP].

p. 7   "As a God," CD, *Diary*, 167; see also August 11, 1833 entry, CD, "Falkland Notebook," 111a–112a; for Rosas, Williamson, *Penguin History of Latin America*, 274–275; and Lynch, *Caudillo*, 28–29, 41–52, 53–56; for his *postas*, Garretón, *Juan Manuel de Rosas*, 17.

CHAPTER TWO

pp. 10–13   "I believe" and other quotations and descriptions in this chapter, unless otherwise cited, CD, *Diary*, 73–87; also Browne, *Voyaging*, 254–258; and Lynch, *Caudillo*, 28–29.

p. 12   "We never read," Susan Darwin to CD, Nov. 22, 1835, DCP.

pp. 12–13   "This operation" and "a man of an," CD, *Journal*, (1839*)*, 121, 86.

p. 13   "This prophecy," CD, *Journal* (1845), 73.

CHAPTER THREE

pp. 18–24   CD, *Auto*, 21–46; Woodall, *Darwin*, 1–17.

p. 18   Charles (1758–78) and Erasmus (1759–99), Browne, *Voyaging*, 41–44.

p. 18   Erasmus Darwin's use of term and speculations on "evolution," Erasmus Darwin, *Zoonomia*, Part One, 401; and Bowler, "Changing," 98.

p. 19   "Somewhat above," Butler, *Evolution*, 174.

p. 19   "about 6 feet," CD, *Auto*, 28.

p. 20   "He was," CD, *Auto*, 39.

p. 20   For CD's early education, Desmond, Moore, *Darwin*, 5–20.

p. 20   "Everyone seems," Woodall, *Darwin*, 12; 28.

p. 20   "the kindest," CD, *Auto*, 28.

p. 20   "My father's mind," CD, *Auto*, 42.

p. 20   Susannah Darwin described, Bowlby, *Darwin*, 46.

p. 21   "I can," CD, *Auto*, 22.

p. 21   "I believe," CD, *Auto*, 22.

p. 21   "early in," CD, *Auto*, 45.

p. 22   "wasting my time," CD, *Auto*, 46.

p. 22   "By the time," CD, *Auto*, 22.

p. 23   "Nothing could," CD, *Auto*, 27.

p. 23   "The only," CD, *Auto*, 43.

p. 23   "As a very young," CD, *Auto*, 25.

p. 23   "I became," CD, *Auto*, 44.

CHAPTER FOUR

p. 25   "You care," CD, *Auto*, 28–29; Desmond, Moore, *Darwin*, 17–20.

p. 26   Early Edinburgh days, CD, *Auto*, 46–48; Desmond, Moore, *Darwin*, 21–22; "little holes," CD to Robert Darwin, [Oct. 23, 1825], DCP.

pp. 26–28   "It is," Douglass quoted, Chaffin, *Giants Causeway*, 114; "We can both," Erasmus Darwin to CD [February, 24, 1825], DCP; "The thought," CD, *Auto*, 30; "great *eclat*" *et al.*, Desmond, Moore, *Darwin*, 27; Snuff, gambling, "laughing gas," library borrowing, *ibid.*, 25.

p. 28   "I am going," CD to Susan Darwin, Jan. 29 [1826], DCP; "I used often," CD, *Auto*, 51; Ashworth, "Edinburgh," 97-100.

pp. 28–30   Desmond, Moore, *Darwin*, 31–44; ; September 1826 hunt at Maer, CD, "Edinburgh Diary, for 1826," Sept. 1–7 entries, NP; "his delicate frame" and Erasmus retirement, [Price], "Recollections of Darwin," 108; "some interesting," CD, *Auto*, 51; for history of term "evolution," see Bowler, "Changing," 95–114; "incredibly dull," Ashworth, "Edinburgh," 99, 112; Dublin, Portrane, and Paris visits, CD, "Journal,"—ms. not to be confused with *Journal and Remarks*—5 verso, 1826–28].

pp. 31, 32   Desmond, Moore, *Darwin*, 45–47; "I never saw," Catherine Darwin to CD, Jan. 15 [1826], DCP; "I must conclude," Fanny Owen to CD, [March 9, 1828] DCP; "Fanny Owen" article, DCP; Browne, *Voyaging*, 111–116.

p. 32   "My father," CD, *Auto*, 56–57; "convinced from," CD, *Auto*, 46; "I asked for," CD, *Auto*, 56–57; Desmond, Moore, *Darwin*, 47–49.

CHAPTER FIVE

pp. 34–43   "I had never," and all other quotations and incidents in this chapter, unless otherwise attributed, derive from CD, *Auto*, 57–58; Desmond, Moore, *Darwin*, 49.

p. 35   Cambridge curriculum and exams, Van Wyhe, *Cambridge*, 82, 83, 93; Desmond, Moore, *Darwin*, 79; Browne, *Voyaging*, 93, 97; "intelligent Creator," Paley, *Natural Theology*, 136; "The logic" and "answering well," CD, *Auto*, 59.

pp. 35–36   "Darwin's scientific," Bowler, *Evolution*, 157; "During the three," CD, *Auto*, "58; There were," CD, *Auto*, 60; "Upon the whole," 68; CD, *Auto*, "Musical set," CD, *Auto*, 61–62; "He inoculated," *Auto*, 61; Glutton Club, Desmond, Moore, *Darwin*, 88.

pp. 36–37   "It was the mere passion," CD, *Auto*, 62; "I concluded," CD, *Auto*, 45; "very soon," CD, "Darwin's Insects," 5; "employed" and "No poet," CD, *Auto*, 62–63.

pp. 36–43   Henslow background, Desmond, Moore, *Darwin*, 80–112; "influenced my whole career," and Henslow's influence on Darwin, CD, *Auto*, 64; "Henslow used to take," CD, *Auto*, 60; "At present," CD to W. D. Fox [April 7, 1831], DCP; "Henslow promises," CD, Caroline Darwin [April 28, 1831], DCP; "for Llangollen" *et al.*, CD, *Auto*, 70–71; Sedgwick

and Wales trip, "Darwin's Introduction to Geology," DCP; "an offer,"
Henslow to CD, August 24, 1831, DCP; return from Wales and invitation letter, CD, *Auto*, 71; "an offer," Wales trip and invitation letter, CD,
Diary, 3; Browne, *Voyaging*, 133–143; Desmond, Moore, *Darwin*, 52–54,
91–97.

CHAPTER SIX

pp. 44–47   "Loss of," Henslow to CD, Aug. 24, 1831, DCP; "The expedition," Peacock to CD [*c.* August 26, 1831], DCP; "I was instantly," CD, *Auto*, 71;
"Mr. Peacocks letter," CD to Henslow 30 [August 1831], DCP; CD,
Diary, 3; Browne, *Voyaging*, 144–153; Desmond, Moore, *Darwin*, 97,
101–102.

pp. 47–51   "If you can find," *Auto*, 71; "Charles will," R. W. Darwin to Josiah
Wedgwood II, August 31, 1831, DCP; "I am afraid," CD to Robert
Darwin, August 31 [1831], DCP; "I feel," Josiah Wedgwood II to Robert
Darwin, August 31, 1831, DCP; "When we arrived," CD, *Auto*, 227;
Browne, *Voyaging*, 153–156; "give him," Robert Darwin to Josiah Wedg-
wood II, Sept. 1, 1831, DCP; Desmond, Moore, *Darwin*, 102–103.

CHAPTER SEVEN

pp. 52–53   "Thence will," CD to Beaufort, Sept. 1 [1831], DCP; "a slight," CD to
Susan Darwin [September 6, 1831], DCP; "The reason," CD to Susan
Darwin [September 4, 1831], DCP; "tremendous hard" and ref to
FitzRoy letter, CD to W. D. Fox, 6 [September 1831], DCP; "*entirely
given it up*," CD to Susan Darwin [Sept. 5, 1831], DCP; Desmond,
Moore, *Darwin*, 101–4.

p. 54   FitzRoy physical description, Nichols, *Captain*, 19–21; "Gloria in
excelsis," CD to Henslow [September 5, 1831], DCP; Desmond, Moore,
Darwin, 103–4.

pp. 54–55   "I had run," CD, *Auto*, 72; "Observativeness," Simms to CD, Sept. 14,
1874, DCP, "Joseph Simms" (article) at DCP; "which I have consulted,"
CD, *Expressions*, 1; the "going about," CD to Henslow, 9 [September
1831], DCP; "It is such," CD to Charles Whitley [Sept. 9, 1831], DCP;
microscope, CD to Susan Darwin [Sept. 6, 1831], DCP; microscope
and pocket compass, CD, *Diary*, 31, 46; Desmond, Moore, *Darwin*,
102–105.

pp. 56–60   Stokes's death, King, *Proceedings*, 181; and Nichols, *Captain*, 15, 16;
transcription of Stokes journal, in King, *Proceedings*, 156–181; enrollment
by FitzRoy of Fuegians in Walthamstow school, FitzRoy, *Proceedings*, 18;
"whether much," CD, *Auto*, 73; for FitzRoy and Fuegians, Hazlewood,
Savage, 17–10; "innovations which" (FitzRoy quoted), "Just 145," and
1831 election, Desmond, Moore, *Darwin's Sacred Cause*, 70–71.

pp. 60–62   "The Conditions," FitzRoy, *Proceedings*, 18; "is not," and "Cap. Fitz," CD
to Susan Darwin [September 9, 1831], DCP; "my beau," CD to Susan

Darwin [September 6, 1831], DCP; "Richard Matthews" (article), at DCP.

CHAPTER EIGHT

pp. 64–67, *Beagle* renovations, FitzRoy, *Proceedings*, 82; Thomson, *"Beagle," American Scientist*, 664–672; Darwin's shipboard quarters and amenities, Thomson, *Beagle*, 62–67, 118–119, 124–125, 127, 151; and "Beagle, ship," *Encyclopedia Britannica* online; open boats, Viens, "Whalers on the Beagle," Beagle Project website; see also Crockatt, "Beagle's Pups"; "The absolute," CD to Henslow, 9 [September 1831], DCP; "My cabin," CD to Susan Darwin, 17 [September 1831], DCP; "My father," Henrietta Darwin, "Recollections," DCP; "I flatter myself," FitzRoy to sister, March 16, 1826, quoted, Darwin Correspondence, Vol. 1, 554; library rules quoted, *ibid.*, 544; "Charles Darwin's *Beagle* Library" (article) at Darwin Online; "Books on the Beagle" (article) at DCP; "I do not think," CD to Henslow, 9 [September 1831], DCP.

CHAPTER NINE

pp. 68–74, Desmond, Moore, *Darwin*, 107–108; Henslow gift of Humboldt book, CD, *Diary*, 24 n. 2; "The men," CD, *Diary*, 4; She looks," CD to Henslow, 15 [Nov. 1831], DCP; "My time," CD to Henslow, Dec. 3, 1831, DCP; "Time, which," CD to W. D. Fox, 17 [November 1831], DCP; "I grieve," CD to Henslow, 15 [Nov. 1831], DCP; Desmond, Moore, *Darwin*, 105–114; "*2nd* Worked all day," CD, *Diary*, 10; FitzRoy, *Proceedings*, 18–23, 42–44; CD, *Diary*, 3–17; Matthews and Fuegians, Christmas 1831, Hazlewood, *Savage*, 104–105; for John Hill and Fanny Owen, see Desmond, Moore, *Darwin*, 83; Armstrong, *Darwin's Luck*, 91; and "Darwin's first love" article at DCP; Fanny Owen to CD, 2 [Dec. 1831], DCP.

CHAPTER TEN

pp. 77–84   "My thoughts," CD, *Diary*, 17; "In the morning" CD, *Diary*, 77; "Although Darwin," Taylor, *Voyage*, 30; "Nothing can," CD, *Diary*, 11; Darwin's typical shipboard schedule described, CD to Susan Darwin, July 14–Aug. 7 [1832], DCP; Darwin's shipboard quarters and amenities, Thomson, *Beagle*, 62–67, 118–119, 124–25, 127, 151; quotidian naval life, Chaffin, *Sea of Gray*, 77, 93; Darwin's count of men onboard, CD, *Diary*, 84; "that in the night," CD to Robert Darwin [Feb. 8–March 1, 1831], DCP; due to additions and departures during the second voyage and possible errors in tabulation of people aboard the ship, tallies of the *Beagle*'s complement vary slightly—Thomson, *Beagle*, 218; FitzRoy, *Proceedings*, 18–21; and Freeman, *Companion*, 30; "are all good friends," CD, *Diary*, 15; list by FitzRoy of all on second *Beagle* expedition who sailed on first voyage, FitzRoy, *Proceedings*, 21. "Although all three" and other descriptions of Fuegians by Darwin, CD, *Journal* [1845 ed.] 207–8; "Jemmy was," Sulivan quoted and other descriptions, Hazlewood, *Savage*, 81–84, 87, 110–111; "wigwam," Nichols, *Captain*, 31.

CHAPTER ELEVEN

pp. 85–95   "Bad & the landing" and all subsequent quotations in this chapter unless otherwise cited, CD, *Diary*, 19–37; "Darwin was," Armstrong, *Other Islands*, 38; "Mosaic account," "Geology is," "We need not dwell," Lyell, *Principles* vol. I, pp. 2, 3, 43, 154; "I always," CD to Leonard Horner, Aug. 29 [1844], DCP; argument that Darwin in *Autobiography* overstated Lyellian influence on him during Jago visit, Pearson, Nicholas, "'Marks of Extreme Violence,'" 239–253; "the very first," "It then," CD, *Auto*, 77; 81; visits to St. Paul's Rocks and Fernando de Noronha, Armstrong, *Other Islands*, 46–54; "I was ... placed ," and other details of Neptune ritual, CD, *Diary*, 35–36.

CHAPTER TWELVE

p. 96   "About 9 o'clock" and Darwin's other description of Salvador de Bahia and forest visited, CD, *Diary*; 41-43; Browne, *Voyaging*, 196–199.

pp. 99–101   Brazilian slavery and Darwin, Parodiz, *Darwin*, 46; "Facts about slavery" *et al.*, CD, *Diary*; 45; "I then asked," CD, *Auto*, 74; Brazilian slavery, Bergad, *Comparative Histories*; British abolitionists, Chaffin, *Fatal Glory*, 21; Historic Centre of Salvador de Bahia," UNESCO World Heritage Centre; "The Captain does," CD to J. S. Henslow, May 18–June 16, 1832, DCP; Browne, *Voyaging*, 196–199; "Hitherto," CD to R. W. Darwin, Feb. 8–March 1, 1832, DCP; "To this day," CD, *Journal* [1845], 499.

CHAPTER THIRTEEN

p. 102   "At night," *et al.*, CD, *Diary*, 48; "various antiscorbutics" *et al.*, FitzRoy, *Proceedings*, 21; "Introduction," *Journal of Syms Covington* [online]; Thomson, "*Beagle*," *American Scientist*, 664–72; and Thomson, *Beagle*, 31, 127–128.

p. 106   R. D. Keynes, "Introduction"—CD, *Diary*, xiii-xviii; Browne, "Introduction"—CD, *Beagle Letters*, x–xii; "I am looking," CD to Caroline Darwin, April 6–2, 1832, DCP; "I send," CD to Caroline Darwin, April 15–6, 1832, DCP; "I am very doubtful," Caroline Darwin to CD, April 28 [1833], DCP.

pp. 106–   Coral-related fears concerns, Sponsel, *Identity*, 2,3 8, 19–20; and Sponsel
108   interview "New Books in Intellectual History" podcast, Feb. 14, 2020; "I commenced" *et al.*, CD, *Diary*, 48; "come round," Desmond, Moore, *Darwin*, 182.

pp. 108–   "All day, "What can be" *et al.*, CD, *Diary*, 49-51; Ships anchored in Rio
111   harbor—HMS *Warspite*, *Tyne*, and *Lightning* and British packet (passenger ship) *Calypso*, McCormick, "Diary," April 4, 1832, 59; Fuegia Basket, in Hazlewood, *Savage*, 113; "The merchandise," Robertson and Robertson, *Letters on Paraguay*, Vol. 1, 143.

CHAPTER FOURTEEN

pp. 112–116 McCormick, Browne, *Voyaging*, 202–210; "an excellent," Caroline
Darwin to CD, July 25 [-August 3], 1832, DCP; "I feel much inclined,"
"I shall," CD to Caroline Darwin, April, 2–6, 1832, DCP; Browne, *Voy-
aging*, 199–202, 212–214; "The Day," "The colours," "Passed through,"
"The Slaves," "Sell them," "How Strange," CD, *Diary*, 52, 53, 56, 58;
"Twiners entwining," CD, "Rio Notebook," 27b; "On such fazendas,"
"As long as," CD, *Journal*, 26; further background on Lennon and his
estate, Mulhern, "After 1833," 146–147; "My horror," "He is," CD to
Caroline Darwin, April 25–26 [1832], DCP.

CHAPTER FIFTEEN

pp. 117–122 "Although I," "The reason," CD to Caroline Darwin, CD, *Diary*, April
25–26 [1832], DCP; "Two or three," CD, *Diary*, 61; "Fevers," FitzRoy,
Proceedings, 64. All other quotes and incidents in this chapter unless otherwise cited, CD, *Diary*, 62–80.

CHAPTER SIXTEEN

pp. 123–
129
All incidents and quotations in this chapter unless otherwise cited, CD,
Diary, 80–85; Spanish-British rivalry in South America, Arana, *Silver,
Sword, and Stone*, 118, 148–49; for a notable expression of the argument
of British domination over post-colonial Latin America, Stein and Stein,
Colonial Heritage of Latin America; specimens sent to Henslow, Henslow
to CD, Jan. 15–21, 1833, DCP.

CHAPTER SEVENTEEN

pp. 133–
142
"Our bottom" *et al.*, CD, *Diary*, 98–115; "Our boats" *et al.*, FitzRoy,
Proceedings, 101–106; "Paseo virtual por la Fortaleza Protectora Argentina" website; "a good pedestrian," Browne, *Voyaging*, 223; "I am" and
"in sad reality," CD to Henslow, [c. Oct. 26–] Nov. 24 [1832], DCP;
for Covington's presence at fossil recovery, "AT Bahía Blanca . . .WE
ALSO found the remains or bones of *Megatherium*," Covington,
Journal [online]; "This was," Keynes, in CD, *Diary*, 106 n.; Ken-
nedy, "Darwin's lost fossils," *Guardian*, April 6, 2018; "I have," CD
to Henslow, July 24–Nov. 7, 1834, DCP; activities in Buenos Aires,
CD, "Buenos Ayres Notebook," 1a–7a; "some enormous bones," CD to
Henslow [c. Oct. 26]–Nov. 24 [1832], DCP; cash withdrawals, Browne,
Voyaging, 228; "Our chief," CD to Caroline Darwin, Oct. 24–Nov. 24,
1832; purchase of Lyell's *Principles of Geology*, Vol. 2, CD to Henslow,
April 11, 1833 and n. 4, DCP.

CHAPTER EIGHTEEN

pp. 143–
155
"The heaviest" *et al.*, CD, *Diary*, 120–133; "waving skins" *et al.*, FitzRoy,
Proceedings, 120–121; Darwin and "Der Freischutz," CD to Robert
Darwin [Oct. 23, 1825], DCP; and De Paolo, *Ethnography*, 83–84; "An

untamed," CD to Caroline Darwin March 30–April 12, 1833, DCP; for
CD and ethnography, see also, De Paolo, *Ethnography*—particularly 82;
"lurid stories," Bridges, *Uttermost Part of the Earth*, 466; "It is proved,"
FitzRoy, *Proceedings*, 183; "Cannibalism was," Nichols, *Captain*, 69–70; for
cannibalism, see also Hazlewood, *Savage*, 5–7, 83, 114, 115, 321, 322; "The
object," CD, *Diary*, 132–133.

CHAPTER NINETEEN

pp. 156–   "Piece of flat land" *et al.*, CD, *Diary*, 133–143; "drag her," *et al.*, FitzRoy,
167   *Proceedings*, 202–222.

CHAPTER TWENTY

pp. 167–   "According to," Said, *Orientalism*, 232–233.
175   "With considerable anxiety" *et al.*, FitzRoy, *Proceedings*, 224–86; "if the
             garden" *et al.*, *Diary*, 143–162; Desmond, Moore, *Darwin*, 136–139;
             "I do not," CD to Catherine Darwin, July 9–20, 1834, DCP; "The Radi-
             cals," Susan Darwin to CD, March 3–6, 1833, DCP; "a sort of," Caro-
             line Darwin to CD, Sept. 12[–18], 1832, DCP; "After the Beagle," CD
             to Henslow, July 18, 1833, DCP.

CHAPTER TWENTY-ONE

pp. 176–   "The surging," Goethe, *Faust*, in *Essential Goethe*, 266; "To the northward,"
185   *Narrative* (1839), 78; "This plain" *et al.*, CD, *Diary*, 163–218; CD,
             Darwin's overland travel plans, FitzRoy, *Proceedings*, 286–287; "irregu-
             larly built," *ibid.*, 298; "fighting with," CD to Charles Whitley [Sept. 9,
             1831,] DCP; "I am bound," CD, *Journal*, footnote p. 83; Thirty or 45
             miles figure, "The horses, &c," "indeed one is nearly," *Scelidotherium* [n.
             2]; "I am now," CD to Caroline Darwin, Sept. 20 [1833], DCP; "law
             of the succession of types," CD, *Journal*, 210; "In the evening," CD,
             Journal 139; "a perfect," *Narrative* (1839). 93; "Northern parts," "peon,"
             "By riding," CD to Caroline Darwin, [October] 23 [1833], DCP; Punta
             Alta site destruction, "A 124 años de la creación de la Base Naval Puerto
             Belgrano," n.d. *Gaceta Marinera* [online]; FitzRoy criticism of preface,
             FitzRoy to CD, Nov. 16, 1837, DCP; and Desmond, Moore, *Darwin*,
             233.

CHAPTER TWENTY-TWO

pp. 186–   "I do not think," *et al.*, CD, *Journal*, 125–128; Viens, "Charles Darwin:
187   Peak Bagger," Beagle Project website, Sept. 12, 2013.

CHAPTER TWENTY-THREE

pp. 188–   "A troop," CD, *Journal*, 129; "I am now," CD to Caroline Darwin,
192   Sept. 20 [1833]; "In the evening," CD, *Journal*, 139; DCP; Lumb's ship-
             ping of *Megatherium* bones, CD to Henslow, Sept. [20–7], 1833, DCP;
             "the Northern," "peon," "By riding," CD to Caroline Darwin, [October]

23 [1833], DCP; Rosas's 1835 return to power, Williamson, *Penguin History of Latin America*, 275; Rosas exile in England, Lynch, *Caudillo*, 162–163; alleged Darwin-Rosas encounter in England, William Erasmus Darwin to CD, June 27 [1863?], DCP; Parodiz, *Darwin in the New World*, 111, and further clarification Rosemary Clarkson (DCP), email to author, May 7, 2021; repatriation of Rosas's body, Eugene Robinson, "Argentines Cheer Returning Hero 112 Years after his Death," *Washington Post*, Oct. 2, 1989; "I went on board," CD, *Diary*, 198.

CHAPTER TWENTY-FOUR

pp. 194–195   Robert Armstrong identified, Porter, "Beagle Collector," 986; described incidents, "harbor . . . a creek which runs" *et al.* CD, *Diary*, 198–209; price of Megatherium head, Desmond, Moore, *Darwin*, 144; for Earle and Martens, FitzRoy to CD, Oct. 4, 1833 and n. 3, DCP; and Smith, "Augustus Earle," *Australian Dictionary of Biography* [online]; Martens, "Journal"; Viens, "Art of the Beagle, Conrad Martens, Part II" Beagle Project website; CD, *Beagle Letters*, 170 n. 7; "stone pounding artist," FitzRoy to CD, Oct. 4, 1833, DCP; Martens boards *Beagle*, Nov. 25, 1833, in Martens, "Journal," 19; "There is nothing," CD to Catherine Darwin, April 6, 1834, DCP; "the Head," CD, "Ornithological Notes," 271.

pp. 197, 199   "Run down" *et al.*, CD, *Diary*, 213–216; "I found some," CD to Henslow, March 1834, DCP; described incidents, "These Indians" *et al.*, CD, *Diary*, 217–218; "They have," CD to Catherine Darwin, April 6, 1834, DCP; "On the 2d, FitzRoy, *Proceedings*, 316–327.

pp. 200–204   "Bold attempt" *et al.*, CD, *Diary*, 225–227; "We anchored," "I thought" and "we hurried," FitzRoy, *Proceedings*, 322, 324; "The Captain offered," CD to Catherine, April 6, 1834, DCP; "Trifling as," Beaufort to FitzRoy, Nov. 11, 1831, quoted in FitzRoy, *Proceedings*, 34–35; Darwin's *Diary* and FitzRoy's *Proceedings* respectively, while substantively consistent in recounting the *Beagle*'s March 1834 visit with Jemmy Button, do differ in minor, mainly chronological, details. When encountering discrepancies in the two accounts, in the absence of other credible primary-sources, I've generally deferred to Darwin's version of events.

pp. 205–206   Marks, *Three Men*, 127–191; "Orundellico (Jemmy Button)" (article), at DCP; Ruth Mayer, "Jemmy Button," 193–215; "The fine," Rosas quoted, Lynch, *Caudillo*, 20; Parker, "Wild Tribes," 261–267; Selk'nam, in Arana, *Silver, Sword, and Stone*, 208–210.

CHAPTER TWENTY-FIVE

pp. 206–208   "The Adventure arrived" and events described, CD, *Diary*, 228–231; "How different," CD to Catherine Darwin, April 6, 1834, DCP; "I cannot," Caroline Darwin to CD, Sept. 27, 1833; DCP; "The fossil portions," Henslow to CD, August 31, 1833, DCP; "alarmed by,"

CD to Henslow, March 1834, DCP; "your name," Frederick Hope to CD, Jan. 15, 1834, DCP; seaman buried, Desmond, Moore, *Darwin,* 151.

pp. 208–212   Subsequently described incidents, FitzRoy *Proceedings,* 336–357; "The captain," CD to Catherine Darwin, April 6, 1834, DCP; "An examination," FitzRoy, *Proceedings,* 336; "One tide" *et al.* and described incidents, CD, *Diary,* 232; "The valley of S. Cruz," CD to Henslow, July 24–Nov. 7, 1834, DCP.

CHAPTER TWENTY-SIX

pp. 213–219   "October Fullness," Neruda, *Poems,* 174–175; Cervantes, *Quixote,* 174; "I never saw" *et al.,* CD, *Diary,* 240–245; patented galley stove, Thomson, *Beagle,* 120–121; "Her main-boom," FitzRoy, *Proceedings,* 360. "Valparaiso is" *et al.* and related events described, CD to Catherine Darwin, July 20–29, 1834, DCP; Valparaiso description, Parodiz, *Darwin,* 123; Corfield identified, CD to Catherine Darwin, July 20–29, 1834, n. 5, DCP; four-hundred British-born residents in Valparaiso, Rock, *British,* 40.

pp. 220–222   "I have already" *et al.,* CD, *Diary,* 250; Covington and Mariano Gonzalez identified as Darwin companions, Chancellor and van Wyhe, "Introduction to the *St. Fe Notebook*," Darwin Online website; "I skirt sierras," Whitman, *Poetry and Prose,* 219; "In consequence," CD to Henslow, March 1834, DCP; "I throughily enjoyed," CD to Caroline Darwin, Oct. 13, 1834, DCP; Browne, *Voyaging,* 276–277; "Rifled," Milton, "Paradise Lost," 252; Desmond, Moore, *Darwin,* 156–157; Bunster, CD, *Valparaiso Notebook,* 55a; "an English Hotel," CD to FitzRoy [August 28, 1834], DCP.

CHAPTER TWENTY-SEVEN

pp. 223–227   Time-line and details of gold-mine visit, illness and return to Valparaíso, CD, *Diary,* 260–263; "Chichi a very weak," "put me right," CD to Caroline Darwin, October 13, 1834, DCP; "scheme," "strange proceedings," "the cold manner," CD to Catherine Darwin, Nov. 8, 1834, DCP; "It was a grievous" and all other Darwin quotations and described events in this chapter not otherwise attributed, CD, *Diary,* 263–264; "As I proposed" *et al.* FitzRoy, *Proceedings,* 361–362; "During the day," CD, *Journal,* 327; "The first Lieutenant," CD, *Auto,* 75.

CHAPTER TWENTY-EIGHT

pp. 228–234   Angelou, "On the Pulse," Poetry Foundation website; "In several places" *et al.* and described events in this chapter, CD, *Diary,* 264–304; and CD, *Journal,* 368–369; for FitzRoy visit to the island—called by Phillip Parker King "Juan Fernández Island"—on which Selkirk was marooned, King, *Proceedings,* 302–308; *Robinson Crusoe,* Selkirk *et al.,* Browne,

Voyaging, 302–03; *Henrietta* crewmen, FitzRoy, *Proceedings*, 370–371; "Obviously Lyell," Bowler, *Evolution*, 158.

CHAPTER TWENTY-NINE

pp. 235–
245

Assistance from Caldcleugh, Wesson, *Darwin's First Theory*, 147–48; Darwin's passport from Prieto, Castro-Le-Fort, *Darwin en Chile*, 27–28; "Six of the mules" *et al.* and all other quotations and incidents in this chapter not otherwise attributed, CD; *Diary*, 307-351; "I saw the spot" *et al.*, CD, *Journal*, 406; for more on petrified forest, CD, *Geological diary*, 517–519; for theory re: South America's geological origins, see entirety of CD, *Geological observations on South America*—and, more specifically, for Uspallata Pass, 206; "most perfect" *et al.*, CD, *Journal*, 409; "I have scarcely," CD to Susan Darwin [Sept.], 3, 1835; DCP; "The very little," CD to Caroline Darwin, July [19]–[Aug. 12], 1835, DCP; "For the last months," CD to W. D. Fox [August 9–12], 1835, DCP; *La Constitución* schooner, Keynes, "Midshipman Forsyth's Log from the voyage of HMS *Beagle*," Intro., Darwin Online.

CHAPTER THIRTY

pp. 246–
257

The weather, now" *et al.* and all other quotations and incidents in this section not otherwise attributed, CD, *Diary*, 351–364; Lawson boards *Beagle*, FitzRoy, *Proceedings*, 490; Lawson background, Sæther, "Making Sense," 31-32; Darwin itinerary within Galápagos, Estes, Grant, Grant, "Darwin in the Galapagos," 343–368; "These birds," CD, "Ornithological Notes," 262; Sulloway, "Darwin and his Finches," 1–53; John Gould, CD, *Diary*, 359–60 n.1; Bowler, *Evolution*, 163; "My attention was," CD, *Journal* [1845 ed.], 394; "Darwin spent" and specifics of his time on individual Galapagos islands, Armstrong, *Other Islands*, 21; "My last letter," CD to Caroline, Dec. 27, 1835, DCP; "I last wrote," CD to Henslow, Jan. [28–29] 1836, DCP; Browne, *Voyaging*, 296–305; Desmond, Moore, *Darwin*; 169–172.

pp. 257–
259

"When I was on board," CD to Otto Zacharias [February 24, 1877], DCP, 350; "character of," CD, "Darwin's Journal," 13 recto [1837]; "After Darwin died" and all other quotes in this section from van Wyhe and Francis Darwin, and re Galápagos Darwin monument and British Association for the Advancement of Science session, van Wyhe, "character of," CD, "Darwin's Journal," 13 recto [1837]; "Where do Darwin's finches come from?" 185–193; "When on board," CD, *Origin*, 1; Horenstein, "Darwin's Busts," 478–488; "After having surveyed," CD, *Diary*, 364.

CHAPTER THIRTY-ONE

pp. 260–
268

"Insignificant patch" *et al.*, CD, *Diary*, 364–395; Darwin's New Zealand collecting, Armstrong, 159–160; "I found," Earle, *Narrative*, 59–60; "The perfect equality," "It was melancholy," CD, *Journal*, 242, 520; Tahiti and

New Zealand visits, Armstrong, *Other Islands*, 138–165; "the strong," FitzRoy, *Proceedings*, 572.

CHAPTER THIRTY-TWO

pp. 269–275   "Beautiful villas" *et al.*, CD, *Diary*, 395–410; "In the evening" and all other quotations and events in this chapter otherwise unattributed, CD, *Journal*, 515–536; "On the whole" and "certainly," CD to Henslow, Jan. [28–29], 1836, DCP; Browne, Voyaging, 314–316; Desmond, Moore, *Darwin*, 176–181; Hobart Town collecting, *ibid.*, 179.

CHAPTER THIRTY-THREE

pp. 276–279   "We staid" *et al.* and all quotations and incidents in this chapter unless otherwise attributed, CD, *Diary*, 410–418; "In his mind's eye," Wesson, *Darwin's First Theory*," 169–170; "if circumstances," Beaufort to FitzRoy, Nov. 11, 1831, in FitzRoy, *Proceedings*, 38; "No other work," CD, *Auto*, 98; "Darwin & Coral Reefs" (article), at DCP; Desmond, Moore, *Darwin*, 176–182; Browne, *Voyaging* 315–320; "To see," Blake, *Portable Blake*, 150; visit to the Cocos (Keeling) atoll, Armstrong, *Other Islands*, 196–213.

pp. 280–291   Writing of coral essay, Armstrong, *Under the Blue Vault*, 103; "Whilst we," "I assure," and "He has proposed," CD to Caroline Darwin, April 29, 1836, DCP; "There being nothing" *et al.* and all subsequent quotations and incidents in this section unless otherwise attributed, CD, *Diary*, 423–447; "rather awful," "I am going," "I am at present," CD to Henslow, July 9, 1836, DCP; "Leaving America," CD to W. D. Fox, Feb. 15, 1836, DCP; "All these finer," Browne, *Voyaging*, 326–335; Cambridge Philo. Society, CD, *Auto*, 81–82; "I have always, CD to Catherine Darwin, June 3, 1836, DCP; "Surely, if three years," FitzRoy and CD, "Darwin-FitzRoy article, *South African Christian Recorder*, Sept 4, 1836, Darwin Online; "I can now walk, CD to Susan Darwin, Aug. 4 [1836], DCP; "I arrived here," CD to FitzRoy, Oct. 6, [1836] DCP.

CHAPTER THIRTY-FOUR

pp. 295–298   "Alexander Selkirk," Borges, *Selected Poems*, 203; "Owning Everything," Cohen, *Selected Poems*, 52–53; "Looking very thin," Caroline Darwin to Sarah [Elizabeth] Wedgwood [Oct. 5, 1836], DCP; "my time," CD to W. D. Fox, Dec. 15 [1836], DCP; Erasmus Darwin (brother of Charles), Browne, *Voyaging*, 375; "I saw more," CD, *Auto*, 100; "Tell no one," Lyell to CD, Dec. 26, 1836, DCP; "Dons in Science," CD to W. D. Fox, Nov. 6 [1836]; in Francis Darwin, *Life and Letters* [of CD], Vol. 1, 277; "I felt," CD to Henslow, [Nov. 1, 1836] DCP; Desmond, Moore, *Darwin*, 195–211; Browne, *Voyaging* 343–356; 441–445.

pp. 298–303   Keynes, R. D., "Introduction," *Journal of Researches* (article), at DCP; R. B. Freeman, "Bibliographical Introduction" for *Journal of Researches et al.*, Darwin Online; "A right," CD to William Whewell, Feb., 16

[1839], DCP; "I hope," Catherine and Caroline Darwin to CD [Feb. 16, 1837], DCP; "We staid there," CD, *Journal*, 241; "I am," CD to William Darwin Fox, [March 12, 1837], DCP; "If I live," CD to J. S. Henslow [November 4, 1837], DCP; "The success," CD, *Auto*, 116; "You will," CD to Caroline Wedgwood [Oct. 27, 1839], DCP; "the fruits," Humboldt to Darwin, Sept. 18, 1839, DCP; Browne, *Voyaging*, 347–348; 360; Desmond, Moore, *Darwin*, 282–285, 292, 294, 314, 323, 327–329.

p. 304 Third *Beagle* expedition and ship's later history, Thomson, *"Beagle," American Scientist* [on-line]; and Thomson, *Beagle*, 264–269.

pp. 304–307 Desmond, Moore, *Darwin*, 233–234, 254, 256–259, 269–272, 276–279, 534; "Before I was engaged," CD, *Auto*, 95; Charles' concerns re: first-cousin marriages, Desmond, Moore, *Darwin*, 575; "We ate," Emma to her mother, *Emma Darwin*, Vol. 2, 26; "The state of mind," Emma Darwin to CD [circa Feb. 1839], DCP; "uncomfortable," CD to Henslow [Sept. 20, 1837], DCP; Browne, *Voyaging*, 379–381, 391–399, 400–422.

CHAPTER THIRTY-FIVE

pp. 306–314 Dylan, "High Water Rising," bobdylan.com; "Did transmutation," Browne, *Voyaging*, 361–362; "uncomfortable palpitation" *et al.*, CD to Henlow [Sept. 20, 1837], DCP; "Population, when," Malthus, "Essay," 4; "In October," CD, *Auto*, 120; "sudden death," CD to Emma Darwin, July 5, 1844, DCP; "fetters," Sedgwick quoted in Browne, *Voyaging*, 468; "big Book," CD to Charles Lyell, November 10, [1856], DCP; "I had good," CD to Hooker, May 9 [1856], DCP; "Some year," CD to Lyell, [June] 18 [1858].

CHAPTER THIRTY-SIX

pp. 315–320 "Beyond the bounds," *Saturday Review* 9 [May 5, 1860]: 573; "Profoundly," J. W. Burrow, intro., CD, *Origin of Species* [Penguin edition, 1968], 15; "the most apparent," CD, *Origin*, 5; "whole Orang," Lyell to Huxley, June 17, 1859, DCP; "I was astounded," CD to Hooker, May 4 [1865], DCP; "I think I shall avoid," CD to Wallace, Dec. 22, 1857, DCP; "The same," CD, *Descent of Man*, Vol. 1, 68; "The Fuegians," CD, *Descent of Man*, Vol. 1, 34; "The main conclusion," CD, *Descent of Man*, Vol. 2, 618–619; "The voyage," CD, *Auto*, 76; more generally for events in chapter, Browne, *Voyaging;* 360–543; and Browne, *Power of Place*, 19–23, 33–90; 264–265; ailments, "Darwin's Health," article, DCP; Odysseus and Poseidon, Homer, *Odyssey*, 464; Darwin never leaves Britain again after return from *Beagle* voyage, Rosemary Clarkson (DCP), email to author, May 7, 2021.

EPILOGUE

pp. 321–322 "In conclusion," CD, *Journal*, 607–609.

INDEX

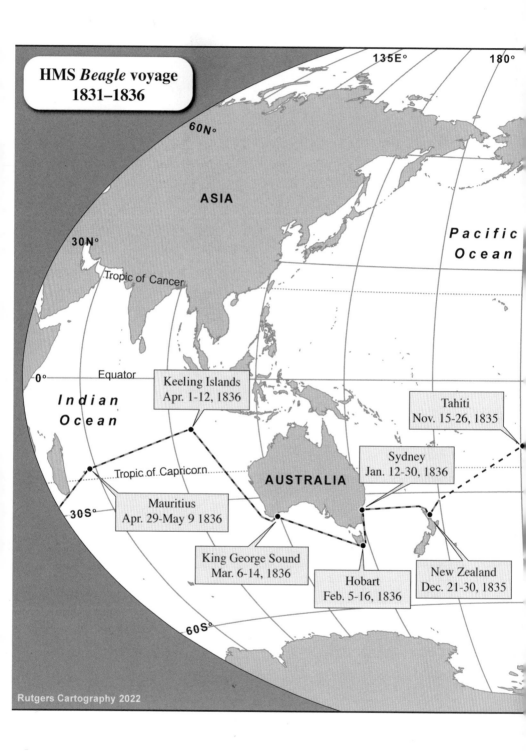

HMS *Beagle* voyage
1831–1836

135E°

180°

60N°

ASIA

30N°

Tropic of Cancer

*Pacific
Ocean*

0°   Equator

*Indian
Ocean*

Keeling Islands
Apr. 1-12, 1836

Tahiti
Nov. 15-26, 1835

Tropic of Capricorn

AUSTRALIA

Sydney
Jan. 12-30, 1836

Mauritius
Apr. 29-May 9 1836

30S°

King George Sound
Mar. 6-14, 1836

Hobart
Feb. 5-16, 1836

New Zealand
Dec. 21-30, 1835

60S°

Rutgers Cartography 2022